Great ANGLING STORIES

Great ANGLING STORIES

Selected and Edited by

JOHN M. DICKIE

Chambers

First published 1941 by W & R Chambers Ltd. Edinburgh
This new edition published 1988.

British Library Cataloguing in Publication Data

Great Angling Stories.
1. Fishing—Literary collections
I. Dickie, John M.
808.8'0355 PN6071.F47

ISBN 0-550-21000-8

Printed in Great Britain at the University Press, Cambridge

PREFACE

HEREIN is an anthology of angling stories—stories in the sense of fiction; and the point may be made though notoriously *all* angling stories are fiction. The casts are in the pools of fancy.

Considering the great flow of angling books, it might have been thought that some such collection would have been made before; but this does not seem to have been so.

Against books on sport the charge may often be laid that they depend too little on merit, too much on a bond of sympathy between author and reader. But angling has a fair literature and no stories have here been included which do not possess, quite apart from their subject, intrinsic literary worth.

The stories given are, it should be said, angling stories proper, stories, that is, where the central theme is angling; they are not stories which have angling merely as a background.

From this it is not to be thought that the reader is thereby doomed to the mere catching, or not catching, of fish. Angling has many aspects, and throughout the aim has been to include in their story guise, and not necessarily by any means for the specialist reader only, as many of these aspects as possible.

Angling stories are as old, of course, as angling itself, and in this respect the collection has been made representative by the inclusion of stories of distant as well as of nearer times.

Further, the collection has been made representative also by country. Thus apart from English, Scottish, and Irish stories, there are also American stories, and as well a story or two from continental Europe and farther away. Concerning Irish stories, it has regretfully to be told that the quest here revealed a sad dearth. For all who have fished with Irish boatmen this will be something hard to believe and harder still to explain.

While the bulk of the stories are in prose, certain others are in verse. But narrative verse of worth on angling is scarce and at times, too, it must be owned, it is no more than slight.

As to the authors of the stories, these will be found to consist on the one hand of those who are writers first and anglers afterwards, and on the other of those who are anglers first and writers afterwards. But if Kingsley, Blackmore, and the other writers knew how to fish, so also, it must be allowed, did Scrope, Francis, and the other anglers know how to write.

Often the stories given are extracts from longer works, and it was fortunate that angling incidents proved mostly readily extractable. But this was not always so, whence sometimes the non-appearance here of authors one might expect to find. Instances are William Black, and none knew better than he how to paint the fishing scene, John Buchan, in respect of his prose, and Maurice Walsh.

At the head of each story there is a brief notice of the author, indication of the source of the story, and, if the author has written other fishing stories, mention of where these stories may be found. It is hoped that in this way the book will be given an added interest and value.

Also at the head of each story, where the material is copyright, specific acknowledgment is made of permission to use the story. Here, however, in the preface, general thanks should be offered to all who have granted permissions. Almost needless to say, every attempt has been made to trace owners of copyrights, but, should any infringement have occurred through failure to accomplish this, apologies are hereby tendered and assurance given that nothing was blameworthy.

There have been various 'complete,' even 'completest,' angling books since Walton's day. Such claims are not for anthologies. It is the hope, however, that by reason of the book's ingredients, Walton, recalling his famous pike, would here have found a second dish 'too good for any but anglers, or very honest men.'

JOHN M. DICKIE

CONTENTS

CROCKER'S HOLE

By R. D. BLACKMORE

RICHARD DODDRIDGE BLACKMORE (1825-1900), shy, reticent, and a lover of nature, was a votary of angling. In chapter VII of *Lorna Doone* there is a fine description of loach-spearing, and in chapter XVIII of *Alice Lorraine* a Triton is taken on fly; but quite the best of Blackmore's fishing is in 'Crocker's Hole,' described by Dr Henry van Dyke (see below, p. 282) as the finest English angling story. It is in *Tales from the Telling-house* (1896) and is here given by permission of Messrs Sampson Low, Marston, & Co.

I

THE CULM, which rises in Somersetshire, and hastening into a fairer land (as the border waters wisely do) falls into the Exe near Killerton, formerly was a lovely trout stream, such as perverts the Devonshire angler from due respect toward Father Thames and the other canals round London. In the Devonshire valleys it is sweet to see how soon a spring becomes a rill, and a rill runs on into a rivulet, and a rivulet swells into a brook; and before one has time to say, 'What are you at?'—before the first tree it ever spoke to is a dummy, or the first hill it ever ran down has turned blue, here we have all the airs and graces, demands and assertions of a full-grown river.

But what is the test of a river? Who shall say? 'The power to drown a man,' replies the river darkly. But rudeness is not argument. Rather shall we say that the power to work a good undershot wheel, without being dammed up all night in a pond, and leaving a tidy back-stream to spare at the bottom of the orchard, is a fair certificate of riverhood. If so, many Devonshire streams attain that rank within five miles of their spring; aye, and rapidly add to it. At every turn they gather aid, from ash-clad dingle and aldered meadow, mossy rock and ferny wall, hedge-trough roofed with bramble netting, where the baby water lurks, and lanes that coming down to ford bring suicidal tribute. Arrogant, all-engrossing river, now it has claimed a great valley of its own; and whatever falls within the hill scoop, sooner or later belongs to itself. Even the crystal 'shutt' that crosses the farm-yard by the wood-rick, and glides down an aqueduct of last year's bark for Mary to fill the kettle from; and even the tricklets that have no organs for telling or knowing their business, but only get into unwary oozings in and among the water-grass, and there make moss and forget themselves among it—one and all, they come to the same thing at last, and that is the river.

The Culm used to be a good river at Culmstock, tormented already by a factory, but not strangled as yet by a railroad. How it is now the present writer does not know, and is afraid to ask, having heard of a vile 'Culm Valley Line.' But Culmstock bridge was a very pretty place to stand and contemplate the ways of trout; which is easier work than to catch them. When I was just big enough to peep above the rim, or to lie upon it with one leg inside for fear of tumbling over, what a mighty river it used to seem, for it takes a treat there and spreads itself. Above the bridge the factory stream falls in again, having done its business, and washing its hands in the innocent half that has strayed down the meadows. Then under the arches they both rejoice and come to a slide of about two feet, and make a short, wide pool below, and indulge themselves in perhaps two islands, through which a little river always magnifies itself, and maintains a mysterious middle. But after that, all of it used to come together, and make off in one body for the meadows, intent upon nurturing trout with rapid stickles, and buttercuppy corners where fat flies may tumble in. And here you may find in the very first meadow, or at any rate you might have found, forty years ago, the celebrated 'Crocker's Hole.'

The story of Crocker is unknown to me, and interesting as it doubtless was, I do not deal with him, but with his Hole. Tradition said that he was a baker's boy who, during his basket-rounds, fell in love with a maiden who received the cottage-loaf, or perhaps good 'Households,' for her master's use. No doubt she was charming as a girl should be, but whether she encouraged the youthful baker and then betrayed him with false *rôle*, or whether she 'consisted' throughout—as our cousins across the water express it—is known to their *manes* only. Enough that she would not have the floury lad; and that he, after giving in his books and money, sought an untimely grave among the trout. And this was the first pool below the bread-walk deep enough to drown a five-foot baker boy. Sad it was; but such things must be, and bread must still be delivered daily.

A truce to such reflections—as our foremost writers always say, when they do not see how to go on with them—but it is a serious thing to know what Crocker's Hole was like; because at a time when (if he had only persevered, and married the maid, and succeeded to the oven, and reared a large family of short-weight bakers) he might have been leaning on his crutch beside the pool, and teaching his grandson to swim by precept (that beautiful proxy for practice)—at such a time, I say, there lived a remarkably fine trout in that hole. Anglers are notoriously truthful, especially as to what they catch, or even more frequently have not caught. Though I may have written fiction, among many other sins—as a nice old lady told me once—now I have to deal with facts; and foul scorn would I count it ever to make believe that I caught that fish. My length at that time was not more than the butt of a four-jointed rod, and all I could catch was a minnow with a pin, which our cook Lydia would not cook, but used to say, 'Oh, what a shame, Master

Richard! they would have been trout in the summer, please God! if you would only a' let 'em grow on.' She is living now, and will bear me out in this.

But upon every great occasion there arises a great man; or to put it more accurately, in the present instance, a mighty and distinguished boy. My father, being the parson of the parish, and getting, need it be said, small pay, took sundry pupils, very pleasant fellows, about to adorn the universities. Among them was the original 'Bude Light,' as he was satirically called at Cambridge, for he came from Bude, and there was no light in him. Among them also was John Pike, a born Zebedee, if ever there was one.

John Pike was a thick-set younker, with a large and bushy head, keen blue eyes that could see through water, and the proper slouch of shoulder into which great anglers ripen; but greater still are born with it; and of these was Master John. It mattered little what the weather was, and scarcely more as to the time of year, John Pike must have his fishing every day, and on Sundays he read about it, and made flies. All the rest of the time he was thinking about it.

My father was coaching him in the fourth book of the *Æneid* and all those wonderful speeches of Dido, where passion disdains construction; but the only line Pike cared for was of horsehair. 'I fear, Mr Pike, that you are not giving me your entire attention,' my father used to say in his mild dry way; and once when Pike was more than usually abroad, his tutor begged to share his meditations. 'Well, sir,' said Pike, who was very truthful, 'I can see a green drake by the strawberry tree, the first of the season, and your derivation of "barbarous" put me in mind of my barberry dye.' In those days it was a very nice point to get the right tint for the mallard's feather.

No sooner was lesson done than Pike, whose rod was ready upon the lawn, dashed away always for the river, rushing headlong down the hill, and away to the left through a private yard, where 'no thoroughfare' was put up, and a big dog stationed to enforce it. But Cerberus himself could not have stopped John Pike; his conscience backed him up in trespass the most sinful when his heart was inditing of a trout upon the rise.

All this, however, is preliminary, as the boy said when he put his father's coat upon his grandfather's tenter-hooks, with felonious intent upon his grandmother's apples; the main point to be understood is this, that nothing—neither brazen tower, hundred-eyed Argus, nor Cretan Minotaur—could stop John Pike from getting at a good stickle. But, even as the world knows nothing of its greatest men, its greatest men know nothing of the world beneath their very nose, till fortune sneezes dexter. For two years John Pike must have been whipping the water as hard as Xerxes, without having ever once dreamed of the glorious trout that lived in Crocker's Hole. But why, when he ought to have been at least on bowing terms with every fish as long as his middle finger, why had he failed to know this champion? The answer is simple—because of his short cuts. Flying as he did like an arrow from a bow, Pike used to hit his beloved river at an elbow, some furlong below Crocker's Hole, where a sweet little stickle sailed away downstream, whereas for the length of a meadow upward the water lay smooth, clear, and shallow; therefore the youth, with so little time to spare, rushed into the downward joy.

And here it may be noted that the leading maxim of the present period, that man can discharge his duty only by going counter to the stream, was scarcely mooted in those days. My grandfather (who was a wonderful man, if he was accustomed to fill a cart in two days of fly-fishing on the Barle) regularly fished downstream; and what more than a cartload need anyone put into his basket?

And surely it is more genial and pleasant to behold our friend the river growing and thriving as we go on, strengthening its voice and enlargening its bosom, and sparkling through each successive meadow with richer plenitude of silver, than to trace it against its own grain and good-will toward weakness, and littleness, and immature conceptions.

However, you will say that if John Pike had fished up stream, he would have found this trout much sooner. And that is true; but still, as it was, the trout had more time to grow into such a prize. And the way in which John found him out was this. For some days he had been tormented with a very painful tooth, which even poisoned all the joys of fishing. Therefore he resolved to have it out, and sturdily entered the shop of John Sweetland, the village blacksmith, and there paid his sixpence. Sweetland extracted the teeth of the village, whenever they required it, in the simplest and most effectual way. A piece of fine wire was fastened round the tooth, and the other end round the anvil's nose, then the sturdy blacksmith shut the lower half of his shop door, which was about breast-high, with the patient outside and the anvil within; a strong push of the foot upset the anvil, and the tooth flew out like a well-thrown fly.

When John Pike had suffered this very bravely, 'Ah, Master Pike,' said the blacksmith, with a grin, 'I reckon you won't pull out thic there big vish'—the smithy commanded a view of the river—'clever as you be, quite so peart as thiccy.'

'What big fish'? asked the boy, with deepest interest, though his mouth was bleeding fearfully.

'Why that girt mortial of a vish as hath his hover in Crocker's Hole. Zum on 'em saith as a' must be a zammon.'

Off went Pike with his handkerchief to his mouth, and after him ran Alec Bolt, one of his fellow-pupils, who had come to the shop to enjoy the extraction.

'Oh, my!' was all that Pike could utter, when by craftily posting himself he had obtained a good view of this grand fish.

'I'll lay you a crown you don't catch him!' cried Bolt, an impatient youth, who scorned angling.

'How long will you give me?' asked the wary Pike, who never made rash wagers.

'Oh! till the holidays if you like; or, if that won't do, till Michaelmas.'

Now the midsummer holidays were six weeks off—boys used not to talk of 'vacations' then, still less of 'recesses.'

'I think I'll bet you,' said Pike, in his slow way, bending forward carefully, with his keen eyes on this monster; 'but it would not be fair to take till Michaelmas. I'll bet you a crown that I catch him before the holidays—at least, unless some other fellow does.'

II

The day of that most momentous interview must have been the 14th of May. Of the year I will not be so sure; for children take more note of days than of years, for which the latter have their full revenge thereafter. It must have been the 14th, because the morrow was our holiday, given upon the 15th of May, in honour of a birthday.

Now, John Pike was beyond his years wary as well as enterprising, calm as well as ardent, quite as rich in patience as in promptitude and vigour. But Alec Bolt was a headlong youth, volatile, hot, and hasty, fit only to fish the Maëlstrom, or a torrent of new lava. And the moment he had laid that wager he expected his crown piece; though time, as the lawyers phrase it, was 'expressly of the essence of the contract.' And now he demanded that Pike should spend the holiday in trying to catch that trout.

'I shall not go near him,' that lad replied, 'until I have got a new collar.' No piece of personal adornment was it, without which he would not act, but rather that which now is called the fly-cast, or the gut-cast, or the trace, or what it may be. 'And another thing,' continued Pike; 'the bet is off if you go near him, either now or at any other time, without asking my leave first, and then only going as I tell you.'

'What do I want with the great slimy beggar?' the arrogant Bolt made answer. 'A good rat is worth fifty of him. No fear of my going near him, Pike. You shan't get out of it that way.'

Pike showed his remarkable qualities that day by fishing exactly as he would have fished without having heard of the great Crockerite. He was up and away upon the mill-stream before breakfast; and the forenoon he devoted to his favourite course—first down the Craddock stream, a very pretty confluent of the Culm, and from its junction, down the pleasant hams, where the river winds toward Uffculme. It was my privilege to accompany this hero, as his humble Sancho; while Bolt and the faster race went up the river ratting. We were back in time to have Pike's trout (which ranged between two ounces and one-half pound) fried for the early dinner; and here it may be lawful to remark that the trout of the Culm are of the very purest excellence, by reason of the flinty bottom, at any rate in these the upper regions. For the valley is the western outlet of the Blackdown range, with the Beacon hill upon the north, and Hackpen long ridge to the south; and beyond that again the Whetstone hill, upon whose western end dark port-holes scarped with white grit mark the pits. But flint is the staple of the broad Culm Valley, under good, well-pastured loam; and here are chalcedonies and agate stones.

At dinner everybody had a brace of trout—large for the larger folk, little for the little ones, with coughing and some patting on the back for bones. What of equal purport could the fierce rat-hunter show? Pike explained many points in the history of each fish, seeming to know them none the worse, and love them all the better, for being fried. We banqueted, neither a whit did soul get stinted of banquet impartial. Then the wielder of the magic rod very modestly sought leave of absence at the tea time.

'Fishing again, Mr Pike, I suppose,' my father answered pleasantly; 'I used to be fond of it at your age; but never so entirely wrapped up in it as you are.'

'No, sir; I am not going fishing again. I want to walk to Wellington, to get some things at Cherry's.'

'Books, Mr Pike? Ah! I am very glad of that. But I fear it can only be fly-books.'

'I want a little Horace for eighteen-pence—the Cambridge one just published, to carry in my pocket—and a new hank of gut.'

'Which of the two is more important? Put that into Latin, and answer it.'

'Utrum pluris facio? Flaccum flocci. Viscera magni.' With this vast effort Pike turned as red as any trout spot.

'After that who could refuse you?' said my father. 'You always tell the truth, my boy, in Latin or in English.'

Although it was a long walk, some fourteen miles to Wellington and back, I got permission to go with Pike; and as we crossed the bridge and saw the tree that overhung Crocker's Hole, I begged him to show me that mighty fish.

'Not a bit of it,' he replied. 'It would bring the blackguards. If the blackguards once find him out, it is all over with him.'

'The blackguards are all in factory now, and I am sure they cannot see us from the windows. They won't be out till five o'clock.'

With the true liberality of young England, which abides even now as large and glorious as ever, we always called the free and enlightened operatives of the period by the courteous name above set down, and it must be acknowledged that some of them deserved it, although perhaps they poached with less of science than their sons. But the cowardly murder of fish by liming the water was already prevalent.

Yielding to my request and perhaps his own desire—manfully kept in check that morning—Pike very carefully approached that pool, commanding me to sit down while he reconnoitred from the meadow upon the right bank of the stream. And the place which had so sadly quenched the fire of the poor baker's love filled my childish heart with dread and deep wonder at the cruelty of women. But as for John Pike, all he thought of was the fish and the best way to get at him.

Very likely that hole is 'holed out' now, as the Yankees well express it, or at any rate changed out of knowledge. Even in my time a very heavy flood entirely altered its character; but to the eager eye of Pike it seemed pretty much as follows, and possibly it may have come to such a form again.

The river, after passing through a hurdle fence at the head of the meadow, takes a little turn or two of bright and shallow indifference, then gathers itself into a good strong slide, as if going down a slope instead of steps. The right bank is high and beetles over with yellow loam and grassy fringe; but the other side is of flinty shingle, low and bare and washed by floods. At the end of this rapid, the stream turns sharply under an ancient alder tree into a large, deep, calm repose, cool, unruffled, and sheltered from the sun by branch and leaf—and that is the hole of poor Crocker.

At the head of the pool (where the hasty current rushes in so eagerly, with noisy excitement and much ado) the quieter waters from below, having rested and enlarged themselves, come lapping up round either curve, with some recollection of their past career, the hoary experience of foam. And sidling toward the new arrival of the impulsive column, where they meet it, things go on, which no man can describe without his mouth being full of water. A 'V' is formed, a fancy letter V, beyond any designer's tracery, and even beyond his imagination, a perpetually fluctuating limpid wedge, perpetually crenelled and rippled into by little ups and downs that try to make an impress, but can only glide away upon either side or sink in dimples under it. And here a grey bough of the ancient alder stretches across, like a thirsty giant's arm, and makes it a very ticklish place to throw a fly. Yet this was the very spot our John Pike must put his fly into, or lose his crown.

Because the great tenant of Crocker's Hole, who allowed no other fish to wag a fin there, and from strict monopoly had grown so fat, kept his victualling yard—if so low an expression can be used concerning him—within about a square yard of this spot. He had a sweet hover, both for rest and recreation, under the bank, in a placid antre, where the water made no noise, but tickled his belly in digestive ease. The loftier the character is of any being, the slower and more dignified his movements are. No true psychologist could have believed—as Sweetland the blacksmith did, and Mr Pook the tinman—that this trout could ever be the embodiment of Crocker. For this was the last trout in the universal world to drown himself for love; if truly any trout has done so.

'You may come now, and try to look along my back,' John Pike, with a reverential whisper, said to me. 'Now don't be in a hurry, young stupid; kneel down. He is not to be disturbed at his dinner, mind. You keep behind me, and look along my back; I never clapped eyes on such a whopper.'

I had to kneel down in a tender reminiscence of pasture land, and gaze carefully; and not having eyes like those of our Zebedee (who offered his spine for a camera, as he crawled on all fours in front of me), it took me a long time to descry an object most distinct to all who have that special gift of piercing with their eyes the water. See what is said upon this subject in that delicious book, *The Gamekeeper at Home*.

'You are no better than a muff,' said Pike, and it was not in my power to deny it.

'If the sun would only leave off,' I said. But the sun, who was having a very pleasant play with the sparkle of the water and the twinkle of the leaves, had no inclination to leave off yet, but kept the rippling crystal in a dance of flashing facets, and the quivering verdure in a steady flush of gold.

But suddenly a May-fly, a luscious grey-drake, richer and more delicate than canvas-back or woodcock, with a dart and a leap and a merry zigzag, began to enjoy a little game above the stream. Rising and falling like a gnat, thrilling her gauzy wings, and arching her elegant pellucid frame, every now and then she almost dipped her three long tapering whisks into the dimples of the water.

'He sees her! He'll have her as sure as a gun!' cried Pike, with a gulp, as if he himself were 'rising.' 'Now, can you see him, stupid?'

'Crikey, crokums!' I exclaimed, with classic elegance; 'I have seen that long thing for five minutes; but I took it for a tree.'

'You little'—animal quite early in the alphabet—'now don't you stir a peg, or I'll dig my elbow into you.'

The great trout was stationary almost as a stone, in the middle of the 'V' above described. He was gently fanning with his large clear fins, but holding his own against the current mainly by the wagging of his broad-fluked tail. As soon as my slow eyes had once defined him, he grew upon them mightily, moulding himself in the matrix of the water, as a thing put into jelly does. And I doubt whether even John Pike saw him more accurately than I did. His size was such, or seemed to be such, that I fear to say a word about it; not because language does not contain the word, but from dread of exaggeration. But his shape and colour may be reasonably told without wounding the feeling of an age whose incredulity springs from self-knowledge.

His head was truly small, his shoulders vast; the spring of his back was like a rainbow when the sun is southing; the generous sweep of his deep elastic belly, nobly pulped out with rich nurture, showed what the power of his brain must be, and seemed to undulate, time for time, with the vibrant vigilance of his large wise eyes. His latter end was consistent also. An elegant taper run of counter, coming almost to a cylinder, as a mackerel does, boldly developed with a hugeous spread to a glorious amplitude of swallow-tail. His colour was all that can well be desired, but ill-described by any poor word-palette. Enough that he seemed to tone away from olive and umber, with carmine stars, to glowing gold and soft pure silver, mantled with a subtle flush of rose and fawn and opal.

Swoop came a swallow, as we gazed, and was gone with a flick, having missed the May-fly. But the wind of his passage, or the skir of wing, struck the merry dancer down, so that he fluttered for one instant on the wave, and that instant was enough. Swift as the swallow, and more true of aim, the great trout made one dart, and a sound, deeper than a tinkle, but as silvery as a bell, rang the poor ephemerid's knell. The rapid water scarcely showed a break; but a bubble sailed down the pool, and the dark hollow echoed with the music of a rise.

'He knows how to take a fly,' said Pike; 'he has had too many to be tricked with mine. Have him I must; but how ever shall I do it?'

All the way to Wellington he uttered not a word, but shambled along with a mind full of care. When I ventured to look up now and then, to surmise what was going on beneath his hat, deeply-set eyes and a wrinkled forehead, relieved at long intervals by a solid shake, proved that there are meditations deeper than those of philosopher or statesman.

III

Surely no trout could have been misled by the artificial May-fly of that time, unless he were either a very young fish, quite new to entomology, or else one afflicted with a combination of myopy and bulimy. Even now there is room for plenty of improvement in our counterfeit presentment; but in those days the body was made with yellow mohair, ribbed with red silk and gold twist, and as thick as a fertile bumble-bee. John Pike perceived that to offer such a thing to Crocker's trout would probably consign him—even if his great stamina should overget the horror—to an uneatable death, through just and natural indignation. On the other hand, while the May-fly lasted, a trout so cultured, so highly refined, so full of light and sweetness, would never demean himself to low bait, or any coarse son of a maggot.

Meanwhile Alec Bolt allowed poor Pike no peaceful thought, no calm absorption of high mind into the world of flies, no placid period of cobbler's wax, floss-silk, turned hackles, and dubbing. For in making of flies John Pike had his special moments of inspiration, times of clearer insight into the everlasting verities, times of brighter conception and more subtle execution, tails of more elastic grace and heads of a neater and nattier expression. As a poet labours at one immortal line, compressing worlds of wisdom into the music of ten syllables, so toiled the patient Pike about the fabric of a fly comprising all the excellence that ever sprang from maggot. Yet Bolt rejoiced to jerk his elbow at the moment of sublimest art. And a swarm of flies was blighted thus.

Peaceful, therefore, and long-suffering, and full of resignation as he was, John Pike came slowly to the sad perception that arts avail not without arms. The elbow, so often jerked, at last took a voluntary jerk from the shoulder, and Alec Bolt lay prostrate, with his right eye full of cobbler's wax. This put a desirable check upon his energies for a week or more, and by that time Pike had flown his fly.

When the honeymoon of spring and summer (which they are now too fashionable to celebrate in this country), the hey-day of the whole year marked by the budding of the wild rose, the start of the wheatear from its sheath, the feathering of the lesser plantain, and flowering of the meadow-sweet, and, foremost for the angler's joy, the caracole of May-flies—when these things are to be seen and felt (which has not happened at all this year), then rivers should be mild and bright, skies blue and white with fleecy cloud, the west wind blowing softly, and the trout in charming appetite.

On such a day came Pike to the bank of Culm, with a loudly beating heart. A fly there is, not ignominious, or of cowdab origin, neither gross and heavy-bodied, from cradlehood of slimy stones, nor yet of menacing aspect and suggesting deeds of poison, but elegant, bland, and of sunny nature, and obviously good to eat. Him or her—why quest we which?—the shepherd of the dale, contemptuous of gender, except in his own species, has called, and as long as they two co-exist will call, the 'Yellow Sally.' A fly that does not waste the day in giddy dances and the fervid waltz, but undergoes family incidents with decorum and discretion. He or she, as the case may be—for the natural history of the river bank is a book to come hereafter, and of fifty men who make flies not one knows the name of the fly he is making—in the early morning of June, or else in the second quarter of the afternoon, this Yellow Sally fares abroad, with a nice well-ordered flutter.

Despairing of the May-fly, as it still may be despaired of, Pike came down to the river with his masterpiece of portraiture. The artificial Yellow Sally is generally always—as they say in Cheshire—a mile or more too yellow. On the other hand, the 'Yellow Dun' conveys no idea of any Sally. But Pike had made a very decent Sally, not perfect (for he was young as well as wise), but far above any counterfeit to be had in fishing-tackle shops. How he made it, he told nobody. But if he lives now, as I hope he does, any of my readers may ask him through the G.P.O., and hope to get an answer.

It fluttered beautifully on the breeze, and in such living form, that a brother or sister Sally came up to see it, and went away sadder and wiser. Then Pike said: 'Get away, you young wretch,' to your humble servant who tells this tale; yet being better than his words, allowed that pious follower to lie down upon his digestive organs and with deep attention watch. There must have been great things to see, but to see them so was difficult. And if I huddle up what happened, excitement also shares the blame.

Pike had fashioned well the time and manner of this overture. He knew that the giant Crockerite was satiate now with May-flies, or began to find their flavour failing, as happens to us with asparagus, marrow-fat peas, or strawberries, when we have had a month of them. And he thought that the first Yellow Sally of the season, inferior though it were, might have the special charm of novelty. With the skill of a Zulu, he stole up through the branches over the lower pool till he came to a spot where a yard-wide opening gave just space for spring of rod. Then he saw his desirable friend at dinner, wagging his tail, as a hungry gentleman dining with the Lord Mayor agitates his coat. With one dexterous whirl, untaught by any of the many books upon the subject, John Pike laid his Yellow Sally (for he cast with one fly only) as lightly as gossamer upon the rapid, about a yard in front of the big trout's head. A moment's pause, and then, too quick for words, was the thing that happened.

A heavy plunge was followed by a fearful rush. Forgetful of current the river was ridged, as if with a plough driven under it; the strong line, though given out as fast as might be, twanged like a harp-string as it cut the wave, and then Pike stood up, like a ship dismasted, with the butt of his rod snapped below the ferrule. He had one of those foolish things, just invented, a hollow butt of hickory; and the finial ring of his spare top looked out, to ask what had happened to the rest of it. 'Bad luck!' cried the fisherman; 'but never mind, I shall have him next time, to a certainty.'

When this great issue came to be considered, the cause of it was sadly obvious. The fish, being hooked, had made off with the rush of a shark for the bottom of the pool. A thicket of saplings below the alder tree had stopped the judicious hooker from all possibility of following; and when he strove to turn him by elastic pliance, his rod broke at the breach of pliability. 'I have learned a sad lesson,' said John Pike, looking sadly.

How many fellows would have given up this matter, and glorified themselves for having hooked so grand a fish, while explaining that they must have caught him, if they could have done it! But Pike only told me not to say a word about it, and began to make ready for another tug of war. He made himself a splice-rod, short and handy, of well-seasoned ash, with a stout top of bamboo, tapered so discreetly, and so balanced in its spring, that verily it formed an arc, with any pressure on it, as perfect as a leafy poplar in a stormy summer. 'Now break it if you can,' he said, 'by any amount of rushes; I'll hook you by your jacket collar; you cut away now, and I'll land you.'

This was highly skilful, and he did it many times; and whenever I was landed well, I got a lollypop, so that I was careful not to break his tackle. Moreover he made him a landing net, with a kidney-bean stick, a ring of wire, and his own best nightcap of strong cotton net. Then he got the farmer's leave, and lopped obnoxious bushes; and now the chiefest question was: what bait, and when to offer it? In spite of his sad rebuff, the spirit of John Pike had been equable. The genuine angling mind is steadfast, large, and self-supported, and to the vapid, ignominious chaff, tossed by swine upon the idle wind, it pays as much heed as a big trout does to a dance of midges. People put their fingers to their noses and said: 'Master Pike, have you caught him yet?' and Pike only answered: 'Wait a bit.' If ever this fortitude and perseverance is to be recovered as the English Brand (the one thing that has made us what we are, and may yet redeem us from niddering shame), a degenerate age should encourage the habit of fishing and never despairing. And the brightest sign yet for our future is the increasing demand for hooks and gut.

Pike fished in a manlier age, when nobody would dream of cowering from a savage because he was clever at skulking; and when, if a big fish broke the rod, a stronger rod was made for him, according to the usage of Great Britain. And though the young angler had been defeated, he did not sit down and have a good cry over it.

About the second week in June, when the May-fly had danced its day, and died—for the season was an early one—and Crocker's trout had recovered from the wound to his feelings and philanthropy, there came a night of gentle rain, of pleasant tinkling upon window ledges, and a soothing patter among young leaves, and the Culm was yellow in the morning. 'I mean to do it this afternoon,' Pike whispered to me, as he came back panting. 'When the water clears there will be a splendid time.'

The lover of the rose knows well a gay voluptuous beetle, whose pleasure is to lie embedded in a fount of beauty. Deep among the incurving petals of the blushing fragrance, he loses himself in his joys sometimes, till a breezy waft reveals him. And when the sunlight breaks upon his luscious dissipation, few would have the heart to oust him, such a gem from such a setting. All his back is emerald sparkles; all his front red Indian gold, and here and there he grows white spots to save the eye from aching. Pike put his finger in and fetched him out, and offered him a little change of joys, by putting a Limerick hook through his thorax, and bringing it out between his elytra. *Cetonia aurata* liked it not, but pawed the air very naturally, and fluttered with his wings attractively.

'I meant to have tried with a fern-web,' said the angler; 'until I saw one of these beggars this morning. If he works like that upon the water, he will do. It was hopeless to try artificials again. What a lovely colour the water is! Only three days now to the holidays. I have run it very close. You be ready, younker.'

With these words he stepped upon a branch of the alder, for the tone of the water allowed approach, being soft and sublustrous, without any mud. Also Master Pike's own tone was such as becomes the fisherman, calm, deliberate, free from nerve, but full of eye and muscle. He stepped upon the alder bough to get as near as might be to the fish, for he could not cast this beetle like a fly; it must be dropped gently and allowed to play. 'You may come and look,' he said to me; 'when the water is so, they have no eyes in their tails.'

The rose-beetle trod upon the water prettily, under a lively vibration, and he looked quite as happy, and considerably more active, than when he had been cradled in the anthers of the rose. To the eye of a fish he was a strong individual, fighting courageously with the current, but sure to be beaten through lack of fins; and mercy suggested, as well as appetite, that the proper solution was to gulp him.

'Hooked him in the gullet. He can't get off!' cried John Pike, labouring to keep his nerves under; 'every inch of tackle is as strong as a bell-pull. Now, if I don't land him, I will never fish again!'

Providence, which had constructed Pike, foremost of all things, for lofty angling—disdainful of worm and even minnow—Providence, I say, at this adjuration, pronounced that Pike must catch that trout. Not many anglers are heaven-born; and for one to drop off the hook halfway through his teens would be infinitely worse than to slay the champion trout. Pike felt the force of this, and rushing through the rushes, shouted: 'I am sure to have him, Dick! Be ready with my nightcap.'

Rod in a bow, like a springle-riser; line on the hum, like the string of Paganini; winch on the gallop, like a harpoon wheel, Pike, the head-centre of everything, dashing through thick and thin, and once taken overhead—for he jumped into the hole, when he must have lost him else, but the fish too impetuously towed him out, and made off in passion for another pool, when, if he had only retired to his hover, the angler might have shared the baker's fate—all these things (I tell you, for they all come up again, as if the day were yesterday) so scared me of my never very steadfast wits, that I could only holloa! But one thing I did, I kept the nightcap ready.

'He is pretty nearly spent, I do believe,' said Pike; and his voice was like balm of Gilead, as we came to Farmer Anning's meadow, a quarter of a mile below Crocker's Hole. 'Take it coolly, my dear boy, and we shall be safe to have him.'

Never have I felt, through forty years, such tremendous responsibility. I had not the faintest notion how to use a landing net; but a mighty general directed me. 'Don't let him see it; don't let him see it! Don't clap it over him; go under him, you stupid! If he makes another rush, he will get off, after all. Bring it up his tail. Well done! You have him!'

The mighty trout lay in the nightcap of Pike, which was half a fathom long, with a tassel at the end, for his mother had made it in the winter evenings. 'Come and hold the rod, if you can't lift him,' my master shouted, and so I did. Then, with both arms straining, and his mouth wide open, John Pike made a mighty sweep, and we both fell upon the grass and rolled, with the giant of the deep flapping heavily between us, and no power left to us, except to cry, 'Hurrah!'

THE FIRST FLY

By ÆLIAN

CLAUDIUS ÆLIANUS (flourished 3rd century A.D.), Roman writer, author in Greek of *Various History* and of *On the Nature of Animals*, both containing much curious lore. 'The First Fly' is from Book XV, 1, of the second work, and, with Ælian, 'the honey-tongued,' as an apt teller, is the first known specific mention of fly-fishing with an artificial fly. The translation is by Dr A. J. Butler as given in chapter X of his *Sport in Classic Times* (1930), and is here reproduced by kind permission of his son. *On the Nature of Animals* has also, in Book XIV, 25, a good story of river-fishing with a team of horses; it is translated in chapter XVII of William Radcliffe's *Fishing from the Earliest Times* (1921).

THERE is a form of fishing in Macedonia of which I have heard and have knowledge. Between Berœa and Thessalonica runs a river called the Astræus containing fish of a speckled colouring: as to their local name you had better ask the Macedonians. They feed on flies which hover about the river—peculiar flies, quite unlike those found elsewhere—not resembling wasps in aspect, nor can one match them rightly in shape with what are called anthedons or wild bees, nor with hive bees: but they have something in common with all these. They rival in boldness an ordinary fly: in size you might rank them with wild bees: their colour is modelled from the wasp, and they buzz like bees. The people of the place invariably call them horsetails.

These flies settle on the stream in search of their special food, but cannot avoid being seen by the fish swimming below. When, therefore, a fish detects a fly floating on the surface, he swims towards it very quietly under water, taking care not to stir the water above, which would scare his prey. So coming close up on the side away from the sun, the fish opens its mouth, snaps the fly down its gullet, like a wolf seizing a lamb from the fold, or an eagle seizing a goose from the farmyard: and then retreats under the ripple.

Anglers are aware of the whole procedure, but never by any chance use the natural fly as bait: for when the flies are handled, they lose their proper colour, their wings are battered, and the fish refuse to feed upon them. Anglers accordingly leave the flies alone, resenting their cursed behaviour when captured: but they get the better of the fish by a clever and wily contrivance of their art. They wrap dark red wool round a hook and tie on to it two feathers which grow under the wattles of a cock and resemble wax in colour. The fishing rod is six feet in length and the line the same. When the tricky fly is lowered, a fish is attracted by the colour and rises madly at the pretty thing that will give him a rare treat, but on opening his jaws is pierced by the hook and finds poor enjoyment of the feast when he is captured.

THE LAW OV IT

By FRANCIS FRANCIS

FRANCIS FRANCIS (1822-86), one of the best known of English anglers and writers on angling, and also a novelist. In 1856-83 he was the first angling editor of *The Field*. His *A Book on Angling* (1867; latest ed. 1920 by Sir Herbert Maxwell) is still counted a standard work on all-round angling. He wrote with fine virility, exuberance, and humour, and one feels he must have been good to fish with, both at the time and after. 'The Law Ov It' is from 'A Christmas Retrospect' in *Angling Reminiscences* (1887), and Francis has also angling stories in *Hot Pot* (1880); while in the novels there are fishing passages in *Newton Dogvane* (3 vols 1859; vol. I, chaps II and X, and vol. III, chap. V) and in *Sidney Bellew* (2 vols 1870; vol. I, chaps V, IX, X, XII, XIII, and vol. II, chap. VI). See also pp. 163, 235, 326.

I WAS fishing the —— some years ago, and I met a Yankee, Jed Chewlick, who was making a tour of the Highlands. He had some sympathy with fishermen, and we interchanged ideas about sport at the table d'hôte. One day I had been trouting below the weir at ——, and as I came up the water I met friend Jed, who was surveying the weir with a rapt gaze while sharpening the blade of a penknife on a piece of soft stick, which he had in his hand preparatory to whittling the same. 'Say, stranger,' said he, nodding towards the weir, at which several salmon were jumping ineffectively, 'who does the water belong to above that dam?—for everything belongs to someone in this durn country o' yourn.' I mentioned the name of the next proprietor. 'And is that dam hisn?' 'Oh, dear, no! That belongs to a Mr So-and-so, who lives down south, and who lets it to a tacksman, who catches the fish in that cage yonder.' Jedediah sniffed, and began to whittle softly. 'And does Mr up above there approve of that erection?' 'No, of course he doesn't; it ruins his fishery, but what can he do?' 'The Tarnal! Wal, I mind when father busted at New York, we went to New Brunswick, and took up a location on Swanstone Creek, and when we first located, there was a sprinklin' o' salmon in that creek, and we made dollars out of it. Wal, by-m-by comes a durn Scotchman who sets up a saw-mill below and puts up a dam across that creek, and, arter that, we didn't get no salmon nohow; but he just raked 'em up in piles. Wal, father goes to him fair and easy, and says, "My friend, you must just make a hole in that dam o' yourn, and let some o' them salmon come up to me." "No," says McSandy, "I hev bought the water privilege, and I mean to hev that water privilege." "Very good," says my father, "I am a peaceable citizen. I am a-goin' up to *Saint* John's nex' week, and I guess I'll inquire into the law ov the case." "Do," says McSandy. So my father goes up to *Saint* John's nex' week, and he comes back with three cocoanuts done up very careful in a box, and I chanced to see them. "What air them nuts, father?" says I. "Them is the law ov the case, my son," says he.

'The nex' day father was busy in his workshop with a piece o' board, some friction tubes, and some string; and, arter supper in the evenin', he just says to mother, gentle-like (he was always quiet and gentle, was my father, unless he was real riz, and then he worn't), "My dear," he says, "I am just a-goin' out a-communin' with the stars," says he; and I see him take out one o' them cocoanuts careful-like, and, with a bit o' board about a foot square under his arm, he went out softly, a-whistlin' the proverbs o' Solomon set to music. I thought this was odd; so, after an interval, I went out to commune with the stars likewise, or to see how 'twas done. About a hundred yards below our house the creek took a bend, and just here the road ran 'longside of the stream which swept round the pint. There had been a freshet the day before, and there was a good deal o' water in the creek, so that it was a-runnin' perhaps nine inches or a foot deep over McSandy's dam down below; and there was a heavy run o' fish up there. Wal, father goes 'long down to that bend, and stops at the bank over the river. The water was pretty deep there, and ran close round that pint, and the stream set off from there towards the middle pretty sharp. Wal, as I comes up to father I hears a splash in the water, and I see suthin' like a square bit o' timber float away out into the stream. "What's that, father?" says I. "That, my son? That *is* the law ov it." "Is it?" says I. "It is," says he; "and now run right away home, and tell mother to get them nets ready agin to-morrer," says he. "Whatever for, father?" says I; "there ain't no fish now since the dam was up." "Never you mind, sonny," says he; "always you do as your parents tells you and don't ax no questions," says he. Wal, I went home mighty kewrious, you bet. I kud 'ardly sleep for thinkin' o't. Nex' mornin' sure as sun-up, word comes up from below that suthin' had happened to McSandy's dam, and there was a hole in it as big as a hayrick, and all Swanstone was a-runnin' threw merrily. I never did see my father look so surprised. Naterally he would anyhow,' said Jed. 'But he *did* look that extra astonished that—"Why, lor a massy!" says he to that there messenger as brought the noos, "I shouldn't wonder a mite or mossel if them durned salmon ain't some ov 'em come up into our water." "I shouldn't wonder neither," said that messenger drily, for he was a dry chap was that messenger, and chips worn't a circumstance to him. Wal, how it came to happen no one kud tell. There was the hole, which daily growed larger, and we had the most splendaciousest season's fishin' as we ever had. McSandy then set to work to repair that dam, and it cost him a matter of three or four hundred dollars to make it sound and good again. Not very long arter there come on another nice little freshet, which I knew would bring up fish, and father he was very busy all day in that workshop of hisn agin.

'In the evenin' arter supper he took another walk to commune with the stars with another square board under his arm, down to that pint agin. There was another splash, you guess. "What is that, father?" said I. "That is the second section ov the law ov it, sonny," says he; "now run right way hum, and get them nets and boxes ready." Then I begun to think that father was kinder of an astronomer, as communed and astrologised along with them stars to larn what was a-goin' to happen. And dog-durn me if the very nex' mornin' that there messenger didn't come up agin and say as there was another hole in McSandy's dam, big as a house this time; and such fishin' as we had that fall we never did afore. No, sir. Then McSandy pranced around consi'r'ble, and thought that someone had a-done it out o' malice like, as if anyone would be that malicious to injure a feller cretur so. He made consi'r'ble of a muss about it, but nothin' come of it, so he just mended up his tarnal old dam the second time—nuther four hundred dollars, and no lumber, and no fish, 'cause they'd all come up to us. Wal, it was just one o' the most astonishin' facts, but the same thing actilly happened all straight over again. McSandy mended his dam, and set people to watch it this time. Father went out and studied the stars a third time to see what was a-goin' to happen; and, as he said, the sidereal inflooences was favourable to fishin', and Pisces was in the ascendant, so he estimated that there would be salmon to-morrer. And them fellers was a-watchin' and a-watchin' McSandy's dam, when all of a sudden, just about half an hour arter supper, as we heerd nex' mornin', believe me if that there dam didn't cave in all of a sudden with a regler bust for the third time; and this time there was a hole in it as big as two houses. Then, what with mendin' the old dam, the stoppage o' business, and gettin' no fish, McSandy was nigh about stone-broke and played out, and he just chucked up that there dam, and moved on; and long arter he'd gone father explained to me the law in cases of this sort.

"Them three cocoanuts, my son, was charged with the execution ov the law, and the board was the officer who supported and had charge ov it; and when that board slumphed over the weir into the down draft, it'd have drawed out a ton, leave alone a friction tube; and when that old cocoar took that dam kerchunk in the middle, six foot below, that dam just moved on about as quick as it knowed how." And that *is* the law in cases of this sort, you bet, young man, and there's a pint about two hundred yards above the dam yonder that you could arguey the case from most *con*vincin'. Ef that there water was mine, I guess I'd have my share o' them salmon, anyhow.' And Jedediah walked away reflectively, picking his teeth with the stump of the peg he had whittled.

UNDER THE SYCAMORE

By IZAAK WALTON

Izaak Walton (1593-1683), by employing the colloquy as his form, gave a slight narrative framework to his *The Compleat Angler* (1653), and below a representative passage is given from Part I, chapter V. As for the colloquy as a form, it must be said that from this much has since had to be borne by angling readers because of unhappy imitators.

Venator. O my good master, this morning walk has been spent to my great pleasure and wonder: but, I pray, when shall I have your direction how to make artificial flies, like to those that the trout loves best; and, also, how to use them?

Piscator. My honest scholar, it is now past five of the clock: we will fish till nine, and then go to breakfast. Go you to yonder sycamore-tree, and hide your bottle of drink under the hollow root of it; for about that time, and in that place, we will make a brave breakfast with a piece of powdered beef, and a radish or two, that I have in my fish-bag: we shall, I warrant you, make a good, honest, wholesome, hungry breakfast. And I will then give you direction for the making and using of your flies: and in the meantime, there is your rod and line; and my advice is, that you fish as you see me do. And let's try which can catch the first fish.

Venator. I thank you, master. I will observe and practise your direction as far as I am able.

Piscator. Look you, scholar; you see I have hold of a good fish; I now see it is a trout. I pray, put that net under him; and touch not my line, for if you do, then we break all. Well done, scholar; I thank you.

Now for another. Trust me, I have another bite.

Come, scholar, come lay down your rod, and help me to land this as you did the other. So now we shall be sure to have a good dish of fish for supper.

Venator. I am glad of that; but I have no fortune: sure, master, yours is a better rod and better tackling.

Piscator. Nay, then take mine, and I will fish with yours. Look you, scholar, I have another. Come, do as you did before. And now I have a bite at another. Oh me! he has broke all; there's half a line and a good hook lost.

Venator. Aye, and a good trout, too.

Piscator. Nay, the trout is not lost; for pray take notice, no man can lose what he never had.

Venator. Master, I can neither catch with the first nor second angle: I have no fortune.

Piscator. Look you, scholar, I have yet another. And now, having caught three brace of trouts, I will tell you a short tale as we walk towards our breakfast. A scholar (a preacher I should say) that was to preach to procure the approbation of a parish that he might be their lecturer, had got from his fellow pupil the copy of a sermon that was first preached with great commendation by him that composed it; and though the borrower of it preached it, word for word, as it was at first, yet it was utterly disliked as it was preached by the second to his congregation: which the sermon-borrower complained of to the lender of it, and was thus answered: 'I lent you, indeed, my fiddle, but not my fiddlestick; for you are to know, that every one cannot make music with my words, which are fitted for my own mouth.' And so, my scholar, you are to know, that as the ill pronunciation or ill accenting of words in a sermon spoils it, so the ill carriage of your line, or not fishing even to a foot in a right place, makes you lose your labour; and you are to know, that though you have my fiddle, that is, my very rod and tacklings with which you see I catch fish, yet you have not my fiddlestick, that is, you yet have not skill to know how to carry your hand and line, nor how to guide it to a right place: and this must be taught you (for you are to remember, I told you angling is an art) either by practice or a long observation, or both.

But now let's say grace, and fall to breakfast. What say you, scholar, to the providence of an old angler? Does not this meat taste well? And was not this place well chosen to eat it, for this sycamore-tree will shade us from the sun's heat?

Venator. All excellent good, and my stomach excellent good too. And I now remember, and find that true which devout Lessius says, That poor men, and those that fast often, have much more pleasure in eating than rich men and gluttons, that always feed before their stomachs are empty of their last meat and call for more; for by that means they rob themselves of that pleasure that hunger brings to poor men. And I do seriously approve of that saying of yours, That you had rather be a civil, well-governed, well-grounded, temperate, poor angler, than a drunken lord. But I hope there is none such; however, I am certain of this, that I have been at many very costly dinners that have not afforded me half the content that this has done, for which I thank God and you.

Piscator. And now, scholar, I think it will be time to repair to our angle-rods, which we left in the water to fish for themselves; and you shall choose which shall be yours; and it is an even lay, one of them catches.

And, let me tell you, this kind of fishing with a dead rod, and laying night-hooks, are like putting money to use; for they both work for the owners when they do nothing but sleep, or eat, or rejoice, as you know we have done this last hour, and sat as quietly and as free from cares under this sycamore, as Virgil's Tityrus and his Melibœus did under their broad beech-tree. No life, my honest scholar, no life so happy and so pleasant as the life of a well-governed angler; for when the lawyer is swallowed up with business, and the statesman is preventing or contriving plots, then we sit on cowslip-banks, hear the birds sing, and possess ourselves in as much quietness as these silent silver streams, which we now see glide so quietly by us. Indeed, my good scholar, we may say of angling, as Dr Boteler said of strawberries, 'Doubtless God could have made a better berry, but doubtless God never did'; and so, if I might be judge, God never did make a more calm, quiet, innocent recreation than angling.

I'll tell you, scholar, when I sat last on this primrose-bank, and looked down these meadows, I thought of them as Charles the Emperor did of the city of Florence: That they were too pleasant to be looked on, but only on holy-days. As I then sat on this very grass, I turned my present thoughts into verse: 'twas a wish, which I'll repeat to you:

THE ANGLER'S WISH

I in these flow'ry meads would be:
These crystal streams should solace me;
To whose harmonious bubbling noise
I with my angle would rejoice:
Sit here, and see the turtle-dove
Court his chaste mate to acts of love:
Or, on that bank, feel the west wind
Breathe health and plenty: please my mind,
To see sweet dew-drops kiss these flowers,
And then washed off by April showers:
Here hear my Kenna [1] sing a song;
There see a blackbird feed her young,
Or a leverock build her nest:
Here give my weary spirits rest,
And raise my low-pitch'd thoughts above
Earth, or what poor mortals love:
Thus, free from law-suits and the noise
Of princes' courts, I would rejoice:

---

[1] Anne Ken, Walton's second wife.

Or, with my Bryan,[1] and a book,
Loiter long days near Shawford [2]-brook;
There sit by him, and eat my meat,
There see the sun both rise and set:
There bid good morning to next day;
There meditate my time away,
And angle on; and beg to have
A quiet passage to a welcome grave.

---

[1] Walton's dog.

[2] Also Shallowford, Meece, or Meese, a Staffordshire rivulet entering the Sow, four miles NW. of Stafford.

AN OLD SALMON-POACHING STORY

By GILFRID W. HARTLEY

GILFRID WILLIAM HARTLEY (1852-1940), English devotee of wild sports, author of the fine *Wild Sport with Gun, Rifle, and Salmon Rod* (1903) and *Wild Sport and Some Stories* (1912), from which last 'An Old Salmon-poaching Story' is here given by kind permission of Mrs Hartley and of Messrs W. Blackwood & Sons.

THE sun was barely peeping round the shoulder of Ben Bhurich when Archie MacCorquodale got on the high bit of tableland where he could look down on the river Awe. The day gave promise of being a very hot one, but as yet a dull white frosty mist lay over the hills, filling up the hollows and corries with its cotton-wool-like masses: every step he took left its trace behind (how often must it have happened in old fighting days that a man has been followed to his death by such trail as this!), and he was soon wet above the knee by the drip from the heather and long grass. In these times, when salmon are scarce and wary, the frosty morning which ushers in a broiling day is not loved by a fisherman, but at that happy period things were different, and better, and he must have been a novice indeed who could not do something almost any time during the season with the fish in the Awe.

When MacCorquodale reached the watershed, he looked down on a district which, save in one respect, sixty years have done little to change. The dark river, flecked with white here and there, made its rapid way to the sea; beyond it stood up the bare grey-green face of Ben Cruachan; and the woods of Inverawe showed, as they show nowadays, against Loch Etive, and the granite face of Bonawe. Far away to the west you can see Morvern, and the higher peaks of Mull. Till quite recently the place must have looked just the same as it has looked for centuries. The railway is the only change—a mighty convenience, but the thin line of iron doubtless takes something from the loneliness of what used to be one of the wildest passes in Scotland.

Archie ran quickly down the hillside till he came to a great rock in the shelter of which lay his rod, with reel and line on it ready for work. Rod and line and fisherman have long been resolved into their component parts, but the reel lies before the writer now—a large wooden one, black-painted, worm-eaten, but still in good order; it has a hole in it through which the rod was run. He put on a fly, dark-bodied, with grey heron-wings, very different from the brilliant 'Doctors' and 'Butchers' which are chiefly in use now, and began to fish his pool. Carefully he fished it—a step and a cast—a step and a cast, the while going through the mental process of anticipation at the start, surprise at the negative result of the first half-dozen throws, disappointment when no boil in the water or pull beneath it awaited him at the first likely place. Before, however, disappointment had time to change into disgust he felt the pull, raised his rod a little, and found the strain increase; saw the water open enough to let him catch a glimpse of some part of a salmon, and then as rapidly close.

Archie came up the hill a little to have more command over the fish; a thrill of joyful exultation ran through him, and the frown on his face indicated only concentrated attention. With feet well apart, finger ready to check the line, and eyes following anxiously the point where it, slowly moving, cut the water tight as a strained steel wire, he stood on the bank, perhaps at that moment the happiest man in all the far-stretching parish of Glenorchy and Innishail. But near are joys and sorrows in this world; close together, ever watching mankind, sit Fortuna and the Fates.

From behind a grey rock on the opposite side of the river rose up now a grey man—long of leg, tough in sinew, stern of countenance; no greeting gave he to the fisherman, no friendly congratulations or applause. He stalked down to a convenient boulder, which commanded a good view of the pool, and sat down on it; he got out his pipe—his eye the while glued to the point of interest—and soon the gentle wind carried over to Archie's nostrils the fragrant scent of his tobacco.

A Prime Minister who, thinking he had a certain majority on a critical division, finds the Opposition have it instead, could hardly be more overwhelmed than Archie was at this bodeful appearance. Fishing was fairly free at the time we are writing of, because, as a rule, it was of little value, but on this part of the Awe the owner had lately been asserting his rights and warning off trespassers. Archie had offended, and had been caught; had offended again, with the same result; had offended again—and the patience of the authorities had at length been worn out. So the edict had gone forth that if ever again—only once—he was caught dipping a fly in the river, then would he have to leave his little cottage in Glen Nant, and the tiny well-loved farm—that never more on all those wide lands would he find a resting-place for his feet, 'Not if you lived for a hundred and seventy years!' added the factor, shaking a quill pen at him. But word had come to Archie the previous night that his enemy the keeper had been summoned to see a sick son far away up at Loch Tulla in the Blackmount, a long day's journey for an active man. And lo! regardless of that affection which is felt by all but the basest of men, this unnatural father was lying in wait for him here!

So it came about that Archibald MacCorquodale stood chained to the river by a big salmon within seventy yards of a man whom he looked on as a natural enemy—from whom he always felt inclined to fly even when merely pursuing his natural lawful occupation. His first thought was to break his line and be off. But what would he gain by that? He would not so shake off his foe. And there was another reason. There is a grim story of a laird of the old school who was busily engaged in playing a very heavy fish when a messenger came to tell him of the sudden and serious illness of his wife. The fisherman, reasoning that his wife might recover, but that he was never likely to get hold of such a monstrous specimen of the *Salar* tribe again, could not bring himself to loose his hold, so sent for further tidings. 'The mistress is dying,' was the answer: but the laird now found that he was engaged in a struggle with such a creature as Tweedside in all its history had never seen the like of, and again he hardened his heart; and it was only when he heard that all was over that he reluctantly broke, and went up to the house. 'She was a good wife to you, laird!' cried a weeping and sympathising retainer. 'Ay, she was that, Jeanie, she was a' that!' said the disconsolate widower; 'but eh, woman! yon was the varra mucklest fish that eyes of man ever yet saw on Tweed!'

The crofter felt something like the old laird: he had not seen the fish, beyond the merest glimpse of it as it slowly edged away out into the stream after being hooked, but he judged from the weight put on his hand and arm, and from the strain on the rod, that if it were only once on the bank, good kipper to eat with his porridge would be plentiful in his house for many a day to come. Always provided—and this was indeed a very large 'if'—no one prevented him carrying it off when it *was* landed. So in a swither of discomfiture and uncertainty Archie played his fish for five or ten minutes, and then, unable to bear the silence any longer, cried out to the man on the other shore—

'It's a fine day this!'

'It'll be a day you'll be wishing it was night, before

I've done wi' ye!' was the grim answer that came back, and Archie almost fell into the river at the response.

'It'll be a bad day's work for me this!' he cried out almost in a whine.

'It'll be all that, my man!' replied the keeper cheerfully.

The fish, so passive hitherto, had behaved as large fish often do behave—he had shown no hurry or undignified alarm. The disagreeable thing he had got into his mouth would soon be swallowed or spat out. So he sailed up and down the pool, unwilling to allow that there was any force guiding or compelling him from above. Then all of a sudden he got irritated, and made a furious rush across and down the stream without breaking water. The stiff unoiled reel screeched as it had never done before, and a red streak showed on the man's thumb as the coarse horse-hair line cut it almost to the bone. The salmon nearly ran aground in the shoaling water on the keeper's side, and then turned and went upstream again, and the latter saw the great white belly flash under the thin water as the mighty rudder of a tail twisted it round as on a pivot. Something like five feet of blue-brown back came shooting up the pool close to the bank, and then disappeared like a ghost in the deep stream above. Archie thought he had hold of a prize, but the other knew it, and his experienced eye told him that he had just seen the heaviest salmon which had ever come into his ken either in or out of the Awe. 'By ——, he is a fish!' he cried to himself, as with straining eyes he followed the wake in the water.

Great, indeed, was this keeper's wrath and indignation. It was bad enough that this poaching crofter should be at the river at all, but that he should fall on such a piece of luck as this was almost more than mortal man could bear. It made matters still worse for the spectator to think that he had been sitting for half an hour within twenty yards of the fish, and might have been playing him himself—if only he had known. The thought flashed through his brain that perhaps this was the way in which he was to be punished for the elaborate manœuvre by which MacCorquodale had been decoyed to the river.

If Rory MacGilp was miserable, Archibald was in a much more parlous state. He would have felt very diffident at working a salmon before this keeper's critical eye under the most favourable and lawful circumstances, and to do justice to himself he would require the ever-ready help of a thoroughly sympathetic friend. Indeed it would be incorrect to speak at this period of the fish as a captive. Archie was the captive: the creature did what it liked with him; moved up and down the slack water just as it chose; stopped and sank, and dug its nose down into the bottom when it wanted without asking any leave from the man on the bank. If such things were to be done in the green tree, what might be expected in the dry? If the salmon was all-powerful in the smooth, quiet pool, what would be his proceedings when he went seawards—into the wild rapids, and among the dangerous sunken rocks down the stream? Archie felt he *would* go down sooner or later—it was merely a question of time; and the perspiration poured from his forehead, his legs shook, and his hands trembled as he moved to and fro along the grassy bank. Whether he landed it, or whether it broke him, the end would be the same; certainly this time the offence would not be overlooked: he might say farewell to Barrachander, and bonnie Loch Tromlie, and green primrose-haunted Glen Nant.

The fish moved down to the tail of the pool, and sunk himself there; he got his nose upstream, and began to 'jig' at the line, each jig taking him a little farther down, and each vibration communicating a dreadful shock to the heart of the man above. 'In five minutes,' thought Archie, 'I'll be likely a mile down, with my rod broken, and that old heathen grinning at me!' Oh, for a friend now!

'Rory!' he cried out softly to his enemy—'Rory!' But no answer came back across the water. Rory sat like a carved statue on his rock.

'Mr MacGilp!—my fingers is cut to the quick! Will ye no' pitch a stone in below him and turn him up?' Still there was no answer. 'My back's fairly broken!' cried Archie piteously.

'I'm right glad to hear it,' roared back the keeper—'of that same back!'

'He's forty pounds weight!' cried Archie appealingly.

'HE'S SIXTY!' screamed Rory, jumping off his rock, and dancing about on the bank. 'You poaching deevil! I hope he'll break your neck and drown you afterwards!'

'Oh—what'll I do if he goes down?' howled the other man; 'he's off—he's off—what'll I do if he goes down?'

The fish lay now on the top of the rapid stream, furiously flapping his tail.

'Give him line!' shouted Rory, 'you great ——!' 'But what am I doing?' he cried to himself. 'Let him break—I hope he will!'

Archie lowered the point of his rod, and the fish—as fish so often will—stopped at the strain being taken off. But he was too far down to get back—foot by foot he walloped down; he was fairly out of the pool, he got into the stream, he struggled against it for a moment, and the next he was raging away down the river: now deep down in it, now showing his huge breadth of tail at the top, turning over and over like a porpoise, careless where he went so long as he got clear.

Archie stood in the old place on the bank with his mouth open and most of his hundred yards of line run out, as incapable of checking its movements as if it had been a hundredweight of iron.

'Rin! rin! after him!' roared Rory, forgetting himself again. 'Keep him in—— But let him alone, you fool!'

was again his second thought; 'let him be! he'll never get by the point!'

The keeper ran down the bank, hopping highly over the boulders, and never taking his eye off the bit of foaming water where he judged the runaway to be; and Archie, his first stupefaction over, did the same, and got a slight pull on the salmon some two hundred yards farther down.

Rory, when coming up in the morning, had left his rod here, and now got possession of it, and of his gaff, which latter he slung over his back. A little lower the river turned, and the two men and the fish followed the curve, and got—the last at any rate—into a bad bit of rock-protected stream, dangerous enough now, though much worse in low water. Whatever knowledge the fisherman had of the place was clean driven out of him by the agitation he was in, and it would have been purely by luck, and not by any sort of guidance, that he would have found a safe passage through. But every inch of the passage was known to the other: every rock and shoal was as clearly photographed on his mind as if it lay before him in bodily shape; the information which for fifty years had slowly percolated to his brain was complete; his hands twitched and his heart leapt when he saw the salmon make for a bad bit of water, and he was quite unable to stop himself from shouting out directions, though all the time he was heartily hoping that the fish would break his hold. The advice, which was plentifully accompanied with abuse of Archie, was always immediately followed by denunciation of himself—the giver of it.

'Keep your rod west and bring him in!' roared the keeper; 'are ye no' seeing the muckle rock there?'—the said rock being at the time six feet under water. Then to himself, 'Whisht, you old fool, and let him cut!' 'Let him come in my side, you black thief!' he thundered again, 'or he'll be round yon stob!—and I hope he will, and be damned to him! If it isn't enough to sicken a fox to see him wi' such a fish as that!'

By that time Archie had got three-quarters of a mile down the river, and was much more exhausted than the salmon. What with keeping a tight hold on it when sulking, and hopping among slippery smooth rocks and stones when it was lively, listening to the threatening advice from the other side—the penalty, moreover, which he would have to pay for his sport ever being present in his mind—he thought he had never had such a time of it since he was born, and felt that the hardest day's work he had ever done was child's play to what he was going through.

'If I was only quit of this cursed fish for good and all!' he now thought to himself; 'ay, if I was lying on my back wi' lumbago like Johnnie Ross, as I was pityin' sae much!'

The playing of a salmon is not often monotonous, and is sometimes exciting in the very highest degree, but, alas! how hopeless a task it is to attempt to communicate the exhilaration by written words! The reel 'screeches' or 'whirrs,' according as it is well-oiled, or a rusty implement like our poacher's. The line 'cuts the water,' the gaff 'went with a soft plunge' into the thick back. 'Fresh up from the sea with the lice on him.' All these words are appropriate and expressive, and they have been used over and over again hundreds and hundreds of times; scarce an account of a day's salmon-fishing is complete without them. The horrid vibration of the line as a big fish 'jigs' at it, and every thrill runs like an electric shock right into the very heart of the rod-holder, has been referred to in almost every account of a tussle with a heavy salmon. How stale the words are! how difficult to put in fresher or better ones! and yet how very freshly every individual shock comes home in practice! Each jig you think will be the last—will find out the weak place in the hold, or the gear, and he will be off.

At six o'clock Archie rose his fish; at half-past seven he was more than a mile down the river, pretty well beaten. He had passed through all the mental phases of apprehension, hope, and deadly fear; and now, after all this manœuvring, it seemed as if the end had come, and he would be able to reel up—what he had left—and go home to make arrangements for his 'flitting.' The fish made a wild rush up the river, turned above a big upstanding stone, and then swam slowly down again. The line touched the stone, and Archie could not clear it; the surface was smooth, and it still ran a little, but the end was near: unless the salmon at once retraced his path, he was a free salmon soon.

A good spring landed Rory out on a green-topped slippery boulder with twelve inches of water running over it. He heard the reel opposite give out its contents in sudden uncertain jerks; he caught sight of a huge bar of yellowish-white coming wobbling down towards him—lost it—saw it again, and delivered his stroke. Up came the great wriggling, curling mass—bright silver now—out of the river: with both hands close to the gaff-head, he half lifted, half dragged the fish to shore, struggling, and all but losing his footing in the passage; then up the bank with it till he was able to lie down on it and get his hand into its gills.

Twenty minutes later Archie, with a sinking heart, had crossed the bridge of Awe and travelled up the north bank. The keeper was sitting on a stone, quietly smoking, with no trace of anger on his face, and before him, on a bit of smooth thymy turf, lay a salmon such as many a man has dreamt about, but few, indeed, seen with mortal eyes. Then for the first time that day the poor crofter forgot his troubles: for half a minute his only feeling was one of intense pride—at such a victory.

'Well—he's safe now,' Rory said at length.

'Ay!' replied Archie, still gaping at him.

'Erchibald,' went on the keeper, 'oh, man! you worked

him just deevilish!' The other shook his head deprecatingly. 'Just deevilish!—frae start tae finish!'

'That was no' a bad bit o' work for a man o' my years,' the keeper continued. 'Gin I hadna been waiting for him there when he came by, it's little you'd have ever seen of your fish!'

'I ken that fine,' said Archie.

'Gin I had no' been quick enough to slip it into him there—it would be at Bonawe he would be by this time.'

'I'm believing that,' replied the crofter.

'It was no' an easy job neither. Stand you on yon stane and see what footing you'll have.'

'There was few could do it, indeed, Mr MacGilp.'

'He was far more like a stirk to lift out of the water than a decent saumon!'

'He was, Mr MacGilp—far more, indeed, like a very heavy stirk!'

'If it hadna been my knowledge of all they sunken rocks, and shouting myself hoarse to guide you, where would you have been, my man, by this time?'

'It was your inteemate acquaintance with the stanes which saved me, indeed,' once more agreed the crofter.

'There's no' anither man in the whole wide world could have steered you down yon places as I did!'

'There is certainly not one in many hundred score would have taken such a vast o' trouble about it.'

'I gaffed him—an' I told you the road to take him—an' saved him many a time——'

'You did all that an' more, Mr MacGilp. It's much obleeged——'

'I doubt I made the varra fly that rose him?'

'You did that, indeed,' said poor Archie, hopelessly. (He had made it himself the night before.)

'Dod!' cried the keeper, 'I believe I got yon muckle fish *mysell!!*'

The other stared at him.

'Erchie, lad,' said the keeper—and the voice of the man was changed now, and he spoke so softly and low it was difficult to recognise the same organ which a few minutes before had been hurling denunciations across the river—'I've been fishing here all my life; man and boy I've been fishing here for nearly fifty years, an' I never yet had the luck to get the grip of such a fish as that!'

MacCorquodale looked at him curiously, and he was never able to say positively—he was never quite sure in his own mind—whether it was a tear which rolled down over the rough cheek or not. Then there was long silence.

'An' where will it be ye'll be flitting to?' the old man asked, in quite another tone, and so suddenly that it made the crofter—deep in reverie—jump.

'Where'll I be—where—oh!—Mr MacGilp!'

'I believe I got yon muckle fish MYSELL!' with great emphasis on the last word.

Archie looked north and east and west, and then at the salmon.

'MYSELL!' as if finally and for the last time.

'I believe—that—too,' said Archie, with a groan. The last three words came out with a gulp.

'Well—he'll be an ugly burden to bear away doun. But a man canna pick an' choose as he would in this world! Good day to you then, Erchibald. And you might be going on wi' that new bit o' garden you're sae proud of; I'll gie you a wheen grand potatoes—next year—for seed for't.'

So MacCorquodale set out under the hot sun homewards. Once more he had a reprieve, and he wondered how it was he did not feel happier. During the exciting fight he had many times pictured to himself the little house from which he would be banished at Whitsunday, its rough meadow in front, and the peat-stacks, and the sunny untidy bit of garden, half filled with currant bushes and ribes and southernwood, over which the bees came in the gloaming, slow flying after their afternoon labour on the moor. Now he thought only of the battle he had won, which was not to bring him in any honour now, or happy reminiscences afterwards.

''Deed, I'll never have the chance of doing the like of yon again!' muttered the poor crofter to himself.

THE TAKING OF THE ANTHIAS

By OPPIAN

OPPIANOS (flourished 2nd century A.D.), Cilician author, famous in antiquity for his Greek poem *Halieutica* ('On Fishing'), and formerly believed, it would now appear wrongly, to have been also the author of the much inferior *Cynegetica* ('On Hunting') and of the now lost *Ixeutica* ('On Bird-catching'). The *Halieutica* contains a wealth of information, true and fancied, both on the habits of fish and on the ways of catching them. The poem confines itself to the sea and to sea-fishing, but, as will be seen from the extract given from Book III (ll. 220-334), there is an elemental quality which belongs to all fishing. What kind of fish the anthias was is not known. The translation is by Dr A. W. Mair and is here given from his *Oppian, Colluthus, Tryphiodorus* (1928) by permission of the editors of the Loeb Classical Library and of Messrs William Heinemann. The verse translation (1722) of the *Halieutica* by W. Diaper and J. Jones cannot be said to be of much merit.

THE belly bears sway over wild beasts and over reptiles and over the flocks of the air, but it has its greatest power among fishes; for them evermore the belly proves their doom.

Hear first the cunning mode of taking the Anthias which is practised by the inhabitants of our glorious fatherland above the promontory of Sarpedon, those who dwell in the city of Hermes, the town of Corycus, famous for ships, and in sea-girt Eleusa. A skilful man observes those rocks near the land, under which the Anthias dwell: caverned rocks, cleft with many a covert. Sailing up in his boat he makes a loud noise by striking planks together; and the heart of the Anthias rejoices in the din, and one haply rises presently from the sea, gazing at the boat and the man. Then the fisher straightway lets down into the waves the ready bait of perch or crowfish, offering a first meal of hospitality. The fish rejoices and greedily feasts on the welcome banquet and fawns upon the crafty fisherman. As to the house of a hospitable man there comes one famous for deeds of hand or head, and his host is glad to see him at his hearth and entreats him well with gifts and feast and all manner of loving-kindness; and at the table both rejoice and take their pleasure in pledging cup for cup; even so the fisher rejoices in hope and smiles while the fish delights in new banquets. Thenceforward the fisherman journeys to the rock every day and relaxes not his labour and ceases not to bring food. And straightway the Anthias gather all together in the place to feast, as if a summoner brought them. Always for more and readier fishes he provides the coveted food, and they have no thought of other paths or other retreats, but there they remain and linger, even as in the winter days the flocks abide in the steadings of the shepherds and care not to go forth even a little from the fold. And when the fishes descry the boat that feeds them starting from the land and speeding with the oars, immediately they are all alert and gaily they wheel over the sea, sporting delightfully, and go to meet their nurse. As when the mother swallow, the bird that first heralds the west wind of spring, brings food to her unfledged nestlings and they with soft cheeping leap for joy about their mother in the nest and open their beaks in their desire for food, and all the house of some hospitable man resounds with the shrill crying of the mother bird; even so the fishes leap joyfully to meet their feeder as he comes, even as in the circle of a dance. And the fisherman fattening them with dainty after dainty and with his hand stroking them and proffering them his gifts from his hand, tames their friendly heart, and anon they obey him like a master, and wheresoever he indicates with his finger, there they swiftly rush. Now behind the boat, now in front, now landward he points his hand; and thou shalt see them, like boys in a place of wrestling, according to the wisdom of a man, rushing this way or that as their master bids. But when he has tended them enough and bethinks him of taking them, then he seats himself with a line in his left hand and fits thereto a hook, strong and sharp. Then all the fishes alike he turns away, commanding them with his hand, or he takes a stone and casts it in the water, and they dive after it, thinking it to be food. One picked fish alone he leaves, whichsoever he will—unhappy fish, rejoicing in a banquet which is to be its last. Then he reaches down the hook over the sea and the fish swiftly seizes its doom; and the bold fisher draws it in with both hands, winning a speedy prey by his cunning. And he avoids the notice of the rest of the company of Anthias; for if they see or hear the din of the unhappy victim being landed, then the fisher will never more have banquets enough to tempt the fishes to return, but they spurn with loathing both his attentions and the place of destruction. But the fisher should be a powerful man and land his fish by force of strength or else a second man should lend a hand in his labour. For so, unwitting of their crafty doom, fattened themselves they fitly fatten others; and always when thou wilt, successful fishing shall be thine.

Others trust in their valiant might and strength of limb when they array the great adventure against the Anthias, not cultivating friendship nor proffering food but having recourse at once to the pointed hook and overcoming the fish by their valour. The hook is fashioned of hard bronze or iron, and two separate barbs are attached to the great rope of twisted flax. On it they fix a live basse—if a live one be at hand; but if it be a dead one, speedily one puts in its mouth a piece of lead, which they call a dolphin; and the fish, under the weight of the lead, moves his head to and fro, as if alive. The line is strong and well-woven. When the Anthias hear the noise and leap from the sea, then some attend to the labour of the oar, while the fisherman from the stern-end lets down the crooked snare into the sea, gently waving it about. And the fishes all straightway follow the ship and seeing before their eyes what seems to be a fleeing fish, they rush in haste after the banquet, each striving to outstrip the other: thou wouldst say it was a foeman plying swift knees in pursuit of a routed foe: and they are eager for goodly victory. Now whichever fish the fisher sees to be best, to it he offers the banquet, and with eager gape it rushes after the gift that is no gift. Thereupon thou shalt see the valour of both, such a struggle there is as man and captive fish contend. His strong arms and brows and shoulders and the sinews of his neck and ankles swell with might and strain with valour; while the fish, chafing with pain, makes a fight, pulling against the pulling fisher, striving to dive into the sea, raging incontinently. Then the fisher bids his comrades plunge in their oars; and as the ship speeds forward, he on the stern is dragged bodily backward by the rush of the fish, and the line whistles, and the blood drips from his torn hand. But he relaxes not the grievous contest. As two keen men of mighty valour stretch their grasp about one another and endeavour each to pull the other, hauling with backward strain; and long time both, enduring equal measure of toil, pull might and main and are pulled; even so between those, the fisher and the fish, strife arises, the one eager to rush away, the other eager to pull him in. Nor do the other Anthias fishes desert the captive in his agony, but are fain to help him and violently hurl their backs against him and fall each one upon him, foolishly, and know not that they are afflicting their comrade. Often also when they are fain to tear through the line with their jaws, they are helpless, since their mouth is unarmed. At last when the fish is weary with labour and pain and the quick rowing, the man overpowers him and pulls him in. But if the fisher yield to him even a little, he cannot pull him in—so tremendous is his strength. Often he tears and cuts the line on his sharp spine and rushes away, leaving the fisherman empty-handed.

FIRST OF APRIL

By WILLIAM SENIOR

WILLIAM SENIOR (pseudonym 'Red Spinner'; 1838-1920), one of the best known of English anglers and writers on angling. He was, succeeding Francis Francis, angling editor of *The Field* in 1884-99 and editor-in-chief in 1900-9. 'First of April' is from Part I, chapter VII, of *Near and Far* (1888) and is here given by permission of Messrs Sampson Low, Marston, & Co. Other angling stories by Senior are in his *A Mixed Bag* (1895) and *Lines in Pleasant Places* (1920).

WHAT struck me more than anything else, standing by the waterside in the somewhat dull morning of the 1st of April with which I am now concerned, was the extreme backwardness of the season. There was not the slightest spring of grass to be seen in the meadows, and you had to examine very closely to find the signs of budding in the trees. The hawthorns were beginning to shoot, no doubt, and the blackthorns, according to their custom, had flowered. But the clump of willows near which I stood arrested my attention, because I remembered that on the 1st of April of the previous year they were fairly towards development of leaf. Even now they had begun to sprout. But the willow shoots in a curious way, and the sprouting leaf at a little distance looks like something which has decayed, rather than like something which is about to burst into life. Flowers also were few and far between. I was treading on some ground ivy, which had fairly blossomed, and in the marshy places and near the river, a few celandines had opened their large yellow stars to catch what there was of sun. But, on the whole, it was a very wintry-looking 1st of April prospect, and, of course, a moment's reflection would convince one, that this was only natural, for the series of floods had been long and vexatious, and, when the water had gone down, there had supervened nipping frosts and blighting east winds, which had put a strong check upon the forwardness which early in February was being remarked.

But looking about one to make notes of what there was or what there was not in meadow, wood, marsh, or hedgerow was not angling, and the ten minutes, which I must confess had been spent in the above observations, might probably lose me that fish, of whose existence I was well aware. I knew of his being there during the first week of March. I saw him twice moving about between St David's Day and Lady Day, and on the previous evening, just before the sun went down, as I stood on the little wooden bridge spanning a turbulent torrent, which constituted a sort of extra byfall a short distance removed from the weir proper, I was delighted to find that my gentleman had not departed for foreign parts.

A very simple-looking man, in that queer combination of nautical and farmyard costume so often to be seen by the riverside, sucked his short black pipe as he leaned upon the rail. He looked so innocent and confiding, and seemed so indifferent to anything connected with the water, gazing as he did at the moment with a far-off style at a distant hill crowned by clumps of trees, that I entered into conversation with him. Yes; he had no doubt there were some trout in the weir pool, and, indeed, he remembered that last year towards the fag end of the season a seven-pounder had been taken between the lasher and weir, and, now he came to think of it, he was also able to state that Tim Bridges, a 'stoopid sort o' feller,' working on the railway, had not more than two months ago been fined by the magistrates thirty shillings for taking a trout out of season from the very weir pool which was thundering in our ears. I was glad to hear that Mr Bridges had suffered for his breach of the law, although, as the man had gone about from village to village showing his prize, and swiping at each exhibition, it was evident that he was unaware, until too late, of the crime he had wrought. It was a bad case, however, the fish being in miserable condition.

I ought, perhaps, to remark that the weir pool at the spot of which I am writing was a very peculiar one. There was the small byfall to which I have referred; there was the weir proper; there was a broadish lasher, the whole between them making a very fair description of tumbling bay, flanked by strong individual streams. A little below, however, there were three small islands ranged at almost equal distances along the bed of the river, and as the bed had silted up between these islands, the stream from the byfall ran swiftly, close under the bank, which was hollowed out and steep. It was in one of the swift streams of this by-water, not far from where it roared under the little bridge, that the trout upon which I had fixed my affections was located.

'There's a pretty good trout feeding yonder,' I said to the rustic, who still smoked on upon the bridge, with the bowl of his pipe in an inverted position.

'No,' he said, 'I don't know much about fishing; but you may depend on't there's no trout there.'

'Oh,' I said, 'I beg your pardon, you are mistaken. I have seen him there several times myself, and I mean to get him if I can to-morrow morning.'

'Well, sir, I wish yer luck,' he replied. 'There'll be two or three gents a-fishing, I expect, off the ware-beams in the morning. I see 'em going to the White Bull wi' their baskets and rods as I come along just now. You had better be early.'

This, I told him, I intended to be, and the civility and intelligence of the man so impressed me that I offered him the choice of any cigar he might fancy from my case. On the morning of April the first I kept the resolution which I had informed my rustic companion I had made, and was at the waterside right early. It was very little after daylight, and, although the wind seemed to be backing a little towards the north, and, although it was a cold air, it was nothing like so piercing as it had been during the previous month.

I soon got to work, spinning over the spot where my trout had taken lodgings, but without success. I worked the stream thoroughly down to the end until breakfast-time, toiling hard and executing every dodge with which I was acquainted. My marked trout would have none of me. Then I winched up my line, and, disposing safely of the flight, strolled across within hail of two London anglers who had been similarly occupied for three hours over the weir pool. One of them said he had been broken away by a big trout; the other said he had had repeated attacks made upon his bleak; but neither had anything to show for their operations. So I left them still trying, and cheering themselves with the interchange of an opinion that the sun would soon shine and infuse something of warmth into the chilly atmosphere.

For myself, I walked back to the White Bull, and resolved that if I could get no trout I would at least get breakfast. I was not a little surprised, though very much delighted, to find that when John, the waiter, with a look of triumph, whipped off the cover from the dish, there lay exposed to view a very shapely Thames trout that, in the full enjoyment of its physical proportions, would have weighed over three pounds. I asked no questions but attacked the meat, which did not, however, eat with the flavour which betokens the well-conditioned fish. Still, there it was upon the table, as the *pièce de résistance* of the feast, and I did it ample justice.

'Where did you manage to get your trout, John?' I said, as the waiter came to see how I was getting on.

'Well, sir, I cannot exactly say where he came from, but I believe as he was caught in the river here this morning.'

'Oh, nonsense,' I said; 'impossible! I was out there

at daylight myself, and there was not a soul about at that time, although the gentlemen who are stopping here came down to the weir soon after.'

'Well, sir, to tell you the truth, I don't know; but I heard them say that the fish had been caught this morning.'

Hereupon, when breakfast was over, I strolled round to the bar and into the smoking-parlour, where, as I expected, I found the landlord. I knew this gentleman of old, and scarcely hoped to receive any information from him; but I felt bound, as a matter of duty, to put him through the leading questions one asks on such an occasion.

'Well, I really don't know,' he said. 'The trout, of course, has been caught to-day. I shouldn't think of buying a fish out of season, but I never ask any questions. All I can tell you is that the trout was alive when he was brought here.'

'What time did you get it?' I inquired.

'I can answer that question very exactly,' he replied with a smile, 'for the clock in the old church at Longton-cum-Burton was striking seven as I handed over two shillings and took in return the fish, which was still gasping, his gills opening slowly but unmistakably.'

'May I ask from whom you bought it?' I then inquired.

'I bought it,' he said, 'from Bridges.'

'What,' I said, 'do you mean Bridges, the same man that was fined thirty shillings for taking a trout out of season this side of Christmas?'

'Yes,' he said, 'that is the man, but he learned a lesson that time.'

'Do you think Bridges caught the trout?'

'That I cannot say; as I told you, I never ask questions, because I know that if I did, in cases of that kind, I should generally hear lies in answer to them.'

I did not quite understand the matter, nor did I feel satisfied about this Thames trout; and as I stood in front of the inn, looking up at the waxen buds which tipped all the branches of the great chestnut-tree, and blowing up clouds of tobacco smoke to reach them if they could, I heard the voice of a man who was evidently in some stage of liquor—a voice thick and droning, and the words he spoke, run into each other as they were, at once attracted my attention, for those words were—

'And a blanked good trout it was, I can tell you.'

I knew where the voice came from, and strolled round leisurely through the stable-yard, past the kitchen, and so to the taproom, where I saw a labouring man stretched on a settle, with a small measure, apparently of gin, on the table, and an empty glass by its side. There were two other men sitting on each side of the fire smoking stolidly, and not paying, apparently, much attention to the gentleman on the settle. One of them spoke, remarking in a careless sort of tone—

'Well, that is two bob off the thirty, anyhow, Jim.'

Here, then, was Mr Bridges, who had sold the fish; and without beating about the bush, I said, pretending that we were old acquaintances—

'Hallo, Bridges, how are you? That was a good trout you got this morning.'

''Scuse me, sir,' he said, 'you've got the better on me, for I'm blest if I remember you. Howsomedever, that's neither here nor there; but I didn't catch the trout, you know.'

'Who did, then?'

'A man we calls Swankey hereabouts.'

'A fisherman?'

'Not exactly to say a fisherman—a sort of poacher feller.'

'When did he catch it?'

'I should say it were about three this morning he got that trout, but in the most queerest place you'd think on. What Swankey was partickerly pleased about was that one of them swells that is stopping here put him on to the fish last night. Then, d'ye see, Swankey, who never meant to go fishing this morning, comes and borrows my old rod and goes and gets a bleak, and, by George! he'd not been gone an hour afore he comes back wi' a bloomin' trout.'

The reader will naturally observe at once that the person called Swankey was my innocent friend, to whose agreeable manners I had offered the generous tribute of a good cigar on the previous evening, and who had abused my confidence by slinking out in the raw, dark morning, and capturing the fish upon which I had set my desire for a good month past.

I am too much of a philosopher to fly into a rage over a trifle of this kind; but I must confess, as I took my rod and tackle, and strolled down once more to the river, I felt that Mr Swankey had got, not only a Thames trout, but a thorough-paced April fool in my humble self.

THE KING O' THE CAULD

By THOMAS TOD STODDART

THOMAS TOD STODDART (1810-1880), famous Border angler, the laureate of angling and the author of the first practical Scottish manual on angling. Born in Edinburgh, he adopted Kelso as his home, and, living in the classic days of Scottish angling, had 'Christopher North' and James Hogg as friends. His angling manual was first published as *The Art of Angling as Practised in Scotland* (1835), but after being recast and enlarged appeared under the new name of *The Angler's Companion to the Rivers and Lochs of Scotland* (1847) and held the field till the publication of W. C. Stewart's *The Practical Angler* (1857). The body of Stoddart's angling verse is in *Songs and Poems* (1839; new ed., entitled *Angling Songs*, with a memoir by his daughter, 1889); and other angling books of his are *Angling Reminiscences* (1837) and *An Angler's Rambles and Angling Songs* (1866). 'The King o' the Cauld' is from *Songs and Poems*, where, however, it has the title 'Ower at the Cauld-foot'; the present title is that in *An Angler's Rambles and Angling Songs*. See also p. 277.

OWER at the cauld[1]-foot
There bides an auld troot,
No mony there be that are wiser;
It baffles a' skill
To tether his gill
An' gie the sly boy a surpriser.

He's thick an' he's braid
Wi' sprecks[2] like a taed[3]
An' spangles o' ilka dimension,
Mirk spangles an' reid
Frae his waem[4] to his heid,
In number ayont comprehension.

[1] weir. [2] spots. [3] toad. [4] belly.

Sic a swasher[1] I ween
Is rare to be seen,
An' no to be grippit wi' thinkin';
It gars[2] ilka chiel
Lay his loof[3] on his reel
An' sets e'en the wisest a-blinkin'.

Auld Purdie cam doon
Ane braw afternoon.
(Ilk angler taks choice o' his weather),
Quoth he, 'I'll soon bring
The knave to the spring
An' teach him the taste o' a feather.'

Sae e'en he set till 't,
Like ane muckle skill 't,
But faith, let the braggin' come last o't;
Frae the mirk till the dawin',[4]
In spite o' his crawin',
He ne'er could mak oot the richt cast o't.

There was Foster an' Kerse
An' a chiel frae the Merse
Wad set a' the water a-seethin';
Watty Grieve an' Jock Hay
Cam ower the way
Wi' Scougal o' fair Innerleithen.

The mair were the han's,
The rifer the wan's,
Our king o' the cauld got the braver;
He bobbit aboot
Wi' his wonnerfu' snoot
An' cock't up his tail oot o' favour.

[1] big fellow. [2] causes. [3] hand. [4] dawning.

But fling as they micht,
To the left or the richt,
Wi' mennin,[1] mawk,[2] lob, leech or rawin[3];
No a rug[4] wad he gie,
For weel ettled[5] he
O' the gear whilk the wind was a-blawin'.

Come, anglers, come a',
Baith meikle an' sma',
Tak yer chance o' the cunnin' auld reiver;
For aught that ye ken,
Mither Fortune may len'
Gude speed to yer wan's an' ye deive[6] her.

[1] minnow. [2] maggot. [3] roe.
[4] tug. [5] knew. [6] deafen, by persistence.

THE ONE-EYED PERCH

By LORD LYTTON

EDWARD GEORGE EARLE LYTTON BULWER-LYTTON, 1ST BARON LYTTON (1803-1873), in the writing of some thirty novels, touched on most themes, angling among the rest. 'The One-eyed Perch' is from Book Sixth, chapter VIII, of *My Novel* (1853); and in *Eugene Aram* (1832) is a fine description of an angler's meadow (Bk I, chap. VI), an indictment of the cruelty of fishing (also in Bk I, chap. VI), and a fishing incident given below on p. 279.

THE weather was singularly lovely, with that combination of softness and brilliancy which is only known to the rare, true summer days of England; all below so green, above so blue—days of which we have about six in the year, and recall vaguely when we read of Robin Hood and Maid Marian, of Damsel and Knight in Spenser's golden Summer Song—or of Jacques, dropped under the oak-tree, watching the deer amidst the dells of Ardennes. So, after a little pause at their inn, they strolled forth, not for travel but pleasure, towards the cool of sunset, passing by the grounds that once belonged to the Duke of Kent, and catching a glimpse of the shrubs and lawns of that beautiful domain through the lodge-gates; then they crossed into some fields, and came to a little rivulet called the Brent. Helen had been more sad that day than on any during their journey. Perhaps because, on approaching London, the memory of her father became more vivid; perhaps from her precocious knowledge of life, and her foreboding of what was to befall them, children that they both were. But Leonard was selfish that day; he could not be influenced by his companion's sorrow; he was so full of his own sense of being, and he already caught from the atmosphere the fever that belongs to anxious capitals.

'Sit here, sister,' said he imperiously, throwing himself under the shade of a pollard tree that overhung the winding brook, 'sit here and talk.'

He flung off his hat, tossed back his rich curls, and sprinkled his brow from the stream that eddied round the roots of the tree that bulged out, bald and gnarled, from the bank, and delved into the waves below. Helen quietly obeyed him, and nestled close to his side.

A step was heard, and a shadow fell over the stream. A belated angler appeared on the margin, drawing his line impatiently across the water, as if to worry some dozing fish into a bite before it finally settled itself for the night. Absorbed in his occupation, the angler did not observe the young persons on the sward under the tree, and he halted there, close upon them.

'Curse that perch!' said he aloud.

'Take care, sir,' cried Leonard; for the man, in stepping back, nearly trod upon Helen.

The angler turned. 'What's the matter? Hist! you have frightened my perch. Keep still, can't you?'

Helen drew herself out of the way, and Leonard remained motionless. He felt a sympathy for the angler.

'It is the most extraordinary perch, that!' muttered the stranger, soliloquising. 'It has the devil's own luck. It must have been born with a silver spoon in its mouth, that damned perch! I shall never catch it—never! Ha! —no—only a weed. I give it up.' With this, he indignantly jerked his rod from the water and began to disjoint it. While leisurely engaged in this occupation, he turned to Leonard.

'Humph! are you intimately acquainted with this stream, sir?'

'No,' answered Leonard. 'I never saw it before.'

Angler (solemnly). 'Then, young man, take my advice, and do not give way to its fascinations. Sir, I am a martyr to this stream; it has been the Delilah of my existence.'

Leonard (interested, the last sentence seemed to him poetical). 'The Delilah, sir, the Delilah!'

Angler. 'The Delilah. Young man, listen, and be warned by example. When I was about your age, I first came to this stream to fish. Sir, on that fatal day, about 3 p.m., I hooked up a fish—such a big one, it must have weighed a pound and a half. Sir, it was that length'; and the angler put finger to wrist. 'And just when I had got it nearly ashore, by the very place where you are sitting, on that shelving bank, young man, the line broke, and the perch twisted himself among those roots, and—cacodæmon that he was—ran off, hook and all. Well, that fish haunted me; never before had I seen such a fish. Minnows I had caught in the Thames and elsewhere, also gudgeons, and occasionally a dace. But a fish like that—a PERCH—all his fins up, like the sails of a man-of-war—a monster perch—a whale of a perch!—No, never till then had I known what leviathans lie hid within the deeps. I could not sleep till I had returned; and again, sir—I caught that perch. And this time I pulled him fairly out of the water. He escaped; and how did he escape? Sir, he left his eye behind him on the hook. Years, long years, have passed since then; but never shall I forget the agony of that moment.'

Leonard. 'To the perch, sir?'

Angler. 'Perch! agony to him! He enjoyed it—agony to me. I gazed on that eye, and the eye looked as sly and as wicked as if it were laughing in my face. Well, sir, I had heard that there is no better bait for a perch than a perch's eye. I adjusted that eye on the hook, and dropped in the line gently. The water was unusually clear; in two minutes I saw that perch return. He approached the hook; he recognised his eye—frisked his tail—made a plunge—and, as I live, carried off the eye, safe and sound; and I saw him digesting it by the side of that water-lily. The mocking fiend! Seven times since that day, in the course of a varied and eventful life, have I caught that perch, and seven times has that perch escaped.'

Leonard (astonished). 'It can't be the same perch; perches are very tender fish—a hook inside of it, and an eye hooked out of it—no perch could withstand such havoc in its constitution.

Angler (with an appearance of awe). 'It does seem supernatural. But it *is* that perch; for harkye, sir, there is ONLY ONE perch in the whole brook! All the years I have fished here, I have never caught another perch; and this solitary inmate of the watery element I know by sight better than I knew my own lost father. For each time that I have raised it out of the water, its profile has been turned to me, and I have seen with a shudder, that it has had only—One Eye! It is a most mysterious and a most diabolical phenomenon, that perch! It has been the ruin of my prospects in life. I was offered a situation in Jamaica: I could not go with that perch left here in triumph. I might afterwards have had an appointment in India, but I could not put the ocean between myself and that perch: thus have I frittered away my existence in the fatal metropolis of my native land. And once a week, from February to December, I come hither. Good Heavens! if I should catch the perch at last, the occupation of my existence will be gone.'

Leonard gazed curiously at the angler, as the last thus mournfully concluded. The ornate turn of his periods did not suit with his costume. He looked woefully threadbare and shabby—a genteel sort of shabbiness too—shabbiness in black. There was humour in the corners of his lip; and his hands, though they did not seem very clean—indeed his occupation was not friendly to such niceties—were those of a man who had not known manual labour. His face was pale and puffed, but the tip of the nose was red. He did not seem as if the watery element was as familiar to himself as to his Delilah—the perch.

'Such is Life!' recommenced the angler, in a moralising tone, as he slid his rod into its canvas case. 'If a man knew what it was to fish all one's life in a stream that has only one perch—to catch that one perch nine times in all, and nine times to see it fall back into the water, plump—if a man knew what it was—why, then'—here the angler looked over his shoulder full at Leonard—'why then, young sir, he would know what human life is to vain ambition. Good evening.'

Away he went treading over the daisies and kingcups. Helen's eyes followed him wistfully.

'What a strange person!' said Leonard, laughing.

'I think he is a very wise one,' murmured Helen; and she came close up to Leonard, and took his hand in both hers, as if she felt already that he was in need of the Comforter—the line broken, and the perch lost!

THE WAY BILLY HARRIS DROVE THE DRUM-FISH TO MARKET

By T. C. HALIBURTON

THOMAS CHANDLER HALIBURTON (1796-1865), Nova Scotian humorist and satirist, the creator of 'Sam Slick' and a founder of the American school of humour. In volume II, chapter I, of *Sam Slick's Wise Saws and Modern Instances* (2 vols 1853) the hero combines angling and love-making and it must be said engagingly. 'The Way Billy Harris Drove the Drum-fish to Market' is from *Traits of American Humour* (1852). See also p. 371.

THE afternoon of a still, sultry day, found us at the Bankhead spring, on Chaptico Bay, Maryland—Billy Harris, old 'Blair,' and myself. Billy was seated on the head of his canoe, leisurely discussing a bone and a slice of bread, the remnant of his midday's repast on the river; old 'Blair' was busily engaged in overhauling and arranging the fish that he had taken in the course of the morning: while I, in a state of half-listlessness, half-doziness, was seated on the trunk of an uprooted cedar near the spring, with my head luxuriously reclining against the bank.

'Well, this is about as pooty a fish as I've had the handling ov for some time,' remarked old 'Blair,' holding up and surveying with much satisfaction a rock about two feet and a half in length.

'Smart rock that,' said Billy, as he measured the fish with his eye. 'What an elegint team a couple o' dozen o' that size would make!'

'Elegint *what*, Mr Harris?' inquired old 'Blair,' depositing the fish under the bushes in the bow of his canoe, and turning round towards Billy.

'Why, an elegint team for a man to travel with,'

replied Billy. 'Did I never tell you 'bout my driving the drums to the Alexandri' market?' he added, at the same time casting a furtive glance in the direction of the spot where I was seated.

'Well, I've hearn a right smart of your exploits, Mr Harris, in our meetin's down here on the bay,' said 'Blair,' 'but I don't remember ov hearin' you tell about that.'

'The fact is,' said Billy, 'it's a little out o' the usual run o' things, and it's not everyone that I care about telling it to. Some people are so hard to make believe, that there's no satisfaction in telling them anything; seeing it's you, though, Lewis, I don't mind relating that little spree—'specially as the tide won't serve us up the narrows for some time yet, and Mr ——, there, seems inclined to do a little napping. Well, to begin at the beginning,' he continued, as old 'Blair' assumed the attitude of an attentive listener at the head of his canoe, 'it's just seven years ago the tenth day of this here last month, that I went down to the drumming-ground off the salt-works to try my luck among the thumpers. I know'd the gents were about, for I'd heard 'em drumming the day before while I was out rocking on the outer eend o' Mills's; so I got everything ready the over night, and by an hour by sun the next morning I had arrived upon the ground, ready for action. For the first half-hour or so I done nothing. Sometimes an old chanu'ler or a greedy cat would pay his respects to my bait in a way that would make my heart jump up into my mouth, and get me kind o' excited like, but that was all. Devil the drum ever condescended to favour me with a nibble. A'ter a while I begun to get tired o' that kind o' sport, and concluded that I'd just up-stake and shove a little nearer in shore. Just as I was preparing to pull in my line, though, I spied a piece o' pine bark 'bout twenty yards off, floating down towards me. "Now," says I, "gents, I'll give you until that bit of bark passes my line, to bite in, and if you don't think proper to do it in that time, you may breakfast as you can—I'll not play the waiting-boy any longer." Well, the piece of bark got right off against my line without my getting so much as a nibble, and I begun wind up; but I hadn't got more'n a foot or so o' the line outer the water, when I felt something give me a smart tug. At first I thought it might be a crab or an oyster-shell that I'd hooked, but presently my line begun to straighten under a strong, steady pull, and then I know'd what was about. I give one sangorous jerk, and the dance commenced.'

'What was it—a drum?' inquired old 'Blair,' a little eagerly.

'Yes, a drum, and a regular scrouger, at that. I wish you had only been there, Lewis, to see the fun. Of all the hard fish to conquer that ever I took in hand, that chap was the Major. I got him alongside at last, though, and lifted him in. I then run a rope through his gills, and sent him overboard agin, makin' the two eends of the line fast to a staple in the stern o' the boat, just behind me.

'Well, this put me in first-rate spirits, and out went my line agin in the twinklin' of an eye. Before it had time to touch the bottom, it was jerked through my hand for the matter of a yard or so, and then cum another interestin' little squabble. Just as I got that chap to the top o' the water, 'way went t'other line!'

'My patience!' exclaimed old 'Blair,' who had probably never taken a drum in the whole course of his life, '*two* goin' at once?'

'Yes, *two* at once.'

'And did you save 'em both, Mr Harris?'

'Save 'em!' said Billy; 'did you ever know me to lose a fish a'ter I'd once struck him?'

'Well, exceptin' that big rock this mornin',' replied 'Blair,' as a scarcely perceptible smile crept over his ebony visage, 'I don't remember as I ever did.'

'But that, you know, was the fault o' the hook—the beard wasn't quite long enough,' said Billy. 'But to come back to the drums,' he continued, quickly. 'In about three hours from the time I staked down I had no less than thirty-nine fine fish floating at the eend o' my little corner; so I concluded that I'd just up-stake, and make a push for the narrows.

'"But how am I to get the drums along?" said I to myself; "that's the next question. If I take 'em in the boat, I shall be swamped to a certainty; and if I undertake to tow 'em straight up the river, it's a school o' pilchers to a single crocus that I'm run away with."

'A'ter debating the matter for a little while with myself, I concluded that I'd just shove in quietly towards the land, until I got into shoal water, and then follow the shore. So I bent over as easy as I could, pulled up the stake, and commenced shoving along; but no sooner did the drums feel themselves moving through the water, than they turned tack, and, with a flirt of their tails, dashed smack off down the river, like so many terrified colts.'

'Thar, bless the Lord!' ejaculated old 'Blair,' suddenly rising from his seat, and then resuming it again.

'My first thought,' continued Billy, 'was to cut the rope, and let the whole batch of 'em go; but on turning round for that purpose, I found that the stern of the boat was buried so low in the water, that a little stream was beginning to run over the top; so I jist travelled to the other eend of the boat, and tried to bear down. But the thing wasn't to be done so easy. The drums had taken the bit between their teeth, and were pulling down with a regular forty-horse power. Seeing no other way of saving myself from the crabs, I just got a-straddle o' the boat, and worked my way backwards, until I reached the last half-inch o' the bow, and there I sot, with my legs dangling in the water, 'till the gents begun to cool down, and come to the top. By this time we had got over Cobb Bar, and the drums were looking straight up the Potomac. I never knowed how to account for it, but just then a queer notion struck me:

'"'Spose, now," said I to myself, "I was to take these chaps in hand, and drive 'em to Alexandri'; wouldn't it be something to talk about when I got back!"

'The thing sorter pleased me, and I determined to try it, come what might of it. So I reached down, and got hold o' my drum-line, and carefully doubled it. I then got down into the boat, and crawled along on my hands and knees to the other eend o' the corner, where the drums were, and looked over. Finding that they were all moving along quietly, I tied my line to the two eends o' the rope that they were fastened with, and then cut the rope loose from the staple. This made the reins about twenty-five yards long, but I only let out about one-half ov 'em. I was afraid, you see, if I give the gents too much play room, that they might get into tantrums, and give me more trouble. Seeing, a'ter a while, though, that I could manage 'em pretty well, I just wound the line round my left hand, picked up my angel rod for a whip, took my seat in the stern of the boat, and told 'em to travel. And *didn't* they travel! I wish you could only have seen me, Lewis. Old Neption, that Mr ——, there, sometimes tells about, wasn't a circumstance. I had a thundering big red drum in the lead, and nineteen as pretty matches o' black ones following after, as ever a man could wish to look at; and they all moved along as nicely as so many well-broke carriage-horses. It's true, a chap would sometimes become a little fractious like, and sheer off towards the Ma'yland or Virginny shore, but I'd just fetch a draw on t'other tack, and give him a slight touch with the rod near the back fin, and he'd fall into line agin as beautiful as could be. Well, Lewis, to make a long story short, it was about ten o'clock in the day when I took the gentlemen in hand, and by three hours by the sun that evening, I pitched the reins over one o' the posts on the Alexandri' wharf. A crowd o' people had collected together to see me land, and as the thing ov a man's drivin' fish to market seemed to tickle 'em, I soon sold out my whole team, at a dollar and a half a head. I at first thought of holding on to about half a dozen ov 'em to travel home with; but as I expected they were pretty well tired out, and the wind happened to be fair, I bought me a sail, laid in a supply ov eatables, and a jug of the best old rye that ever tickled a man's throat' (a slight working of old 'Blair's' mouth was here perceptible), 'and at day-break the next morning was snoozing it away nicely under my own shingles at home.'

'Didn't you see no steam-boats, nor nothin', on your way up, Mr Harris?' inquired old 'Blair.'

'Oh yes,' said Billy. ''Bout twenty miles this side o' Alexandri' I met the old Columbria coming down under a full head o' steam. She was crowded with people, and as I passed close along by the wheel-house, and bowed my head to 'em, they all clapped their hands and hollered mightily. I hearn afterwards that the captin, or somebody else, had it all put in the papers, but I can't say from my own knowledge whether it was so or not. I also overtook two or three brigs, but didn't stop to talk—just give 'em a nod, and passed on.'

'My patience!' exclaimed old 'Blair'; 'well you *was* a-travellin'.'

'Just t'other side o' Nangem'y Reach, too,' continued Billy, 'I fell in with a sa'cy little pungy, that brushed up alongside, and seemed inclined to keep company. As the wind happened to freshen up just then, I couldn't get away from her nohow; and the son of a blood of a captin kept bearing me in towards the land until he got me almost right upon a long bar before I know'd it. As the water was several feet deep at the eend of the bar, the pungy could pass right by it without touching; so I had either to cross the bar or go round the pungy. It was a desperate undertaking to try the bar, for 'bout a yard or so wide it was perfectly bare; but I couldn't think of being beat, so I just stood up in the boat, gathered the line well together in my hands, and with a whoop to the drums, rushed 'em at it.'

'And did you *raily* cross it, Mr Harris?' said 'Blair,' a little staggered.

'Without turning a shell,' replied Billy.

'And what became o' the pungy?'

'Why in a little while the wind died away, and she dropped behind, and I saw nothing more of her. I reckon it mad the captin open his eyes though, to see the way I crossed the bar. But the greatest expl'it ov all was——'

'What, you unconscionable liar—what?' exclaimed I, determined to put a stop to any further drafts upon old 'Blair's' credulity.

'Why, the one you was tellin' me t'other day 'bout old Neption's hitching his sea-horses to some big island or 'nother, and pulling it up by the roots, and towing it off with the people and all on it, and anchorin' it down in some other place that he liked better,' was the unexpected rejoinder.

A reply was deemed unnecessary; and in a few minutes more the cheerful plash of the Bankhead spring was among the sounds we heard not.

LANG SYNE

By 'IAN MACLAREN'

JOHN WATSON (pseudonym 'Ian Maclaren'; 1850-1907), Scottish clergyman and author, one of the founders of the 'Kailyard' school of fiction. 'Lang Syne' is from chapter I of 'Drumsheugh's Love Story' in *The Days of Auld Langsyne* (1895) and is here given by permission of the author's executor and of Messrs Hodder & Stoughton.

THE wind came in gusts, roaring in the chimney, and dying away with a long moan across the fields, while the snowdrift beat against the window. Drumsheugh's dog, worn out with following his master through the drifts, lay stretched before the fire sound asleep, but moved an ear at the rattling of a door upstairs, or a sudden spark from the grate.

Drumsheugh gazed long into the red caverns and saw former things, till at last he smiled and spake.

'Hoo lang is't since ye guddled [1] for troot, Weelum?'

'Saxty year or sae. Div ye mind yon hole in the Sheuchie burn, whar it comes doon frae the muir? They used to lie and feed in the rin o' the water.

'A' wes passin' that wy laist hairst,[2] an' a' took a thocht and gaed ower tae the bank. The oak looks juist the same, an' a' keekit through, an' if there wesna a troot ablow the big stane. If a' hedna been sae stiff a' wud hae gane doon and tried ma luck again.'

'A' ken the hole fine, Weelum,' burst out Drumsheugh. 'Div ye mind whar a' catchit yon twa-punder in the dry simmer? It wes the biggest ever taen oot o' the Sheuchie. A' telt ye a' next day at schule.'

'Ye did that, an' ye blew aboot that troot for the hale

[1] groped with the hands. [2] harvest.

winter, but nane o's ever saw't, an' it wes juist a bare half-pund tae begin wi'; it's been growin', a' doot; it'ill be five afore ye're dune wi't, Drum.'

'Nane o' yir impidence, Weelum. A' weighed it in Luckie Simpson's shop as a' gaed hame, an' it made twa pund as sure as a'm sittin' here; but there micht be a wecht left in the scale wi't.'

'Fishers are the biggest leears a' ever cam across, and ye've dune yir best the nicht, Drum; but eh! man, guddlin' wes a graund ploy,' and the doctor got excited.

'A' think a'm at it aince mair, wi' ma sleeves up tae the oxters,[1] lyin' on ma face, wi' naething but the een ower the edge o' the stane, an' slippin' ma hands intae the caller water, an' the rush o' the troot, and grippin' the soople, slidderin' body o't an' throwin't ower yir head, wi' the red spots glistenin' on its white belly. It wes michty.'

'Ay, Weelum, an' even missin't wes worth while; tae feel it shoot atween yir hands an' see it dash doon the burn, makin' a white track in the shallow water, an' ower a bit fall an' oot o' sicht again in anither hole.'

They rested for a minute to revel in the past, and in the fire the two boys saw water running over gravel, and deep, cool holes beneath overhanging rocks, and little waterfalls, and birch boughs dipping into the pools, and speckled trout gleaming on the grass.

Maclure's face kindled into mirth, and he turned in his chair.

'Ye're sayin' naething o' the day when the burn was settlin' aifter a spate, and ye cam tae me an' Sandy Baxter an' Netherton's brither "Squinty," an' temptit us tae play the truant, threepin'[2] ye hed seen the troot juist swarmin' in the holes.'

'A' tried John Baxter tae,' interrupted Drumsheugh, anxious for accuracy since they had begun the story, 'though he didna come. But he wudna tell on's for a'

[1] armpits. [2] insisting.

that. Hillocks lat it oot at the sicht o' the tawse. "They're up the Sheuchie aifter the troot," he roared, an' the verra lassies cried "clype"[1] at him gaein' hame.'

'What a day it wes, Drum! A' can see Sandy's heels in the air when he coupit[2] intae the black hole abune Gormack, an' you pullin' him oot by the seat o' his breeks, an' his Latin Reader, 'at hed fa'en oot o' his pocket, sailin' doon the water, an' "Squinty" aifter it, scrammellin' ower the stanes'; and the doctor laughed aloud.

'Ye've forgot hoo ye sent me in tae beg for a piece frae the gudewife at Gormack, an' she saw the lave o' ye coorin'[3] ahint the dyke, an' gied us a flytin'[4] for playin' truant.'

'Fient a bit o't,'[5] and Maclure took up the running again; 'an' then she got a sicht o' Sandy like a drooned rat, and made him come in tae dry himsel', and gied us pork an' oatcake. Ma plate hed a burn on it like the Sheuchie—a' cud draw the pattern on a sheet o' paper till this day. That wes Gormack's mither, it's no' sae lang since she dee'd; a' wes wi' her the laist nicht.'

'An' the tawse next day frae the auld dominie, him 'at wes afore Domsie; he hed a fine swing. A' think a' feel the nip still,' and Drumsheugh shuffled in his chair. 'An' then we got anither lickin' frae oor faithers; but, man,' slapping his knee, 'it wes worth it a'; we've never hed as gude a day again.'

'It's juist like yesterday, Drum, but it cam tae an end. An' div ye mind hoo we were feared tae gae hame, and didna start till the sun wes weel doon ahint Ben Urtach?'

[1] tell-tale. [2] fell. [3] cowering.
[4] scolding. [5] not a bit of it.

THE RIVER LEGEND OF ÆGLE

By PATRICK R. CHALMERS

PATRICK REGINALD CHALMERS (born 1879), Scots-born banker and author—poet, novelist, and writer of many books on wild sports, including fishing, which he celebrates also in his verse. 'The River Legend of Ægle' is from chapter IX of *At the Tail of the Weir* (1932), and is here given by permission of the author. See also p. 266.

NAIADS they were called, those good little sisters of the Golden Age who were part and parcel of the waters of Cephissus and his hundred blue and kindred streams, and who played, tumbling over each other as pretty and slippery as so many otter cubs, in his pools and golden shallows, or hid pale as Loddon lilies among the green rushes.

And Ægle was the prettiest of them all. Her eyes were as blue as rivers seen through beechwoods on a blue May morning and, all amber shadows, her bright hair poured about her gleaming little body. So pretty was she indeed that when the early Sun saw her as she sat on a stone to dry herself, he of a sudden fell in love with her; and I for one can but admire his very good taste.

But Ægle, smoothly as an otter, slipped off her stone into the river again and was gone. Not because she wasn't rather flattered but because she didn't want to have to make up her mind about anything before breakfast. At least let us think so. But the Sun was inconsolable and kept looking for Ægle from different angles all the day long; and all the next day and the day after that. And Ægle kept peeping at him from under a lily-pad, and she thought what fun it was to be loved by so fine and splendid a young gentleman, '*and,*' she added to herself in a little, small voice, 'to love him back again.' But still she didn't want to make up her mind about anything before breakfast, and, if you think in that way, you can put off the making up of your mind for ever so long, for you can always pretend that you mean *to-morrow's* breakfast. Besides Ægle, you see, only had water-melon and water-biscuits for breakfast anyhow, and perhaps that isn't having breakfast at all. So don't let's blame her a bit.

But the Sun—he was young then and impetuously impatient—said fiercely, 'I'll show her,' and then he added fatuously, 'the darling!' And show her he did, for he was both powerful and a personage and precious inconsiderate of others when he wanted anything. But there—so are lots of good people, people too who have not got the excuse *he* had of wanting so lovely a thing as Ægle. So he shone—for days he shone, till the skies were hot and blue and hazy and never a raindrop fell. And Ægle said to herself, 'I see what he's up to,' and she was frightfully frightened but frightfully happy at the same time.

But the trout and the chub and the caddises and all the funny little creatures that live in rivers were not happy a bit. How could they be when they saw their home gradually getting littler and littler? And so they gathered, huddled in a dark cloud, under the shrunken splash of the falls, just as you saw the barbel huddle in that drought of a few years back; and there they held a council, all their tails and fins fanning at once, faintly but in the most agitated fashion.

'It is all Ægle's fault,' they said, for gossip on her affairs had of course been quite unavoidable; 'how *can* she put us in a position of so much discomfort and danger?'

'And yet,' said a handsome old trout whom Ægle had guided out of a fisherman's drag-net only recently, 'Ægle has a heart of gold; why not appeal to it?'

'You wish to make a *sacrifice* of me?' said Ægle, trying

hard not to dance about and clap her hands; for can anything be more satisfactory than to be implored to do just what you are simply dying to do and then be hailed as a heroine for saying 'Yes'?

For, of course, 'Yes' is just what Ægle did say.

'I told you that the child had a heart of gold,' said the old trout importantly.

And so the next morning, when the Sun, who had got up earlier than ever because it was Midsummer Day, came tiptoe and golden through the big oaks and down to the river, there sat little Ægle on the rock under the fall, her blue eyes dancey and her bright hair glancey, and a nibbled little bit of water-melon beside her to show that she'd had her breakfast at last.

And the Sun took her in both his burning arms, and together they stood a minute, he and she, one with the joyful dazzle of water before he caught her up with him into the morning.

And did Ægle never come back to her fishes at all, at all? Why, of course she did, and every day when the Sun shines you'll see her and her lover in any Thames weir pool; for, when Sun and Water were blent all those years ago, they, with the dancing blue eyes of Ægle and with the brightness of her gleaming hair to help them, made, in their moment, a rainbow in the whiteness of the fall—the same little occasional rainbow that you may see any sunny afternoon under the weir at Mapledurham. And when the great arc of glory stands across our valley and we know that it stands for The Promise of the continual kindness of Sun and Water, may we not still say that therein little Ægle and her lover go riding down to the river again with the sunny showers—the singing showers which make the running rivers which were, and are, her home?

THE PEARLY FISH

By SVEND FLEURON

SVEND FLEURON (born 1874), Danish writer of animal stories. 'The Pearly Fish' is from chapter v of *Grim: the Story of a Pike* (English translation, 1920, published by Gyldendal).

BETWEEN a cloudy sky and rough water the wind tore through reeds and rushes.

Grim was lurking at the edge of the bottom vegetation; she had not seen fish-food since the previous evening.

There is a splash in front of her, a broad foot is pushed obliquely down into the water and forces a large, heavy 'swimming-bird'[1] past her.

A little later there is a sudden gleam. A small fugitive of a fish darts past as though taking advantage of the wake of the big bird, from one reedy shelter to another.

Grim has already eaten so many bleak and roach that they are beginning to be everyday fare; and now, there goes a new kind of food, a fish that shines all red and green and blue and black, with large, glittering, beady eyes!

At a distance she follows the tit-bit that swims through the water like no other fish, turning incessantly round and round on its own axis.

How hard it works! There is a bright starry light all round it, and its tail-fin quivers behind in a long thick trail.

She cannot look at it unmoved. 'After it!' say her eyes; 'after it!' echoes her empty stomach.

She does not succeed in seizing it across as she generally does, but has to swim up and swallow it from behind in one mouthful.

[1] boat.

It is a curiously sharp-spined little fish! Now that she has it in her mouth, it is not nearly so tempting to her palate as it was before to her eyes. Well, she has taken the trouble to catch it, so down it shall go!

She cannot get it to move in her mouth; it will not stir! She takes a firmer hold, turns with it, and hastens back into her hiding-place.

Then it begins to bite her in the throat! And now—she becomes quite uneasy—her throat suddenly tries to go the opposite way to her tail! What can be the matter?

She forcibly sets her teeth into her refractory captive, when suddenly she is pulled over.

How strange! The simple little pearly fish takes the form of a master, and drags her after it through the water; no matter how much she tries to back, no matter what powerful strokes she makes to force it to obey her will, she is obliged to yield and go with it. Her brain is bursting; she cannot comprehend this powerlessness: the fish is in her mouth and on its way down her throat, and yet it is dragging her along with it.

No! *No!* And she sets to work and lashes the water into foam with her tail; but the little pearly fish is inexorable; it is too strong for her.

There must be some strange witchcraft about it all!

Instead of her swimming away with it, here it goes swimming away with her, and on they go, nearer and nearer up towards the light and the surface, which she instinctively shuns. All at once the pearly fish leaps into the air with her. She wants to let go, to spit it out, but she is too late; for the moment she is not quite conscious.

Her eyes ache; she feels as if they would jump out of her head. Her sight is gone, and a bright red mist surrounds her. She tries to swim, but cannot get her balance; she tries to strike with her tail in order to escape, but the water round her offers no resistance.

A suffocating feeling seems suddenly to contract her

gills; she cannot open them far enough. She opens her mouth to let water in, but only swallows dry wind.

The next moment she is lying floundering in a boat, and then a human hand takes her up.

'A pickerel! under-sized!' mutters the angler. And he carefully takes out the revolving bait and weighs the fish in his hand. Alas! not even a miserable two pounds!

He takes out his sheath-knife and marks her dorsal fin; and then, in the hope of finding favour with the gods on account of his magnanimity, and catching the fish again at some future time, he tosses her over the side of the boat, and Grim is given back to life.

It was much the same feeling as when she was ejected from the heron's throat; her intestines seem bursting, and her breath to be leaving her. Then she reaches the water, where she lies floating on her side, and slowly wakens as though from a long fit of unconsciousness.

And in a trice she has disappeared into the depths.

Her suspicion was aroused. The world was full of villainies, more than those that she herself committed!

Twilight was falling.

The sun's fiery columns, that stood obliquely over the lake, suddenly separated and flowed out, their glowing fragments lying like burning oil upon the surface of the water. Then they were gradually extinguished; the darkness of evening shed its deep blue tones over them.

Long and black, the shadows crept out from the banks; the little fish made their way in to the shelter of the reeds, and the pursuing pike went to rest. And while the surface still sparkled with a peculiar mother-of-pearl brilliancy, the darkness of night already brooded closely beneath the water.

THE SALMON OF FINN MAC COOL

By CÆSAR OTWAY

CÆSAR OTWAY (1780-1842), Irish Protestant clergyman and miscellaneous writer. 'The Salmon of Finn Mac Cool,' a popular rendering of the Salmon of Knowledge story of the Fenian Cycle of Irish heroic romance, is from Letter IV of 'Sketches in Donegal' in Otway's anonymous *Sketches in Ireland* (1827).

IN days of yore, Cormac, son of Art, ruled Ireland, and a hospitable prince was he. His house was always open, many were the retainers kept in his hall; and thereby, like more modern princes, his expenses outran both his ready money and his tardy credit, and he was at his wit's end how to supply with meat and strong drink those who honoured his quality by feeding at his expense.

After all the most obvious recipe that can occur to any prince, when desirous of aggrandising himself, is to go to war with one of his neighbours.

Now, Fiachadh Muilliathan, King of Munster, had some fat pasture-lands along the banks of the Suir, which preserve their credit for fertility unto this very day, and go under the name of the Golden Vein. On these plentiful plains Cormac cast his longing eye, assuring himself that, were he once possessed of such mensal lands, he should never want a sirloin or baron of beef to grace his board. Go to war, therefore, he should; but withal, Fiachadh of Munster was potent and wise, and he valued those very fields as the apple of his eye; and his merry men of Ormond and Desmond were as fond of fighting as their descendants are at this very day.

In this difficulty Cormac resorted for advice to a Druid, who was a Caledonian, for even in these early days the Scotch itched after foreign travel, and were everywhere at hand to give advice to those who could pay for it; and the Druid, being an enchanter and depositary of old prophecies, told the King that in one of those rivers that run underground in the western land now called Mayo, and not far from that lofty mountain now named Croagh Patrick, there was a salmon, which, if caught and eaten, would communicate such wisdom, prowess, and good fortune to the eater, that, from that day forth, fame and prosperity would attend him in all his wars. You may be sure Cormac lost no time in setting out on his fishing excursion into Connaught, and, attending to the directions of his adviser, he arrived at the banks of a river that rises in the mountain-chain surrounding the reek of Croagh Patrick; and pursuing the river's course through a fertile valley, he at length came to where the turbulent stream falls into a fearful cavern and is lost, to be seen no more; and whether it seeks by some unknown passage the depths of the ocean, or whether it plunges into the earth's abyss and goes to cool the raging of its central fires, was never yet ascertained; but close to the jaws of the engulfing cavern, there is a dark, deep pool, where the stream, as if in terror, whirls about in rapid eddies, and here, amidst multitudes of fish, it was supposed the Salmon of Knowledge spent its days. On the banks of this pool Cormac and his Caledonian adviser sat day after day, and complain they could not of want of sport, for many a fine fish they caught and broiled on the live coals which they kept for their accommodation on the bank. But still Cormac became not a whit the wiser; and after feeding on salmon, firm and curdy enough to satisfy the *goût* of the Lord Mayor of Dublin, he at length grew so tired of fish, it palled so much upon his appetite, that the Milesian monarch began to sigh after the fat mutton that the broad pastures of Tara supplied.

At length the fish were caught with such rapidity that if he got thereby the wisdom of Solomon he could not be brought to taste of every one taken in this populous pool.

And now he and his adviser presumed to make selections, and applying the arbitrary principles of physiognomy to fish, ventured to throw back some into the stream, while others, as more plump and well favoured, were elected to the honour of being broiled; and here, methinks, the discretion of the King and his Druid was not evinced, for many a time and oft, ugly heads contain capacious brains, and sleek skins fail to enclose shining intellects. So it proved here, for one evening a little fish was taken—a poor, long, lank, spent thing, with a hooked snout, just such another as a poacher spears by the light of a blazing wisp of potato-stalks on a dark night in October. Now, who would suppose that anyone who had his pick and choice would think of feeding on a spent salmon? So this good-for-nothing fish was thrown on the bank, leaving it to its own fancy to bounce and wriggle back into the river; and just as it was in the very act of eloping into the stream, an idle gorsoon who was looking on, caught it by the gills, and says he to himself, 'Though this be not plump enough for a king's palate, it may not come amiss to me.' So, choosing a snug place behind a rock, just within the cavern's mouth, he blew up a fire and set about to broil his fish.

Now it is time to tell who this boy was, for questionless his match Ireland has not produced from that day to this. No one else he was than the famous Finn, the son of Cumhall, and grandson of Trein the Big, who was sent to these shores of the Western Sea, from his native hills of Almhuin, in order to save him from the enchantments of the tribe of Morni, that sought to take his life; and here he lived sporting along these wild hills, and here he might have died, unknowing and unknown, were it not for the circumstance I now record. Thank therefore he may his stars that he was not so squeamish in the choice of his fish as King Cormac.

So, having lit up his fire, he was not long in clapping his salmon, all alive as it was, on the coals; for, alas, sportsmen, as well as cooks, think little of the pain they may inflict on fowl or fish. And thus on the live coals the poor animal was not long until a great swelling blister arose by the force of the fire on its heretofore bright and silver side; and Finn, seeing the broiling salmon, was uneasy, not at its sufferings, but in apprehension lest all the nutritious juices of his game should be wasted in the fire if the blister should rise any more. So, pressing his left thumb to it, he caused it to burst, and the said thumb feeling a sensation of burning, he claps it into his mouth to cool. And oh, what a change! He, who until that moment was as little troubled with knowledge as with care, and, as the saying is, 'knew not a B from a bull's foot'—the instant his thumb came between his teeth he felt as wise and prudent as if he were a hundred years old. All his future glories, all the failures of his foes, and all his own achievements flashed before his eyes, and he saw prospectively how that Ireland and Caledonia would ring with his fame, and both contend for the honour of giving him birth.

Thus it was that Finn Mac Cool, instead of King Cormac, happened on the Salmon of Knowledge; and time and your patience, good reader, would fail me to recount all his succeeding renowned deeds.

TWICE GRUPPIT

By 'CHRISTOPHER NORTH'

JOHN WILSON (pseudonym 'Christopher North'; 1785-1854), professor of moral philosophy in the University of Edinburgh, but better known for his work on *Blackwood's Magazine* at its beginning, was renowned in his day as an athlete and as a sportsman, whence such distinctions as M.A., 'Master of Angling,' and F.R.S., 'Fisherman Royal of Scotland.' He lived, the contemporary of James Hogg, Thomas Tod Stoddart, and William Scrope, in the classic days of Scottish angling, and these days are drawn exuberantly here and there in the *Noctes Ambrosianæ* (vols I-IV of Wilson's works, 12 vols 1855-8) and in *The Recreations of Christopher North* (vols IX and X of the works). Both the *Noctes* and the *Recreations* consist of material collected from *Blackwood's Magazine*, the *Noctes* being dialogue records of festive gatherings at Ambrose's Tavern, Edinburgh. 'Twice Gruppit' is from the *Noctes* for November 1831. See also p. 299.

North. By the by, James, who won the salmon medal this season on the Tweed?

Shepherd. Wha, think ye, could it be, you coof, but masel'? I beat them a' by twa stane wecht. Oh, Mr North, but it would hae done your heart gude to hae daunner'd alang the banks wi' me on the 25th and seen the slauchter. At the third thraw the snoot o' a famous fish sookit in ma flee—and for some seconds keepit steadfast in a sort o' eddy that gaed sullenly swirlin' at the tail o' yon pool—I needna name 't—for the river had risen just to the proper pint, and was black as ink, accept when noo and then the sun struggled out frae atween the cludchinks, and then the water was purple as heather-moss, in the season o' blaeberries. But that verra instant the flee began to bite him on the tongue, for by a jerk o' the wrist I had slichtly[1] gi'en him the butt—and sunbeam

[1] deftly.

never swifter shot frae heaven, than shot that saumon-beam doon intil and oot o' the pool below, and alang the sauch-shallows or you come to Juniper Bank. Clap—clap—clap—at the same instant played a couple o' cushats frae an aik aboon my head, at the purr o' the pirn, that let oot in a twinklin' a hunner yards o' Mr Phin's best, strang aneuch to haud a bill or a rhinoceros.

North. Incomparable tackle!

Shepherd. Far, far awa' doon the flood, see till him, sir—see till him—loup—loup—loupin' intil the air, describin' in the spray the rinnin' rainbows! Scarcely could I believe, at sic a distance, that he was the same fish. He seemed a saumon divertin' himsell, without ony connection in this warld wi' the Shepherd. But we were linked thegither, sir, by the inveesible gut o' destiny—and I chasteesed him in his pastime wi' the rod o' affliction. Windin' up—windin' up, faster than ever ye grunded coffee—I keepit closin' in upon him, till the whalebone was amaist perpendicular outowre him, as he stapped to tak' breath in a deep plum. You see the savage had gotten sulky, and ye micht as weel hae rugged at a rock. Hoo I leuch[1]! Easin' the line ever so little, till it just muved slichtly[2] like gossamer in a breath o' wun'—I half persuaded him that he had gotten aff; but na, na, ma man, ye ken little about the Kirby-bends, gin ye think the peacock's harl and the tinsy[3] hae slipped frae your jaws! Snuvin'[4] up the stream he goes, hither and thither, but still keepin' weel in the middle—and noo strecht and steddy as a bridegroom ridin' to the kirk.

North. An original image.

Shepherd. Say rather application! Maist majestic, sir, you'll alloo, is that flicht o' a fish, when the line cuts the surface without commotion, and ye micht imagine that he was sailin' unseen below in the style o' an eagle about to fauld his wings on the cliff.

North. Tak' tent, James. Be wary, or he will escape.

[1] laughed. [2] slightly. [3] tinsel. [4] boring.

Shepherd. Never fear, sir. He'll no pit me aff my guard by keepin' the croon o' the causey in that gate. I ken what he's ettlin' at [1]—and it's naething mair nor less nor yon island. Thinks he to himsell, wi' his tail, gin I get abreist o' the broom, I'll roun' the rocks, doon the rapids, and break the Shepherd. And nae sooner thocht than done—but bauld in my cork-jacket——

North. That's a new appurtenance to your person, James; I thought you had always angled in bladders.

Shepherd. Sae I used—but last season they fell doon to my heels, and had nearly droon'd me—sae I trust noo to my bodyguard.

North. I prefer the air life-preserver.

Shepherd. If it bursts you're gone. Bauld in my cork-jacket I took till the soomin',[2] haudin' the rod aboon my head——

North. Like Cæsar his Commentaries.

Shepherd. And gettin' footin' on the bit island—there's no a shrub on't, ye ken, aboon the waistband o' my breeks—I was just in time to let him easy owre the fa', and Heaven safe us! he turned up, as he played wallop, a side like a house! He fand noo that he was in the hauns o' his maister, and began to lose heart; for naething cows the better pairt o' man, brute, fule, or fish, like a sense o' inferiority. Sometimes in a large pairty it suddenly strikes me dumb——

North. But never in the Snuggery, James—never in the Sanctum——

Shepherd. Na—na—na—never i' the Snuggery, never i' the Sanctum, my dear auld man! For there we're a' brithers, and keep bletherin' withouten ony sense o' propriety—I ax pardon—o' inferiority—bein' a' on a level, and that lichtsome, like the parallel roads in Glenroy, when the sunshine pours upon them frae the tap o' Benevis.

North. But we forget the fish.

[1] aiming at. [2] swimming.

Shepherd. No me. I'll remember him on my death-bed. In body the same, he was entirely anither fish in sowle. He had set his life on the hazard o' a die, and it had turned up blanks. I began first to pity—and then to despise him—for frae a fish o' his appearance, I ex-peckit that nae act o' his life would hae sae graced him as the closin' ane—and I was pairtly wae and pairtly wrathfu' to see him *dee saft!* Yet, to do him justice, it's no impos-sible but that he may hae druv his snoot again' a stane, and got dazed—and we a' ken by experience that there's naething mair likely to cawm courage than a brainin' knock on the head. His organ o' locality had gotten a clour,[1] for he lost a' judgment atween wat and dry, and came floatin', belly upmost, in amang the bit snail-bucky-shells on the san' around my feet, and lay there as still as if he had been gutted on the kitchen dresser—an enormous fish.

North. A sumph.

Shepherd. No sic a sumph as he looked like—and that you'll think when you hear tell o' the lave o' the adventur'. Bein' rather out o' wun, I sits doon on a stane, and was wipin' ma broos, wi' ma een fixed upon the prey, when a' on a sudden, as if he had been galvaneesed, he stotted up intil the lift, and wi' ae squash played plunge into the pool, and awa' doon the eddies like a porpus. I thocht I soud hae gane mad, Heaven forgie me—and I fear I swore like a trooper. Loupin' wi' a spang[2] frae the stane, I missed ma feet, and gaed head-owre-heels intil the water—while amang the rushin' o' the element I heard roars o' lauchter as if frae the kelpie himsell, but what afterwards turned out to be guffaws frae your friens Boyd and Juniper Bank, wha had been wutnessin' the drama frae commencement to catastrophe.

North. Ha! ha! ha! James! it must have been excessively droll.

Shepherd. Risin' to the surface wi' a guller,[3] I shook

[1] blow. [2] spring. [3] gurgle.

ma nieve[1] at the ne'er-do-weels, and then doon the river after the sumph o' a saumon, like a verra otter. Followin' noo the sight and noo the scent, I wasna lang in comin' up wi' him—for he was as deid as Dawvid—and lyin' on his back, I protest, just like a man restin' himsell at the soomin'. I had forgotten the gaff—so I fasten'd ma teeth intil the shouther o' him, and like a Newfoundlan' savin' a chiel frae droonin', I bare him to the shore, while, to do Boyd and Juniper justice, the lift rang wi' acclamations.

North. What may have been his calibre?

Shepherd. On puttin' him intil the scales at nicht, he just turned three stane trone.

Tickler (*stretching himself out to an incredible extent*). Alas! 'twas but a dream!

Shepherd. Was ye dreamin', sir, o' bein' hanged?

[1] fist.

FISH ARE SUCH LIARS!

By ROLAND PERTWEE

ROLAND PERTWEE (born 1886), English dramatist, novelist, and short-story writer. 'Fish Are Such Liars!' is from *Fish Are Such Liars! and other stories* (1931) and is here given by permission of the author and of Messrs William Heinemann Ltd. In *May We Come Through?* (1940) there are also some fishing stories; and 'The River God' (*Saturday Evening Post*, July 1928, *Strand Magazine*, November 1928) is a fine story, largely autobiographical, of boyhood fishing.

THERE had been a fuss in the pool beneath the alders, and the small rainbow trout, with a skitter of his tail, flashed upstream, a hurt and angry fish. For three consecutive mornings he had taken the rise in that pool, and it injured his pride to be jostled from his drift just when the Mayfly was coming up in numbers. If his opponent had been a half-pounder like himself, he would have stayed and fought, but when an old hen fish weighing fully three pounds, with a mouth like a rat hole and a carnivorous, cannibalistic eye rises from the reed beds and occupies the place, flight is the only effective argument.

But Rainbow was very much provoked. He had chosen his place with care. Now the Mayfly was up, the little French chalk stream was full of rising fish, and he knew by experience that strangers are unpopular in that season. To do one's self justice during a hatch, one must find a place where the fly drifts nicely overhead with the run of the stream, and natural drifts are scarce even in a chalk stream. He was not content to leap at the fly like a hysterical youngster who measured his weight in ounces and his wits in milligrams. He had reached that time of life which demanded that he should feed off the surface by suction rather than exertion. No living thing is more particular about his table manners than a trout, and Rainbow was no exception.

'It's a sickening thing,' he said to himself, 'and a hard shame.' He added: 'Get out of my way,' to a couple of fat young chub with negroid mouths who were bubbling the surface in the silly, senseless fashion of their kind.

'Chub indeed!'

But even the chub had a home and he had none—and the life of a homeless river dweller is precarious.

'I will not and shall not be forced back to midstream,' he said.

For, save at eventide or in very special circumstances, trout of personality do not frequent open water where they must compete for every insect with the wind, the lightning-swift sweep of swallows and martins, and even the laborious pursuit of predatory dragon-flies with their bronze wings and bodies like rods of coloured glass. Even as he spoke he saw a three-ouncer leap at a dapping Mayfly which was scooped out of his jaws by a passing swallow. Rainbow heard the tiny click as the Mayfly's body cracked against the bird's beak. A single wing of yellowy gossamer floated downward and settled upon the water. Under the shelving banks to right and left, where the fly, discarding its nymph and still too damp for its virgin flight, drifted downstream, a dozen heavy trout were feeding thoughtfully and selectively.

'If only some angler would catch one of them, I might slip in and occupy the place before it gets known there's a vacancy.'

But this uncharitable hope was not fulfilled, and with another whisk of his tail he propelled himself into the unknown waters upstream. A couple of strands of rusty barbed wire, relic of the war, spanned the shallows from bank to bank. Passing beneath them he came to a narrow reach shaded by willows, to the first of which was nailed a board bearing the words Pêche Réservée. He had passed out of the communal into private water—water running languidly over manes of emerald weed between clumps of alder, willow herb, tall crimson sorrel and masses of yellow iris. Ahead, like an apple-green rampart, rose the wooded heights of a forest; on either side were flat meadows of yellowing hay. Overhead, the vast expanse of blue June sky was tufted with rambling clouds. 'My scales!' said Rainbow. 'Here's water!'

But it was vain to expect any of the best places in such a reach would be vacant, and to avoid a recurrence of his unhappy encounter earlier in the morning, Rainbow continued his journey until he came to a spot where the river took one of those unaccountable right-angle bends which result in a pool, shallow on the one side, but slanting into deeps on the other. Above it was a water break, a swirl, smoothing, as it reached the pool, into a sleek, swift run, with an eddy which bore all the lighter floating things of the river over the calm surface of the little backwater, sheltered from above by a high shelving bank and a tangle of bramble and herb. Here in this backwater the twig, the broken reed, the leaf, the cork, the fly floated in suspended activity for a few instants until drawn back by invisible magnetism to the main current.

Rainbow paused in admiration. At the tail of the pool two sound fish were rising with regularity, but in the backwater beyond the eddy the surface was still and unbroken. Watching open-eyed, Rainbow saw not one but a dozen Mayflies, fat, juicy and damp from the nymph, drift in, pause, and carried away untouched. It was beyond the bounds of possibility that such a place could be vacant, but there was the evidence of his eyes to prove it; and nothing if not a trier, Rainbow darted across the stream and parked himself six inches below the water to await events.

It so happened that at the time of his arrival the hatch of fly was temporarily suspended, which gave Rainbow leisure to make a survey of his new abode. Beyond the eddy was a submerged snag—the branch of an apple-tree borne there by heavy rains, water-logged, anchored, and intricate—an excellent place to break an angler's line. The river bank on his right was riddled under water with old rat holes, than which there is no better sanctuary. Below him and to the left was a dense bed of weeds brushed flat by the flow of the stream.

'If it comes to the worst,' said Rainbow, 'a smart fish could do a get-away here with very little ingenuity, even from a cannibalistic old hen like—hullo!'

The exclamation was excited by the apparition of a gauzy shadow on the water, which is what a Mayfly seen from below looks like. Resisting a vulgar inclination to leap at it with the violence of a youngster, Rainbow backed into the correct position which would allow the stream to present the morsel, so to speak, upon a tray. Which it did—and scarcely a dimple on the surface to tell what had happened.

'Very nicely taken, if you will accept the praise of a complete stranger,' said a low, soft voice, one inch behind his line of sight.

Without turning to see by whom he had been addressed, Rainbow flicked a yard upstream and came back with the current four feet away. In the spot he had occupied an instant before lay a great old trout of the most benign aspect, who could not have weighed less than four pounds.

'I beg your pardon,' said Rainbow, 'but I had no idea that any one—that is, I just dropped in *en passant*, and finding an empty house, I made so bold——'

'There is no occasion to apologise,' said Old Trout seductively. 'I did not come up from the bottom as early to-day as is my usual habit at this season. Yesterday's hatch was singularly bountiful and it is possible I did myself too liberally.'

'Yes, but a gentleman of your weight and seniority can hardly fail to be offended at finding——'

'Not at all,' Old Trout broke in. 'I perceive you are a well-conducted fish who does not advertise his appetite in a loud and splashing fashion.'

Overcome by the charm of Old Trout's manner and address, Rainbow reduced the distance separating them to a matter of inches.

'Then you do not want me to go?' he asked.

'On the contrary, dear young sir, stay by all means and take the rise. You are, I perceive, of the rainbow or, as they say here in France, of the Arc-en-ciel family. As a youngster I had the impression that I should turn out a rainbow, but events proved it was no more than the bloom, the natural sheen of youth.'

'To speak the truth, sir,' said Rainbow, 'unless you had told me to the contrary, I would surely have thought you one of us.'

Old Trout shook his tail. 'You are wrong,' he said. 'I am from Dulverton, an English trout farm on the Exe, of which you will have heard. You are doubtless surprised to find an English fish in French waters.'

'I am indeed,' Rainbow replied, sucking in a passing Mayfly with such excellent good manners that it was hard to believe he was feeding. 'Then you, sir,' he added, 'must know all about the habits of men.'

'I may justly admit that I do,' Old Trout agreed. 'Apart from being hand-reared, I have in my twelve years of life studied the species in moods of activity, passivity, duplicity, and violence.'

Rainbow remarked that such must doubtless have proved of invaluable service. It did not, however, explain the mystery of his presence on a French river.

'For, sir,' he added, 'Dulverton, as once I heard when enjoying "A Chat about Rivers" delivered by a much-travelled sea trout, is situated in the west of England, and without crossing the Channel I am unable to explain how you arrived here. Had you belonged to the salmon family, with which, sir, it is evident you have no connection, the explanation would be simple, but in the circumstances it baffles my understanding.'

Old Trout waved one of his fins airily. 'Yet cross the

Channel I certainly did,' said he, 'and at a period in history which I venture to state will not readily be forgotten. It was during the war, my dear young friend, and I was brought in a can, in company with a hundred yearlings, to this river, or rather the upper reaches of this river, by a young officer who wished to further an entente between English and French fish even as the war was doing with the mankind of these two nations.'

Old Trout sighed a couple of bubbles and arched his body this way and that.

'There was a gentleman and sportsman,' he said. 'A man who was acquainted with our people as I dare to say very few are acquainted. Had it ever been my lot to fall victim to a lover of the rod, I could have done so without regret to his. If you will take a look at my tail, you will observe that the letter *W* is perforated on the upper side. He presented me with this distinguishing mark before committing me, with his blessing, to the water.'

'I have seldom seen a tail more becomingly decorated,' said Rainbow. 'But what happened to your benefactor?'

Old Trout's expression became infinitely sad. 'If I could answer that,' said he, 'I were indeed a happy trout. For many weeks after he put me into the river I used to watch him in what little spare time he was able to obtain, casting a dry fly with the most exquisite precision and likeness to nature in all the likely pools and runs and eddies near his battery position. Oh, minnows! It was a pleasure to watch that man, even as it was his pleasure to watch us. His bravery too! I call to mind a dozen times when he fished unmoved and unstartled while bullets from machine-guns were pecking at the water like herons and thudding into the mud banks upon which he stood.'

'An angler!' remarked Rainbow. 'It would be no lie to say I like him the less on that account.'

Old Trout became unexpectedly stern.

'Why so?' he retorted severely. 'Have I not said he was also a gentleman and a sportsman? My officer was neither a pot-hunter nor a beast of prey. He was a purist —a man who took delight in pitting his knowledge of nature against the subtlest and most suspicious intellectual forces of the wild. Are you so young as not yet to have learned the exquisite enjoyment of escaping disaster and avoiding error by the exercise of personal ingenuity? Pray, do not reply, for I would hate to think so hard a thing of any trout. We as a race exist by virtue of our brilliant intellectuality and hypersensitive selectivity. In waters where there are no pike and only an occasional otter, but for the machinations of men, where should we turn to school our wits? Danger is our mainstay, for I tell you, Rainbow, that trout are composed of two senses—appetite, which makes of us fools, and suspicion, which teaches us to be wise.'

Greatly chastened not alone by what Old Trout had said but by the forensic quality of his speech, Rainbow rose short and put a promising Mayfly on the wing.

'I am glad to observe,' said Old Trout, 'that you are not without conscience.'

'To tell the truth, sir,' Rainbow replied apologetically, 'my nerve this morning has been rudely shaken, but for which I should not have shown such want of good sportsmanship.'

And with becoming brevity he told the tale of his eviction from the pool downstream. Old Trout listened gravely, only once moving, and that to absorb a small blue dun, an insect which he keenly relished.

'A regrettable affair,' he admitted, 'but as I have often observed, women, who are the gentlest creatures under water in adversity, are a thought lacking in moderation in times of abundance. They are apt to snatch.'

'But for a turn of speed she would certainly have snatched me,' said Rainbow.

'Very shocking,' said Old Trout. 'Cannibals are disgusting. They destroy the social amenities of the river. We fish have but little family life and should therefore aim to cultivate a freemasonry of good-fellowship among ourselves. For my part, I am happy to line up with other well-conducted trout and content myself with what happens along my own particular drift. Pardon me!' he added, breasting Rainbow to one side. 'I invited you to take the rise of Mayfly, but I must ask you to leave the duns alone.' Then, fearing this remark might be construed to reflect adversely upon his hospitality, he proceeded: 'I have a reason which I will explain later. For the moment we are discussing the circumstances that led to my presence in this river.'

'To be sure—your officer. He never succeeded in deluding you with his skill?'

'That would have been impossible,' said Old Trout, 'for I had taken up a position under the far bank where he could only have reached me with a fly by wading in a part of the river which was in view of a German sniper.'

'Wily!' Rainbow chuckled. 'Cunning work, sir.'

'Perhaps,' Old Trout admitted, 'although I have since reproached myself with cowardice. However, I was at the time a very small fish and a certain amount of nervousness is forgivable in the young.'

At this gracious acknowledgment the rose-coloured hue in Rainbow's rainbow increased noticeably—in short, he blushed.

'From where I lay,' Old Trout went on, 'I was able to observe the manœuvres of my officer and greatly profit thereby.'

'But excuse me, sir,' said Rainbow, 'I have heard it said that an angler of the first class is invisible from the river.'

'He is invisible to the fish he is trying to catch,' Old Trout admitted, 'but it must be obvious that he is not invisible to the fish who lie beside or below him. I would also remind you that during the war every tree, every scrap of vegetation, and every vestige of natural cover had been torn up, trampled down, razed. The river banks were as smooth as the top of your head. Even the buttercup, that very humorous flower that tangles up the back cast of so many industrious anglers, was absent. Those who fished on the Western Front had little help from nature.'

Young Rainbow sighed, for, only a few days before, his tongue had been badly scratched by an artificial alder which had every appearance of reality.

'It would seem,' he said, 'that this war had its merits.'

'My young friend,' said Old Trout, 'you never made a greater mistake. A desire on the part of our soldiery to vary a monotonous diet of bully beef and biscuit often drove them to resort to villainous methods of assault against our kind.'

'Nets?' gasped Rainbow in horror.

'Worse than nets—bombs,' Old Trout replied. 'A small oval black thing called a Mills bomb, which the shameless fellows flung into deep pools.'

'But surely the chances of being hit by such a——'

'You reveal a pathetic ignorance,' said Old Trout. 'There is no question of being hit. The wretched machine exploded under water and burst our people's insides or stunned us so that we floated dead to the surface. I well remember my officer coming upon such a group of marauders one evening—yes, and laying about him with his fists in defiance of King's Regulations and the Manual of Military Law. Two of them he seized by the collar and the pants and flung into the river. Spinning minnows, that was a sight worth seeing! "You low swine," I heard him say; "you trash, you muck! Isn't there enough carnage without this sort of thing?" Afterward he sat on the bank with the two dripping men and talked to them for their souls' sake.

'"Look ahead, boys. Ask yourselves what are we fighting for? Decent homes to live in at peace with one another, fields to till and forests and rivers to give us a day's sport and fun. It's our rotten job to massacre each other, but, by gosh, don't let's massacre the harmless rest of nature as well. At least, let's give 'em a running chance. Boys, in the years ahead, when all the mess is cleared up, I look forward to coming back to this old spot, when there is alder growing by the banks, and willow herb and tall reeds and the drone of insects instead of the rumble of those guns. I don't want to come back to a dead river that I helped to kill, but to a river ringed with rising fish—some of whom were old comrades of the war." He went on to tell of us hundred Dulverton trout that he had marked with the letter *W*. "Give 'em their chance," he said, "and in the years to come those beggars will reward us a hundred times over. They'll give us a finer thrill and put up a cleaner fight than old Jerry ever contrived." Those were emotional times, and though you may be reluctant to believe me, one of those two very wet men dripped water from his eyes as well as his clothing.

'"Many's the 'appy afternoon I've 'ad with a roach pole on Brentford Canal," he sniffed, "though I've never yet tried m' hand against a trout." "You shall do it now," said my officer, and during the half-hour that was left of daylight that dripping soldier had his first lesson in the most delicate art in the world. I can see them now—the clumsy, wet fellow and my officer timing him, timing him—"one and two, and one and two, and——" The action of my officer's wrist with its persuasive flick was the prettiest thing I have ever seen.'

'Did he carry out his intention and come back after the war?' Rainbow asked.

'I shall never know,' Old Trout replied. 'I do not even know if he survived it. There was a great battle—a German drive. For hours they shelled the river front, and many falling short exploded in our midst with terrible results. My own bank was torn to shreds and our people suffered. How they suffered! About noon the infantry came over—hordes in field grey. There were pontoons, rope bridges, and hand-to-hand fights on both banks and even in the stream itself.'

'And your officer?'

'I saw him once, before the water was stamped dense into liquid mud and dyed by the blood of men. He was in the thick of it, unarmed, and a German officer called on him to surrender. For answer he struck him in the face with a light cane. Ah, that wrist action! Then a shell burst, smothering the water with clods of fallen earth and other things.'

'Then you never knew?'

'I never knew, although that night I searched among the dead. Next day I went downstream, for the water in that place was polluted with death. The bottom of the pool in which I had my place was choked with strange and mangled tenants that were not good to look upon. We trout are a clean people that will not readily abide in dirty houses. I am a Dulverton trout, where the water is filtered by the hills and runs cool over stones.'

'And you have stayed here ever since?'

Old Trout shrugged a fin. 'I have moved with the times. Choosing a place according to the needs of my weight.'

'And you have never been caught, sir, by any other angler?'

'Am I not here?' Old Trout answered with dignity.

'Oh, quite, sir. I had only thought, perhaps, as a younger fish enthusiasm might have resulted to your disadvantage, but that, nevertheless, you had been returned.'

'Returned! Returned!' echoed Old Trout. 'Returned to the frying-pan! Where on earth did you pick up that expression? We are in France, my young friend; we are not on the Test, the Itchen, or the Kennet. In this country it is not the practice of anglers to return anything, however miserable in size.'

'But nowadays,' Rainbow protested, 'there are Englishmen and Americans on the river who show us more consideration.'

'They may show you consideration,' said Old Trout, 'but I am of an importance that neither asks for nor expects it. Oblige me by being a little more discreet with your plurals. In the impossible event of my being deceived and caught, I should be introduced to a glass case with an appropriate background of rocks and weeds.'

'But, sir, with respect, how can you be so confident of your unassailability?' Rainbow demanded, edging into position to accept an attractive Mayfly with yellow wings that was drifting downstream toward him.

'How?' Old Trout responded. 'Because——' Then suddenly: 'Leave it, you fool!'

Rainbow had just broken the surface when the warning came. The yellow-winged Mayfly was wrenched off the water with a wet squeak. A tangle of limp cast lapped itself round the upper branches of a willow far upstream and a raw voice exclaimed something venomous in French. By common consent the two fish went down.

'Well, really,' expostulated Old Trout, 'I hoped you were above that kind of thing! Nearly to fall victim to a downstream angler. It's a little too much! And think of the effect it will have on my prestige. Why, that incompetent fool will go about boasting that he rose me. Me!'

For some minutes Rainbow was too crestfallen even to apologise. At last:

'I am afraid,' he said, 'I was paying more heed to what you were saying than to my own conduct. I never expected to be fished from above. The fly was an uncommonly good imitation and it is a rare thing for a Frenchman to use Four-X gut.'

'Rubbish,' said Old Trout testily. 'These are mere half-pound arguments. Four-X gut, when associated with a fourteen-stone shadow, should deceive nothing over two ounces. I saved your life, but it is all very provoking.

If that is a sample of your general demeanour, it is improbable that you will ever reach a pound.'

'At this season we are apt to be careless,' Rainbow wailed. 'And nowadays it is so hard, sir, to distinguish the artificial fly from the real.'

'No one expects you to do so,' was the answer, 'but common prudence demands that you should pay some attention to the manner in which it is presented. A Mayfly does not hit the water with a splash, neither is it able to sustain itself in midstream against the current. Have you ever seen a natural insect leave a broadening wake of cutwater behind its tail? Never mind the fly, my dear boy, but watch the manner of its presentation. Failure to do that has cost many of our people their lives.'

'You speak, sir,' said Rainbow, a shade sulkily, 'as though it were a disgrace for a trout ever to suffer defeat at the hands of an angler.'

'Which indeed it is, save in exceptional circumstances,' Old Trout answered. 'I do not say that a perfect upstream cast from a well-concealed angler, when the fly alights dry and cocked and dances at even speed with the current, may not deceive us to our fall. And I would be the last to say that a grasshopper skilfully dapped on the surface through the branches of an overhanging tree will not inevitably bring about our destruction. But I do most emphatically say that in such a spot as this, where the slightest defect in presentation is multiplied a hundredfold by the varying water speeds, a careless rise is unpardonable. There is only one spot—and that a matter of twelve yards downstream—from which a fly can be drifted over me with any semblance to nature. Even so, there is not one angler in a thousand who can make that cast with success, by reason of a willow which cramps the back cast and the manner in which these alders on our left sprawl across the pool.'

Rainbow did not turn about to verify these statements

because it is bad form for a trout to face downstream. He contented himself by replying, with a touch of acerbity:

'I should have thought, sir, with the feelings you expressed regarding sportsmanship, you would have found such a sanctuary too dull for your entertainment.'

'Every remark you make serves to aggravate the impression of your ignorance,' Old Trout replied. 'Would you expect a trout of my intelligence to put myself in some place where I am exposed to the vulgar assaults of every amateur upon the bank? Of the green boy who lashes the water into foam, of the purblind peasant who slings his fly at me with a clod of earth or a tail of weed attached to the hook? In this place I invite attention from none but the best people—the expert, the purist.'

'I understood you to say that there were none such in these parts,' grumbled Rainbow.

'There are none who have succeeded in deceiving me,' was the answer. 'As a fact, for the last few days I have been vastly entranced by an angler who, by any standard, is deserving of praise. His presentation is flawless and the only fault I can detect in him is a tendency to overlook piscine psychology. He will be with us in a few minutes, since he knows it is my habit to lunch at noon.'

'Pardon the interruption,' said Rainbow, 'but there is a gallant hatch of fly going down. I can hear your two neighbours at the tail of the pool rising steadily.'

Old Trout assumed an indulgent air. 'We will go up if you wish,' said he, 'but you will be well advised to observe my counsel before taking the rise, because if my angler keeps his appointment you will most assuredly be *meunièred* before nightfall.'

At this unpleasant prophecy Rainbow shivered. 'Let us keep to weed,' he suggested.

But Old Trout only laughed, so that bubbles from the river bed rose and burst upon the surface.

'Courage,' said he; 'it will be an opportunity for you to learn the finer points of the game. If you are nervous,

8

lie nearer to the bank. The natural fly does not drift there so abundantly, but you will be secure from the artificial. Presently I will treat you to an exhibition of playing with death you will not fail to appreciate.' He broke off and pointed with his eyes. 'Over you and to the left.'

Rainbow made a neat double rise and drifted back into line. 'Very mellow,' he said—'very mellow and choice. Never tasted better. May I ask, sir, what you meant by piscine psychology?'

'I imply that my angler does not appreciate the subtle possibilities of our intellect. Now, my officer concerned himself as vitally with what we were thinking as with what we were feeding upon. This fellow, secure in the knowledge that his presentation is well-nigh perfect, is content to offer me the same variety of flies day after day, irrespective of the fact that I have learned them all by heart. I have, however, adopted the practice of rising every now and then to encourage him.'

'Rising? At an artificial fly? I never heard such temerity in all my life,' gasped Rainbow.

Old Trout moved his body luxuriously. 'I should have said, appearing to rise,' he amended. 'You may have noticed that I have exhibited a predilection for small duns in preference to the larger *Ephemeridæ*. My procedure is as follows: I wait until a natural dun and his artificial Mayfly are drifting downstream with the smallest possible distance separating them. Then I rise and take the dun. Assuming I have risen to him, he strikes, misses, and is at once greatly flattered and greatly provoked. By this device I sometimes occupy his attention for over an hour and thus render a substantial service to others of my kind who would certainly have fallen victim to his skill.'

'The river is greatly in your debt, sir,' said Young Rainbow, with deliberate satire.

He knew by experience that fish as well as anglers are notorious liars, but the exploit his host recounted was a trifle too strong. Taking a sidelong glance, he was surprised to see that Old Trout did not appear to have appreciated the subtle ridicule of his remark. The long, lithe body had become almost rigid and the great round eyes were focused upon the surface with an expression of fixed concentration.

Looking up Rainbow saw a small white-winged Mayfly with red legs and a body the colour of straw swing out from the main stream and describe a slow circle over the calm surface above Old Trout's head. Scarcely an inch away a tiny blue dun, its wings folded as closely as the pages of a book, floated attendant. An upward rush, a sucking kerr-rop, and when the broken water had calmed, the dun had disappeared and the Mayfly was dancing away downstream.

'Well,' said Old Trout, 'how's that, my youthful sceptic? Pretty work, eh?'

'I saw nothing in it,' was the impertinent reply. 'There is not a trout on the river who could not have done likewise.'

'Even when one of those two flies was artificial?' Old Trout queried tolerantly.

'But neither of them was artificial,' Rainbow retorted. 'Had it been so the angler would have struck. They always do.'

'Of course he struck,' Old Trout replied.

'But he didn't,' Rainbow protested. 'I saw the Mayfly go down with the current.'

'My poor fish!' Old Trout replied. 'Do you presume to suggest that I am unable to distinguish an artificial from a natural fly? Are you so blind that you failed to see the prismatic colours in the water from the paraffin in which the fly had been dipped? Here you are! Here it is again!'

Once more the white-winged insect drifted across the backwater, but this time there was no attendant dun.

'If that's a fake I'll eat my tail,' said Rainbow.

'If you question my judgment,' Old Trout answered, 'you are at liberty to rise. I dare say, in spite of a shortage of brain, that you would eat comparatively well.'

But Rainbow, in common with his kind, was not disposed to take chances.

'We may expect two or three more casts from this fly and then he will change it for a bigger. It is the same programme every day without variation. How differently my officer would have acted. By now he would have discovered my little joke and turned the tables against me. Aye me, but some men will never learn! Your mental outfit, dear Rainbow, is singularly like a man's,' he added. 'It lacks elasticity.'

Rainbow made no retort and was glad of his forbearance, for every word Old Trout had spoken was borne out by subsequent events. Four times the white-winged Mayfly described an arc over the backwater, but in the absence of duns Old Trout did not rise again. Then came a pause, during which, through a lull in the hatch, even the natural insect was absent from the river.

'He is changing his fly,' said Old Trout, 'but he will not float it until the hatch starts again. He is casting beautifully this morning and I hope circumstances will permit me to give him another rise.'

'But suppose,' said Rainbow breathlessly, 'you played this game once too often and were foul hooked as a result?'

Old Trout expanded his gills broadly. 'Why, then,' he replied, 'I should break him. Once round a limb of that submerged apple bough and the thing would be done. I should never allow myself to be caught and no angler could gather up the slack and haul me into midstream in time to prevent me reaching the bough. Stand by.'

The shadow of a large, dark Mayfly floated cockily over the backwater and had almost returned to the main stream when a small iron-blue dun settled like a puff of thistledown in its wake.

The two insects were a foot nearer the fast water than

the spot where Old Trout was accustomed to take the rise. But for the presence of a spectator, it is doubtful whether he would have done so, but Young Rainbow's want of appreciation had excited his vanity, and with a rolling swoop he swallowed the dun and bore it downward.

And then an amazing thing happened. Instead of drifting back to his place as was expected, Old Trout's head was jerked sideways by an invisible force. A thin translucent thread upcut the water's surface and tightened irresistibly. A second later Old Trout was fighting, fighting, fighting to reach the submerged apple bough with the full weight of the running water and the full strength of the finest Japanese gut strained against him.

Watching, wide-eyed and aghast, from one of the underwater rat holes into which he had hastily withdrawn, Rainbow saw the figure of a man rise out of a bed of irises downstream and scramble upon the bank. In his right hand, with the wrist well back, he held a light split-cane rod whose upper joint was curved to a half-circle. The man's left hand was detaching a collapsible landing net from the ring of his belt. Every attitude and movement was expressive of perfectly organised activity. His mouth was shut as tightly as a steel trap, but a light of happy excitement danced in his eyes.

'No, you don't, my fellar,' Rainbow heard him say. 'No, you don't. I knew all about that apple bough before ever I put a fly over your pool. And the weed bed on the right,' he added, as Old Trout made a sudden swerve half down and half across stream.

Tucking the net under his arm the man whipped up the slack with a lightning-like action. The manœuvre cost Old Trout dear, for when, despairing of reaching the weed and burrowing into it, he tried to regain his old position, he found himself six feet farther away from the apple bough than when the battle began.

Instinctively Old Trout knew it was useless to dash downstream, for a man who could take up slack with the speed his adversary had shown would profit by the expedient to come more quickly to terms with him. Besides, lower down there was broken water to knock the breath out of his lungs. Even where he lay straining and slugging this way and that, the water was pouring so fast into his open mouth as nearly to drown him. His only chance of effecting a smash was by a series of jumps, followed by quick dives. Once before, although he had not confessed it to Rainbow, Old Trout had saved his life by resorting to this expedient. It takes the strain off the line and returns it so quickly that even the finest gut is apt to sunder.

Meanwhile the man was slowly approaching, winding up as he came. Old Trout, boring in the depths, could hear the click of the check reel with increasing distinctness. Looking up, he saw that the cast was almost vertical above his head, which meant that the moment to make the attempt was at hand. The tension was appalling, for ever since the fight began his adversary had given him the butt unremittingly. Aware of his own weight and power, Old Trout was amazed that any tackle could stand the strain.

'Now's my time,' he thought, and jumped.

It was no ordinary jump, but an aërial rush three feet out of the water, with a twist at its apex and a cutting lash of the tail designed to break the cast. But his adversary was no ordinary angler, and at the first hint of what was happening he dropped the point of the rod flush with the surface.

Once and once more Old Trout flung himself into the air, but after each attempt he found himself with diminishing strength and with less line to play with.

'It looks to me,' said Rainbow mournfully, 'as if my unhappy host will lose this battle and finish up in that glass case to which he was referring a few minutes ago.' And greatly affected, he burrowed his nose in the mud and wondered, in the event of this dismal prophecy coming true, whether he would be able to take possession of the pool without molestation.

In consequence of these reflections he failed to witness the last phase of the battle, when, as will sometimes happen with big fish, all the fight went out of Old Trout, and rolling wearily over and over, he abandoned himself to the clinging embraces of the net. He never saw the big man proudly carry Old Trout back into the hayfield, where, before proceeding to remove the fly, he sat down beside a shallow dyke and lit a cigarette and smiled largely. Then, with an affectionate and professional touch, he picked up Old Trout by the back of the neck, his forefinger and thumb sunk firmly in the gills.

'You're a fine fellar,' he said, extracting the fly; 'a good sportsman and a funny fish. You fooled me properly for three days, but I think you'll own I outwitted you in the end.'

Rummaging in his creel for a small rod of hard wood that he carried for the purpose of administering the quietus, he became aware of something that arrested the action. Leaning forward, he stared with open eyes at a tiny *W* perforated in the upper part of Old Trout's tail.

'Shades of the war! Dulverton!' he exclaimed. Then with a sudden warmth: 'Old chap, old chap, is it really you? This is red-letter stuff. If you're not too far gone to take another lease of life, have it with me.'

And with the tenderness of a woman, he slipped Old Trout into the dyke and in a tremble of excitement hurried off to the *auberge* where the fishermen lodged, to tell a tale no one even pretended to believe.

For the best part of an hour Old Trout lay in the shallow waters of the dyke before slowly cruising back to his own place beneath the overhanging bank. The alarming experience through which he had passed had made him a shade forgetful, and he was not prepared for the sight of Young Rainbow rising steadily at the hatch of fly.

'Pardon me, but a little more to your right,' he said, with heavy courtesy.

'Diving otters!' cried Young Rainbow, leaping a foot clear of the water. 'You, sir! You!'

'And why not?' Old Trout replied. 'Your memory must be short if you have already forgotten that this is my place.'

'Yes, but——' Rainbow began and stopped.

'You are referring to that little circus of a few minutes ago,' said Old Trout. 'Is it possible you failed to appreciate the significance of the affair? I knew at once it was my dear officer when he dropped the artificial dun behind the natural Mayfly. In the circumstances I could hardly do less than accept his invitation. Nothing is more delightful than a re-union of comrades of the war.' He paused and added: 'We had a charming talk, he and I, and I do not know which of us was the more affected. It is a tragedy that such friendship and such intellect as we share cannot exist in a common element.'

And so great was his emotion that Old Trout dived and buried his head in the weeds. Whereby Rainbow did uncommonly well during the midday hatch.

HIAWATHA'S FISHING

By HENRY W. LONGFELLOW

HENRY WADSWORTH LONGFELLOW (1807-1882) in 'Hiawatha's Fishing' in *The Song of Hiawatha* (1855) produced that rare thing—a piece of narrative verse of quality on fishing.

FORTH upon the Gitche Gumee,
On the shining Big-Sea-Water,
With his fishing-line of cedar,
Of the twisted bark of cedar,
Forth to catch the sturgeon Nahma,
Mishe-Nahma, King of Fishes,
In his birch canoe exulting
All alone went Hiawatha.
Through the clear, transparent water
He could see the fishes swimming
Far down in the depths below him:
See the yellow perch, the Sahwa,
Like a sunbeam in the water,
See the Shawgashee, the craw-fish,
Like a spider on the bottom,
On the white and sandy bottom.
At the stern sat Hiawatha,
With his fishing-line of cedar;
In his plumes the breeze of morning
Played as in the hemlock branches;
On the bows, with tail erected,
Sat the squirrel, Adjidaumo;
In his fur the breeze of morning
Played as in the prairie grasses.
On the white sand of the bottom
Lay the monster Mishe-Nahma,

Lay the sturgeon, King of Fishes;
Through his gills he breathed the water,
With his fins he fanned and winnowed,
With his tail he swept the sand-floor.
  There he lay in all his armour;
On each side a shield to guard him,
Plates of bone upon his forehead,
Down his sides and back and shoulders
Plates of bone with spines projecting!
Painted was he with his war-paints,
Stripes of yellow, red, and azure,
Spots of brown and spots of sable;
And he lay there on the bottom,
Fanning with his fins of purple,
As above him Hiawatha
In his birch canoe came sailing,
With his fishing-line of cedar.
'Take my bait!' cried Hiawatha
Down into the depths beneath him,
'Take my bait, O Sturgeon, Nahma!
Come up from below the water,
Let us see which is the stronger!'
And he dropped his line of cedar
Through the clear, transparent water,
Waited vainly for an answer,
Long sat waiting for an answer,
And repeating loud and louder,
'Take my bait, O King of Fishes!'
  Quiet lay the sturgeon, Nahma,
Fanning slowly in the water,
Looking up at Hiawatha,
Listening to his call and clamour,
His unnecessary tumult,
Till he wearied of the shouting;
And he said to the Kenozha,
To the pike, the Maskenozha,
'Take the bait of this rude fellow,

Break the line of Hiawatha!'
  In his fingers Hiawatha
Felt the loose line jerk and tighten;
As he drew it in, it tugged so
That the birch canoe stood endwise,
Like a birch log in the water,
With the squirrel, Adjidaumo,
Perched and frisking on the summit.
  Full of scorn was Hiawatha
When he saw the fish rise upward,
Saw the pike, the Maskenozha,
Coming nearer, nearer to him,
And he shouted through the water,
'Esa! esa! shame upon you!
You are but the pike, Kenozha,
You are not the fish I wanted,
You are not the King of Fishes!'
  Reeling downward to the bottom
Sank the pike in great confusion,
And the mighty sturgeon, Nahma,
Said to Ugudwash, the sun-fish,
'Take the bait of this great boaster,
Break the line of Hiawatha!'
  Slowly upward, wavering, gleaming
Like a white moon in the water,
Rose the Ugudwash, the sun-fish,
Seized the line of Hiawatha,
Swung with all his weight upon it,
Made a whirlpool in the water,
Whirled the birch canoe in circles,
Round and round in gurgling eddies.
Till the circles in the water
Reached the far-off sandy beaches,
Till the water-flags and rushes
Nodded on the distant margins.
  But when Hiawatha saw him
Slowly rising through the water,

Lifting his great disc of whiteness,
Loud he shouted in derision,
'Esa! esa! shame upon you!
You are Ugudwash, the sun-fish,
You are not the fish I wanted,
You are not the King of Fishes!'
  Slowly downward, wavering, gleaming,
Sank the Ugudwash, the sun-fish,
And again the sturgeon, Nahma,
Heard the shout of Hiawatha,
Heard his challenge of defiance,
The unnecessary tumult,
Ringing far across the water.
  From the white sand of the bottom
Up he rose with angry gesture,
Quivering in each nerve and fibre,
Clashing all his plates of armour,
Gleaming bright with all his war-paint;
In his wrath he darted upward,
Flashing leaped into the sunshine,
Opened his great jaws and swallowed
Both canoe and Hiawatha.
  Down into that darksome cavern
Plunged the headlong Hiawatha,
As a log on some black river
Shoots and plunges down the rapids,
Found himself in utter darkness,
Groped about in helpless wonder,
Till he felt a great heart beating,
Throbbing in that utter darkness.
  And he smote it in his anger,
With his fist, the heart of Nahma,
Felt the mighty King of Fishes
Shudder through each nerve and fibre,
Heard the water gurgle round him
As he leaped and staggered through it,
Sick at heart, and faint and weary.

Crosswise then did Hiawatha
Drag his birch canoe for safety,
Lest from out the jaws of Nahma,
In the turmoil and confusion
Forth he might be hurled and perish.
And the squirrel, Adjidaumo,
Frisked and chattered very gaily,
Toiled and tugged with Hiawatha
Till the labour was completed.
Then said Hiawatha to him,
'O my little friend, the squirrel,
Bravely have you toiled to help me;
Take the thanks of Hiawatha,
And the name which now he gives you;
For hereafter and for ever
Boys shall call you Adjidaumo,
Tail-in-air the boys shall call you!'
And again the sturgeon, Nahma,
Gasped and quivered in the water,
Then was still, and drifted landward
Till he grated on the pebbles,
Till the listening Hiawatha
Heard him grate upon the margin,
Felt him strand upon the pebbles,
Knew that Nahma, King of Fishes,
Lay there dead upon the margin.
Then he heard a clang and flapping,
As of many wings assembling,
Heard a screaming and confusion,
As of birds of prey contending,
Saw a gleam of light above him,
Shining through the ribs of Nahma,
Saw the glittering eyes of sea-gulls,
Of Kayoshk, the sea-gulls, peering,
Gazing at him through the opening,
Heard them saying to each other,
''Tis our brother, Hiawatha!'

And he shouted from below them,
Cried exulting from the caverns,
'O ye sea-gulls! O my brothers!
I have slain the sturgeon, Nahma;
Make the rifts a little larger,
With your claws the openings widen,
Set me free from this dark prison,
And henceforward and for ever
Men shall speak of your achievements,
Calling you Kayoshk, the sea-gulls,
Yes, Kayoshk, the Noble Scratchers!'
And the wild and clamorous sea-gulls
Toiled with beak and claws together,
Made the rifts and openings wider
In the mighty ribs of Nahma,
And from peril and from prison,
From the body of the sturgeon,
From the peril of the water,
Was released my Hiawatha.
He was standing near his wigwam,
On the margin of the water,
And he called to old Nokomis,
Called and beckoned to Nokomis,
Pointed to the sturgeon, Nahma,
Lying lifeless on the pebbles,
With the sea-gulls feeding on him.
'I have slain the Mishe-Nahma,
Slain the King of Fishes!' said he;
'Look! the sea-gulls feed upon him,
Yes, my friends Kayoshk, the sea-gulls;
Drive them not away, Nokomis,
They have saved me from great peril
In the body of the sturgeon.
Wait until their meal is ended,
Till their craws are full with feasting,
Till they homeward fly, at sunset,
To their nests among the marshes;

Then bring all your pots and kettles,
And make oil for us in Winter.'
  And she waited till the sunset,
Till the pallid moon, the night-sun,
Rose above the tranquil water,
Till Kayoshk, the sated sea-gulls,
From their banquet rose with clamour,
And across the fiery sunset
Winged their way to far-off islands,
To their nests among the rushes.
  To his sleep went Hiawatha,
And Nokomis to her labour,
Toiling patient in the moonlight,
Till the sun and moon changed places,
Till the sky was red with sunrise,
And Kayoshk, the hungry sea-gulls,
Came back from the reedy islands,
Clamorous for their morning banquet.
  Three whole days and nights alternate
Old Nokomis and the sea-gulls
Stripped the oily flesh of Nahma,
Till the waves washed through the rib-bones,
Till the sea-gulls came no longer,
And upon the sands lay nothing
But the skeleton of Nahma.

THE SWIM

By GUY DE MAUPASSANT

Henri René Albert Guy de Maupassant (1850-93), the great French short-story writer, wrote two fishing stories—'*Le Trou*' ('The Hole' or, in fishing parlance, 'The Swim') in *Le Horla* (1887) and '*Deux Amis*' ('Two Friends') in *Mademoiselle Fifi* (1883). 'The Swim' (translation by the editor) is here given. As for 'Two Friends,' it is really a picture of Prussian brutality, heightened in effect by being painted against the peace of an angling background.

Inflicting blows and wounds causing death. Such was the charge on which M. Léopold Renard, upholsterer, appeared before the assizes.

In court were the chief witnesses, Mme Flamèche, widow of the victim; Louis Ladureau, cabinetmaker; and Jean Durdent, plumber: while close to the accused was his wife, in black—small, ugly, like a monkey dressed up as a woman.

And here is Renard (Léopold) 's account of the drama.

'As God is my witness, this is a catastrophe where, far from being the cause, I was all along the chief victim. The facts speak for themselves, My Lord. I am a decent man, a hard-working man, upholsterer these sixteen years in the same street, known, liked, respected, well thought of by all, as you've heard the neighbours say, even the house-porter, who speaks a sane word now and then. I'm fond of work, I'm fond of thrift, I'm fond of honest folk and of harmless pleasures. That's been my undoing, worse luck. Still, as I did nothing of intent, I feel no shame.

'Well, every Sunday for five years my wife here and I have spent the day at Poissy. That takes us into the open air—to say nothing of our love of fishing. Why, we're as keen on that as on spring onions! Mélie's the one that gave me the craze, the wretch, and that she's madder on it than I am, the sinner, you can see from all this trouble having come about through her, as assuredly it did, as you'll learn.

'As for me, I'm no soft one, yet I'm easy-going, without a pennyworth of wickedness. But as for her, well, well! You'd think her quite harmless, she's so small and skinny. Let me tell you, though, she's more spiteful than a cat. I'm not denying that she has her points; indeed she has, and important ones for one like me in business. But her disposition! Just you ask the neighbours, and even the house-porter, who put in a word for me a moment ago—she can tell you things.

'Day in day out she kept harping on about my softness. "I wouldn't put up with this. I wouldn't put up with that." Had I listened to her, My Lord, I'd have been in three scraps a month at least.'

Mme Renard cut in: 'Keep on. He laughs best who laughs last.'

He turned towards her, not mincing his words: 'Oh well, I can say what I like about you, seeing it's not you that's on trial, you.'

Then turning to the judge again, he said:

'I proceed. We always went, then, to Poissy on Saturday evenings to be able to start our fishing next morning at daybreak. That custom became a kind of second nature, as the saying goes. Three years past this summer I discovered a swim—and such a swim! Shaded, eight feet of water at the least, perhaps ten. What a spot it was with its hollows under the bank—a regular lair of fishes! Talk about an angler's heaven! This hole, My Lord, I could look on as my own, seeing I was its Christopher Columbus. Everyone in the district knew it for mine, everyone—not a soul to dispute it. "That, oh, that's Renard's spot," they'd say, and nobody dreamt of going there, not even M. Plumeau, who is notorious, and no offence meant in saying it, for pinching the places of others.

'Well, certain always of my place, I went back and back to it just like an owner. The moment I arrived on Saturdays I boarded *Dalila* with my wife. *Dalila*, I should explain, is a Norwegian boat I had made for me by Fournaise—light yet strong. I was saying, then, that we boarded *Dalila*, and we would set about baiting the swim. As for baiting, there's no one to touch me, and well my pals all know it. You want to hear what I bait with? Well, I can't tell you. It has nothing to do with the case, I just can't tell you. It's my secret. Hundreds have asked me for it. I've been offered drinks and dainties no end to make me part with it. But just go and see if the chub come! Oh yes, they've tried to pet my patent out through my tummy. But not another soul knows it apart from my wife, and she won't tell it any more than I shall. Isn't that so, Mélie?'

The judge interrupted: 'Just get to the point as soon as you can.'

Whereupon the accused went on: 'I'm getting to it, I'm getting to it. Well, on Saturday, the 8th of July, we left by the 5.25 train, and, as we always did on Saturdays, went before dinner to bait the swim. The weather promised to be fine. I said to Mélie: "Great work to-morrow, great work." And she answered: "Looks like it." We never talk more than that to each other.

'Then we came back to dinner. I was feeling good, and I was dry. That's where the whole trouble began, My Lord. I said to Mélie: "Look here, Mélie, I think it would be an idea if I had a bottle of 'nightcap.'" That's a light white wine we've christened so, because, if you drink too much of it, it keeps you awake and is just the opposite of a nightcap. You get the idea?

'She replied: "Have your way, but you'll be upset again and won't be able to get up to-morrow." There for you was truth, wisdom, prudence, discernment—I own it.

Still I couldn't resist, and back I knock the bottle. Whence the whole trouble.

'Well, I couldn't sleep. Good Lord! that grape-juice nightcap kept me awake till two in the morning. Then in a twinkling, over I go, and so soundly that I'd have been deaf to the last trump itself.

'To be brief, my wife woke me at six. Out of bed I spring. On in a jiffy with my trousers and jersey, a dash of water on my mug, and into *Dalila* we jump. Too late. When I get to the swim it is already taken. Never had that happened before, My Lord, never in three years. Why, I was being robbed before my very eyes! "Well I'm damned, I'm damned, I'm damned," I cried. And then my wife began to rail at me: "That's your nightcap for you. Get out, you soaker. Are you satisfied now, you stupid fool?"

'I answered nothing. Everything she said was true.

'I went ashore, however, near the spot, by way of making the best of a bad job. Perhaps the fellow wouldn't catch anything after all, and would clear out.

'He was a little skinny chap, in white drill and with a large straw hat. His wife was with him, a fat woman, who was sitting behind, sewing.

'When she saw us taking up our position near the spot, what do you think she muttered?

'"Is this, then, the only place on the river?"

'And my wife, fuming, replied:

'"People of ordinary decency usually make a point of finding out local ways. It keeps them off others' preserves."

'As I didn't want a row, I said to her:

'"Hold your tongue, Mélie. Don't answer back, don't answer back. We'll see about this all right."

'Well, we had tied up *Dalila* under the willows and had got out and were fishing side by side, Mélie and I, right beside the other two.

'Here, My Lord, I must go into detail.

'We hadn't been there five minutes, when down went

my neighbour's line twice, thrice, and lo and behold, he hauled out a chub, big as my thigh, a bit less perhaps, but not much! My heart gave a jump, my brow broke into a sweat, and Mélie cried: "Hi, you toper, did you see that?"

'Just then, M. Bru, the grocer of Poissy, a dab with the gudgeon, passed by in his boat and shouted:

'"So somebody's taken your place, M. Renard?" "Yes, M. Bru," I replied, "there are some toughs in this world who don't know how to behave."

'The little fellow in drill at my side pretended not to hear. His fat lump of a wife likewise, the cow.'

The judge interrupted a second time: 'Careful of your language. You insult the widow, Mme Flamèche, here.'

Renard made excuse: 'Pardon me, pardon me, my feelings ran away with me.

'Well, a quarter of an hour had hardly gone, when what should the little devil in drill do but yank out another fish, a chub, and then another on top of it, and still another five minutes later.

'I tell you I was on the verge of tears, and I could sense Mme Renard bursting with rage. She kept on rating me without pausing for breath: "You miserable fool, don't you see you're being robbed of your fish? Don't you see it? You'll catch nothing, you, nothing, nothing, not even a frog. Don't my hands itch merely to think of it?"

'All I said, and to myself, was: "Just wait till noon. He'll go to lunch then, this poaching fellow, and you'll get back your place." You see, My Lord, we lunch every Sunday on the spot. We bring food with us in *Dalila*.

'Bah! Twelve struck. The wretch had a chicken wrapped up in a newspaper, and, would you believe it, while he ate he actually caught another chub!

'Mélie and I had a crumb, hardly anything. As things were, we didn't feel like it.

'Then to aid digestion I took up my newspaper. Every Sunday I read *Gil Blas* like that in the shade by the waterside. Sunday is Columbine's day, Columbine, you know, who writes articles in *Gil Blas*. I've a way of infuriating Mme Renard by pretending to know this Columbine. It's all a yarn. I don't know her at all, have never even seen her. Still she writes well, hits out and to the point, for a woman. She suits me down to the ground. After all, there're not so many of her kind.

'Well, then, I began ragging my wife, but at once she got angry, furiously angry, and then angrier still. So I said no more.

'Just at this moment our two witnesses here, M. Ladureau and M. Durdent, appeared on the other bank. We know each other by sight.

'The little fellow had begun fishing again and to such tune that I shook from sheer vexation. Then his wife said: "This is a thundering good spot, we'll keep on coming here, Désiré."

'A cold shiver ran down my spine, and Mme Renard kept on saying: "Call yourself a man, call yourself a man! You chicken heart!"

'"Look here," I said quickly, "I'd rather clear out. I shall only do something I'll regret."

'She hissed as if she'd scald me: "Call yourself a man! Now you're running away, giving up your place! Run away then, you Bazaine!"

'That went home. Still I did not wince.

'Then what does the other fellow do but drag out a bream! Never had I seen such a thumper before. Never.

'And now my wife began to talk loud out—pretending to be merely thinking. You see what a she-devil she is. "This is what one might call stolen fish," she said, "seeing it was we who baited the swim. They ought at least to pay us for the bait."

'Whereupon the little drill-clad bloke's fat wife chipped in: "Is it us you're getting at, madam?"

'"I'm getting at fish thieves, those who profit by what's been spent by others."

'"Are you calling us fish thieves then?"

'Then they began explaining—then slanging. Good Lord! they knew the words all right—real stingers. They bawled so, that our two witnesses, who were on the other bank, called out by way of a joke: "Hi, you, over there, less row, you'll spoil your husbands' sport!"

'The fact is that the little fellow in drill and myself remained stock still. We stuck where we were, our noses glued to the water, as if we'd never heard.

'But Lord help me, we heard all right!

'"You're nothing but a liar."—"And you a strumpet." —"And you a trollop."—"And you a trull." And so on and so on. A sailor couldn't have beat them.

'Suddenly I heard a noise behind me and turned round. There was the other woman, the great fat thing, belabouring my wife with her parasol. Whack! whack! Mélie took a couple. But now she was fairly roused, and when Mélie's roused she lams about, I tell you. She seized the fat dame by the hair and then smack! smack! smack! the blows fell like a shower of ripe plums.

'I'd have left them to it—the women to themselves, the men to themselves. Why mix the thing? But up like a devil comes the little drill-suit chap making to spring at my wife. "No, no, hardly that, my hearty," says I, and I received the old cock-sparrow flush on the end of my fist. Biff! biff! One on the nose, the other in the guts. Up go his arms, up go his legs, and he falls on his back clean in the river, right in the middle of the swim.

'Most certainly I would have fished him out, My Lord, if I'd had the time just then. But now, to crown all, the fat woman gained the upper hand and was making mincemeat of Mélie. I know well I shouldn't have rescued her while the other was drinking his fill. Still I didn't think he would be drowned. I said to myself: "Ugh! that'll cool him down."

'I ran, then, to separate the women. I was pommelled, scratched, bitten. Good Lord, what vixen!

'The long and the short of it was that it took me a good five minutes, nearer ten, perhaps, to part this pair of clingers.

'I turned round. There was nothing to be seen. The water was as smooth as a lake. And the fellows on the other bank kept shouting: "Fish him out, fish him out."

'That was all very well, but I can't swim, much less dive, believe me.

'At last, after more than a quarter of an hour it would be, the lock-keeper came along and two men with boat-hooks. They found him at the bottom of the pool, under eight feet of water, as I have said, but there he was, the little fellow in his drill suit.

'These are the facts as I swear to them. On my word of honour I am innocent.'

The witnesses having testified in the same sense, the accused was acquitted.

ST ANTHONY TO THE FISHES

Translation by JOSEPH ADDISON

JOSEPH ADDISON (1672-1719), in the part of his *Remarks on Several Parts of Italy* (1705) dealing with Brescia, Verona, Padua, gives in Italian, from a life of St Anthony of Padua by an unnamed author, an account of the discourse of that saint to an assembly of fish, and adds his own translation. Surely it would have rejoiced Izaak Walton.

WHEN the heretics would not regard his preaching, St Anthony betook himself to the seashore, where the river Marecchia disembogues itself into the Adriatic. He here called the fish together in the name of God, that they might hear his holy word. The fish came swimming towards him in such vast shoals, both from the sea and from the river, that the surface of the water was quite covered with their multitudes. They quickly ranged themselves, according to their several species, into a very beautiful congregation, and, like so many rational creatures, presented themselves before him to hear the word of God. St Anthony was so struck with the miraculous obedience and submission of these poor animals, that he found a secret sweetness distilling upon his soul, and at last addressed himself to them in the following words.

'Although the infinite power and providence of God (my dearly beloved Fish) discovers itself in all the works of his creation, as in the heavens, in the sun, in the moon, and in the stars, in this lower world, in man, and in other perfect creatures; nevertheless the goodness of the Divine Majesty shines out in you more eminently, and appears after a more particular manner, than in any other created beings. For notwithstanding you are comprehended under the name of reptiles, partaking of a middle nature between stones and beasts, and imprisoned in the deep abyss of waters; notwithstanding you are tost among billows, thrown up and down by tempests, deaf to hearing, dumb to speech, and terrible to behold: notwithstanding, I say, these natural disadvantages, the Divine Greatness shows itself in you after a very wonderful manner. In you are seen the mighty mysteries of an infinite goodness. The holy scripture has always made use of you, as the types and shadows of some profound sacrament.

'Do you think that, without a mystery, the first present that God Almighty made to man, was of you, O ye Fishes? Do you think that without a mystery, among all creatures and animals which were appointed for sacrifices, you only were excepted, O ye Fishes? Do you think there was nothing meant by our Saviour Christ, that next to the paschal lamb he took so much pleasure in the food of you, O ye Fishes? Do you think it was by mere chance, that when the Redeemer of the World was to pay a tribute to Cæsar, he thought fit to find it in the mouth of a fish? These are all of them so many mysteries and sacraments, that oblige you in a more particular manner to the praises of your Creator.

'It is from God, my beloved Fish, that you have received being, life, motion, and sense. It is he that has given you, in compliance with your natural inclinations, the whole world of waters for your habitation. It is he that has furnished it with lodgings, chambers, caverns, grottoes, and such magnificent retirements as are not to be met with in the seats of kings, or in the palaces of princes. You have the water for your dwelling, a clear transparent element, brighter than crystal; you can see from its deepest bottom everything that passes on its surface; you have the eyes of a lynx, or of an argus; you are guided by a secret and unerring principle, delighting in everything that may be beneficial to you, and avoiding everything that may be hurtful; you are carried on by a hidden instinct to preserve yourselves, and to propagate your species; you obey, in all your actions, works and motions, the dictates and suggestions of nature, without the least repugnancy or contradiction.

'The colds of winter, and the heats of summer, are equally incapable of molesting you. A serene or a clouded sky are indifferent to you. Let the earth abound in fruits, or be cursed with scarcity, it has no influence on your welfare. You live secure in rains and thunders, lightnings and earthquakes; you have no concern in the blossoms of spring, or in the glowings of summer, in the fruits of autumn, or in the frosts of winter. You are not solicitous about hours or days, months or years; the variableness of the weather, or the change of seasons.

'In what dreadful majesty, in what wonderful power, in what amazing providence did God Almighty distinguish you among all the species of creatures that perished in the universal deluge! You only were insensible of the mischief that had laid waste the whole world.

'All this, as I have already told you, ought to inspire you with gratitude and praise towards the Divine Majesty, that has done so great things for you, granted you such particular graces and privileges, and heaped upon you so many distinguishing favours. And since for all this you cannot employ your tongues in the praises of your Benefactor, and are not provided with words to express your gratitude; make at least some sign of reverence; bow yourselves at his name; give some show of gratitude, according to the best of your capacities; express your thanks in the most becoming manner that you are able, and be not unmindful of all the benefits he has bestowed upon you.'

He had no sooner done speaking, but behold a miracle! The fish, as though they had been endued with reason, bowed down their heads with all the marks of a profound humility and devotion, moving their bodies up and down with a kind of fondness, as approving what had been spoken by the blessed Father St Anthony.

The legend adds, that after many heretics, who were present at the miracle, had been converted by it, the saint gave his benediction to the fish, and dismissed them.

TOM PURDIE'S MUCKLE FISH

By WILLIAM SCROPE

WILLIAM SCROPE (1772-1852), English landscape painter and writer on wild sport, the author of *The Art of Deerstalking* (1838) and of *Days and Nights of Salmon Fishing in the Tweed* (1843; new ed. by H. T. Sheringham, 1921), the last-named one of the angling classics. He lived with 'Christopher North,' James Hogg, and Thomas Tod Stoddart in the grand days of Scottish angling, and at his fishing quarters on the Tweed near Melrose had Sir Walter Scott as his intimate friend. 'Tom Purdie's Muckle Fish' is from chapter IX of *Days and Nights of Salmon Fishing in the Tweed.* See also pp. 243, 384.

'WHILE I was wi' Mr Anderson, and shepherd at West Bold, one Sunday,' says Tom, 'I didna go up to Traquair to the kirk, but took a walk by the riverside; there war a vast o' fish i' the water, and I saw ane or twae great rowaners [1] turnin', a sure sign there war mickle kippers [2] too. I had dandered doon to near the burn fit, and had a pair o' good stilts aye lyin' there. My first wife was than a lass, and lived at Caberston; and the stilts war ready to cross the water at an orra time. I took a thought that I would like to see what was steerin' on Caberston throat; and sae I lap on the stilts and went through at the rack [3]; and whan I was on the other side, I thought I might as weel tak a keek at the throat. I keepit weel off the water-side until I was doon aneth where the fish began to work. I kend by a clour [4] i' the water a gay bit afore me, that there was a big redd there, and drew cannily forrit. 'Od, sir! my verra heart lap to my mouth whan I gat the glisk o' something mair like a red stirk [5] than aught else

[1] female salmon with roe. [2] male salmon during spawning-time.
[3] shallow. [4] heaving. [5] young bullock or heifer.

muve off the redd, and hallans [1] doon the water and mak for the south side. I fand my hair crap on my head. I minded it was the Sabbath, and I shouldna hae been there. It might be a delusion o' the enemy, if it wasna the deil himsel'. I stude and consider'd. I had never seen the deil i' daylight, and forbye there was just than a great brown rowaner slade off the redd after him. If it was the deil, what could he be doin' wi' the rowaner? The water was breast deep at the least; it might be a fish after a', and I had heard the auld folk speak o' verra muckle anes. I lookit up the brae to the toon.[2] Peggy aiblins [3] hadna likit my hankerin' about the throat on sic a day, and she had slippit in to the house, and didna come out again. Sae whan I saw it was sae, I held up the waterside for my stilts, keepin', for a' that, an e'e to the redds. Heaven forgie me! I never saw sic a water o' fish! If it wasna the deil I had seen, I was sure he wasna far off. I saw eneugh to temp a better man than me; and I began to think I had better be at hame readin' a chapter o' the gude book, if no a leaf or twae o' *The Four-fold State*; sae I took the stilts and cam through again by the rack, and wan hame just a wee thought afore the master and the mistress, honest woman!, cam hame thrae the kirk. I haflins wist I had been there too; but yet I was only lookin' at the warks o' the creation, and couldna say I had done ony great wrang; an' if I hadna seen Peggy come out o' the byre [4] at Caberston, I aiblins hadna stiltit the water after a'. But I fand I couldna read a styme; for, do as I might, I couldna get the appearance that I had seen out o' my mind; and yet whan I consider'd about the mickle rowaner, that I was sure eneugh was a yirthly [5] thing, I couldna help believin' that it was, after a', a fish I had seen; but I never saw sic another.

'Weel, a' the time the master was at the readin', I couldna keep the glisk o' the awesome mickle fish out o'

[1] slanting. [2] farmstead. [3] perhaps.
[4] cow-house. [5] earthly.

my head, and whan we raise thrae the prayers, I popit [1] the shouther o' the nowtherd [2] callant, and said quietly, "Sandy, if I raise ye about twal o'clock ye needna wonder; sleep as fast as ye can till than, and tak' nae notice to Jamie whan ye rise." I had aft ta'en this lad wi' me afore to haud the light, for he was a stout loon o' his age, and could haud a light weel eneugh, havin' a natural cast rather bye common for a' kin-kind o' mischief and ploys. I believe he was sound asleep in five minutes.

'As for mysel', I need hardly say I never steekit [3] an e'e. I kend fu' weel that if we warna at Queedside by the first o' the Monanday mornin', the hempies [4] out o' twae or three o' the toons o' the north side o' the water wad be bleezin' up afore us; and some devilrie cam owre the cock that sat on the byre balks [5] aside us, for he never mist to skirl every ten minutes thrae the time I lay doon; sae I was as often grapin' [6] the hands o' my watch, which I had gotten in a coup [7] thrae Geordie Matheson three weeks afore.

'At last, whan I had a gude guess it was drawin' near to twal o'clock, and nae fear o' breakin' the Sabbath, I gat up and shook Sandy by the shouther, who was out o' bed in a jiffy. We went to the barn and tyed up twae prime heather lights thrae a bunch or twae which I had gar'd the miller lad dry on the kiln ten days afore. They may talk o' ruffies [8] and birk bark baith; but gie me a good heather light, weel dried on the kiln, for a throat o' the Queed. However, I got the lights on my back, Sandy carried a weel-dried bairdie,[9] and I took in my hand my cloddin' waster.[10] I had gi'en the Runchies o' Yarrowford seven white shillings for her; but nane could mak a waster wi' the Runchies, nor track an otter either; they had clean the best terriers in the hale countryside; and they had an art o' their ain in temperin' the taes o' a waster that

[1] tapped. [2] cattle-herd. [3] closed. [4] scamps.
[5] beams. [6] looking at. [7] swap. [8] tarred sacking.
[9] straw rope to keep the ligh+ in. [10] a throwing pronged salmon-spear.

they took to the grave wi' them. I could hae thrawn mine off the head o' a scaur; and if she had stracken a whinstane rock she wad hae been nae mair blunted than gif I had thrawn her on a haystack.

'On our way to the water I was nae little fashed [1] wi' the unsonsie [2] callant blowin' up the bairdie every now and than to mak sure that it wasna out, and I had ance or twice to shake him by the neck; for I wasna sure that the Caberston folk, who war aye devilash yap [3] whan there war mony fish i' the water, mightna be lyin' at the side o' the throat ready to blaw up whan it past twal o'clock; and gude truly, if they had gotten a blink o' our bairdie, they wad hae ta'en that instead o' the hour. At any rate there was little use in warnin' a' the north side o' the water that Tam Purdie was ga'an out to the fishin'; and, to tell the truth, the Sabbath day was little mair than owre.

'But some had clippit the wings o' the Sabbath closer than us after a'; I saw the twinkle o' a coal every now and than commin doon Caberston peat-road; and I weel kend it was just the Sandersons o' Priesthope bent for the same place wi' oursels. It was ill bein' afore them on a Monanday mornin' wi' fair play, whan the water was in good trim. Faith I lost nae time whan I saw the twinkle o' their peat-coal (there was nae strae for bairdies at Priesthope) in tyin' the lights on the callant's back and thrawin' him and the clod-waster on my shouther and stiltin' the water as I hàd done in the daylight. I kend fu' weel the place where the big redd was, and blew up about thirty step below, sae that the light might be at the best whan we cam fornent [4] it. Sandy held the light weel; his e'en war glentin' in his head wi' eagerness; and just whan we cam to the tail o' the redd, I saw the muckle kipper lyin' like a flain wedder.[5] I had, as I thought, the advantage on my side, for the brae was three or four feet

[1] annoyed. [2] mischievous. [3] alert.
[4] opposite. [5] flayed wether.

aboon the water, and I strack him wi' a' my pith Whither the mid grain had stracken him on the back fin, I took nae time than to consider; but the fourteen-pund waster stottit off his back as if he had been a bag o' wool.

'A cauld sweet cam owre me, an' I believe every hair on my body crap. I was dead sure it was the deil himsel' that had been permitted to throw himsel' i' my way for breakin' the Sabbath! For I had begun to tye up the lights as soon as I shook up the callant; an' it was hardly twal o'clock. I pu'd the burnin' light out o' his hand, and dash'd it i' the Queed, threw him on my back as fast as I could, an' was hardly able to stilt the water again for verra dread.

'I needna say we war soon in our beds; and I took the callant in aside me, for he was to the full as feard, poor fellow, as I was—an' mair. For whan I got time, an' turn'd calm eneugh to consider, I began to see it couldna weel be Auld Clutie, for I could mind o' seein' the verra e'en, an' gib an' teeth and the gapin' mouth o' the kipper. And by and by, I cam to be certain sure it was neither mair nor less than the big monster I had seen i' daylight. Sae wi' that settlement there cam the question; how could I get another chance? Aweel, I lay still till just afore sky-break, which I kend baith by my watch, and the cock that had been through the night as quiet as the kye [1] aneth him. I waken'd Sandy wi' muckle ado this time, and he had nae grit broo' [2] o' the business: but, however, be that as it may, we tyed up another light an' set off again. But there was still a hankerin' i' the callant's mind anent ga'an back to the same place, where he had gotten sic a fleg.[3] He was like a colt that has been scar'd wi' a grey stane, an's no willing to venture back to see that it's nae bogle.[4] "But is ye *sure*, Tam, it wasna the deil?" "Deil a bit o' Satan it was, Sandy, ma man," says I, "for I saw him afore you; an' the deil darena show himsel' i' daylight on sic a day." Weel, we gat through the

[1] cows. [2] liking. [3] fright. [4] apparition.

Queed again, an' kindled up the auld place. Whan we cam up to the muckle redd, the fiend a haed [1] was there but twae or three rowangatherers [2] whiddin' [3] about; sae we cam up the waterside for the light was only at the best, whan, gonshens! there was the great brute o' a kipper, that, whan he had gotten a glint o' the light had minded the dunt he got on the back, an' was glidin' up the side o' the water within three step o' the channel. I scraucht to Sandy to haud up the light, and keepin' clear o' the back fin this time, I strack him atween the back fin an' the gills, at the same time shakin' the lyams [4] off my arm. Peace be here! if he didna stem the throat four feet deep wi' the waster stickin' straight up in his back as if he never fand it, wi' the lyams about him ! I durstna draw however. I had nae fear o' their breakin', for they were spun o' the hair o' the grey auld buck that gaed for mony years on the Plora craig; but had I pu'd at the lyams, the kipper behooved to turn, an' he might ha' taen doon the throat tap water, an' I wad ha' lost my waster an' lyams or pu'd it out o' his back. That I had nae mind to do.

'I never was feard for drownin' in my life; at ony rate never i' the Queed. I strack into the water breast deep, an' wonder sin syne [5] how I keepit my feet; but I had on a pair o' gude clouted shoon. The kipper tired o' the trade o' ga'an against the strength o' the throat, an' tralin' the lyams, turned doon the deep side o' the water atween me an' the brae. I got haud o' the shaft o' the waster, but to try to grund him was needless, sae I keepit doon the shank, an' that made the force o' the water raise the fish to the tap, an' I push'd him to the side, followin' as I best could, an' pressed him to the brae, whan I lifted him out. Wi' the help o' Sandy (who had, whan he saw the blood, gotten rid o' his fear o' the deil), I carried him to the head o' the rack, and whan I got him on my back,

[1] devil a thing. [2] roe-gatherers, *i.e.* trout. [3] flitting.
[4] hair-rope attached to the waster. [5] since.

my certie I was a massy[1] man! I was aye vext I didna weigh him, but my belief was he was forty gude punds, Dutch weight. As I waded the water wi' him, leadin' Sandy by the hand, his neb was above my head, an' his tail plash'd in the water on my heels.

'My father was then miller o' Bold Milln, an' I took him doon to be reisted[2] in the kilIn; but we war a' sae thrang[3] wi' talkin' about his size, that we forgot to lay him on the broads,[4] and that, as I was sayin', vexes me to this day.'

[1] proud. [2] dried. [3] busy. [4] scales.

'TWIXT CUP AND LIP

By RICHARD FRANCK

Richard Franck (1624?-1708), Cromwellian soldier, religious mystic, fisherman, and traveller, the author of *Northern Memoirs* (written 1658; published 1694; new ed. 1821, with an anonymous preface by Sir Walter Scott), etc. The *Memoirs*, an excellent example of euphuistic literature, describe in dialogue a journey made into the 'little artick world' of Scotland about 1656 or 1657. A chief purpose of the visit to Scotland was 'to rummage and rifle her rivers and rivulets, and examine her flourishing streams for entertainment' (how many were to follow!), and scattered throughout the *Memoirs* for the benefit of 'Virtuosos of the Rod' and of 'Gentlemen Piscatorians' is 'The Contemplative and Practical Angler,' wherein, still in dialogue, is given practical instruction to a tyro in 'the mystical art and the intrigues of angling.' Franck's rules for fly-fishing are admirable, and the *Memoirs* are noteworthy for this; so also are they for containing a first account of salmon-fishing in Scotland; but most of all, perhaps, they are memorable for their onslaughts on Walton. Scott did not much like Franck's style by contrast with Walton's, yet is constrained to admit that as a fly-fisher and as an instructor he far outdid 'the excellent patriarch,' and adds also 'Franck's contests with salmon are painted to the life.' ''Twixt Cup and Lip' is in pp. 75-82 of the 1821 edition of the *Memoirs*.

Theophilus (*a tyro*). Shall we spread the water this morning with our angling artillery, and examine the fords before we feast ourselves? Resolve this morning's exercise, my benevolence; only stand by, and furnish me with directions.

Arnoldus (*the mentor*). Your motion inclines me to promote the adventure, and the rather because to introduct you into the anglers' society. Hold forth your hand, and grasp this rod; take also this box, and this dubbing bag of flies, and select a choice. The complexion of the water must also be considered; and depths and shallows are necessary observations. But, above all, mind carefully the clifts of those craggy rocks, from whence you must expect the head of your game, if you angle for trout. And be circumspect and cautious when and how you strike, lest peradventure passion provoke your discretion, so indanger the loss of what you labour for.

Theophilus. These are soveraign admonitions.

Arnoldus. Mind, therefore, your directions, and fish like an artist; for here, if your line but reach the water, you raise a trout, or, it may be, a salmon. Where, note, if you be indigent of this generous art, and unskilful to manage so eminent an encounter, perchance you'l sacrifice your labours to loss, so in conclusion lose your reputation.

Theophilus. I shall be mindful of that.

Arnoldus. Then direct your eye to those bubbling streams, at whose murmuring descents are most profound deeps. But then, again, there's cataracts and falls of water; from whose fair invitations neither doubt nor despair of incomparable entertainments. That's the Sirene's seat of trophies, where trouts tumble up and down for diversion. Don't you see them pick, and cast themselves on the surface of the streams amongst those knotty stumpy rocks, almost drown'd in water? Lay but your line in at the tail of that stream, where it's sheltred with craggy rocky stones, and manage your game with art and discretion, I'le uphold you sport enough; but be circumspect (be sure) and look well to your line, lest peradventure your tackle be torn to pieces.

Theophilus. Doubt not of my care and circumspection.

Arnoldus. Then take your lot, and cast in your line; and flourish your fly, for it's dub'd with bear's hair; and the point of your hook, it's so snug and so sharp, that, as it ought, it must always hang downward. Moreover, it's proportioned of an excellent compass, wing'd also with the dapple feather of a teal; a dangerous novel to invite a desperate fish; and sutable to the day and season, in regard it's bright.

Theophilus. Why thus to capitulate? Let us in amongst them.

Arnoldus. Two words to a bargain; be better advised.

Theophilus. It's past that now, and I'm past my senses, to feel such trepidations on a sudden invade me. What's the matter with me that I'm thus out of order?

Arnoldus. I perceive you disordred, but not much deliciated.

Theophilus. If I were, it's folly to complain, when past all hope to expect redress.

Arnoldus. How know you that?

Theophilus. I know you won't tell me what it is that tugs thus.

Arnoldus. It may be a trout; or it may be a salmon.

Theophilus. Or it may be both, for ought I know; for it's almost impossible that one single fish should raise the water to such eruptions.

Arnoldus. And impossible for you (I perceive) to reclaim him.

Theophilus. Do but resolve me what it is, and then I'le resolve myself what to do.

Arnoldus. Make your own choice, what would you have it?

Theophilus. I would have it a fish.

Arnoldus. So it is; and it may be a fish of the largest size; therefore, look well about you.

Theophilus. I may look which way I will, and despair at last; what makes the water swell with ebullitions?

Arnoldus. Nothing I suppose but a change of elements, the fish has no mind to come ashore.

Theophilus. And I have as little inclination to go to fetch him.

Arnoldus. Then were your hazards equal; and hitherto, as I apprehend, you have much the odds.

Theophilus. Odd or even, I know not how to manage him.

Arnoldus. Would you put a force upon Neptune, to compel his subjects ashore?

Theophilus. Had I skill enough, I would certainly do it.

Arnoldus. So I perceive; but you'r now almost at a stand. Pull.

Theophilus. On the other hand, he strives to pull all in pieces; which he will certainly do, if I do not reclaim him. But where is he now?

Arnoldus. Gone to the bottom, it may be.

Theophilus. And it may be, I begin to smell the plot; he courts the deep for self-security.

Arnoldus. Then you fancy the streams won't protect him; because there's no plot in them.

Theophilus. Plots for the most part, you know, lie deepest; so he sinks to the bottom for self-preservation, and creeps to death as if of old acquaintance.

Arnoldus. Rash results reap repentance; mistake not your self by dooming his death; he's but slipt to the bottom to recruit himself, and indenture with stones to oblige their protection.

Theophilus. What, must we have now another vagary? Is my scaly companion surrounded and compounded of nothing but frolicks? which, for ought I know, may cost him his life, if he is not mindful to look to his hitts.[1]

Arnoldus. And you must be advised to look well to yours; for he'l not come ashore to beg his life. Stand fast, therefore, and call to mind your former rudiments; for trust me, I shall give you no other supply than some friendly admonishments to reconcile you together.

Theophilus. What, no directions; nor any farther instructions?

Arnoldus. If two to one be odds at football, and against the rules and law of fair play, the very thought on't would make me blush, and appear shamefac'd, if but to think

[1] chances.

two anglers should at once consult together to encounter one fish.

Theophilus. Then I'le fight him myself, and run my own destiny. See where he comes, tumbling and tossing, and volting himself in the stiffest streams. Can no element contain his active violence? Will he twist his tail to cut my line for an experiment? But this kind of cunning may perchance defeat him; he may prick his chaps and yet miss my bait.

Arnoldus. And you may miss him, that won't stand upon a trifle.

Theophilus. A trifle did you say? I'le trifle him no longer. Ha, boys! he's gone again.

Arnoldus. I suppose he's gone where you can't come at him; and that's to the bottom for another insurrection.

Theophilus. So it appears, for he's invisible in a moment. This is a kind of *hocus pocus*: Surely I fancy he has outliv'd his time.

Arnoldus. Flatter not yourself with that fly-blown opinion; for I'm apt to perswade myself he'l live beyond the art of your exercise; this I know and perceive by his working, that if you work not wisely, he'l work a reprieve.

Theophilus. Then I'le work with him, and trifle him ashore, to examine the point, and exchange of elements. I see he's convulst by fluttering his fins; and I'm sure he's half dead by rigling his tail; nay, more than that, he lies still without motion: And are not all these mortal signs of submission?

Arnoldus. And if he submits, he dies without redemption; and death, you know, is a total submission.

Theophilus. I'le kill this fish, or forfeit my reputation.

Arnoldus. Take your chance, for I know you are resolute.

Theophilus. I'le take my chance, and return victorious.

Arnoldus. But there's no triumph, you know, till possest of the trophies.

Theophilus. And I am pretty near them, was it not

that one or two stratagems strangely amuse me; the one of them is the casting himself on the surface, as if designing thereby to cut my line; and the other, his fastning himself in the bottom, thinking, as I apprehend, to tear all in pieces; which, if he do, I lose my reputation: besides I grow weary, and would fain horse him out.

Arnoldus. You may do what you please, you are lord of your own exercise; the law is in your hand, manage with discretion.

Theophilus. I'le manage it with all the industry I have.

Arnoldus. Do so, and you will see the event.

Theophilus. Then have at[1] all.

Arnoldus. And what have you got?

Theophilus. I have got nothing but the foot-steps of folly.

Arnoldus. And nothing out of nothing is folly in the abstract; was not I prophetick?

Theophilus. An oracle too true to confirm my loss; for what have I left? Nothing but folly, to lament and condole this fatal conclusion: to be rob'd by a fish that I reckoned my reward: is not this felony, to steal my tackle, and ruin an angler?

[1] try.

OL' SETTLER OF DEEP HOLE

By IRVING BACHELLER

IRVING ADDISON BACHELLER (born 1859), American journalist and novelist. 'Ol' Settler of Deep Hole' is chapter x of *Eben Holden* (1900) and is here given by kind permission of the author. The same writer's *Eben Holden's Last Day a-Fishing* (1907) has only little of fishing.

UNCLE Eb was a born lover of fun. But he had a solemn way of fishing that was no credit to a cheerful man. It was the same when he played the bass viol, but that was also a kind of fishing at which he tried his luck in a roaring torrent of sound. Both forms of dissipation gave him a serious look and manner, that came near severity. They brought on his face only the light of hope and anticipation or the shadow of disappointment.

We had finished our stent early the day of which I am writing. When we had dug our worms and were on our way to the brook with pole and line, a squint of elation had hold of Uncle Eb's face. Long wrinkles deepened as he looked into the sky for a sign of the weather, and then relaxed a bit as he turned his eyes upon the smooth sward. It was no time for idle talk. We tiptoed over the leafy carpet of the woods. As soon as I spoke he lifted his hand with a warning 'Sh-h!' The murmur of the stream was in our ears. Kneeling on a mossy knoll we baited the hooks; then Uncle Eb beckoned to me.

I came to him on tiptoe.

'See that there foam 'long side o' the big log?' he whispered, pointing with his finger.

I nodded.

'Cre-e-ep up jest as ca-a-areful as ye can,' he went on whispering. 'Drop in a leetle above an' let 'er float down.'

Then he went on, below me, lifting his feet in slow and stealthy strides.

He halted by a bit of driftwood and cautiously threw in, his arm extended, his figure alert. The squint on his face took a firmer grip. Suddenly his pole gave a leap, the water splashed, his line sang in the air, and a fish went up like a rocket. As we were looking into the tree tops it thumped the shore beside him, quivered a moment, and flopped down the bank. He scrambled after it and went to his knees in the brook, coming up empty handed. The water was slopping out of his boot legs.

'Whew!' said he, panting with excitement as I came over to him. 'Reg'lar ol' he one,' he added, looking down at his boots. 'Got away from me—consarn him! Hed a leetle too much power in the arm.'

He emptied his boots, baited up, and went back to his fishing. As I looked up at him he stood leaning over the stream jiggling his hook. In a moment I saw a tug at the line. The end of his pole went under water like a flash. It bent double as Uncle Eb gave it a lift. The fish began to dive and rush. The line cut the water in a broad semicircle and then went far and near with long, quick slashes. The pole nodded and writhed like a thing of life. Then Uncle Eb had a look on him that is one of the treasures of my memory. In a moment the fish went away with such a violent rush that, to save him, he had to throw his pole into the water.

'Heavens an' airth!' he shouted, 'the ol' settler!'

The pole turned quickly and went lengthwise into the rapids. He ran down the bank and I after him. The pole was speeding through the swift water. We scrambled over logs and through bushes, but the pole went faster than we. Presently it stopped and swung around. Uncle Eb went splashing into the brook. Almost within reach of the pole he dashed his foot upon a stone, falling headlong in the current. I was close upon his heels and gave him a hand. He rose hatless, dripping from head to foot, and pressed on. He lifted his pole. The line clung to a snag and then gave way; the tackle was missing. He looked at it silently, tilting his head. We walked slowly to the shore. Neither spoke for a moment.

'Must have been a big fish,' I remarked.

'Powerful!' said he, chewing vigorously on his quid of tobacco as he shook his head and looked down at his wet clothing. 'In a desp'rit fix, ain't I?'

'Too bad!' I exclaimed.

'Seldom ever hed sech a disapp'intment,' he said. 'Ruther counted on ketchin' thet fish—he was s' well hooked.'

He looked longingly at the water a moment. 'If I don't go hum,' said he, 'an' keep my mouth shet I'll say sumthin' I'll be sorry fer.'

He was never quite the same after that. He told often of his struggle with this unseen, mysterious fish, and I imagined he was a bit more given to reflection. He had had hold of the 'ol' settler of Deep Hole'—a fish of great influence and renown there in Faraway. Most of the local fishermen had felt him tug at the line one time or another. No man had ever seen him, for the water was black in Deep Hole. No fish had ever exerted a greater influence on the thought, the imagination, the manners or the moral character of his contemporaries. Tip Taylor always took off his hat and sighed when he spoke of the 'ol' settler.' Ransom Walker said he had once seen his top fin and thought it longer than a razor. Ransom took to idleness and chewing tobacco immediately after his encounter with the big fish, and both vices stuck to him as long as he lived. Everyone had his theory of the 'ol' settler.' Most agreed he was a very heavy trout. Tip Taylor used to say that in his opinion ''twas nuthin' more'n a plain, overgrown, common sucker,' but Tip came from the Sucker Brook country where suckers lived in colder water and were more entitled to respect.

Mose Tupper had never had his hook in the 'ol' settler,' and would believe none of the many stories of adventure at Deep Hole that had thrilled the township.

'Thet fish hes made s' many liars 'round here ye dunno who t' b'lieve,' he had said at the corners one day, after Uncle Eb had told his story of the big fish. 'Somebody 't knows how t' fish hed oughter go 'n ketch him fer the good o' the town—thet's what I think.'

Now Mr Tupper was an excellent man, but his incredulity was always too bluntly put. It had even led to some ill-feeling.

He came in at our place one evening with a big hook and line from 'down east'—the kind of tackle used in salt water.

'What ye goin' t' dew with it?' Uncle Eb inquired.

'Ketch thet fish ye talk s' much about—goin' t' put him out o' the way.'

''Tain't fair,' said Uncle Eb, 'it's reedic'lous. Like leading a pup with a log chain.'

'Don't care,' said Mose, 'I'm goin' t' go fishin' t' morrer. If there reely is any sech fish—which I don't believe there is—I'm goin' t' rassle with him an' mebbe tek him out o' the river. Thet fish is sp'ilin' the moral character o' this town. He oughter be rode on a rail—thet fish hed.'

How he would punish a trout in that manner Mr Tupper failed to explain, but his metaphor was always a worse fit than his trousers—and that was bad enough.

It was just before haying, and, there being little to do, we had also planned to try our luck in the morning. When, at sunrise, we were walking down the cow path to the woods, I saw Uncle Eb had a coil of bed cord on his shoulder.

'What's that for?' I asked.

'Wall,' said he, 'goin' t' hev fun anyway. If we can't ketch one thing we'll try another.'

We had great luck that morning, and when our basket

was near full we came to Deep Hole and made ready for a swim in the water above it. Uncle Eb had looped an end of the bed cord and tied a few pebbles on it with bits of string.

'Now,' said he presently, 'I want t' sink this loop t' bottom an' pass the end o' the cord under the driftwood so 't we can fetch it 'crost under water.'

There was a big stump, just opposite, with roots running down the bank into the stream. I shoved the line under the drift with a pole and then hauled it across, where Uncle Eb drew it up the bank under the stump roots.

'In 'bout half an hour I cal'late Mose Tupper'll be 'long,' he whispered. 'Wisht ye'd put on yer clo's an' lay here back o' the stump an' hold on t' the cord. When ye feel a bite give a yank er two an' haul in like Sam Hill —fifteen feet er more quicker 'n scat. Snatch his pole right away from him. Then lay still.'

Uncle Eb left me shortly, going up stream. It was near an hour before I heard them coming. Uncle Eb was talking in a low tone as they came down the other bank.

'Drop right in there,' he was saying, 'an' let her drag down, through the deep water, deliberate like. Git clus t' the bottom.'

Peering through a screen of bushes, I could see an eager look on the unlovely face of Mose. He stood leaning toward the water and jiggling his hook along the bottom. Suddenly I saw Mose jerk and felt the cord move. I gave it a double twitch and began to pull. He held hard for a jiffy and then stumbled and let go, yelling like mad. The pole hit the water with a splash and went out of sight like a diving frog. I brought it well under the foam and driftwood. Deep Hole resumed its calm, unruffled aspect. Mose went running toward Uncle Eb.

''S a whale!' he shouted. 'Ripped the pole away quicker 'n lightnin'.'

'Where is it?' Uncle Eb asked.

'Tuk it away f'm me,' said Mose. 'Grabbed it jes' like thet,' he added, with a violent jerk of his hand.

'What d' he dew with it?' Uncle Eb inquired.

Mose looked thoughtfully at the water and scratched his head, his features all a-tremble.

'Dunno,' said he. 'Swallered it mebbe.'

'Mean t' say ye lost hook, line, sinker 'n pole?'

'Hook, line, sinker, 'n pole,' he answered mournfully. 'Come nigh haulin' me in tew.'

''Tain't possible,' said Uncle Eb.

Mose expectorated, his hands upon his hips, looking down at the water.

'Wouldn't eggzac'ly say 'twas possible,' he drawled, 'but 'twas a fact.'

'Yer mistaken,' said Uncle Eb.

'No, I hain't,' was the answer, 'I tell ye I see it.'

'Then if ye see it, the nex' thing ye orter see 's a doctor. There's sumthin' wrong with you sumwheres.'

'Only one thing the matter o' me,' said Mose, with a little twinge of remorse. 'I'm jest a natural born perfec' dum fool. Never c'u'd b'lieve there *was* any sech fish.'

'Nobody ever said there was any *sech* fish,' said Uncle Eb. 'He's done more t' you 'n he ever done t' me. Never served me no sech trick as thet. If I was you I'd never ask nobody t' b'lieve it. 'S a leetle tew much.'

Mose went slowly and picked up his hat. Then he returned to the bank and looked regretfully at the water.

'Never see the beat o' thet,' he went on. 'Never see sech power 'n a fish. Knocks the spots off any fish I ever hearn of.'

'Ye riled him with that big tackle o' yourn,' said Uncle Eb. 'He wouldn't stan' it.'

'Feel jest as if I'd hed holt uv a wil' cat,' said Mose. 'Tuk the hull thing—pole an' all—quicker 'n lightnin'. Nice a bit o' hickory as a man ever see. Gol' durned if I ever hearn o' the like o' that, *ever*.'

He sat down a moment on the bank.

'Got t' rest a minute,' he remarked. 'Feel kind o' wopsy after thet squabble.'

They soon went away. And when Mose told the story of the 'swallered pole' he got the same sort of reputation he had given to others. Only it was real and large and lasting.

'Wha' d' ye think uv it?' he asked, when he had finished.

'Wall,' said Ransom Walker, 'wouldn't want t' say right out plain t' yer face.'

''Twouldn't be p'lite,' said Uncle Eb soberly.

'Sound a leetle ha'sh,' Tip Taylor added.

'Thet fish has jerked the fear o' God out o' ye—thet's the way it looks t' me,' said Carlyle Barber.

'Yer up 'n the air, Mose,' said another. 'Need a sinker on ye.'

They bullied him—they talked him down, demurring mildly, but firmly.

'Tell ye what I'll do,' said Mose sheepishly, 'I'll b'lieve you fellers if you'll b'lieve me.'

'What, swop even? Not much!' said one, with emphasis. ''Twouldn't be fair. Ye've ast us t' b'lieve a genuwine out 'n out *im*possibility.'

Mose lifted his hat and scratched his head thoughtfully. There was a look of embarrassment in his face.

'Might a ben dreamin',' said he slowly. 'I swear it's gittin' so here 'n this town a feller can't hardly b'lieve himself.'

'Fur's my experience goes,' said Ransom Walker, 'he'd be a fool 'f he did.'

''Minds me o' the time I went fishin' with Ab Thomas,' said Uncle Eb. 'He ketched an ol' socker the fust thing. I went off by myself 'n got a good-sized fish, but 'twa'nt s' big 's hisn. So I tuk 'n opened his mouth 'n poured in a lot o' fine shot. When I come back Ab he looked at my fish 'n begun t' brag. When we weighed 'em mine was a leetle heavier.

'"What!" says he. "'Tain't possible thet leetle cuss uv a trout's heavier 'n mine."

'"'Tis sartin," I said.

'"Dummed deceivin' business," said he, as he hefted 'em both. "Gittin' so ye can't hardly b'lieve the still-yurds."'

THE SAUMON

By GEORGE OUTRAM

GEORGE OUTRAM (1805-1856), Scottish advocate and journalist, editor in 1837-56 of the *Glasgow Herald*, collaborator for a time with 'Christopher North,' and author of the humorous *Legal and Other Lyrics* (privately printed 1851; publicly issued 1874). He was an enthusiastic angler. 'The Saumon' is from the *Legal and Other Lyrics*.

By Tweedside a-standin',
Wi' lang rods our hands in,
In great hopes o' landin' a saumon were we;
I took up my station,
Wi' much exultation,
While Morton fell a-fishin' farther doun upon the lea.

Across the stream flowin'
My line I fell a-throwin',
Wi' a sou-'wester blowin' right into my e'e;
I jumpt when my hook on
I felt something pookin' [1];
But upon further lookin' it proved to be a tree.

But deep, deep the stream in,
I saw his sides a-gleamin',
The king o' the saumon, sae pleasantly lay he;
I thought he was sleepin',
But on further peepin',
I saw by his teeth he was lauchin' at me.

[1] pulling.

The flask frae my pocket
I poured into the socket,
For I was provokit unto the last degree;
And to my way o' thinkin',
There's naething for't like drinkin',
When a saumon lies winkin' and lauchin' at ye.

There's a bend in the Tweed, ere
It mingles with the Leader—
If you go you will see there a wide o'er-spreadin' tree;
That's a part o' the river
That I'll revisit never—
'Twas there that scaly buffer lay lauchin' at me.

PISCATOR'S PROGRESS

By ANDREW LANG

ANDREW LANG (1844-1912), a native of the Scottish Borders, was nurtured in angling and wrote of it memorably in verse; in *Letters to Dead Authors* (1886), one of the letters being to Walton; in *Lost Leaders* (1889); in *Old Friends* (1890), from which 'Piscator's Progress' is taken by permission of the author's representatives and of Messrs Longmans, Green, & Co.; and in *Angling Sketches* (1891), which has a fishing story or two, though not, it must be said, of much account. See also p. 179.

Walton and Bunyan were men who should have known each other. It is a pleasant fancy, to me, *that they may have met on the banks of Ouse, while John was meditating a sermon, and Izaak was* '*attentive of his trembling quill.*'

From Christian to Piscator

SIR, Being now come into the Land of Beulah; here, whence I cannot so much as see Doubting Castle; here, where I am solaced with the sound of voices from the City—my mind, that is now more at peace about mine own salvation, misgives me sore about thine. Thou wilt remember me, perchance, for him that met thee by a stream of the Delectable Mountains, and took thee to be a man fleeing from the City of Destruction. For beholding thee from afar, methought that thou didst carry a burden on thy back, even as myself before my deliverance did bear the burden of my sins and fears. Yet when I drew near I perceived that it was but a fisherman's basket on thy back, and that thou didst rather seek to add to the weight of thy burden than to lighten it or fling it away. But, when we fell into discourse, I marvelled much how thou camest so far upon the way, even among the sheep and the shepherds of that country. For I found that thou hadst little experience in conflict with Apollyon, and that thou hadst never passed through the Slough of Despond nor wandered in the Valley of the Shadow. Nay, thou hadst never so much as been distressed in thy mind with great fear, nor hadst thou fled from thy wife and children, to save, if it might be, thy soul for thyself, as I have done. Nay, rather thou didst parley with the shepherds as one that loved their life; and I remember, even now, that sweet carnal song:

The Shepherd swains shall dance and sing,
For thy delight, each May morning;
If these delights thy mind may move,
Then live with me and be my love.

These are not the songs that fit the Delectable Country; nay, rather they are the mirth of wantons. Yet didst thou take pleasure in them; and therefore I make bold to ask how didst thou flee at all from the City of Destruction, and come so far upon thy way? Beware lest, when thou winnest to that brook wherein no man casts angle, even to that flood where there is no bridge to go over and the River is very deep—beware, I say, of one Vain Hope, the Ferryman! For I would not have thee lost, because thou art a kindly man and a simple. Yet for Ignorance there is an ill way, even from the very gates of the City.—Thy fellow-traveller,

CHRISTIAN.

From Piscator to Christian

SIR, I do indeed remember thee; and I trust thou art amended of these gripings which caused thee to groan and moan, even by the pleasant streams from the hills of the Delectable Mountains. And as for my 'burden' 'twas pleasant to me to bear it; for, like not the least of the Apostles, I am a fisher, and I carried trout. But I take no shame in that I am an angler; for angling is somewhat like poetry; men are to be born so, and I would not be otherwise than my Maker designed to have me. Of the antiquity of angling I could say much; but I misdoubt me that thou dost not heed the learning of ancient times, but art a contemner of good learning and virtuous recreations. Yet it may a little move thee that in the Book of Job mention is made of fish-hooks, and without reproof; for let me tell you that in the Scriptures angling is always taken in the best sense.

Touching my flight from the City of Destruction, I love that place no more than thou dost; yet I fear not its evil communications, nor would I so hastily desert it as to leave my wife and children behind therein. Nor have I any experience of conflict with the Evil One; wherefore I thank Him that hath set me in pleasant fields, by clear waters, where come no wicked whispers (be they from Apollyon or from our own hearts); but there is calmness of spirit, and a world of blessings attending upon it. And hence can no man see the towers of Doubting Castle, for the green trees and the hedges white with May. This life is not wholly vile, as some of thy friends declare (Thou, who makest thy pilgrims dance to the lute, knowest better); and, for myself, I own that I love such mirth as does not make men ashamed to look upon each other next morning. Let him that bears a heavy heart for his ill-deeds turn him to better, but not mourn as though the sun were taken out of the sky. What says the song?—nay, 'tis as good balm for the soul as many a hymn:

A merry heart goes all the day,
Your sad one tires in a mile-a!

He that made the world made man to take delight in it; even as thou saw'st me joyful with the shepherds—ay, with godly Mr Richard Hooker, 'he being then tending his small allotment of sheep in a common field,' as I recount in a brief life of a good man. As to what awaits me on the other side of that River, I do expect it with a peaceful heart, and in humble hope that a man may reach the City with a cheerful countenance, no less than through groans and sighs and fears. For we have not a tyrant over us, but a Father, that loveth a cheerful liver no less than a cheerful giver. Nevertheless, I thank thee for thy kind thought of one that is not of thy company, nor no Nonconformist, but a peaceful Protestant. And, lest thou be troubled with apparitions of hobgoblins and evil spirits, read that comfortable sermon of Mr Hooker's to weak believers, on the *Certainty of Adherence*, though they want the inward testimony of it.

But now falls there a sweet shower, 'a singing shower' saith old George Chapman, and methinks I shall have sport; for I do note that the Mayfly is up; and, seeing all these beautiful creatures playing in the air and water, I feel my own heart play within me; and I must out and dape under yonder sycamore tree. Wherefore, prithee, pardon me a longer discourse as at this time.—Thy friend,

PISCATOR.

WI'OUT A WORD O' A LEE

By FRANCIS FRANCIS

For Francis Francis, see p. 29. 'Wi'out a Word o' a Lee' is from volume I, chapter X, of *Sidney Bellew* (2 vols 1870).

From the starting-point the major and Sidney, accompanied by the boy-ghillie Johnnie, pursued their way upstream to join their companions, Mr Cameron and Allan. They had walked about a mile up the river, when they saw the point of a rod projecting above a low bank, idly; and coming to the spot they found Mr Cameron comfortably bestowed in a dry snug corner—the relics of a big lunch about him—fast asleep in the sun, and snoring above the rush of the waters. The rod was planted between his knees, and his fly idly trailed in the water just over the bank. He had got tired with the scrambling and fishing, and being indisposed to move, Allan made him snug and went up the reach to look for the seal of an otter. They had, apparently, been unsuccessful—the creel lying at his feet empty; but Mr Cameron was not much better with the rod than with the gun. Considering him for a moment or two, a smile broke over the face of the major. 'I will,' he said, softly, 'be the powers I will'; and he looked like a boy with a tempting bit of mischief in hand. 'Faith, it'll be a great joke intirely. See here, Johnnie, lad, reach me that large stone there wid the hole in it. Now, then, we'll take off the castin'-line, and put that round his hat, so.' There was no fear of his waking, as a solid lunch, with plenty of punch, had put Mr Cameron as *hors de combat* as Mr Pickwick himself under similar circumstances. 'Now, Johnnie, run across over the foot-bridge above: I'll run the line through this big stone'—

passing it through a hole in a large stone which Johnnie had picked up from the strand and brought him, and which was rounded and smooth as ivory from long friction of the water—'then I pitch the end across to you, and drop the big stone in the water, and do you get into that water-course opposite, out of sight, and conduct yourself as much like a salmon as you can—without noise, mind—and don't give the first tug till you hear me whistle—and let all go when I say "Mind your eye."' Johnnie's face expanded into a broad grin at a little bit of mischief so much after his own heart, and in which he was to play so noble a part: he darted off to the footbridge, and speedily stood on the other bank. The major then, without disturbing the sleeper, drew as much line as he required gently off the reel, passed the end through the aforesaid large stone, tied a small pebble to the end, and threw it across the river to Johnnie, who immediately caught and secured it. The big stone, which was now strung on the line like an enormous bead, was then carefully conveyed to the pool, and pitched into the middle of it, where it went plumb down to the bottom in twenty feet of water, carrying the bight of the line with it. The slack was then wound carefully on the reel, and the rod placed between Mr Cameron's knees, in the same position as they had found it. Opposite the point where they stood, a little rill poured into the river between high banks, much concealed and hidden with brush and large stones. Into this crept Johnnie, where he was completely out of sight, and the line was thus conveyed across the stream up into the waters of the little rill, and so did not make its appearance above water until it almost reached Johnnie's hand. All being arranged, the major and our friend retired over the bank out of sight, lying down behind a bush, through which they could see without being seen, and then communicated the signal to Johnnie with a low whistle. The excellent ex-merchant slept—wotting nothing of practical jokers—when suddenly there was a deuce of a tug at the point of the rod, which almost pulled it out of his hand, and woke him up with a start.

'Odds guds!' Jag, jag, went the rod. 'I'm in him! I'm in him! A fusshe—a fusshe! Odds, he's a whopper!' Jag—jag—jag—whirr! And away scud Johnnie up the ditch as hard as he could pelt, taking out the line in royal style; and then, with a sulky shake now and then, allowing his capturer to wind him grudgingly in again, this, however, only to be succeeded by fresh jags and more runs. In the midst of all this, Mr Cameron vociferated, danced about, and rushed here and there like one demented, shouting for some one 'to come on wi' the gaff.' The major and Sidney lay over on their backs roaring with laughter, but there was little fear of Mr Cameron hearing them, so intent was he on his *fish*, while the row he made over it would have drowned the yells of a pack of hyenas. It certainly was a huge joke, and they enjoyed it thoroughly. At length, as though summoned by his cries, they put in an appearance.

'Is he a good fish?' asked the major, apparently much out of breath and greatly interested. 'Have ye *seen* him?'

'Seen him! Why he's been dancing awl ower the pool; joomped yairds high times an' times. Twal poonds if he's an oonce, I gie ye my word.'

'Bravo!' said the major, while Sidney was compelled to make a precipitate retreat over the bank again.

'He's got ye round a rock,' said the major with wicked sympathy. 'He'll cut ye! Don't ye see how straight the line goes down into the pool, while the fish is evidently yards and yards away? Very odd *we* see nothing of him; he's a very strong fish. Can't you lead him this way a bit? I can't possibly gaff him until I can see him. Can't you bring him up here?'

'Hoo the de'il can I, when I canna left 'm an eench, an' he joost stacks till the bottom like a big stane?'

'He *is* just like a big stone,' said the major, with such a power of comparison that Sidney was obliged to retire again. All this time Mr Cameron was dancing about, sloping the point of his rod now this way now that; now butting Johnnie severely, and now 'letting him go,' according as the major directed, when suddenly, just when there was a great strain on the rod, the major shouted 'Ah! he'll cut ye! Mind yer eye!' Immediately the rod sprung up, released from its strain, and the line came trailing loosely through the water. 'Ah! I told ye he would,' said the major, looking like a sage. 'They always do it in this pool. It's a way they've got. Cut off casting-line and all, you see—ah! bad job—very. If you'd only,' etc., etc., etc. But Mr Cameron was quite in despair.

'Saxteen poonds if he was an oonce. Joomped just aboon the rock there, three times—sax fut if he joomped an eench.' He grieved over it sorely, and he lied over it still more sorely, and to the end of his days he so told the story, and actually believed that he had seen the fish. Nor could he at all account for it, when he found on reaching home his casting-line and fly round his hat. That was a little incomprehensible, to be sure; possibly he might have been supplied with two casting-lines, but it was hardly worthy of deep consideration. If it was impossible to account for it, why attempt impossibilities? As for the fish, that was a great fact, and continued to increase in greatness—for the last time he told the story, which was only a few weeks ago, it 'was twenty-sax poonds if it was an oonce, and joomped saxteen times in succession a height o' ten fut clear *wi'out a word o' a lee.*'

TOM BROWN, POACHER

By THOMAS HUGHES

THOMAS HUGHES (1822-1896) was a devotee of rural sports and had for a fishing friend Charles Kingsley, from whom he received a famous verse invitation to fish, beginning: 'Come away with me, Tom.' Angling figures both in *Tom Brown's School Days* (1857) and in *Tom Brown at Oxford* (3 vols 1861). 'Tom Brown, Poacher,' is from Part I, chapter IX, of *Tom Brown's School Days*. See also p. 312.

NOW came on the Mayfly season. The soft hazy summer weather lay sleepily along the rich meadows by Avon side, and the green and grey flies flickered with their graceful lazy up-and-down flight over the reeds and the water and the meadows, in myriads upon myriads. The Mayflies must surely be the lotus-eaters of the ephemeræ—the happiest, laziest, carelessest fly that dances and dreams out his few hours of sunshiny life by English rivers.

Every little pitiful coarse fish in the Avon was on the alert for the flies, and gorging his wretched carcass with hundreds daily, the gluttonous rogues! And every lover of the gentle craft was out to avenge the poor Mayflies.

So one fine Thursday afternoon, Tom, having borrowed East's new rod, started by himself to the river. He fished for some time with small success—not a fish would rise at him; but as he prowled along the bank he was presently aware of mighty ones feeding in a pool on the opposite side, under the shade of a huge willow-tree. The stream was deep here, but some fifty yards below was a shallow, for which he made off hotfoot; and forgetting landlords, keepers, solemn prohibitions of the Doctor, and everything else, pulled up his trousers, plunged across, and in three minutes was creeping along on all-fours towards the clump of willows.

It isn't often that great chub, or any other coarse fish, are in earnest about anything, but just then they were thoroughly bent on feeding, and in half-an-hour Master Tom had deposited three thumping fellows at the foot of the giant willow. As he was baiting for a fourth pounder, and just going to throw in again, he became aware of a man coming up the bank not one hundred yards off. Another look told him that it was the under-keeper. Could he reach the shallow before him? No, not carrying his rod. Nothing for it but the tree; so Tom laid his bones to it, shinning up as fast as he could, and dragging up his rod after him. He had just time to reach and crouch along upon a huge branch some ten feet up, which stretched out over the river, when the keeper arrived at the clump. Tom's heart beat fast as he came under the tree. Two steps more and he would have passed, when, as ill-luck would have it, the gleam on the scales of the dead fish caught his eye, and he made a dead point at the foot of the tree. He picked up the fish one by one; his eye and touch told him that they had been alive and feeding within the hour. Tom crouched lower along the branch, and heard the keeper beating the clump. 'If I could only get the rod hidden,' thought he, and began gently shifting it to get it alongside him; 'willow-trees don't throw out straight hickory shoots twelve feet long with no leaves, worse luck!' Alas! the keeper catches the rustle, and then a sight of the rod, and then of Tom's hand and arm.

'Oh, be up ther', be 'ee?' says he, running under the tree. 'Now you come down this minute!'

'Tree'd at last!' thinks Tom, making no answer and keeping as close as possible, but working away at the rod, which he takes to pieces. 'I'm in for it, unless I can starve him out.' And then he begins to meditate getting along the branch for a plunge and scramble to the other side; but the small branches are so thick and the opposite bank so difficult that the keeper will have lots of time to get round by the ford before he can get out, so he gives that up. And now he hears the keeper beginning to scramble up the trunk. That will never do; so he scrambles himself back to where his branch joins the trunk, and stands with lifted rod.

'Hullo, Velveteens, mind your fingers if you come any higher.'

The keeper stops and looks up, and then with a grin says, 'Oh! be you, be it, young measter? Well, here's luck! Now I tells 'ee to come down at once, an 't'll be best for 'ee.'

'Thank'ee, Velveteens, I'm very comfortable,' said Tom, shortening the rod in his hand and preparing for battle.

'Werry well, please yourself,' says the keeper, descending, however, to the ground again and taking his seat on the bank. 'I beant in no hurry, so you med take yer time. I'll larn 'ee to gee honest folk names afore I've done with 'ee.'

'My luck as usual!' thinks Tom. 'What a fool I was to give him a black! If I'd called him "keeper," now, I might get off. The return match is all his way.'

The keeper quietly proceeded to take out his pipe, fill, and light it, keeping an eye on Tom, who now sat disconsolately across the branch, looking at keeper—a pitiful sight for men and fishes. The more he thought of it the less he liked it. 'It must be getting near second calling-over,' thinks he. Keeper smokes on stolidly. 'If he takes me up, I shall be flogged, safe enough. I can't sit here all night. Wonder if he'll rise at silver?

'I say, keeper,' said he meekly, 'let me go for two bob?'

'Not for twenty neither,' grunts his persecutor.

And so they sat on till long past second calling-over,

and the sun came slanting in through the willow-branches and telling of locking-up near at hand.

'I'm coming down, keeper,' said Tom at last with a sigh, fairly tired out. 'Now, what are you going to do?'

'Walk 'ee up to school and give 'ee over to the Doctor; them's my orders,' says Velveteens, knocking the ashes out of his fourth pipe, and standing up and shaking himself.

'Very good,' said Tom; 'but hands off, you know. I'll go with you quietly, so no collaring or that sort of thing.'

Keeper looked at him a minute. 'Werry good,' said he at last; and so Tom descended, and wended his way drearily by the side of the keeper up to the schoolhouse, where they arrived just at locking-up. As they passed the school gates, the Tadpole and several others who were standing there caught the state of things, and rushed out, crying 'Rescue!' But Tom shook his head; so they only followed to the Doctor's gate, and went back sorely puzzled.

How changed and stern the Doctor seemed from the last time that Tom was up there, as the keeper told the story, not omitting to state how Tom called him blackguard names. 'Indeed, sir,' broke in the culprit, 'it was only "Velveteens."' The Doctor only asked one question.

'You know the rule about the banks, Brown?'

'Yes, sir.'

'Then wait for me to-morrow after first lesson.'

'I thought so,' muttered Tom.

'And about the rod, sir?' went on the keeper. 'Master's told we as we might have all the rods——'

'Oh, please, sir,' broke in Tom, 'the rod isn't mine!'

The Doctor looked puzzled; but the keeper, who was a good-hearted fellow and melted at Tom's evident distress, gave up his claim. Tom was flogged next morning, and a few days afterwards met Velveteens and presented him with half a crown for giving up the rod claim, and they became sworn friends; and I regret to say that Tom had many more fish from under the willow that Mayfly season, and was never caught again by Velveteens.

FAST DAY

By NEIL MUNRO

NEIL MUNRO (1864-1930), Scottish novelist and short-story writer. 'Fast Day' is from 'The *Vital Spark*' in *Para Handy and other tales* (1931), where it has the title 'Para Handy—Poacher'; it is here given by permission of Dr Neil Munro's trustees and of Messrs William Blackwood & Sons.

THE *Vital Spark* was lying at Greenock with a cargo of scrap-iron, on the top of which was stowed loosely an extraordinary variety of domestic furniture, from bird-cages to cottage pianos. Para Handy had just had the hatches off when I came to the quay-side, and he was contemplating the contents of his hold with no very pleasant aspect.

'Rather a mixed cargo!' I ventured to say.

'Muxed's no' the word for't,' he said bitterly. 'It puts me in mind of an explosion. It's a flittin' from Dunoon. There would be no flittin's in the *Fital Spark* if she wass my boat. But I'm only the captain, och aye! I'm only the captain, thirty-five shullin's a-week and liberty to put on a pea-jecket. To be puttin' scrap-iron and flittin's in a fine smert boat like this iss carryin' coals aboot in a coach and twice. It would make any man use Abyssinian language.'

'Abyssinian language?' I repeated, wondering.

'Chust that, Abyssinian language—swearing, and the like of that, you ken fine, yoursel', withoot me tellin' you. Fancy puttin' a flittin' in the *Fital Spark*! You would think she wass a coal-laary, and her with two new coats of pent out of my own pocket since the New Year.'

'Have you been fishing?' I asked, desirous to change the subject, which was, plainly, a sore one with the

Captain. And I indicated a small fishing-net which was lying in the bows.

'Chust the least wee bit touch,' he said, with a very profound wink. 'I have a bit of a net there no' the size of a pocket-naipkin, that I use noo and then at the river-mooths. I chust put it doon—me and Dougie—and whiles a salmon or a sea-troot meets wi' an accident and gets into 't. Chust a small bit of a net, no' worth speakin' aboot, no' mich bigger nor a pocket-naipkin. They'll be calling it a splash-net, you ken yoursel' withoot me tellin' you.' And he winked knowingly again.

'Ah, Captain!' I said, 'that's bad! Poaching with a splash-net! I didn't think you would have done it.'

'It's no' me; it's Dougie,' he retorted promptly. 'A fair duvvle for high jeenks, you canna keep him from it. I told him many a time that it wasna right, becaause we might be found oot and get the jyle for 't, but he says they do it on aal the smertest yats. Yes, that iss what he said to me—"They do it on aal the first-cless yats; you'll be bragging the *Fital Spark* is chust ass good ass any yat, and what for would you grudge a splash-net?"'

'Still it's theft, Captain,' I insisted. 'And it's very, very bad for the rivers.'

'Chust that!' he said complacently. 'You'll likely be wan of them fellows that goes to the hotels for the fushing in the rivers. There's more sport aboot a splash-net; if Dougie wass here he would tell you.'

'I don't see where the sport comes in,' I remarked, and he laughed contemptuously.

'Sport!' he exclaimed. 'The best going. There wass wan time yonder we were up Loch Fyne on a Fast Day, and no' a shop open in the place to buy onything for the next mornin's breakfast. Dougie says to me, "What do you think yoursel' aboot takin' the punt and the small bit of net no' worth mentionin', and going doon to the river mooth when it's dark and seeing if we'll no' get a fush?"

12

'"It's a peety to be poaching on the Fast Day," I said to him.

'"But it's no' the Fast Day in oor parish," he said. "We'll chust give it a trial, and if there's no fush at the start we'll come away back again." Oh! a consuderate fellow, Dougie; he saw my poseetion at wance, and that I wasna awfu' keen to be fushin' wi' a splash-net on the Fast Day. The end and the short of it wass that when it wass dark we took the net and the punt and rowed doon to the river and began to splash. We had got a fine haul at wance of six great big salmon, and every salmon Dougie would be takin' oot of the net he would be feeling it all over in a droll way, till I said to him, "What are you feel-feelin' for, Dougie, the same ass if they had pockets on them? I'm sure they're all right."

'"Oh, yes," he says, "right enough, but I wass frightened they might be the laird's salmon, and I wass lookin' for the luggage label on them. There's none. It's all right; they're chust wild salmon that nobody planted."

'Weel, we had got chust ass many salmon ass we had any need for when somebody birled a whustle, and the river watchers put off in a small boat from a point outside of us to catch us. There wass no gettin' oot of the river mooth, so we left the boat and the net and the fush and ran ashore, and by-and-by we got up to the quay and on board the *Fital Spark*, and paused and consudered things.

'"They'll ken it's oor boat," said Dougie, and his clothes wass up to the eyes in salmon scales.

'"There's no doo't aboot that," I says. "If it wassna the Fast Day I wouldna be so vexed; it'll be an awful disgrace to be found oot workin' a splash-net on the Fast Day. And it's a peety aboot the boat, it wass a good boat, I wish we could get her back."

'"Aye, it's a peety we lost her," said Dougie; "I wonder in the wide world who could have stole her when we were doon the fo'c'sle at oor supper?" Oh, a smert fellow,

Dougie! When he said that I saw at wance what he meant.

'"I'll go up this meenute and report it to the polis office," I said quite firm, and Dougie said he would go with me too, but that we would need to change oor clothes, for they were covered with fush-scales. We changed oor clothes and went up to the sercheant of polis, and reported that somebody had stolen oor boat. He wass sittin' readin' his Bible, it bein' the Fast Day, wi' specs on, and he keeked up at us, and said, "You are very spruce, boys, with your good clothes on at this time of the night."

'"We aalways put on oor good clothes on the *Fital Spark* on a Fast Day," I says to him; "it's as little as we can do, though we don't belong to the parish."

'Next day there wass a great commotion in the place aboot some blackguards doon at the river mooth poachin' with a splash-net. The factor wass busy, and the heid gamekeeper wass busy, and the polis wass busy. We could see them from the dake of the *Fital Spark* goin' aboot buzzin' like bum-bees.

'"Stop you!" said Dougie to me aal of a sudden. "They'll be doon here in a chiffy, and findin' us with them scales on oor clothes—we'll have to put on the Sunday wans again."

'"But they'll smell something if they see us in oor Sunday clothes," I said. "It's no' the Fast Day the day."

'"Maybe no' here," said Dougie, "but what's to hinder it bein' the Fast Day in oor own parish?"

'We put on oor Sunday clothes again, and looked the Almanac to see if there wass any word in it of a Fast Day any place that day, but there wass nothing in the Almanac but tides, and the Battle of Waterloo, and the weather for next winter. That's the worst of Almanacs; there's nothing in them you want. We were fair bate for a Fast Day any place, when The Tar came up and asked me if he could get to the funeral of a cousin of his in the place at two o'clock.

'"A funeral!" said Dougie. "The very thing. The Captain and me'll go to the funeral too. That's the way we have on oor Sunday clothes." Oh, a smert, smert fellow, Dougie!

'We had chust made up oor mind it wass the funeral we were dressed for, and no' a Fast Day any place, when the polisman and the heid gamekeeper came doon very suspeecious, and said they had oor boat. "And what's more," said the gamekeeper, "there's a splash-net and five stone of salmon in it. It hass been used, your boat, for poaching."

'"Iss that a fact?" I says. "I hope you'll find the blackguards"; and the gamekeeper gave a grunt, and said somebody would suffer for it, and went away busier than ever. But the polis sercheant stopped behind. "You're still in your Sunday clothes, boys," said he; "what iss the occasion to-day?"

'"We're going to the funeral," I said.

'"Chust that! I did not know you were untimate with the diseased," said the sercheant.

'"Neither we were," I said, "but we are going oot of respect for Colin." And we went to the funeral, and nobody suspected nothin', but we never got back the boat, for the gamekeeper wass chust needin' wan for a brother o' his own. Och, aye! there's wonderful sport in a splash-net.'

OF A FISHER AND A LITTLE FISH

From *THE DIALOGUES OF CREATURES MORALISED*

'Of a Fisher and a Little Fish' is dialogue XLVIII in *The Dialogues of Creatures Moralised*, a translation, made in Paris, conjecturally in 1520, of the anonymous Latin work *Dyalogus Creaturarum Moralizatus* (Gouda 1480). In the story as here given the spelling has been modernised. Dialogues XLIV and XLVI are also of fish.

A FISHER as he fished caught a little fish. When he would have killed him, the fish spake and said: O gentle fisher, have mercy upon me, for, if thou kill me, thou shalt have but little advantage of me. But, if thou wilt suffer me to go free and deliver me from this danger and captivity, I promise to God and to thee that I shall cause thee to have great winning, for I shall return unto the dale with great multitude of fishes, and I shall lead them into thy nets. To whom the fisher said: How shall I know thee among so many fishes? Then said the fish: Cut off a little of my tail that thou mayst know me among all other. The fisher gave credence to his words and cut off his tail and let him go. This little fish was ever uncourteous, for contrary to his promise he letted the fisher as often as he should fish, and withdrew the fishes from him, and said: Fathers and worshipful seniors, be ye ware of that deceiver, for he deceived me, and cut off my tail; and so shall he serve you if ye be not ware, and if ye believe not me, believe his works that appear upon me. And this saying, the fish shewed them his tail that was cut. Wherefore the fishes abhorred the fisher, and fled from him in all possible haste. The fisher had no more fishing, wherefore he lived in great poverty. Of fortune it happed so that a long while after the fisher caught again the same fish among others. And when he knew him he killed him cruelly, and said:

> He that hath a good turn and is uncourteous again,
> It is very rightful that he be therefore slain.

THE FISHERMAN'S DREAM

By THEOCRITUS (?)

The piece here given in three renderings is one of the most celebrated in classical literature on fishing. It is included as Idyll XXI (Ἁλιεῖς ; 'Fishers') in the works of the great Greek pastoral poet Theocritus (flourished 3rd century B.C.), but is now commonly believed to have been the work, not of Theocritus, but of the contemporaneous Leonidas of Tarentum or of some imitator of Leonidas.

I

Prose translation by ANDREW LANG (see above, p. 159) from his *Theocritus, Bion, and Moschus rendered into English Prose* (1880), and here given by permission of Messrs Macmillan & Co.

'TIS Poverty alone, Diophantus, that awakens the arts; Poverty, the very teacher of labour. Nay, not even sleep is permitted, by weary cares, to men that live by toil, and if, for a little while, one close his eyes in the night, cares throng about him, and suddenly disquiet his slumber.

Two fishers, on a time, two old men, together lay and slept; they had strown the dry sea-moss for a bed in their wattled cabin, and there they lay against the leafy wall. Beside them were strewn the instruments of their toilsome hands, the fishing-creels, the rods of reed, the hooks, the sails bedraggled with sea-spoil, the lines, the weels, the lobster pots woven of rushes, the seines, two oars, and an old coble upon props. Beneath their heads was a scanty matting, their clothes, their sailor's caps. Here was all their toil, here all their wealth. The threshold had never a door, nor a watch-dog; all things, all, to them seemed superfluity, for Poverty was their sentinel. They had no neighbour by them, but ever against their narrow cabin gently floated up the sea.

The chariot of the moon had not yet reached the mid-point of her course, but their familiar toil awakened the fishermen; from their eyelids they cast out slumber, and roused their souls with speech.

Asphalion

They lie all, my friend, who say that the nights wane short in summer, when Zeus brings the long days. Already have I seen ten thousand dreams, and the dawn is not yet. Am I wrong, what ails them, the nights are surely long?

The Friend

Asphalion, thou blamest the beautiful summer! It is not that the season hath wilfully passed his natural course, but care, breaking thy sleep, makes night seem long to thee.

Asphalion

Didst ever learn to interpret dreams? for good dreams have I beheld. I would not have thee to go without thy share in my vision; even as we go shares in the fish we catch, so share all my dreams! Sure, thou art not to be surpassed in wisdom; and he is the best interpreter of dreams that hath wisdom for his teacher. Moreover, we have time to idle in, for what could a man find to do, lying on a leafy bed beside the wave and slumbering not? Nay, the ass is among the thorns, the lantern in the town hall, for, they say, it is always sleepless.

The Friend

Tell me, then, the vision of the night; nay, tell all to thy friend.

Asphalion

As I was sleeping late, amid the labours of the salt sea (and truly not to full-fed, for we supped early if thou dost remember, and did not over-tax our bellies), I saw myself busy on a rock, and there I sat and watched the fishes, and kept spinning the bait with the rods. And one of the fish nibbled, a fat one, for in sleep dogs dream of bread, and of fish dream I. Well, he was tightly hooked, and the blood was running, and the rod I grasped was bent with his struggle. So with both hands I strained, and had a sore tussle for the monster. How was I ever to land so big a fish with hooks all too slim? Then just to remind him he was hooked, I gently pricked him, pricked, and slackened, and, as he did not run, I took in line. My toil was ended with the sight of my prize; I drew up a golden fish, lo you, a fish all plated thick with gold! Then fear took hold of me, lest he might be some fish beloved of Posidon, or perchance some jewel of the sea-grey Amphitrite. Gently I unhooked him, lest ever the hooks should retain some of the gold of his mouth. Then I dragged him on shore with the ropes, and swore that never again would I set foot on sea, but abide on land, and lord it over the gold.

This was even what wakened me, but, for the rest, set thy mind to it, my friend, for I am in dismay about the oath I swore.

The Friend

Nay, never fear, thou art no more sworn than thou hast found the golden fish of thy vision; dreams are but lies. But if thou wilt search these waters, wide awake, and not asleep, there is some hope in thy slumbers; seek the fish of flesh, lest thou die of famine with all thy dreams of gold!

II

Verse translation by CHARLES STUART CALVERLEY (1831-1884) from his facile *Theocritus translated into English Verse* (1869).

Want quickens wit: Want's pupils needs must work,
O Diophantus: for the child of toil
Is grudged his very sleep by carking cares:

Or, if he taste the blessedness of night,
Thought for the morrow soon warns slumber off.

Two ancient fishers once lay side by side
On piled-up sea-wrack in their wattled hut,
Its leafy wall their curtain. Near them lay
The weapons of their trade, basket and rod,
Hooks, weed-encumbered nets, and cords and oars,
And, propped on rollers, an infirm old boat.
Their pillow was a scanty mat, eked out
With caps and garments: such the ways and means,
Such the whole treasury of the fishermen.
They knew no luxuries: owned nor door nor dog;
Their craft, their all, their mistress Poverty:
Their only neighbour Ocean, who for aye
Round their lorn hut came floating lazily.

Ere the moon's chariot was in mid-career,
The fishers girt them for their customed toil,
And banished slumber from unwilling eyes,
And roused their dreamy intellects with speech:

Asphalion

'They say that soon flit summer-nights away,
Because all lingering is the summer day:
Friend, it is false; for dream on dream have I
Dreamed, and the dawn still reddens not the sky.
How? am I wandering? or does night pass slow?'

His Comrade

'Asphalion, scout not the sweet summer so.
'Tis not that wilful seasons have gone wrong,
But care maims slumber, and the night seems long.'

Asphalion

'Didst thou e'er study dreams? For visions fair
I saw last night; and fairly thou shouldst share

The wealth I dream of, as the fish I catch.
Now, for sheer sense, I reckon few thy match;
And, for a vision, he whose motherwit
Is his sole tutor best interprets it.
And now we've time the matter to discuss:
For who could labour, lying here (like us)
Pillowed on leaves and neighboured by the deep,
Or sleeping amid thorns no easy sleep?
In rich men's halls the lamps are burning yet;
But fish come alway to the rich man's net.'

Comrade

'To me the vision of the night relate;
Speak, and reveal the riddle to thy mate.'

Asphalion

'Last evening, as I plied my watery trade,
(Not on an o'erfull stomach—we had made
Betimes a meagre meal, as you can vouch),
I fell asleep; and lo! I seemed to crouch
Among the boulders, and for fish to wait,
Still dangling, rod in hand, my vagrant bait.
A fat fellow caught it (e'en in sleep I'm bound
To dream of fishing, as of crusts the hound):
Fast clung he to the hooks; his blood outwelled;
Bent with his struggling was the rod I held:
I tugged and tugged: my efforts made me ache:
"How, with a line thus slight, this monster take?"
Then gently, just to warn him he was caught,
I twitched him once; then slacked and then made taut
My line, for now he offered not to run;
A glance soon showed me all my task was done.
'Twas a gold fish, pure metal every inch
That I had captured. I began to flinch:
"What if this beauty be the sea-king's joy,
Or azure Amphitrite's treasured toy?"

With care I disengaged him—not to rip
With hasty hook the gilding from his lip:
And with a tow-line landed him, and swore
Never to set my foot on ocean more,
But with my gold live royally ashore.
So I awoke: and, comrade, lend me now
Thy wits, for I am troubled for my vow.'

Comrade

'Ne'er quake: you're pledged to nothing, for no prize
You gained or gazed on. Dreams are nought but lies.
Yet may this dream bear fruit; if, wide-awake
And not in dreams, you'll fish the neighbouring lake.
Fish that are meat you'll there mayhap behold,
Not die of famine, amid dreams of gold.'

III

A free rendering in verse by JOHN BUCHAN, 1ST BARON TWEEDSMUIR (1875-1940), who, a Tweedside angler from boyhood, compiled *Musa Piscatrix* (1896; an anthology of angling verse) and himself wrote on angling in *Scholar Gipsies* (1896; youthful essays), *Grey Weather* (1899; 'prentice stories), *Poems Scots and English* (1917), *John Macnab* (1925; a novel), 'Pilgrim's Rest' (two chapters of an unfinished book on angling, given as an appendix to *Memory Hold-the-Door*, 1940). The rendering of Theocritus is from *Poems Scots and English* and is here given by permission of Messrs Thomas Nelson & Sons.

'Tis puirtith [1] sooples heid and hand
And gars [2] inventions fill the land;
And dreams come fast to folk that lie
Wi' nocht atween them and the sky.

Twae collier lads frae near Lasswade,
Auld skeely [3] fishers, fand their bed
Ae simmer's nicht aside the shaw
Whaur Manor runs by Cademuir Law.

[1] poverty. [2] makes. [3] skilful.

Dry flowe-moss made them pillows fine,
And, for a bield [1] to kep the win',
A muckle craig owerhung the burn,
A' thacked [2] wi' blaeberry and fern.
Aside them lay their rods and reels,
Their flee-books and their auncient creels.
The pooches o' their moleskin breeks
Contained unlawfu' things like cleeks,
For folk that fish to fill their wame [3]
Are no fasteedious at the game.
The twae aye took their jaunts thegither;
Geordie was ane and Tam the ither.
Their chaumer [4] was the mune-bricht sky,
The siller stream their lullaby.

When knocks [5] in touns were chappin' three,
Tam woke and rubbed a blinkin' ee.
It was the 'oor when troots are boun'
To gulp the May-flee floatin' doun,
Afore the sun is in the glens
And dim are a' the heughs and dens.

Tam

'Short is the simmer's daurk, they say,
But this ane seemed as lang's the day;
For siccan dreams as passed my sicht
I never saw in Januar' nicht.
If some auld prophet chiel were here
I wad hae cürious things to speir.' [6]

Geordie

'It's conscience gars the nichtmares rin,
Sae, Tam my lad, what hae ye dune?'

[1] shelter. [2] thatched. [3] belly.
[4] chamber. [5] clocks. [6] ask.

Tam

'Nae ill; my saul is free frae blame,
Nor hae I wrocht ower hard my wame,
For last we fed, as ye maun awn,
On a sma' troot and pease-meal scone.
But hear my dream, for aiblins [1] you
May find a way to riddle 't true . . .

I thocht that I was castin' steady
At the püle's tail ayont the smiddy,[2]
Wi' finest gut and sma'est flee,
For the air was clear and the water wee;
When sudden wi' a rowst [3] and swish
I rase a maist enormous fish . . .
I struck and heuked the monster shüre,
Guidsakes! to see him loup in air!
It was nae saumon, na, nor troot;
To the last yaird my line gaed oot,
As up the stream the warlock ran
As wild as Job's Leviathan.
I got him stopped below the linn,
Whaur verra near I tummled in,
Aye prayin' hard my heuk wad haud;
And syne he turned a dorty [4] jaud,
Sulkin' far doun amang the stanes.
I tapped the butt to stir his banes.
He warsled [5] here and plowtered [6] there,
But still I held him ticht and fair,
The water rinnin' oxter-hie,[7]
The sweat aye drippin' in my ee.
Sae bit by bit I wysed [8] him richt
And broke his stieve [9] and fashious [10] micht,

[1] perhaps. [2] smithy. [3] commotion. [4] peevish.
[5] struggled. [6] floundered. [7] armpit-high. [8] guided.
[9] stiff. [10] troublesome.

Till sair fordone he cam to book
And walloped in a shallow crook.
I had nae gad,[1] sae doun my wand
I flang and pinned him on the sand.
I claucht him in baith airms and peched [2]
Ashore—he was a michty wecht;
Nor stopped till I had got him shüre
Amang the threshes [3] on the muir.

Then, Geordie lad, my een I rowed [4]—
The beast was made o' solid gowd [5]!—
Sic ferlie [6] as was never kenned,
A' glitterin' gowd frae end to end!
I lauched, I grat,[7] my kep [8] I flang,
I danced a sprig, I sang a sang.
And syne I wished that I micht dee
If wark again was touched by me . . .

Wi' that I woke; nae fish was there—
Juist the burnside and empty muir.
Noo tell me honest, Geordie lad,
Think ye yon daftlike aith will haud?'

Geordie

'Tuts, Tam ye fule, the aith ye sware
Was like your fish, nae less, nae mair.
For dreams are nocht but simmer rouk,[9]
And him that trusts them hunts the gowk [10] . . .
It's time we catched some fish o' flesh
Or we will baith gang breakfastless.'

[1] gaff. [2] panted. [3] rushes. [4] rolled.
[5] gold. [6] wonder. [7] wept. [8] cap.
[9] madness. [10] cuckoo, *i.e.* goes on a fool's errand.

THE FISHERMAN

By MARTIN ARMSTRONG

Martin Donisthorpe Armstrong (born 1882), English poet, novelist, and short-story writer. 'The Fisherman' is from *Sir Pompey and Madame Juno* (1927) and is here given by permission of the author.

The road, diving downwards off the bridge, slid away to the left; but tucked into a low recess on the right, so that it looked down upon the river and up at the high, foreshortened mass of the bridge, the George Inn opened its comfortable, L-shaped front, thick with climbing greenery. Behind it a flourishing kitchen-garden stood embanked above the river to which steps descended under a canopy of ancient elm-trees.

Michael Dunne, having finished his breakfast, appeared in the doorway and stood looking up at the sky. Then he lowered his eyes to the scene before him and slowly drew in his breath. It was delicious to be in the country again. The trees, loaded mound upon mound with fresh young green; the pervading hush of the river; the soft clean air tinged with the smell of wet earth and standing water breathed up from the river edge, thrilled him with indescribable delight. He glanced again at the sky. It was bright, too bright, at present, but there were light clouds in the blue and a gentle breeze: there would certainly be intervals of dullness. Not, on the whole, a bad day for fishing. He had made up two fishing-casts overnight, seated in the bow-window of the sitting-room with half a dozen trout-flies hanging from his mouth. When the gut was sufficiently soaked, he drew out the flies one by one and carefully knotted them on to the cast. He had decided to use nothing but March Browns, and old Wales, the landlord, had entirely agreed when Dunne had mentioned it to him.

He was ready to start now at any moment, and he stood there in the doorway with his hands in his breeches-pockets, impatiently waiting for the sun to stop shining. From time to time in the inn behind him footsteps tapped along the stone-floored passage and died away. But at last he was roused by some that came closer and closer still and finally stopped just behind his back. He swung round. Somebody was waiting to be allowed to pass: a young woman. With a quick apology Dunne moved out of her way and she came out, thanking him with a smile as she passed him, and moved away along the front of the inn, a slim figure in a brown coat and skirt. A white-handled umbrella hung from her left arm: her right hand carried a camp-stool and a satchel.

Dunne stood watching her. It was as if in its flying course an invisible flame had swept over him, for the brief glimpse of her face had thrilled him suddenly and profoundly. Only two or three times before had that curious experience befallen him, for he was not easily attracted by women. He stood now, immovable, gazing after her with flushed face, till she vanished round the corner of the house: then he turned back into the inn, his sense resounding with the impression of her. In a few minutes, he reappeared, preceded by the slim point of his rod. He had put on his waders and an old cap stuck with one or two gaudy salmon-flies; a creel hung at his left side. His emotion at the sight of the beautiful girl had died down; he was calm again, and now he began to make his way down the little garden path under the elm-trees, carefully pointing the wavering tip of the rod into the spaces between the thick hanging foliage. At the river's edge he paused to survey again the grey and golden bridge whose four stone arches towered above him a stone's throw away to his right. Under the two nearest, at this time of the year, there was nothing but dry gravel, thickly overgrown near the bank with a jungle of wild rhubarb. Under the third, the water, brown and clear as ale, babbled shallow over the pebbles. It was only under the fourth, where it washed the farther bank, that the water was deep.

Dunne clambered down, holding his rod carefully in front of him, and began to push through the great funnel-shaped rhubarb leaves. Then, crunching across the gravel-bed, he waded through the shallows to a little island within a short cast of a round pool, the very place for a trout. He had watched them rising there on the previous evening as he stood, an hour after his arrival, leaning idly over the parapet of the bridge. It was a deep, round pool, slowly stirred by a circular eddy which swung the streaks of floating spume into narrowing whorls, so that it looked, from above, like a huge polished ammonite. He had decided to fish upstream from that point.

It was years, four years at least, since he had last had a day's fishing, but as he began casting up to the head of the pool, he recovered at once that delicious mood peculiar to the fisherman—a mood composed of conscious craft, expectation, and at the same time a quiet passivity laying the mind open to streams of thoughts and ideas which flow through the brain easily as the flowing of the river, washing it clean of complexities.

The breeze had almost died down. Not a fish was stirring. And, moving slowly upstream, he worked leisurely on for half an hour without getting a single bite. But just as he reached the lower end of another promising pool—a gently swirling pool fed by a narrow and copious flow—the breeze freshened again and the day clouded over. It was ideal now—grey, and with just the right purl on the water.

The fish were beginning to feed. A small one rose in the pool a few yards from where he stood; then, just under the bank, another, a larger one. The sudden musical splash sounded clear and sharp above the monotonous babbling of the water. Then, as though his line were a nerve identifying the finger that held it with every movement of the floating fly, he felt three electric tugs. The end of his rod curved into a hoop, and he began to play the trout.

It was only, he knew at once, a small one—something over a quarter of a pound perhaps; and, though it fought gamely, as a trout always does, Dunne landed it at once. It lay for a moment motionless on the pebbles with helpless, gaping mouth: but as he stooped to take hold of it, suddenly it began to twist and wriggle, tense as a steel spring. Dunne caught it, grasping the firm, wincing body in his left hand while with his right he began to work the hook free of its mouth, twisting and wrenching the pale, talc-like flesh. Then, stooping again, he struck its head against a stone. It lay motionless in his palm now, a limp, exquisite shape of silver, gold, and brown. The delicate cucumber scent of it rose to his nostrils. Between a quarter and half a pound he thought, and dropped it into his creel.

A few minutes later, soon after he had begun to cast again, Dunne experienced a curious repetition of the physical sensation of striking the soft, unresisting creature against the stone. A little shudder ran through his vitals. Curious! Could it have been something disagreeable in the sound of it, or in the sense of the too hard striking the too soft? He shuddered again, but less perceptibly, and then the ceaseless tinkle of the water smoothed the faint scar from his mind. Peaceably, incoherently his thoughts swirled with the swirling clusters of bubbles.

But soon he was thinking coherently again. What was it that happened when he struck the trout's head against the stone and all its exquisite mechanism stopped for ever? Was it nothing more than that he broke the delicate motor housed in the little box in the skull? No more than the smashing of a watch? Years ago, old Mr Worston, the peppery old gentleman who always gave him a sovereign when he went back to school after the summer holidays, smashed his watch against the wall in Hexham station because it was slow and had made him miss the express. Smash! Swinging it the full length of the heavy gold chain. A pulp of little gold wheels and broken glass. Delightful thought! It had delighted him as a boy and it delighted him still. But a watch is hard. To smash something hard . . . a bottle or an egg against a wall . . . how satisfying! But to hit a fish . . . a limp, soft fish . . . and alive! Another faint shudder. All the leaves on the river bank hissed and rustled suddenly: hurrying grey spearheads shot along the surface of the stream. The wind was freshening.

A twitch. A palpitating tug. He had hooked another; and a few minutes after that there was another, and then another—a much larger one. Such a game one it was that Dunne thought for a moment that it must be a salmon-trout. When he landed it, the hook was fixed in the extreme tip of the lower jaw: it was a wonder it had held. A fine fish, fully a pound, the tarnished silver sides spotted with rose. Dunne gazed at it fascinated, curiously inspecting the staring, expressionless eyes, set like the work of a master jeweller in the subtly moulded bronze of the head. The slippery body thrilled and stiffened spasmodically in his clenched fingers. Its slipperiness was beginning already to grow viscous against his palm. The foolish mouth gaped patiently, sufferingly, and Dunne suddenly recalled the blanched, tight-lipped mouth of a dying man whom, years ago, he had visited in hospital. He felt his heart contract under his ribs. Then, throwing off his morbid fancies, he stooped down and struck the trout's head against a stone, as he had struck the other. The body stiffened: the tail curved up tensely like a spring. He struck it again and then loosened his grip. The second blow had done it: the body was limp and flaccid now: the life was gone.

Gone where? Could the life be something distinct from the body actuated . . . could it fly out and escape from the killed fish? A shadow . . . a little puff of cigarette-smoke, detaching itself from the fish's mouth . . . floating away? Life must be the same as what some people call the soul. . . . The immortality of the soul. . . . A fish's soul. . . . Jesu, lover of my soul. A flood of the emotion which that hymn always produced in him as a boy. Ancient memories . . . sentimental . . . absurd!

A touch on his face, soft, fluttering. Here he was, standing up to his thighs in water, fishing. A gust of wind was furrowing the water and blowing his line along in a great bow. He reeled in a few yards of it. The breeze stiffened: all his fisherman's skill was needed now, and for the next few minutes his attention was concentrated on throwing a clean line in defiance of the breeze. But it had only been a momentary flurry: soon it had swept on downstream and with the return of calm Dunne dropped back into his former line of thought. . . .

Fishes are cold-blooded creatures without feeling. A comforting idea, but false—mere metaphor and simile drawn from human experience. We know nothing outside our own narrow circle of experience, can never escape into the universal where everything is true and equal. A simple thing to beat the life out of a trout; and yet, when we have done it, what have we done? A mystery. A tremendous act of whose consequences we know nothing. Who can tell? perhaps the death of a fish changes irrevocably the whole hidden scheme of things. And yet, wherever there is life, there must be death. All life devours life, even the sheep and cows that munch grass. Life feeding on life. Life destroying life that it may live. An endless process . . . process . . . progress . . . progression . . . the scheme of things . . . stream of things. . . .

The stream had caught his mind again, caressing it, floating it safely away from all those jarring, sharp-edged thoughts. But now the fish had stopped taking and during the next hour Dunne caught nothing. Yet he fished on, soothed by the peacefully sliding river, his mind sliding with the water over rough and smooth, deep and shallow. Then, discovering that he was hungry, he looked at his watch and began to wade towards the bank.

There he sat down and took out his flask and sandwiches. But before beginning to eat he opened his creel, tumbled out the contents, and arranged them in a row on the grass. They were a nice lot—seven fish ranging from a quarter to half a pound and, at the end, the noble one-pounder. They were dull and gummy now; their clean slipperiness was gone, their iridescence faded. Dunne gazed at them until his mind slipped out of the grooves of habit and again he was gazing at fish for the first time in his life. Strange, unbelievable creatures; mysterious slips of life, swift and spear-like, marvellously designed and coloured. He stared at their eyes; for a man, baffled by man or beast, always stares at the eye, that smouldering window of the spirit, and there finds some partial answer to his question. But these quaint metallic disks, stark as the painted eyes of a mask, told his nothing except that their secret was undiscoverable or that there was nothing to discover. They did not even rebuke him, like the eye of a dead bird or animal, for snatching them from their secret world and slaughtering them. Dunne sighed and next moment shrugged his shoulders. After all, such questions as he was asking have no answer. Neither philosophy nor religion casts any light on them. To what category, then, can they belong? To poetry, perhaps: and Dunne, being no poet, but a solicitor and a fisherman, threw the trout back one by one into the creel and began to eat his sandwiches.

The sun came out. He looked anxiously at the sky: this would play the devil with his afternoon. But meanwhile it was delicious to feel its warmth on his back, stealing through coat and shirt. He finished his last sandwich, lit a cigarette, and leaned back full length on the grass. Although the sun was still shining, clouds covered more than half the sky: there was certainly some hope, now, for the afternoon. A luxurious drowsiness overcame him: he closed his eyes for a moment, then opened them again. Then he closed them again, and this time they remained closed. The cigarette fell from his fingers and lay twining a blue spiral among the tall green grass-blades. . . .

He was still fishing. The little brass rings on his rod had sprouted into green leaf-buds. He was fishing in a stream of liquid gold, the Gulf Stream. All at once he noticed that his line was running out noiselessly . . . longer . . . longer . . . longer. He clasped it to the butt of the rod, gripped it with all his strength. When he had almost given up hope, he succeeded at last in holding it. Then slowly he began to reel in, and as he did so the reel tinkled a little tune like a musical-box. It was a heavy fish—a pound at least. He reeled away strenuously until he had reeled the cast right out of the water.

A beautiful wooden fish, streaked with scarlet and blue, hung from the end of it. A Chinese fish. Each eye was a gold disk with a daisy in the centre of it. He began to sway the rod so that the fish swung to and fro. When it was at the top of its swing he suddenly dipped the rod and the fish dropped on the bank. But the moment it touched earth it began to cry—a horrible human cry. 'No! No!' it cried. 'No! No! No!' He stood staring at it, appalled, not daring to touch it. Then, bracing himself, he suddenly put his foot on it and immediately swooped upon it to remove the hook. The fish did not move, but its mouth opened and shut spasmodically like an automatic toy and, to his horror, it began to cry again. But soon its voice flagged, died away, fainter . . . fainter. . . . It had become almost inaudible when suddenly, as if summoning its last strength, it shouted aloud a single sharp 'Ah!'

Dunne awoke. A shaggy dog stood looking at him,

wagging its tail. He held out his hand to it and sat up, but the dog flounced away and trotted off along the bank with its tail down. Dunne looked about him. The sun had gone in: conditions were perfect once again. He felt refreshed and clear-headed after his sleep and, scrambling to his feet, he pocketed his flask, took up his rod and creel, and began to work slowly downstream.

During the afternoon he added eight good fish to his catch, and by five o'clock he had got back to the point from which he had started. He reeled in and, securing his cast, waded to the bank. He was looking forward to showing the fish to old Wales. Mrs Wales would fry the best of them for dinner: she knew how to fry trout perfectly, rolling them first in oatmeal and serving them with melted butter. He climbed up the bank to the little path and, with his rod pointed in front of him, began to make his way cautiously under the elm-trees. In the creel behind him a trout not yet dead kept up a dry, persistent rustling.

As he came out in front of the inn he became aware of something unusual. A little group of people was moving towards the door. They were stooping as if carrying something. A few yards from the bridge an empty motor stood at the roadside.

When Dunne came up with the moving group they had reached the inn door. They were carrying something laid on a large sack, as on a stretcher, and with a sudden constriction of the heart he caught sight, between two of the bearers, of an end of brown skirt hanging over the edge of the sack. Hardly knowing what he did, he propped his rod against the house-wall and, turning his back on the door, walked away towards the standing car. His instinct had been to escape from something unbearable. Then, pausing dazed where the road dipped from the bridge, he saw lying at the roadside between him and the car a white-handled umbrella. He stooped and gently picked it up and began to carry it to the inn. He felt vaguely that he had found something that he could do for her.

The bearers had vanished indoors. Dunne entered the stone-flagged hall with its pleasant, humble smell of beer and sawdust. A group of women—Mrs Wales and the three servants—stood with their backs to him at an open door, their heads craning into a great bare room. It was a room unused except in summer-time when large parties came to the inn for lunch or tea. Several people were inside. A table was being moved. Dunne, still holding her umbrella, paused beside the women.

'What happened?' he whispered.

One of the maids turned a white face to him. 'The car knocked her down,' she replied. 'It must have come on her when she was crossing the road.'

Another turned. 'They come so unexpected over that bridge,' she said.

Old Mrs Wales was leaning against the door-post with her apron to her eyes. Dunne touched her arm. 'Is she . . . is she much hurt?' he asked.

The old woman raised her bleared face from the apron and stared at him vacantly. Then her chin began to tremble. 'Hurt? She's dead, poor thing!' she whispered.

Twenty-five years later Dunne himself died. He was a bachelor, and his things went to his nephews. They had spent several days in his house, going through cupboards and drawers. Last of all they looked into the attic. It was half dark, but one of them rummaging among old hat-boxes and portmanteaux, pulled out a creel and a fishing-rod in a canvas case. Both the creel and the case were cloaked with the grey wool of cobwebs.

'I say, look at this!' the young man called to his brother. 'I never knew the Uncle was a fisherman.'

THE WICKHAM

By H. T. SHERINGHAM

HUGH TEMPEST SHERINGHAM (1876-1930), one of the best known of English anglers and writers on angling, and also a novelist. In 1903-30 he was angling editor of *The Field.* His works on angling consist of instructional books (he was the 'complete' angler) and of books descriptive and reflective. There is little of fiction, but *An Angler's Hours* (1905) has a fishing story, while 'The Wickham,' one of several like pieces, is from *Fishing: its Cause, Treatment, and Cure* (1925) and is here given by kind permission of Mrs Sheringham. In the novels, there are fishing passages in *The Court of Sacharissa* (1904) and in *The Enemy's Camp* (1906), both written in collaboration with N. Meakin, and also in *Syllabub Farm* (1919) and in *Ourselves When Young* (1922).

SCENE I

A fine fresh morning of May. Scene, a wooden seat overlooking the river. Thereon an angler regardant. Another angler standing, also regardant. Two rods, spiked, in middle distance.

A. (*gloomily*). So he told me.

B. Do you know how he got them?

A. One has one's ideas, of course.

B. (*dramatic, spreading his hands*). Out of the Black Hatch with a wet Wickham. Both of them. Told me himself.

A. And this is supposed to be a dry-fly stream!

B. Ruining the water, that's what it is. What's the committee doing? Is this dry-fly fishing or is it not? That's what I want to know.

A. He says he comes fishing to catch trout.

B. That 'fly only' rule wants altering, that's what it wants. It's simply an invitation to pot-hunters. (*Scornfully*) Coming fishing to catch trout! This is a hideous age.

(*Both meditate in profound gloom on the age. Presently a happier thought occurs to A., whose brow clears. He takes a fly-box from his pocket and extracts a fly with a small pair of forceps, placing it in the palm of B.'s hand.*)

A. What do you think of that for a pale watery?

B. (*considers it attentively*). Not bad, not bad at all. Very nice, in fact. But there's a shade too much white in the third segment, and the right seta is about two millimetres too long.

A. (*nods appreciatively*). Yes, you're quite right. Exactly what I said. They *will* make these silly mistakes. And they had my pattern to work to, too. But for a shop fly, it's not bad. Hullo, what's that?

(*He rises and looks fixedly upstream. B. turns and gazes with equal fixity.*)

B. A rise, or was it a dabchick? No, it was a rise, I think. Yes, there it is again. I can't see what he's taking. (*Raises binoculars, slung round his neck, to his eyes.*) There's an olive coming down over him.

A. (*who has also brought his binoculars into action*). He wouldn't have it. Ah, I thought so. He's bulging. He was doing that yesterday. He's no good. (*Resumes his seat.*)

B. Aren't you going to have a chuck?

A. No. He isn't rising.

B. He might take a medium olive.

A. (*with a little scorn in his voice*). Oh yes, he might *take*. There was a period when I should have had that fish out with a Wickham in no time. But I don't care about that sort of thing now, naturally.

B. (*still looking regretfully at the fish, which is feeding with vigour*). Yes, perhaps you're right. But it looked that time as though he took a fly, an iron blue, I believe.

A. (*tolerant*). Well, try a female iron blue over him yourself.

B. (*firmly*). No, no, my dear fellow, he's your fish. I'm off downstream. There's a good trout at the third stile I want to interview, and the rise seems to be beginning. Well, good-bye.

A. Good-bye.

(*B. takes his rod, goes off downstream, and is soon out of sight. A. gets up from the seat, goes to his rod, ties a large Wickham to the end of the cast, and proceeds to cover, rise, hook, and land the trout, which he taps on the head, weighs, and places in his creel. Afterwards he goes slowly upstream.*)

Scene II

The bridge at 4 p.m. A. is leaning on the parapet and looking over into the water. B. gets over the stile and comes on to the bridge.

B. I had a look for your bulger as I came up, but he wasn't moving any more.

A. No, he wouldn't be. I caught him—in the long run.

B. The deuce you did. So he came on properly at last.

A. Yes, at last. A pound and three-quarters.

B. Iron blue, I suppose. (*A. gives silent assent.*) Any others?

A. I've got a couple of brace. What have you done?

B. I've got a brace and a half. But they wouldn't look at iron blue or olive, or spinners, or anything.

A. What did you get them on, then?

B. Well—(*hesitates, then decides to brazen it out*)—well, I got them on a Wickham. After all, one does want something to show for a day's fishing. To tell you the truth, what you said suggested it.

A. Oh, I've no quarrel with the Wickham. It makes a very tolerable sedge. One prefers, of course, something a little more exact, but there *are* times—and the Wickham is certainly a killing fly. In my time I've done very well with the Wickham.

PLAIN FISHING

By FRANK R. STOCKTON

FRANCIS RICHARD STOCKTON (1834-1902), American humorous story writer. His fishing fun was praised by Andrew Lang. 'Plain Fishing' is from *Amos Kilbright, his Adscititious Experiences* (1888) and is here given by kind permission of Messrs Ernest Benn Ltd.

'WELL, sir,' said old Peter, as he came out on the porch with his pipe, 'so you come here to go fishin'?'

Peter Gruse was the owner of the farmhouse where I had arrived that day, just before supper-time. He was a short, strong-built old man, with a pair of pretty daughters, and little gold rings in his ears. Two things distinguished him from the farmers in the country round about: one was the rings in his ears, and the other was the large and comfortable house in which he kept his pretty daughters. The other farmers in that region had fine large barns for their cattle and horses, but very poor houses for their daughters. Old Peter's earrings were indirectly connected with his house. He had not always lived among those mountains. He had been on the sea, where his ears were decorated, and he had travelled a good deal on land, where he had ornamented his mind with many ideas which were not in general use in the part of his State in which he was born. This house stood a little back from the highroad, and if a traveller wished to be entertained, Peter was generally willing to take him in, provided he had left his wife and family at home. The old man himself had no objection to wives and children, but his two pretty daughters had.

These two young women had waited on their father and myself at supper-time, one continually bringing hot griddle cakes, and the other giving me every opportunity to test the relative merits of the seven different kinds of preserves, which, in little glass plates, covered the unoccupied spaces on the table-cloth. The latter, when she found that there was no further possible way of serving us, presumed to sit down at the corner of the table and begin her supper. But in spite of this apparent humility, which was only a custom of the country, there was that in the general air of the pretty daughters which left no doubt in the mind of the intelligent observer that they stood at the wheel in that house. There was a son of fourteen, who sat at table with us, but he did not appear to count as a member of the family.

'Yes,' I answered, 'I understood that there was good fishing hereabouts, and, at any rate, I should like to spend a few days among these hills and mountains.'

'Well,' said Peter, 'there's trout in some of our streams, though not as many as there used to be, and there's hills a plenty, and mountains too, if you choose to walk fur enough. They're a good deal furder off than they look. What did you bring with you to fish with?'

'Nothing at all,' I answered. 'I was told in the town that you were a great fisherman, and that you could let me have all the tackle I would need.'

'Upon my word,' said old Peter, resting his pipe-hand on his knee and looking steadfastly at me, 'you're the queerest fisherman I've seed yet. Nigh every year, some two or three of 'em stop here in the fishin' season, and there was never a man who didn't bring his jinted pole, and his reels, and his lines, and his hooks, and his dry-good flies, and his whisky-flask with a long strap to it. Now, if you want all these things, I haven't got 'em.'

'Whatever you use yourself will suit me,' I answered.

'All right, then,' said he. 'I'll do the best I can for you in the mornin'. But it's plain enough to me that you're not a game fisherman, or you wouldn't come here without your tools.'

To this remark I made answer to the effect, that though I was very fond of fishing, my pleasure in it did not depend upon the possession of all the appliances of professional sport.

'Perhaps you think,' said the old man, 'from the way I spoke, that I don't believe them fellers with the jinted poles can ketch fish, but that ain't so. That old story about the little boy with the pin-hook who ketched all the fish, while the gentleman with the modern improvements, who stood alongside of him, kep' throwin' out his beautiful flies and never got nothin', is a pure lie. The fancy chaps, who must have ev'rythin' jist so, gen'rally gits fish. But for all that, I don't like their way of fishin', and I take no stock in it myself. I've been fishin', on and off, ever since I was a little boy, and I've caught nigh every kind there is, from the big jew-fish and cavalyoes down South, to the trout and minnies round about here. But when I ketch a fish, the first thing I do is to try to git him on the hook, and the next thing is to git him out of the water jist as soon as I kin. I don't put in no time worryin' him. There's only two animals in the world that likes to worry smaller creeturs a good while afore they kill 'em; one is the cat, and the other is what they call the game fisherman. This kind of a feller never goes after no fish that don't mind being ketched. He goes fur them kinds that loves their home in the water and hates most to leave it, and he makes it jist as hard fur 'em as he kin. What the game fisher likes is the smallest kind of a hook, the thinnest line, and a fish that it takes a good while to weaken. The longer the weak'nin' business kin be spun out, the more the sport. The idee is to let the fish think there's a chance fur him to git away. That's jist like the cat with her mouse. She lets the little creetur hop off, but the minnit he gits fur enough down, she jabs on him with her claws, and then, if there's any game left in him, she lets him try agen. Of course, the game fisher could have a strong line and a stout pole and git his fish in a good sight quicker, if he wanted to, but that wouldn't be sport. He couldn't give him the butt and spin him out, and reel him in, and let him jump and run till his pluck is clean worn out. Now, I likes to git my fish ashore with all the pluck in 'em. It makes 'em taste better. And as fur fun, I'll be bound I've had jist as much of that, and more, too, than most of these fellers who are so dreadful anxious to have everythin' jist right, and think they can't go fishin' till they've spent enough money to buy a suit of Sunday clothes. As a gen'ral rule they're a solemn lot, and work pretty hard at their fun. When I work I want to be paid fur it, and when I go in fur fun I want to take it easy and comfortable. Now I wouldn't say so much agen these fellers,' said old Peter, as he arose and put his empty pipe on a little shelf under the porch-roof, 'if it wasn't for one thing, and that is, that they think that their kind of fishin' is the only kind worth considerin'. The way they look down upon plain Christian fishin' is enough to rile a hitchin'-post. I don't want to say nothin' agen no man's way of attendin' to his own affairs, whether it's kitchen gardenin', or whether it's fishin', if he says nothin' agen my way; but when he looks down on me, and grins me, I want to haul myself up, and grin him, if I kin. And in this case, I kin. I s'pose the house-cat and the cat-fisher (by which I don't mean the man who fishes for cat-fish) was both made as they is, and they can't help it; but that don't give 'em no right to put on airs before other bein's, who gits their meat with a square kill. Good night. And sence I've talked so much about it, I've a mind to go fishin' with you to-morrow myself.'

The next morning found old Peter of the same mind, and after breakfast he proceeded to fit me out for a day of what he called 'plain Christian trout-fishin'.' He gave me a reed rod, about nine feet long, light, strong, and nicely balanced. The tackle he produced was not of the fancy order, but his lines were of fine strong linen, and his hooks were of good shape, clean and sharp, and snooded to the lines with a neatness that indicated the hand of a man who had been where he learned to wear little gold rings in his ears.

'Here are some of these feather insects,' he said, 'which you kin take along if you like.' And he handed me a paper containing a few artificial flies. 'They're pretty nat'ral,' he said, 'and the hooks is good. A man who come here fishin' gave 'em to me, but I shan't want 'em to-day. At this time of year grasshoppers is the best bait in the kind of place where we're goin' to fish. The stream, after it comes down from the mountain, runs through half a mile of medder land before it strikes into the woods agen. A grasshopper is a little creetur that's got as much conceit as if his jinted legs was fish-poles, and he thinks he kin jump over this narrer run of water whenever he pleases; but he don't always do it, and them of him that don't git snapped up by the trout that lie along the banks in the medder is floated along into the woods, where there's always fish enough to come to the second table.'

Having got me ready, Peter took his own particular pole, which he assured me he had used for eleven years, and hooking on his left arm a good-sized basket, which his elder pretty daughter had packed with cold meat, bread, butter, and preserves, we started forth for a three-mile walk to the fishing-ground. The day was a favourable one for our purpose, the sky being sometimes overclouded, which was good for fishing, and also for walking on a highroad; and sometimes bright, which was good for effects of mountain scenery. Not far from the spot where old Peter proposed to begin our sport, a small frame-house stood by the roadside, and here the old man halted and entered the open door without knocking or giving so much as a premonitory stamp. I followed, imitating my companion in leaving my pole outside, which appeared to be the only ceremony that the etiquette of those parts required of visitors. In the room we entered, a small man in his shirt sleeves sat mending a basket handle. He nodded to Peter, and Peter nodded to him.

'We've come up a-fishin',' said the old man. 'Kin your boys give us some grasshoppers?'

'I don't know that they've got any ready ketched,' said he, 'for I reckon I used what they had this mornin'. But they kin git you some. Here, Dan, you and Sile go and ketch Mister Gruse and this young man some grass-hoppers. Take that mustard-box, and see that you git it full.'

Peter and I now took seats, and the conversation began about a black cow which Peter had to sell, and which the other was willing to buy if the old man would trade for sheep, which animals, however, the basket-mender did not appear just at that time to have in his possession. As I was not very much interested in this subject, I walked to the back door and watched two small boys in scanty shirts and trousers and ragged straw hats, who were darting about in the grass catching grasshoppers, of which insects, judging by the frequent pounces of the boys, there seemed a plentiful supply.

'Got it full?' said their father when the boys came in.

'Crammed,' said Dan.

Old Peter took the little can, pressed the top firmly on, put it in his coat-tail pocket, and rose to go. 'You'd better think about that cow, Barney,' said he. He said nothing to the boys about the box of bait; but I could not let them catch grasshoppers for us for nothing, and I took a dime from my pocket, and gave it to Dan. Dan grinned, and Sile looked sheepishly happy, and at the sight of the piece of silver an expression of interest came over the face of the father. 'Wait a minute,' said he, and he went into a little room that seemed to be a kitchen. Returning, he brought with him a small string of trout. 'Do you want to buy some fish?' he said. 'These is nice fresh ones. I ketched 'em this mornin'.'

To offer to sell fish to a man who is just about to go out

to catch them for himself might, in most cases, be considered an insult, but it was quite evident that nothing of the kind was intended by Barney. He probably thought that if I bought grasshoppers, I might buy fish. 'You kin have 'em for a quarter,' he said.

It was derogatory to my pride to buy fish at such a moment, but the man looked very poor, and there was a shade of anxiety on his face which touched me. Old Peter stood by without saying a word. 'It might be well,' I said, turning to him, 'to buy these fish, for we may not catch enough for supper.'

'Such things do happen,' said the old man.

'Well,' said I, 'if we have these we will feel safe in any case.' And I took the fish and gave the man a quarter. It was not, perhaps, a professional act, but the trout were well worth the money, and I felt that I was doing a deed of charity.

Old Peter and I now took our rods, and crossed the road into an enclosed lot, and thence into a wide stretch of grassland, bounded by hills in front of us and to the right, while a thick forest lay to the left. We had walked but a short distance, when Peter said: 'I'll go down into the woods, and try my luck there, and you'd better go along upstream, about a quarter of a mile, to where it's rocky. P'raps you ain't used to fishin' in the woods, and you might git your line cotched. You'll find the trout'll bite in the rough water.'

'Where is the stream?' I asked.

'This is it,' he said, pointing to a little brook, which was scarcely too wide for me to step across, 'and there's fish right here, but they're hard to ketch, fur they git plenty of good livin', and are mighty sassy about their eatin'. But you kin ketch 'em up there.'

Old Peter now went down toward the woods, while I walked up the little stream. I had seen trout-brooks before, but never one so diminutive as this. However, when I came nearer to the point where the stream issued from between two of the foot-hills of the mountains, which lifted their forest-covered heights in the distance, I found it wider and shallower, breaking over its rocky bottom in sparkling little cascades.

Fishing in such a jolly little stream, surrounded by this mountain scenery, and with the privileges of the beautiful situation all to myself, would have been a joy to me if I had had never a bite. But no such ill-luck befell me. Peter had given me the can of grasshoppers after putting half of them into his own bait-box, and these I used with much success. It was grasshopper season, and the trout were evidently on the lookout for them. I fished in the ripples under the little waterfalls; and every now and then I drew out a lively trout. Most of these were of moderate size, and some of them might have been called small. The large ones probably fancied the forest shades, where old Peter went. But all I caught were fit for the table, and I was very well satisfied with the result of my sport.

About an hour after noon I began to feel hungry, and thought it time to look up the old man, who had the lunch-basket. I walked down the bank of the brook, and some time before I reached the woods I came to a place where it expanded to a width of about ten feet. The water here was very clear, and the motion quiet, so that I could easily see to the bottom, which did not appear to be more than a foot below the surface. Gazing into this transparent water, as I walked, I saw a large trout glide across the stream, and disappear under the grassy bank which overhung the opposite side. I instantly stopped. This was a much larger fish than any I had caught, and I determined to try for him.

I stepped back from the bank, so as to be out of sight, and put a fine grasshopper on my hook; than I lay, face downward, on the grass, and worked myself slowly forward until I could see the middle of the stream; then quietly raising my pole, I gave my grasshopper a good swing, as if he had made a wager to jump over the stream at its widest part. But as he certainly would have failed in such an ambitious endeavour, especially if he had been caught by a puff of wind, I let him come down upon the surface of the water, a little beyond the middle of the brook. Grasshoppers do not sink when they fall into the water, and so I kept this fellow upon the surface, and gently moved him along, as if, with all the conceit taken out of him by the result of his ill-considered leap, he was ignominiously endeavouring to swim to shore. As I did this, I saw the trout come out from under the bank, move slowly toward the grasshopper, and stop directly under him. Trembling with anxiety and eager expectation, I endeavoured to make the movements of the insect still more natural, and, as far as I was able, I threw into him a sudden perception of his danger, and a frenzied desire to get away. But, either the trout had had all the grasshoppers he wanted, or he was able, from long experience, to perceive the difference between a natural exhibition of emotion and a histrionic imitation of it, for he slowly turned, and, with a few slight movements of his tail, glided back under the bank. In vain did the grasshopper continue his frantic efforts to reach the shore; in vain did he occasionally become exhausted, and sink a short distance below the surface; in vain did he do everything that he knew, to show that he appreciated what a juicy and delicious morsel he was, and how he feared that the trout might yet be tempted to seize him; the fish did not come out again.

Then I withdrew my line, and moved back from the stream. I now determined to try Mr Trout with a fly, and I took out the paper old Peter Gruse had given me. I did not know exactly what kind of winged insects were in order at this time of the year, but I was sure that yellow butterflies were not particular about just what month it was, so long as the sun shone warmly. I therefore chose that one of Peter's flies which was made of the yellowest feathers, and, removing the snood and hook from my line, I hastily attached this fly, which was provided with a hook quite suitable for my desired prize. Crouching on the grass, I again approached the brook. Gaily flitting above the glassy surface of the water, in all the fancied security of tender youth and innocence, came my yellow fly. Backward and forward over the water he gracefully flew, sometimes rising a little into the air, as if to view the varied scenery of the woods and mountains, and then settling for a moment close to the surface, better to inspect his glittering image as it came up from below, and showing in his every movement his intense enjoyment of summer-time and life.

Out from his dark retreat now came the trout; and settling quietly at the bottom of the brook, he appeared to regard the venturesome insect with a certain interest. But he must have detected the iron barb of vice beneath the mask of blitheful innocence, for, after a short deliberation, the trout turned and disappeared under the bank. As he slowly moved away, he seemed to be bigger than ever. I must catch that fish! Surely he would bite at something. It was quite evident that his mind was not wholly unsusceptible to emotions emanating from an awakening appetite, and I believed that if he saw exactly what he wanted, he would not neglect an opportunity of availing himself of it. But what did he want? I must certainly find out. Drawing myself back again, I took off the yellow fly, and put on another. This was a white one, with black blotches, like a big miller moth which had fallen into an ink-pot. It was certainly a conspicuous creature, and as I crept forward and sent it swooping over the stream, I could not see how any trout, with a single insectivorous tooth in his head, could fail to rise to such an occasion. But this trout did not rise. He would not even come out from under his bank to look at the swiftly flitting creature. He probably could see it well enough from where he was.

But I was not to be discouraged. I put on another fly; a green one with a red tail. It did not look like any insect that I had ever seen, but I thought that the trout might know more about such things than I. He did come out to look at it, but probably considering it a product of that modern æstheticism which sacrifices natural beauty to mediæval crudeness of colour and form, he returned without evincing any disposition to countenance this style of art.

It was evident that it would be useless to put on any other flies, for the two I had left were a good deal bedraggled, and not nearly so attractive as those I had used. Just before leaving the house that morning Peter's son had given me a wooden matchbox filled with worms for bait, which, although I did not expect to need, I put in my pocket. As a last resort I determined to try the trout with a worm. I selected the plumpest and most comely of the lot; I put a new hook on my line; I looped him about it in graceful coils, and cautiously approached the water, as before. Now a worm never attempts to leap wildly across a flowing brook, nor does he flit in thoughtless innocence through the sunny air, and over the bright transparent stream. If he happens to fall into the water, he sinks to the bottom; and if he be of a kind not subject to drowning, he generally endeavours to secrete himself under a stone, or to burrow in the soft mud. With this knowledge of his nature I gently dropped my worm upon the surface of the stream, and then allowed him to sink slowly. Out sailed the trout from under the bank, but stopped before reaching the sinking worm. There was a certain something in his action which seemed to indicate a disgust at the sight of such plebeian food, and a fear seized me that he might now swim off, and pay no further attention to my varied baits. Suddenly there was a ripple in the water, and I felt a pull on the line. Instantly I struck; and then there was a tug. My blood boiled through every vein and artery, and I sprang to my feet.

I did not give him the butt: I did not let him run with yards of line down the brook; nor reel him in, and let him make another mad course upstream: I did not turn him over as he jumped into the air; nor endeavour, in any way, to show him that I understood those tricks, which his depraved nature prompted him to play upon the angler. With an absolute dependence upon the strength of old Peter's tackle, I lifted the fish. Out he came from the water, which held him with a gentle suction as if unwilling to let him go, and then he whirled through the air like a meteor flecked with rosy fire, and landed on the fresh green grass a dozen feet behind me. Down on my knees I dropped before him as he tossed and rolled, his beautiful spots and colours glistening in the sun. He was truly a splendid trout, fully a foot long, round and heavy. Carefully seizing him, I easily removed the hook from the bony roof of his capacious mouth thickly set with sparkling teeth, and then I tenderly killed him, with all his pluck, as old Peter would have said, still in him.

I covered the rest of the fish in my basket with wet plantain leaves, and laid my trout-king on this cool green bed. Then I hurried off to the old man, whom I saw coming out of the woods. When I opened my basket and showed him what I had caught, Peter looked surprised, and, taking up the trout, examined it.

'Why, this is a big fellow,' he said. 'At first I thought it was Barney Sloat's boss trout, but it isn't long enough for him. Barney showed me his trout, that gen'rally keeps in a deep pool, where a tree has fallen over the stream down there. Barney tells me he often sees him, and he's been tryin' fur two years to ketch him, but he never has, and I say he never will, fur them big trout's got too much sense to fool round any kind of victuals that's got a string to it. They let a little fish eat all he wants, and then they eat him. How did you ketch this one?'

I gave an account of the manner of the capture, to which Peter listened with interest and approval.

'If you'd a stood off and made a cast at that feller, you'd either have caught him at the first flip, which isn't likely, as he didn't seem to want no feather-flies, or else you'd a skeered him away. That's all well enough in the tumblin' water, where you gen'rally go fur trout, but the man that's got the true feelin' fur fish will try to suit his idees to theyrn, and if he keeps on doin' that, he's like to learn a thing or two that may do him good. That's a fine fish, and you ketched him well. I've got a lot of 'em, but nothin' of that heft.'

After luncheon we fished for an hour or two, with no result worth recording, and then we started for home.

When we reached the farm the old man went into the barn, and I took the fish into the house. I found the two pretty daughters in the large room, where the eating and some of the cooking was done. I opened my basket, and with great pride showed them the big trout I had caught. They evidently thought it was a large fish, but they looked at each other, and smiled in a way that I did not understand. I had expected from them, at least, as much admiration for my prize and my skill as their father had shown.

'You don't seem to think much of this fine trout that I took such trouble to catch,' I remarked.

'You mean,' said the elder girl, with a laugh, 'that you bought of Barney Sloat.'

I looked at her in astonishment.

'Barney was along here to-day,' she said, 'and he told about your buying your fish of him.'

'Bought of him!' I exclaimed indignantly. 'A little string of fish at the bottom of the basket I bought of him, but all the others, and this big one, I caught myself.'

'Oh, of course,' said the pretty daughter, 'bought the little ones and caught all the big ones.'

'Barney Sloat ought to have kept his mough shut,' said the younger pretty daughter, looking at me with an expression of pity. 'He'd got his money, and he hadn't no business to go telling on people. Nobody likes that sort of thing. But this big fish is a real nice one, and you shall have it for your supper.'

'Thank you,' I said, with dignity, and left the room.

I did not intend to have any further words with these young women on this subject, but I cannot deny that I was annoyed and mortified. This was the result of a charitable action. I think I was never more proud of anything than of catching that trout; and it was a very considerable downfall suddenly to find myself regarded as a mere city man fishing with a silver hook. But, after all, what did it matter? But the more I said this to myself, the more was I impressed with the fact that it mattered a great deal.

The boy who did not seem to be accounted a member of the family came into the house, and as he passed me he smiled good-humouredly, and said: 'Buyed 'em!'

I felt like throwing a chair at him, but refrained out of respect to my host. Before supper the old man came out on to the porch where I was sitting. 'It seems,' said he, 'that my gals has got it inter their heads that you bought that big fish of Barney Sloat, and as I can't say I seed you ketch it, they're not willin' to give in, 'specially as I didn't git no such big one. 'Tain't wise to buy fish when you're goin' fishin' yourself. It's pretty certain to tell agen you.'

'You ought to have given me that advice before,' I said, somewhat shortly. 'You saw me buy the fish.'

'You don't s'pose,' said old Peter, 'that I'm goin' to say anythin' to keep money out of my neighbour's pockets. We don't do that way in these parts. But I've told the gals they're not to speak another word about it, so you needn't give your mind no worry on that score. And now let's go in to supper. If you're as hungry as I am, there won't be many of them fish left fur breakfast.'

For two days longer I remained in this neighbourhood, wandering alone over the hills, and up the mountainsides, and by the brooks, which tumbled and gurgled through the lonely forest. Each evening I brought home a goodly supply of trout, but never a great one like the noble fellow for which I anglèd in the meadow stream.

On the morning of my departure I stood on the porch with old Peter waiting for the arrival of the mail driver, who was to take me to the nearest railroad town.

'I don't want to say nothin',' remarked the old man, 'that would keep them fellers with the jinted poles from stoppin' at my house when they comes to these parts a-fishin'. I ain't got no objections to their poles; 'tain't that. And I don't mind nuther their standin' off, and throwin' their flies as fur as they've a mind to; that's not it. And it ain't even the way they have of worryin' their fish. I wouldn't do it myself, but if they like it, that's their business. But what does rile me is the cheeky way in which they stand up and say that there isn't no decent way of fishin' but their way. And that to a man that's ketched more fish, of more different kinds, with more game in 'em, and had more fun at it, with a lot less money and less tomfoolin' than any fishin' feller that ever come here and talked to me like an old cat tryin' to teach a dog to ketch rabbits. No, sir; agen I say that I don't take no money fur entertainin' the only man that ever come out here to go a-fishin' in a plain, Christian way. But if you feel tetchy about not payin' nothin', you kin send me one of them poles in three pieces, a good strong one, that'll lift Barney Sloat's trout, if ever I hook him.'

I sent him the rod; and next summer I am going up to see him use it.

THE BURN TROUT

By GEORGE MACINDOE

GEORGE MACINDOE (1771-1848), Scottish silk-weaver, hotel-keeper, and poet, a friend of the poet Thomas Campbell. 'The Burn Trout' is from Macindoe's *Poems and Songs, chiefly in the Scottish dialect* (1805), and it and one other piece (not of fish or of fishing) are said to be alone worthy of preservation in the volume. The poem is in the form given in volume II of *The Modern Scottish Minstrel* (edited by Charles Rogers, 6 vols 1855-7).

BRITHER Jamie cam west, wi' a braw burn trout,
An' speer'd [1] how acquaintance were 'greeing;
He brought it frae Peebles, tied up in a clout,
An' said it wad just be a preeing,[2] a preeing,
An' said it wad just be a preeing.

In the burn that rins by his grandmother's door
This trout had lang been a dweller,
Ae night fell asleep a wee piece frae the shore,
An' was killed wi' a stane by the miller, the miller,
An' was killed wi' a stane by the miller.

This trout it was gutted an' dried on a nail
That grannie had reested [3] her ham on,
Weel rubbed wi' saut, frae the head to the tail,
An' kipper'd as 't had been a sa'mon, a sa'mon,
An' kipper'd as 't had been a sa'mon.

This trout it was boil'd an' set ben on a plate,
Nae fewer than ten made a feast o't;
The banes and the tail, they were gi'en to the cat,
But we lickit our lips at the rest o't, the rest o't,
But we lickit our lips at the rest o't.

[1] asked. [2] tasting. [3] smoked.

When this trout it was eaten, we were a' like to rive,[1]
   Sae ye maunna think it was a wee ane;
May ilk trout in the burn grow muckle an' thrive,
   An' Jamie bring west aye a preeing, a preeing,
   An' Jamie bring west aye a preeing.

[1] burst.

THE FISH

By ANTON CHEKHOV

Anton Pavlovich Chekhov (1860-1904), Russian author—novelist, dramatist, and one of the great short-story writers of the world. 'The Fish,' translated by Mrs Constance Garnett, is from *The Cook's Wedding and other stories* (1922) and is here given by permission of Messrs Chatto & Windus.

A summer morning. The air is still; there is no sound but the churring of a grasshopper on the river bank, and somewhere the timid cooing of a turtle-dove. Feathery clouds stand motionless in the sky, looking like snow scattered about. . . . Gerassim, the carpenter, a tall gaunt peasant, with a curly red head and a face overgrown with hair, is floundering about in the water under the green willow branches near an unfinished bathing shed. . . . He puffs and pants and, blinking furiously, is trying to get hold of something under the roots of the willows. His face is covered with perspiration. A couple of yards from him, Lubim, the carpenter, a young hunchback with a triangular face and narrow Chinese-looking eyes, is standing up to his neck in water. Both Gerassim and Lubim are in shirts and linen breeches. Both are blue with cold, for they have been more than an hour already in the water.

'But why do you keep poking with your hand?' cries the hunchback Lubim, shivering as though in a fever. 'You blockhead! Hold him, hold him, or else he'll get away, the anathema! Hold him, I tell you!'

'He won't get away. . . . Where can he get to? He's under a root,' says Gerassim in a hoarse, hollow bass, which seems to come not from his throat, but from the depths of his stomach. 'He's slippery, the beggar, and there's nothing to catch hold of.'

'Get him by the gills, by the gills!'

'There's no seeing his gills. . . . Stay, I've got hold of something. . . . I've got him by the lip. . . . He's biting, the brute!'

'Don't pull him out by the lip, don't—or you'll let him go! Take him by the gills, take him by the gills. . . . You've begun poking with your hand again! You are a senseless man, the Queen of Heaven forgive me! Catch hold!'

'Catch hold!' Gerassim mimics him. 'You're a fine one to give orders. . . . You'd better come and catch hold of him yourself, you hunchback devil. . . . What are you standing there for?'

'I would catch hold of him if it were possible. But can I stand by the bank, and me as short as I am? It's deep there.'

'It doesn't matter if it is deep. . . . You must swim.'

The hunchback waves his arms, swims up to Gerassim, and catches hold of the twigs. At the first attempt to stand up, he goes into the water over his head and begins blowing up bubbles.

'I told you it was deep,' he says, rolling his eyes angrily. 'Am I to sit on your neck or what?'

'Stand on a root . . . there are a lot of roots like a ladder.' The hunchback gropes for a root with his heel, and tightly gripping several twigs, stands on it. . . . Having got his balance, and established himself in his new position, he bends down, and trying not to get the water into his mouth begins fumbling with his right hand among the roots. Getting entangled among the weeds and slipping on the mossy roots, he finds his hand in contact with the sharp pincers of a crayfish.

'As though we wanted to see you, you demon!' says Lubim, and he angrily flings the crayfish on the bank.

At last his hand feels Gerassim's arm, and groping its way along it comes to something cold and slimy.

'Here he is!' says Lubim with a grin. 'A fine fellow! Move your fingers, I'll get him directly . . . by the gills. Stop, don't prod me with your elbow. . . . I'll have him in a minute, in a minute, only let me get hold of him. . . . The beggar has got a long way under the roots, there is nothing to get hold of. . . . One can't get to the head . . . one can only feel its belly. . . . Kill that gnat on my neck—it's stinging! I'll get him by the gills, directly. . . . Come to one side and give him a push! Poke him with your finger!'

The hunchback puffs out his cheeks, holds his breath, opens his eyes wide, and apparently has already got his fingers in the gills, but at that moment the twigs to which he is holding on with his left hand break, and losing his balance he plops into the water! Eddies race away from the bank as though frightened, and little bubbles come up from the spot where he has fallen in. The hunchback swims out and, snorting, clutches at the twigs.

'You'll be drowned next, you stupid, and I shall have to answer for you,' wheezes Gerassim. 'Clamber out, the devil take you! I'll get him out myself.'

High words follow. . . . The sun is baking hot. The shadows begin to grow shorter and to draw in on themselves, like the horns of a snail. . . . The high grass warmed by the sun begins to give out a strong, heavy smell of honey. It will soon be midday, and Gerassim and Lubim are still floundering under the willow tree. The husky bass and the shrill, frozen tenor persistently disturb the stillness of the summer day.

'Pull him out by the gills, pull him out! Stay, I'll push him out! Where are you shoving your great ugly fist? Poke him with your finger—you pig's face! Get round by the side! get to the left, to the left, there's a big hole on the right! You'll be a supper for the water-devil! Pull it by the lip!'

There is the sound of the flick of a whip. . . . A herd of cattle, driven by Yefim, the shepherd, saunter lazily down the sloping bank to drink. The shepherd, a decrepit old man, with one eye and a crooked mouth, walks with his head bowed, looking at his feet. The first to reach the water are the sheep, then come the horses, and last of all the cows.

'Push him from below!' he hears Lubim's voice. 'Stick your finger in! Are you deaf, fellow, or what? Tfoo!'

'What are you after, lads?' shouts Yefim.

'An eel-pout! We can't get him out! He's hidden under the roots. Get round to the side! To the side!'

For a minute Yefim screws up his eye at the fishermen, then he takes off his bark shoes, throws his sack off his shoulders, and takes off his shirt. He has not the patience to take off his breeches, but, making the sign of the cross, he steps into the water, holding out his thin dark arms to balance himself. . . . For fifty paces he walks along the slimy bottom, then he takes to swimming.

'Wait a minute, lads!' he shouts. 'Wait! Don't be in a hurry to pull him out, you'll lose him. You must do it properly!'

Yefim joins the carpenters and all three, shoving each other with their knees and their elbows, puffing and swearing at one another, bustle about the same spot. Lubim, the hunchback, gets a mouthful of water, and the air rings with his hard spasmodic coughing.

'Where's the shepherd?' comes a shout from the bank. 'Yefim! Shepherd! Where are you? The cattle are in the garden! Drive them out, drive them out of the garden! Where is he, the old brigand?'

First men's voices are heard, then a woman's. The master himself, Andrey Andreitch, wearing a dressing-gown made of a Persian shawl and carrying a newspaper in his hand, appears from behind the garden fence. He looks inquiringly towards the shouts which come from the river, and then trips rapidly towards the bathing shed.

'What's this? Who's shouting?' he asks sternly, seeing through the branches of the willow the three wet heads of the fishermen. 'What are you so busy about there?'

'Catching a fish,' mutters Yefim, without raising his head.

'I'll give it to you! The beasts are in the garden and he is fishing! . . . When will that bathing shed be done, you devils? You've been at work two days, and what is there to show for it?'

'It . . . will soon be done,' grunts Gerassim; 'summer is long, you'll have plenty of time to wash, your honour. . . . Pfrrr! . . . We can't manage this eel-pout here anyhow. . . . He's got under a root and sits there as if he were in a hole and won't budge one way or another. . . .'

'An eel-pout?' says the master, and his eyes begin to glisten. 'Get him out quickly then.'

'You'll give us half a rouble for it presently . . . if we oblige you. . . . A huge eel-pout, as fat as a merchant's wife. . . . It's worth half a rouble, your honour, for the trouble. . . . Don't squeeze him, Lubim, don't squeeze him, you'll spoil him! Push him up from below! Pull the root upwards, my good man . . . what's your name? Upwards, not downwards, you brute! Don't swing your legs!'

Five minutes pass, ten. . . . The master loses all pateince.

'Vassily!' he shouts, turning towards the garden. 'Vaska! Call Vassily to me!'

The coachman Vassily runs up. He is chewing something and breathing hard.

'Go into the water,' the master orders him. 'Help them to pull out that eel-pout. They can't get him out.'

Vassily rapidly undresses and gets into the water.

'In a minute. . . . I'll get him in a minute,' he mutters. 'Where's the eel-pout? We'll have him out in a trice! You'd better go, Yefim. An old man like you ought to be minding his own business instead of being here. Where's that eel-pout? I'll have him in a minute. . . . Here he is! Let go.'

'What's the good of saying that? We know all about that! You get it out!'

'But there is no getting it out like this! One must get hold of it by the head.'

'And the head is under the root! We know that, you fool!'

'Now then, don't talk or you'll catch it! You dirty cur!'

'Before the master to use such language,' mutters Yefim. 'You won't get him out, lads! He's fixed himself much too cleverly!'

'Wait a minute, I'll come directly,' says the master, and he begins hurriedly undressing. 'Four fools, and can't get an eel-pout!'

When he is undressed, Andrey Andreitch gives himself time to cool and gets into the water. But even his interference leads to nothing.

'We must chop the root off,' Lubim decides at last. 'Gerassim, go and get an axe! Give me an axe!'

'Don't chop your fingers off,' says the master, when the blows of the axe on the root under water are heard. 'Yefim, get out of this! Stay, I'll get the eel-pout. . . . You'll never do it.'

The root is hacked a little. They partly break it off, and Andrey Andreitch, to his immense satisfaction, feels his fingers under the gills of the fish.

'I'm pulling him out, lads! Don't crowd round . . . stand still. . . . I am pulling him out!'

The head of a big eel-pout, and behind it its long black body, nearly a yard long, appears on the surface of the water. The fish flaps its tail heavily and tries to tear itself away.

'None of your nonsense, my boy! Fiddlesticks! I've got you! Aha!'

A honied smile overspreads all the faces. A minute passes in silent contemplation.

'A famous eel-pout,' mutters Yefim, scratching under his shoulder-blades. 'I'll be bound it weighs ten pounds."

'Mm! . . . yes,' the master assents. 'The liver is fairly swollen! It seems to stand out! A-ach!'

The fish makes a sudden, unexpected upward movement with its tail and the fishermen hear a loud splash . . . they all put out their hands, but it is too late; they have seen the last of the eel-pout.

DOWN TO THE SEA!

By CHARLES KINGSLEY

CHARLES KINGSLEY (1819-1875), perhaps the best known of English author-anglers. Like his closest friend Thomas Hughes, he was a devotee of rural sports, and this he combined with a passion for the beautiful in nature and with a power of describing that beauty unsurpassed in English prose. He wrote of angling in verse; in his 'Chalk-stream Studies,' included both in the *Miscellanies* (1859) and in the *Prose Idylls* (1873), produced one of the angling classics; while he touched also on angling in his letters (edited by his wife, 2 vols 1877) and from time to time in his stories, as in *Yeast* (1849) and in *Water-babies* (1863), from chapter III of which last 'Down to the Sea!' is taken.

TOWARD evening it grew suddenly dark, and Tom looked up and saw a blanket of black clouds lying right across the valley above his head, resting on the crags right and left. He felt not quite frightened, but very still; for everything was still. There was not a whisper of wind, nor a chirp of a bird to be heard; and next a few great drops of rain fell plop into the water, and one hit Tom on the nose, and made him pop his head down quickly enough.

And then the thunder roared, and the lightning flashed, and leapt across Vendale and back again, from cloud to cloud, and cliff to cliff, till the very rocks in the stream seemed to shake: and Tom looked up at it through the water, and thought it the finest thing he ever saw in his life.

But out of the water he dared not put his head; for the rain came down by bucketsful, and the hail hammered like shot on the stream, and churned it into foam; and soon the stream rose, and rushed down, higher and higher, and fouler and fouler, full of beetles, and sticks, and straws, and worms, and addle-eggs, and wood-lice, and leeches, and odds and ends, and omnium-gatherums, and this, that, and the other, enough to fill nine museums.

Tom could hardly stand against the stream, and hid behind a rock. But the trout did not; for out they rushed from among the stones, and began gobbling the beetles and leeches in the most greedy and quarrelsome way, and swimming about with great worms hanging out of their mouths, tugging and kicking to get them away from each other.

And now, by the flashes of the lightning, Tom saw a new sight—all the bottom of the stream alive with great eels, turning and twisting along, all downstream and away. They had been hiding for weeks past in the cracks of the rocks, and in burrows in the mud; and Tom had hardly ever seen them, except now and then at night: but now they were all out, and went hurrying past him so fiercely and wildly that he was quite frightened. And as they hurried past he could hear them say to each other, 'We must run, we must run. What a jolly thunder-storm! Down to the sea, down to the sea!'

And then the otter came by with all her brood, twining and sweeping along as fast as the eels themselves; and she spied Tom as she came by, and said:

'Now is your time, eft, if you want to see the world. Come along, children, never mind those nasty eels: we shall breakfast on salmon to-morrow. Down to the sea, down to the sea!'

Then came a flash brighter than all the rest, and by the light of it—in the thousandth part of a second they were gone again—but he had seen them, he was certain of it—three beautiful little white girls, with their arms twined round each other's necks, floating down the torrent, as they sang, 'Down to the sea, down to the sea!'

'Oh stay! Wait for me!' cried Tom; but they were gone: yet he could hear their voices clear and sweet through the roar of thunder and water and wind, singing as they died away, 'Down to the sea!'

'Down to the sea?' said Tom; 'everything is going to the sea, and I will go too. Good-bye, trout.' But the trout were so busy gobbling worms that they never turned to answer him; so that Tom was spared the pain of bidding them farewell.

And now, down the rushing stream, guided by the bright flashes of the storm; past tall birch-fringed rocks, which shone out one moment as clear as day, and the next were dark as night; past dark hovers under swirling banks, from which great trout rushed out on Tom, thinking him to be good to eat, and turned back sulkily, for the fairies sent them home again with a tremendous scolding, for daring to meddle with a water-baby; on through narrow strids and roaring cataracts, where Tom was deafened and blinded for a moment by the rushing waters; along deep reaches, where the white water-lilies tossed and flapped beneath the wind and hail; past sleeping villages; under dark bridge-arches, and away and away to the sea. And Tom could not stop, and did not care to stop; he would see the great world below, and the salmon, and the breakers, and the wide wide sea.

And when the daylight came, Tom found himself out in the salmon river.

And what sort of a river was it? Was it like an Irish stream, winding through the brown bogs, where the wild ducks squatter up from among the white water-lilies, and the curlews flit to and fro, crying 'Tullie-wheep, mind your sheep'; and Dennis tells you strange stories of the Peishtamore, the great bogy-snake which lies in the black peat pools, among the old pine-stems, and puts his head out at night to snap at the cattle as they come down to drink?—But you must not believe all that Dennis tells you, mind; for if you ask him:

'Is there a salmon here, do you think, Dennis?'

'Is it salmon, thin, your honour manes? Salmon?

Cartloads it is of thim, thin, an' ridgmens, shouldthering ache out of water, av' ye'd but the luck to see thim.'

Then you fish the pool all over, and never get a rise.

'But there can't be a salmon here, Dennis! and, if you'll but think, if one had come up last tide, he'd be gone to the higher pools by now.'

'Sure thin, and your honour's the thrue fisherman, and understands it all like a book. Why, ye spake as if ye'd known the wather a thousand years! As I said, how could there be a fish here at all, just now?'

'But you said just now they were shouldering each other out of water?'

And then Dennis will look up at you with his handsome, soft, sleepy, good-natured, Irish grey eye, and answer with the prettiest smile:

'Shure, and didn't I think your honour would like a pleasant answer?'

Or was it like a Welsh salmon river, which is remarkable chiefly (at least, till this last year) for containing no salmon, as they have been all poached out by the enlightened peasantry, to prevent the *Cythrawl Sassenach* from coming bothering into Wales?

Or was it such a salmon stream as I trust you will see among the Hampshire water-meadows before your hairs are grey, under the wise new fishing-laws—when Winchester apprentices shall covenant, as they did three hundred years ago, not to be made to eat salmon more than three days a week; and fresh-run fish shall be as plentiful under Salisbury spire as they are in Holly-hole at Christchurch; in the good time coming, when folks shall see that, of all Heaven's gifts of food, the one to be protected most carefully is that worthy gentleman salmon, who is generous enough to go down to the sea weighing five ounces, and to come back next year weighing five pounds, without having cost the soil or the state one farthing?

Or was it like a Scotch stream, such as Arthur Clough drew in his 'Bothie'?—

> 'Where over a ledge of granite
> Into a granite bason the amber torrent descended . . .
> Beautiful there for the colour derived from green rocks under;
> Beautiful most of all, where beads of foam uprising
> Mingle their clouds of white with the delicate hue of the stillness . . .
> Cliff over cliff for its sides, with rowan and pendant birch boughs. . . .'

Ah, my little man, when you are a big man, and fish such a stream as that, you will hardly care, I think, whether she be roaring down in full spate, like coffee covered with scald cream, while the fish are swirling at your fly as an oar-blade swirls in a boat-race, or flashing up the cataract like silver arrows, out of the fiercest of the foam; or whether the fall be dwindled to a single thread, and the shingle below be as white and dusty as a turnpike road, while the salmon huddle together in one dark cloud in the clear amber pool, sleeping away their time till the rain creeps back again off the sea. You will not care much, if you have eyes and brains; for you will lay down your rod contentedly, and drink in at your eyes the beauty of that glorious place; and listen to the water-ouzel piping on the stones, and watch the yellow roes come down to drink and look up at you with their great soft trustful eyes, as much as to say, 'You could not have the heart to shoot at us?' And then, if you have sense, you will turn and talk to the great giant of a gilly who lies basking on the stone beside you. He will tell you no fibs, my little man; for he is a Scotchman.

No. It was none of these, the salmon stream at Harthover. It was such a stream as you see in dear old Bewick; Bewick, who was born and bred upon them. A full hundred yards broad it was, sliding on from broad pool to broad shallow, and broad shallow to broad pool, over great fields of shingle, under oak and ash coverts, past low cliffs of sandstone, past green meadows, and fair parks, and a great house of grey stone, and brown moors above, and here and there against the sky the smoking chimney of a colliery. You must look at Bewick to see just what it was like, for he has drawn it a hundred times with the care and the love of a true north countryman.

But Tom thought nothing about what the river was like. All his fancy was, to get down to the wide wide sea.

And after a while he came to a place where the river spread out into broad still shallow reaches, so wide that little Tom, as he put his head out of the water, could hardly see across.

And there he stopped. He got a little frightened. 'This must be the sea,' he thought. 'What a wide place it is! If I go on into it I shall surely lose my way, or some strange thing will bite me. I will stop here and look out for the otter, or the eels, or some one to tell me where I shall go.'

So he went back a little way, and crept into a crack of the rock, just where the river opened out into the wide shallows, and watched for some one to tell him his way: but the otter and the eels were gone on miles and miles down the stream.

There he waited, and slept too, for he was quite tired with his night's journey; and, when he woke, the stream was clearing to a beautiful amber hue, though it was still very high. And after a while he saw a sight which made him jump up; for he knew in a moment it was one of the things which he had come to look for.

Such a fish! ten times as big as the biggest trout, and a hundred times as big as Tom, sculling up the stream past him, as easily as Tom had sculled down.

Such a fish! shining silver from head to tail, and here and there a crimson dot; with a grand hooked nose and grand curling lip, and a grand bright eye, looking round him as proudly as a king, and surveying the water right and left as if all belonged to him. Surely he must be the salmon, the king of all the fish.

Tom was so frightened that he longed to creep into a hole; but he need not have been; for salmon are all true gentlemen, and, like true gentlemen, they look noble and proud enough, and yet, like true gentlemen, they never harm or quarrel with any one, but go about their own business, and leave rude fellows to themselves.

The salmon looked at him full in the face, and then went on without minding him, with a swish or two of his tail which made the stream boil again. And in a few minutes came another, and then four or five, and so on; and all passed Tom, rushing and plunging up the cataract with strong strokes of their silver tails, now and then leaping clean out of water and up over a rock, shining gloriously for a moment in the bright sun; while Tom was so delighted that he could have watched them all day long.

And at last one came up bigger than all the rest; but he came slowly, and stopped, and looked back, and seemed very anxious and busy. And Tom saw that he was helping another salmon, an especially handsome one, who had not a single spot upon it, but was clothed in pure silver from nose to tail.

'My dear,' said the great fish to his companion, 'you really look dreadfully tired, and you must not over-exert yourself at first. Do rest yourself behind this rock'; and he shoved her gently with his nose, to the rock where Tom sat.

You must know that this was the salmon's wife. For salmon, like other true gentlemen, always choose their lady, and love her, and are true to her, and take care of her and work for her, and fight for her, as every true gentleman ought; and are not like vulgar chub and roach and pike, who have no high feelings, and take no care of their wives.

Then he saw Tom, and looked at him very fiercely one moment, as if he was going to bite him.

'What do you want here?' he said, very fiercely.

'Oh, don't hurt me!' cried Tom. 'I only want to look at you; you are so handsome.'

'Ah!' said the salmon, very stately but very civilly. 'I really beg your pardon; I see what you are, my little dear. I have met one or two creatures like you before, and found them very agreeable and well-behaved. Indeed, one of them showed me a great kindness lately, which I hope to be able to repay. I hope we shall not be in your way here. As soon as this lady is rested, we shall proceed on our journey.'

What a well-bred old salmon he was!

'So you have seen things like me before?' asked Tom.

'Several times, my dear. Indeed, it was only last night that one at the river's mouth came and warned me and my wife of some new stake-nets which had got into the stream, I cannot tell how, since last winter, and showed us the way round them, in the most charmingly obliging way.'

'So there are babies in the sea?' cried Tom, and clapped his little hands. 'Then I shall have someone to play with there? How delightful!'

'Were there no babies up this stream?' asked the lady salmon.

'No! and I grew so lonely. I thought I saw three last night; but they were gone in an instant, down to the sea. So I went too; for I had nothing to play with but caddises and dragon-flies and trout.'

'Ugh!' cried the lady, 'what low company!'

'My dear, if he has been in low company, he has certainly not learnt their low manners,' said the salmon.

'No, indeed, poor little dear: but how sad for him to live among such people as caddises, who have actually six legs, the nasty things; and dragon-flies, too! why they are not even good to eat; for I tried them once, and they are all hard and empty; and, as for trout, every one knows what they are.' Whereon she curled up her lip, and looked dreadfully scornful, while her husband curled up his too, till he looked as proud as Alcibiades.

'Why do you dislike the trout so?' asked Tom.

'My dear, we do not even mention them, if we can help it; for I am sorry to say they are relations of ours who do us no credit. A great many years ago they were just like us: but they were so lazy, and cowardly, and greedy, that instead of going down to the sea every year to see the world and grow strong and fat, they chose to stay and poke about in the little streams and eat worms and grubs; and they are very properly punished for it; for they have grown ugly and brown and spotted and small; and are actually so degraded in their tastes, that they will eat our children.'

'And then they pretend to scrape acquaintance with us again,' said the lady. 'Why, I have actually known one of them propose to a lady salmon, the little impudent little creature.'

'I should hope,' said the gentleman, 'that there are very few ladies of our race who would degrade themselves by listening to such a creature for an instant. If I saw such a thing happen, I should consider it my duty to put them both to death upon the spot.' So the old salmon said, like an old blue-blooded hidalgo of Spain; and what is more, he would have done it too. For you must know, no enemies are so bitter against each other as those who are of the same race; and a salmon looks on a trout, as some great folks look on some little folks, as something just too much like himself to be tolerated.

SQUARING THE KEEPER

By FRANCIS FRANCIS

For Francis Francis, see p. 29. 'Squaring the Keeper' is from *Hot Pot* (1880).

How I enjoyed that day, to be sure! Some old sportsmen dearly love a little bit of poaching; for my part, it must be a very little bit to suit me. I never feel comfortable under it. In shooting, for example, I have seen some fellows who would rather pot a brace of birds off a neighbour's land than a dozen brace from their own, the stolen sweets are so particularly relishing. I never had any such feeling. If I ever was induced to break bounds, I always felt ashamed of myself from the first. My heart never was in the work, and if I got a shot I was so disturbed by my sense that I had no right to it, that the odds were two to one against the gun, though on other occasions it would be two to one on it; and if a keeper did appear, I would always rather have sneaked off by the shortest cut to my own territory than brazen it out by a bribe of 5s. I don't think, if left to my decision, I would ever willingly—never deliberately—have poached; but, on the occasion I am about to deal with I did it without intent, and cheeked it out afterwards in such a way that I often doubt in my own mind whether it could have been I, and if so, what possessed me.

We had a line from the Three Bridges Station on the Brighton line to Horsham under consideration; and I was engaged in surveying and levelling it. The line has long since been constructed. Our party, consisting of three, put up at the old-fashioned half-way house at Crawley—a queer little village, with a very remarkable old elm tree in it, the root and bole of which are hollowed out and form a small apartment. Crawley was a wonderful place in the old coaching days. The inn was a house of great grandeur and pretension; even then there were some attenuated remnants of old plate that gave one the idea of a lady-like old spinster very much reduced in circumstances. Here, formerly, dozens of coaches stopped daily, and it was rarely that they had not out from thirty to forty pair of post-horses. Now one coach called during the summer at the end of the village, and a pair of post-horses three times a week was good work; a sad falling off! Still the worthies of the village assembled nightly in the common room (greatly shorn of its glories) to have their smoke and talk, and, being a gregarious animal, I preferred to join them rather than to smoke alone. One evening I was listening to the usual Babel of conversation going on round me about pigs, beasts, and whuts, when I heard the word 'trout' close at hand. I immediately pricked up my ears; two men sitting by me were talking:

'Ah, I've had many a voine un out an it, surelye.'

'Out of where?' said I, breaking in upon the talk without scruple.

'Whoy, out o' the stream down agin th' steation.'

'Stream! Why, you don't mean that dead ditch water that runs under the road just above the public?'

'Ah! but I doo tho! There be some voine trout in't, onlikely as't looks.'

'The deuce there are!—and—and—may anyone go and fish it?'

'Ay, surelye. Whoy not?'

'Then dash my wigs if I don't go and have a turn at it to-morrow!' And, as my tackle needed looking up, I retired shortly. My stock was not extensive, for, not expecting any fishing, I had come down without any necessaries; but it so happened that, being at Horsham one day, and seeing in a small stream that flowed—or, as a Yankee would say, 'flew'—through it in those days, some uncommonly fine roach, I went to the only shop in the town (a barber's I think it was) where any approach to fishing-tackle could be purchased, and bought the only rod I could get, a small, trumpery, three-joint, walking-stick rod, a dozen or so of strands of Indian grass—gut he did not possess—a yard or so of silk line, and a few hooks; no reel, no running-line, no anything else. With this I was perforce content. The fishing at Horsham did not result in much, and the place I was going to fish on the next day was pretty much as I have described it—a dead, deep, ditchy-looking bit of water, apparently with very little stream, which ran under the road and past the end of the garden appertaining to a public-house on the other side of the road. I rigged up a line of a yard and a half or so of silk, and to it fastened a strand of Indian grass some two feet long, and on this tied a No. 6 or 7 hook. I had no shot, because, the stream being almost still, the worm would suffice to carry it to the bottom. I forgot to say that worm fishing was my intent; for, even had I had fly tackle, the stream was so grown over and inclosed in a thicket that it would not have been possible to use it.

The next morning I sallied out directly after breakfast, and, having to get some bait, I stopped on the roadside just behind a gipsy's cart, where there was a mound of old road scrapings and cuttings, and, to the astonishment of sundry olive-coloured juveniles, I commenced turning the stuff up with a pointed stick, and soon got together a good stock of worms. Having put in a bit of moss out of the hedge to scour them, I again made tracks for the water, and soon reached it. There was a stile opposite the public-house, and I stepped over it. A footpath ran alongside of a dense sort of hedgerow thicket, which was some twenty or thirty yards or more deep, and in the centre of this the stream ran. Into the thicket I at once plunged, and soon got to the banks of the stream. It was sore work scrambling along them, the tangle was so thick. It did not look as if the stream was often fished. The first twenty or thirty yards or so did not seem tempting. They were straight, even, and dead, and the water looked black and very ditch-like. Presently I came to a bend, which made a sort of pool. It had a profound appearance. There might have been a fish there, and, if there was, he would likely enough be a big one; so, rapidly jointing up my little poker of a rod—for it was not above eight or nine feet long—I unwound the line, stuck a worm on the hook, and dropped it into the spot. It slowly settled down out of sight into some four or five feet of water, and barely had reached the bottom when 'spang' the line went, cutting the surface, out towards the opposite bank. I raised the point sharply as it ran straight out, and struck. I only got one tug, and that nearly pulled the rod out of my hand and smashed everything, and, with a boil which came up to the surface as if the rudder of a boat had been rapidly turned below, a huge fish made his escape. I collapsed. 'Four or five pounds, if he was an ounce, by the boil he made!' I groaned. 'When—when shall I ever have such another chance? When shall I ever hook such another?' It was a dreadful beginning. Of course the miserable grass had broken; but I doubt if even gut would have held him without a little running-line. Had I had but three or four yards of that, so as to have allowed him to reach the opposite side without breaking, no doubt I might have got on terms with him in time; but it was no use crying over spilt milk. As an Irishman would say, there might be 'as good fish in the stream as *hadn't* come out of it,' and luck might be in store yet; so I set to work to repair damages, and, as single-strand grass was not strong enough, I doubled it and twisted it, and so tied another hook on. It was clumsy work enough, but the water was dark and the stream shaded, and the trout apparently very unso*fish*ticated, for I soon began picking them up, here one and there one. They all ran from about ¾ lb. to 1 lb., and I got some three or four brace of them pretty quickly.

Presently I emerged from the thicket, and found that the stream ran under an arch in the railway embankment. Dropping the worm in, I let it glide off under the arch, and got a heavy lug, and, after a turn of pully-hauly, up bolted a fine trout into the open stream above the arch. He was a powerful fish, and I had all my work to play him with my fourteen feet of rod and line without letting him go down under the arch again; but I was up to my work, and by degrees I coaxed him away from it into a little gut, and as soon as he was exhausted I shelved him out with my left hand. As I was doing so a train rattled by, and a row of heads popped out to note my battle with the trout. He was a capital fish, very handsome, and weighed exactly two pounds. I then crossed the railway and plunged once more into the thicket, which was here denser and deeper than ever. It was rare tearing and scrambling work, but the stream here was livelier and shallower, and the fish more plentiful; and, having now filled my pockets, I had to hang fish on the twigs as I went along (having no basket), with a view to retrieving them as I came back; and at every place where I made my way into the stream I left two or three good trout hanging gilled on a branch. I fished on and on, and the afternoon began to grow apace, the stream to get thin and shallow, and the trout small; so I thought I would turn back and fish only a choice spot or two on my return, collecting my fish as I went. Sport had been capital, and on my return journey, though I only caught another fish or two, I filled my pockets, my hat, and my handkerchief, until I left off fishing at last, having nowhere else to stow a single fish more; and I made my way out into the footpath, having tackled up and tied up my rod. By this time I was almost exhausted, for I had had nothing to eat or drink all day; and, crossing the stile, I made for the public-house opposite to recruit the inner man. As I did so, the host came to the door.

'What! Bin a-fishin', sir?' was his accost.

'Yes,' I replied, 'yes, and had some very nice sport—eighteen brace and a half, and one two-pounder.'

'Why, where *have* you been then?'

'Oh, up the ditch in the thicket yonder.'

'What!!!' in a tone of horror. 'Ditch! Why, that's the head of the Mole! Don't you know that I'm the keeper to it? And master's so dreadful particular that he won't give leave to no one, and there hain't been a single rod in there this two year' (I could well believe it) 'and, by jingo, here he comes! Here, bring them fish in out of sight' (I had been untying the handkerchief to show them) 'and give me that there rod. If he sees 'em, there'll be a horful row.'

In we bolted, and a stout, jolly gentleman, with a white hat, drove up in a sulky, and stopped to discourse the landlord. I peeped at him from behind the curtain of the parlour window, and, as he sat flicking at a stone in the road, I thought he had a very 'see-you-hanged-before-I-give-you-leave' kind of a face. They talked for a few minutes, and then he drove on, when the host returned to me. I need not say that my feelings were not the most cheerful in the interval.

'Well, you air as nice a cool sort of young gent as I've met with for some time! To go an' poarch a stream right an' left like this, and then to go and walk slap into the keeper's 'ouse an' show'n the vish! What is to be done about it, danged if I knows. Ye ought to be summoned, that you did!' 'Well,' I replied, 'all right; but first of all let's drink something, and then we'll consider about it. If you've got to do anything professional, why we shan't either of us be the worse of it for a pipe and a glass of brandy-and-water. "You can always take up a quarrel at any time; but a limited portion of spirits and water you cannot,"' quoth I, quoting Dickens, 'and, while you're mixing it, give me a biscuit.' At this he shook his head; but I could see that it was like the shake of a pointer's tail when he is not certain whether he has game before him or no. So I filled up the two big rummers with a stiff dose of mahogany myself, and chirruped invitingly through a fine churchwarden pipe, before filling it with the finest of birdseye, with which my pouch was well stocked.

'Well, I be dashed if I knows what I ought to do! 'Tis clear to me as ye did'n knaw ye was doin' wrong.' The pointer's tail was wagging, and unconsciously his hand stole to the big rummer, and a third of the mahogany vanished at a swig.

'Certainly not; should I have come in here to show you the fish if I had?'

'Naw, naw, that *be* trew; 't bent likely'—and I pushed the big pouch across to him, for I saw that his eyes lightened at the sight of the birdseye, for really good tobacco was by no means so general in the country then as it is now. 'That be trew,' he continued, filling his churchwarden in an absent kind of way, as if the question was still one of uncertainty; and he repeated, slowly, 'That be ver-ry'—puff, puff—pause—''mazin' foine backer this'—puff—'Lor'!'—puff, puff—'it dooes one good, sich a bit o' backer as this.' From that time not another word was said about the poaching, but we branched off into general sport. Mine host was a real enthusiastic sportsman at heart. He enjoyed every kind of sport, and, beyond all, loved a crack about it like the present. We went the whole round of hunting, shooting, coursing, fishing, with a touch of ratting and badger 'droring,' and we both enjoyed ourselves very thoroughly.

Three times were those big jorums of mahogany refilled, and twice three times the contents of the churchwardens came and went, and mine host and myself grew more and more hail fellows, and more pleased with our company. It evidently was an unusual treat for Boniface, and he looked on me as a sort of phenomenon. At length, however, it began to get late, and I rose to go. I paid my score, and left the remains of the prime birdseye for his future pleasure—a delicacy he much appreciated. His last words to me as I left the house were: 'Now look here; if anybody 'ed a seed you as tha went along that theer footpath—and there was lots went along it, 'cos I seed 'em' (this was true enough, and I had heard them, too, but they did not see me), 'I'd 'a lost my place, vor sartin. Now, mind, you must promise me you woan't never goo there no more' (this I readily did, and duty was satisfied). 'But, lookee here' (catching hold of my arm just as I left the door, and whispering in my ear), 'the next time as you cooms, goo up droo my garden, and out at the little gate at the back; there ben't no footpath at all there, and the vishin's a sight better nor 'tis down thik way.'

THREE AN' TWENTY MEAL POUNDS

By WILLIAM SCROPE

For WILLIAM SCROPE, see p. 136. 'Three an' Twenty Meal Pounds' is from chapter VI of *Days and Nights of Salmon Fishing in the Tweed* (1843).

'I HAD,' said Tom Purdie, 'risen a sawmon three successive days at the throat o' Caddon-water fut,[1] and on the fourth day I was determined to bring him to book; and whan he rose as usual, I went up to Caddon Wa's, namely, the pool opposite the ruins o' Caddon Lee, where there had been a terrace garden facin' the south; and on returnin' I tried my old friend, whan he rose again without touchin' the heuck: but I got a glimpse o' him, and saw he was a sawmon o' the biggest sort. I than went doon the river to a lower pool, and in half an hour cam up again and changed my heuck. I began to suspect that havin' raised the fish sae often, I had become too anxious, and gien him too little law—or jerked the heuck away afore he had closed his mouth upon it. And as I had a heavy rod and good line, and the castin'-line, which I had gotten thrae the Sherra,[2] had three fadom o' pleit gut at the end o' it, and the flee was buskit on a three plies o' sawmon gut, sae I wasna feard for my tackle. I had putten a cockle-stane at the side o' the water fornent[3] the place where he raise; forbye I kend fu' weel where he was lyin': it was at the side o' a muckle blue clint[4] that made a clour[5] i' the rough throat, e'en whan the Queed was in a brown flood, as she had been for twa days afore. Aweel, I thocht I wad try a plan o' auld Juniperbank's whan he had risen a sawmon mair nor ance. I keepit my eyne hard closed

[1] foot. [2] sheriff. [3] opposite. [4] rock. [5] break.

whan the heuck was commin' owre the place. Peace be here! I fand as gif I had catched the branch o' an aik tree swingin' and sabbin' in a storm o' wind. Ye needna doobt I opened my eyne! An' what think ye was the sawmon aboot?—turnin' and rowin' [1] doon the tap o' the water owre him and owre him (as ye hae seen a hempie [2] o' a callant row doon a green braeside) at great speed, makin' a fearfu' jumblin' and splashin', and shakin' the tap o' the wand at sic a rate, that deil hae me but I thocht he wad hae shaken my arms aff at the shouther joints, tho' I said to mysel' they were guy firm putten on. I never saw a fish do the like but ane i' the Auld Brig pool in the Darnwick-water. I jalouse [3] they want to unspin the line; for a fish has far mair cunnin' and wiles aboot him than mony ane wad think. At ony rate it was a fashious [4] plan this I fell on; for or he war to the fut o' the pool I was tyrt o' him and his wark, and sae was he, I'se warrant ye. For whan he fand the water turnin' shallow, he wheeled aboot, and I ran up the pool as fast as I could follow him, gien' him a' the line I could at the same time; and whan it was just aboot a' aff the pirn, and he was commin' into the throat, he wheeled again in a jiffy, and cam straight for my feet as if he had been shot out o' a cannon! I thocht it was a' owre atween us, for I fand naethin' at the wand as the line was soomin' [5] i' the pool a' the way doon. I was deed sure I had lost him after a' my quirks; for whan they cast a cantrip [6] o' that kind, it's done to slacken the line to let them draw the heuck out o' their mouths wi' their teethy toung—an' they are amaist sure to do sae. But he was owre weel heuckit, this ane, to work his purpose in that gyse, as ye sal hear; for whan, by dint o' runnin' back thrae the water as fast as I could and windin' up the line, I had brought a bow on the tap o' the rod, I fand the fish had riestit in the deepest part o' the pool, tryin' a' that teeth

[1] rolling. [2] rascal. [3] guess.
[4] troublesome. [5] swimming. [6] trick.

an' toung could do to get haud o' the heuck; and there did he lie for nearly an hour, for I had plenty o' time to look at my watch, and now and than to tak' mony a snuff too. But I was certain by this time that he was fast heuckit, and I raised him again by cloddin'[1] stanes afore him as near as I durst for hittin' the line. But whan I got him up at last there was mickle mair to do than I thocht o'; for he ran up the pool and doon the pool I dar' say fifty times, till my feet wur dour sair wi' gangin' sae lang on the channel: than he gaed owre the stream a'thegither. I was glad to let him change his gait ony way; and he gaed doon to Glenbenna, that was in Whitebank's water, and I wrocht him lang there. To mak' a lang tale short, afore I could get at him wi' the gaff, I was baith hungry an' tyrt; an' after a' he was firm heuckit, in the teughest part o' the body, at the outside o' the edge o' the wick[2] bane. He was a clean sawmon, an' three an' twenty meal pounds.'

[1] throwing. [2] corner of the mouth.

ON IZAAK'S STREAM

By CHARLES COTTON

CHARLES COTTON (1630-1687), angler and intimate of Walton, as well as poet and translator of Montaigne, produced, in some ten days, in fulfilment of an old-standing undertaking with Walton, an addition on fly-fishing, etc., to *The Compleat Angler*. As Part II this was incorporated in the 5th edition of 1676 and has ever since formed an integral part of the book. Cotton with much skill accommodated himself to Walton's method, preserving the dialogue form and the slight narrative interest. 'On Izaak's Stream' is from chapter VI and the scene is the Derbyshire-Staffordshire Dove, Cotton's home water and Walton's favourite stream.

Piscator. You shall now, if you please, make a fly yourself, and try what you can do in the streams with that; and I know a trout taken with a fly of your own making will please you better than twenty with one of mine. Give me that bag again, Sirrah: look you, Sir, there is a hook, towght,[1] silk, and a feather for the wings: be doing with those and I will look you out a dubbing [2] that I think will do.

Viator. This is a very little hook.

Piscator. That may serve to inform you that it is for a very little fly, and you must make your wings accordingly; for as the case stands, it must be a little fly, and a very little one, too, that must do your business. Well said! Believe me, you shift your fingers very handsomely. I doubt I have taken upon me to teach my master. So, here's your dubbing now.

Viator. This dubbing is very black.

Piscator. It appears so in hand; but step to the door

[1] strand of hair-line. [2] dressing.

and hold it up betwixt your eye and the sun, and it will appear a shining red; let me tell you, never a man in England can discern the true colour of a dubbing any way but that; and therefore choose always to make your flies on such a bright sunshine day as this, which also you may the better do, because it is worth nothing to fish in. Here, put it on; and be sure to make the body of your fly as slender as you can. Very good! Upon my word, you have made a marvellous handsome fly.

Viator. I am very glad to hear it; 'tis the first that ever I made of this kind in my life.

Piscator. Away, away! You are a doctor at it: but I will not commend you too much, lest I make you proud. Come, put it on; and you shall now go downward to some streams betwixt the rocks below the little footbridge you see there, and try your fortune. Take heed of slipping into the water as you follow me under this rock. So now you are over: and now throw in.

Viator. This is a fine stream indeed. There's one! I have him!

Piscator. And a precious catch you have of him; pull him out! I see you have a tender hand. This is a diminutive gentleman; e'en throw him in again, and let him grow till he be more worthy your anger.

Viator. Pardon me, Sir, all's fish that comes to the hook with me now. Another!

Piscator. And of the same standing.

Viator. I see I shall have good sport now. Another! and a grayling. Why you have fish here at will.

Piscator. Come, come, cross the bridge; and go down the other side, lower, where you will find finer streams and better sport, I hope, than this. Look you, Sir, here is a fine stream now. You have length enough; stand a little further off, let me entreat you; and do but fish this stream like an artist, and peradventure a good fish may fall to your share. How now! what! is all gone?

Viator. No, I but touched him; but that was a fish worth taking.

Piscator. Why now, let me tell you, you lost that fish by your own fault, and through your own eagerness and haste; for you are never to offer to strike a good fish, if he do not strike himself, till first you see him turn his head after he has taken your fly, and then you can never strain your tackle in the striking, if you strike with any manner of moderation. Come, throw in once again, and fish me this stream by inches; for I assure you, here are very good fish, both trout and grayling lie here; and at that great stone on the other side, 'tis ten to one a good trout gives you the meeting.

Viator. I have him now: but he is gone down towards the bottom. I cannot see what he is, yet he should be a good fish by his weight; but he makes no great stir.

Piscator. Why then, by what you say, I dare venture to assure you 'tis a grayling, who is one of the deadest-hearted fishes in the world; and the bigger he is, the more easily taken. Look you, now you see him plain; I told you what he was. Bring hither the landing-net, boy. And now, Sir, he is your own; and, believe me, a good one; sixteen inches long I warrant him: I have taken none such this year. But move on; for it grows towards dinner-time; and there is a very great and fine stream below, under that rock, that fills the deepest pool in all the river, where you are almost sure of a good fish.

Viator. Let him come, I'll try a fall with him. Here's another skip-jack; and I have raised five or six more at least, whilst you were speaking. Well, go thy way, little Dove! thou art the finest river that ever I saw, and the fullest of fish. Indeed, Sir, I like it so well, that I am afraid you will be troubled with me once a year, so long as we two live.

Piscator. I am afraid I shall not, Sir; but were you once here a May or a June, if good sport would tempt you,

I should then expect you would sometimes see me; for you would then say it were a fine river indeed, if you had once seen the sport at the height.

Viator. Which I will do, if I live, and that you please to give me leave. There was one, and there another.

Piscator. And all this in a strange river, and with a fly of your own making! Why what a dangerous man are you!

Viator. Aye, Sir: but who taught me? And as Dametas says by his man Dorus, so you may say by me,

> If my man such praises have,
> What then have I, that taught the knave?

But what have we got here? A rock springing up in the middle of the river! This is one of the oddest sights that ever I saw.

Piscator. Why, Sir, from that pike that you see standing up there distant from the rock, this is called Pike Pool. And young Mr Izaak Walton was so pleased with it, as to draw it in landscape, in black and white, in a blank book I have at home.

Viator. Has young Mr Izaak Walton been here, too?

Piscator. Yes, marry has he, Sir, and that again and again, too. In the meantime, Sir, to come to this fine stream at the head of this great pool, you must venture over these slippery cobbling stones. Believe me, Sir, there you were nimble, or else you had been down. But now you are got over, look to yourself: for, on my word, if a fish rise here, he is like to be such a one as will endanger your tackle. How now!

Viator. I think you have such command here over the fishes, that you can raise them by your word, as they say conjurers can do spirits, and afterward make them do what you bid them; for here's a trout has taken my fly; I had rather have lost a crown. What luck's this! He was a lovely fish, and turned up a side like a salmon.

Piscator. O Sir, this is a war where you sometimes win, and must sometimes expect to lose. Never concern yourself for the loss of your fly; for ten to one I teach you to make a better.

THE FOUR-POUNDER

By WILLIAM CAINE

WILLIAM CAINE (1873-1925; 'W. Quilliam' of *The Field*), English humorist. He was a keen trout-fisher, combining the pursuit with sketching, and, in addition to his many novels and collections of short stories, he wrote two original books on angling —*An Angler at Large* (1911) and *Fish, Fishing, and Fishermen* (1927), both of which contain, among other things, pleasantly humorous stories on angling. 'The Four-pounder' is from *What a Scream!* (1927). See also pp. 294, 329.

'I HOPE George is all right,' said Basil as he began on his beef.

'Right as ninepence, Selby,' said Major Poole, 'and stouter than ever.'

'What's he weigh this year?' Basil enquired.

'It hasn't yet been definitely ascertained. But it's generally agreed that he's put on flesh since last season. Personally,' said the Major, 'I think he must go quite the four and a quarter pounds now.'

'Not by two ounces,' snapped old Mr Wellington: 'Four two is his weight, or I'll eat my brogues.'

'Who is George?' asked Arethusa Lyne. She sat between Basil (to whom she was affianced) and her mother. These three had descended at the Complete Angler only ten minutes previously; dinner being on, they had come straight into the coffee-room, where Basil had found several habitués to whom he was well known.

'George,' said Basil, 'is a trout that lives in a pool close by here. I'll introduce you to him after dinner. He's a famous fish, for I may tell you that a four-pounder in the Yeoman is simply fantastic. Anything over a pound hereabouts is an absolute whale. And at the end of last season George weighed precisely four pounds and one ounce. He's known throughout Devon and Somerset and there's not a West Country angler of any repute who hasn't had a go at him.'

'Can't they catch him?'

'Some of them can. Not many. The place where he lies is as near as needs be impossible. It takes a broth of an angler to ensnare George, I promise you.' He paused.

'Selby is modestly waiting, Miss Lyne,' said little Willie Rook, 'for one of us to tell you that he, Selby, has had George out no less than three times. Permit me to give you this piece of information. Now, Selby, you can carry on with your tale.'

'It is even so,' said Basil; 'and that's how I know what his weight was last September. Before putting him back——'

'Do you always put him back?' she asked.

'Always,' he said. 'It's an understood thing that anyone who catches George puts him back. It would never do to have George slain. He confers a lustre upon this hotel that is absolutely unique. Anglers come from the United States and New Zealand just to fish for George. His fame is world-wide. He is legendary. To kill George would be a quite unspeakable villainy. I don't believe that even a Norwegian farmer could be wicked enough to kill George. George is sacred.'

'But,' she objected, 'suppose some angler came along who didn't know that George mustn't be killed.'

'Oh,' he replied, 'there's a notice-board by the pool to say so. We had it put up five years ago; the people, I mean, who come here fishing. Besides, it's unlikely that anyone who was man enough to catch George wouldn't know about him. One would as soon expect a plus-four golfer never to have heard of St Andrews.'

'He's very hard to catch, is he?' she asked.

'Well,' he explained, 'I wouldn't say that. If you can get your fly to him properly, he'll generally take it. We have a theory that George knows he won't be killed, and that when he sees a fly properly presented to him, he says to himself, "Now that's a pretty good effort. This fellow deserves his reward," and thereupon he takes the fly, gives the angler a run, and gets off or is netted as the case may be. George, in a word, is a thorough sportsman. I drink long life to him.' And Basil emptied his pot of ale.

'Well,' said Arethusa, '*I* call it pretty hard luck on the trout.'

'What do you mean pretty hard luck on the trout?' Basil cried. 'I tell you George simply loves being caught. Doesn't he, you fellows?' he demanded of the other fishermen. They all swore that to be caught was George's greatest pleasure in life.

Arethusa didn't argue the point. She was too hungry, and the beef was too good.

After dinner Basil led her, according to his promise, out of the hotel, across the road, through a gate and into a wood of young oaks, where they found the Yeoman making its busy way to the sea. Almost at once they stood by the pool where dwelt George, that inconceivable monster. Basil showed Arethusa the notice-board which stood by the pool. It read: 'Any angler who catches the large trout that lives in this pool is earnestly entreated to return him to the water.' Then Basil pointed out the place where George habitually lay. A particular description of it, with diagrams and measurements to the eighth of an inch, would be out of place. I will only say that George's lair was an exceedingly narrow passage, thickly overhung with hazel bushes, at the very head of the pool, and only to be entered by a fly that should be thrown from a point situated some twenty-five yards downstream, because, owing to the depth of the pool, it was impossible, by wading, to get any nearer; and that since the whole place was closely over-arched by the branches of trees, and thickly shrouded in undergrowth, the projection of a line twenty-five yards in length was a feat to tax the powers of the Apostle Peter himself.

Arethusa was duly impressed, and said that she didn't think she would probably waste very much of her time angling for George. In the wood there was very little light, for the sun had been at least three hours gone out of the valley. George, therefore, on this occasion was not to be seen lying in the water. But even as they gazed at the place where he was supposed to be, there came floating upon the oily glide that floored the little green tunnel, a pale insect which fluttered once and again. And lo! an august snout emerged, followed by a broad olive-green back, and the fly was gone, and in the water there was a heavy swirl, while Basil said, 'That's him,' and Arethusa clutched Basil's arm, and emitted an eldritch scream.

'Always the little gentleman, George is,' said Basil as they went back to the hotel. 'He knew you wanted to have a look at him.'

'Oh, Basil,' said the girl, 'if ever I catch a trout like that I shall give up the ghost for sheer beatitude.' Hitherto the young lady had grassed nothing heavier than six ounces.

Basil squeezed her to reward her enthusiasm. 'No, you won't,' he said. 'You'll be too keen to go on living, so that you may catch a still bigger one. And now you'll want to help your mother to unpack and get to bed.' He kissed her good night and repaired to the bar to exchange fishing-boasts with the Major and little Willie Rook and old Mr Wellington and the rest of them.

Nobody fished seriously for George; I mean none of the habitués did. Ambitious strangers might sit down behind the great trout and devote long hours or even whole days to the hopeless siege of him; but the habitués knew better. They were at the Complete Angler to catch fishes, not to lose their time and temper juggling a fly in and out among the leafy defences of George. After breakfast they distributed themselves over the various hotel waters—this man up the Yeoman, that man down the Yeoman, the next up the Cobley Brook, a fourth on the Davy in the next valley, a fifth on the Brewer two miles away. When they fished for George it was before breakfast or after tea or dinner. Anyone, in short, who had an empty half-hour on his hands was as likely as not to take his rod and go and attempt to put a fly over George's nose. This feat was so difficult that it was never undertaken save apologetically and as a sort of joke. Very, very rarely, as we know, it was accomplished, and then George might be risen and missed, or perhaps hooked and lost, or actually brought to the net. But no one who went out to fish for him ever expected anything but failure.

On the third morning of her stay Arethusa came down to breakfast to find Basil just entering the hall with his rod in his hand. 'Well,' she said, '*you've* been at it early.'

'Yes,' he replied, as he put his rod up on its hooks, 'I thought I'd just see if I could land old George. I did, too,' he added casually.

'Basil!' she screamed. 'How could you, and with me not there to see?'

'If you had been,' he told her, 'you wouldn't have seen it, because it wouldn't have come off. George hates a gallery. He weighs four and a quarter pounds, by the way. My balance says so, at any rate. Old Wellington is wrong, and I shall insist on him eating his brogues.'

Basil took it all very lightly, but it was obvious that he was thoroughly pleased with himself. And, indeed, to have taken George four times out of his pool was a very considerable thing to have done. At breakfast Basil was quite the hero, but he didn't succeed in making old

Mr Wellington eat his brogues; for old Mr Wellington simply maintained that Basil must have read his balance wrongly.

Basil put on airs. He announced that he was never going to fish for George again. He'd had enough of catching George. George was altogether too easy, he said.

'Well,' said little Willie Rook, 'I don't fancy anyone else will catch him this summer. You'll have given him a distaste for flies, Selby, that'll last him for some time.'

But little Willie Rook was wrong. Before a week was out he himself had landed George. He, too, reported that George weighed four and a quarter pounds. Old Mr Wellington, however, still declined to eat his brogues. This time he gave no reason for his refusal. He just refused—angrily.

It really looked as if Basil had been right and that George was a thorough sportsman. It looked as if he did positively enjoy having a tussle with an angler. Unless this was the case it was almost incredible that a trout of George's size and age should let himself be caught twice within ten days. Once a season is as much as such a fish's nerves can ordinarily stand. But George was very far from being an ordinary trout. He was, when you come to think of it, more of a pet than anything else.

Arethusa was an honest, humble-minded young fisherwoman. She knew herself to be still a mere bungler, though she was quite tolerably pleased with the advance she had made since, during the previous summer, Basil had entered her at the game. She could catch trout in quite respectable numbers, given that conditions were strongly in her favour, that is to say, if the wind was upstream and the fish were hungry. A basket of half a dozen was nothing out of the way for Arethusa. But she knew her limitations; and she had recognised at once that she would do better not to aspire to the grassing of George. And so, during her first fortnight at the Complete Angler, she was very well satisfied to fish, with Basil, the many miles of the hotel water in which George was not. During these days she covered herself with a moderate glory, wiping on two occasions the eye of old Mr Wellington, to old Mr Wellington's extreme annoyance and the intense delight of all the other habitués.

On her fifteenth day, however, she and Basil having been on the lower Yeoman, she arrived at the hotel about half an hour before tea-time, and, to kill this half-hour, went down to George's pool, just to have a look at him, a thing which she had done many times before. There he lay in his little green tunnel, huge, solid, phenomenal, and almost motionless. To Arethusa wholly inaccessible. 'Oh,' she thought, 'for the skill to put a fly only once over that great brute's nose!' and she cast a baleful eye upon the close-set greenery by which he was surrounded. 'If this were only cleared away,' she said; 'it would be grand,' she murmured.

Suddenly her heart stopped beating, then bounded against her ribs. George had left his tunnel (a thing which he was supposed never to do) and had come down into the pool. Around it he now proceeded slowly to cruise. Arethusa knew that a marvellous, an incredible opportunity had been presented to her, but she did not realise that George was simply behaving like the gentleman he was.

Suspending entirely the movements of her breathing apparatus, she detached from the cork handle of her rod the small red tag with which she had been fishing since lunch, and, letting it and the cast swing clear, lowered her point and held the fly steady, a foot above the surface. Soon George came loafing along with his hands in his pockets and his hat on the back of his head. Arethusa made the red tag dance, and George halted to gaze upwards. Arethusa lowered her point still further and the dry red tag just touched the surface. George—good sportsman—hurled himself upon it and was fast.

A hundred thousand æons later Arethusa lifted him in her net from the water, laid him in the grass, and fell on her knees beside him.

Next moment George had got it in the *medulla oblongata* from the handle of the net—whack! He gave one strong shudder of reproach and was still for ever.

Then Arethusa came to herself. The red mists which had been recently obscuring her vision scattered and were gone, and all things became clear again. She knew what she had done. 'Oh, heaven!' she cried, leaping to her feet, 'I've killed George!' She was chalk-white already from the emotion which her battle had caused her. She could not go whiter. So she went scarlet. 'Oh, my goodness!' she muttered, 'I've killed poor old George!' She stood looking down upon the lovely corpse and was suddenly blinded by tears; three or four great sobs burst from her. The triumphant joy which should attend the slaughter of a four-and-a-quarter-pound trout was singularly to seek within her bosom. She felt much worse than Cain did just after he murdered Abel, for Cain was only scared; whereas Arethusa was filled with remorse as well, not to mention pity for poor gentlemanly, sportsman-like George.

Crying, however, never picked up any spilt milk, and Arethusa, being a sensible girl, knew this perfectly well. She realised further that it behoved her to take speedy counsel with herself as to what she was to do. At any moment an habitué might be inspired to come down to George's pool and have a go at its principal denizen. Suppose she should be found by such an habitué standing red-handed above the corpse of George. Suppose the habitué in question should be Basil. She had left him busy on a fish only a few hundred yards below the hotel. He was certainly not far away. Suppose she should now see him coming towards her through the oaks!

Panic laid hold of her and, tearing up some double handfuls of green stuff, she scattered them hurriedly upon George's body. Then, with the spike that was in the butt of her rod, she began to dig in the clay of the bank. This spike was about an inch and a half long by half an inch broad. The clay was as stiff as soap. Very soon she broke a nail. But she persisted and presently the little grave was prepared. She pulled the remains from their hiding-place, tumbled them in and, with her hands, scrabbled the clay on top of them, trod it flat with her brogues and scattered the loose greenery over it. Then she whispered: 'An otter has killed George. Yes, an otter did it.'

She waded into the Yeoman, cleaned her brogues, cleaned her hands, took her rod and began to move in the direction of the hotel. But at the edge of the wood she paused and looked back. 'This,' she told herself, 'is hopeless. It's childish. Hang it all, they can't eat me. And I caught that trout. I caught it fairly. I did. And if I caught it, I was entitled to kill it.' It becomes evident that her panic had subsided a little.

The truth is that Arethusa was much too young an angler to be able easily to forgo the satisfaction of exhibiting a four-and-a-quarter-pound trout which she had slain. It falls to the lot of very few fisherwomen to land so goodly a fish in their second season, and it was altogether too much to ask of that assemblage of ordinary flesh and blood which went by the name of Arethusa Lyne that George should be left where he lay. What though the whole hotel should turn upon her with imprecations and send her for ever to Coventry. What though Basil should curse her and break off their engagement. She must, she must, she must exhibit George to the habitués assembled for tea in the lounge of the hotel. She must see their eyes protrude. She must hear them gasp. Not one of them—not even Basil had for a moment so much as pretended that he thought her capable of landing George. Well, she *had* landed George; and the only way of making them believe it was to show them George's body. And she was going to do it, if it blinded her!

Of course she was very sorry that she had been so far carried away by excitement as to knock poor old George on the head, but since she had done it—why, it was only common-sense to get the credit of having caught him. Not every girl could have done it.

Besides, it was wicked waste of good food to leave George in the earth.

Those hotel anglers were idiots about George.

Basil too.

She was going to dig George up.

She was.

She did.

Then she washed all the clay off George and squeezed him into her creel. 'There!' she said, and slammed the lid down on him.

When she came into the lounge she found assembled her mother, Basil, old Mr Wellington, little Willie Rook, Major Poole, the Reverend Alfred Jerningham, his wife, and a young man called Butterworth.

'Ah, here you are, child,' said her mother, who was pouring out for the company. 'We were wondering what had become of you.'

'Oh,' said Arethusa carelessly (but her cheeks were devoid of colour), 'I've just been having a try for George.'

Old Mr Wellington (who never fished for George now, and who had never, at his best, so much as risen him) cackled high. 'Indeed, young lady,' he said. 'And you got him, of course.'

'Of course,' said Arethusa, as she slipped her creel off, hung it on the hat-stand and sat down. 'Lots of milk, mother,' she added.

There was a general laugh. It was felt that Miss Lyne had rather scored off old Wellington.

'Splendid!' said Mr Wellington, 'and I suppose you put him back after taking his temperature and counting his teeth. The great advantage about catching George,' Mr Wellington went on nastily, 'is that one doesn't have to show him.' We must remember that Mr Wellington was very old and that he suffered rather often from neuritis. 'One of these days,' he continued, 'I must really go down and catch George myself.'

'You can't,' said Arethusa, as she bit a scone in two—and there was another laugh. 'No,' she cried, 'I didn't mean that. What I meant was that George is in that creel.' With her chin she indicated the receptacle. 'Nobody,' she said, 'can catch him now.'

This time there was not so much as a smile. Basil broke a constrained pause by observing: 'Even in joke, Arethusa, you oughtn't to say things like that. You can't realise how much George means to us or you wouldn't do it. However——'

She got up and fetched her creel, opened it and dragged George out by the tail. She held him aloft, but said no word. An arctic silence fell upon the lounge of the Complete Angler. At last the Reverend Mr Jerningham whispered: 'It's George.' Old Mr Wellington cackled. 'I apologise to Miss Lyne,' he said, and cackled again and coughed horribly. No one patted him on the back.

'She's killed George,' said young Butterworth. 'Oh, I say, dash it, poor old George.'

'But why?' asked Major Poole, 'why kill George, Miss Lyne?' He fixed his eyeglass and glared at her distastefully.

'It isn't,' said little Willie Rook, 'as if we were exactly starving for a bit of fish, you know, is it? Well, well—that's that, isn't it?'

Basil burst. 'What in the name of goodness,' he cried, 'did you *kill* him for, Arethusa? You *knew* we never kill George. Did you think we wouldn't believe you if you told us you'd caught him? Was that it? Was *that* it?'

All this time Arethusa had been cursing herself for not having left George underground. The reasons for digging him up and exhibiting him to the anglers, the reasons for having killed him, which had all seemed so potent down by the river were now in her sight simply foolish. To tell these men, for instance, that having caught George, she was entitled to kill him—what was that but a plain stupidity?

She had nothing to say.

Oh! if she had only left George in his grave and allowed the hotel to make what they pleased of his disappearance. One thing was quite certain; she would never have been connected with it in their thoughts.

She had nothing to say.

'What beats me,' said young Butterworth, obviously communing with himself, 'is how the deuce she got him. *She* can't make that cast. Not in a thousand years, she can't. I've seen her throw a fly. It's not reasonable. It's all *wrong*.'

'Say something, Arethusa,' Basil entreated. 'Say anything. You must have had some reason for doing this. It isn't as if you didn't know that we always put George back.'

With that an argument was vouchsafed to Arethusa. She laid George carefully in her creel and put the creel carefully on the floor by her foot.

'Yes,' she said slowly. 'I'll tell you why I killed him. I did it because I was sorry for him. I did it to put him out of his misery. I did it because I think you're a lot of cruel beasts, catching a miserable trout over and over again. You ought to be prosecuted for the way you've treated that fish. It makes my blood boil even to think of it. Dragging him out with a sharp hook through his nose, or perhaps his tongue, time after time, year after year. It was horrible and hateful. And you call yourselves sportsmen! Why,' she cried, warming to it, 'you're no better than those odious creatures who hunt the carted deer, or the savages who keep a tame badger to bait. Oh, I know you'll tell me that a trout doesn't feel pain from the hook in his horny mouth—and perhaps he doesn't—sometimes; but I'll tell you what he *does* feel when he's hooked, and that's fear. But what do you care for the agonies of terror you've been causing this poor animal? Not a rap. Oh, I'm downright ashamed of the lot of you, and I should be ashamed of myself if I hadn't killed George just now. So there!'

'Bravo!' said old Mr Wellington, who had at last ceased to cough. 'My sentiments entirely, Miss Lyne. Bravo!' He got up and went to his room for a dose of his cherry pectoral. Arethusa ignored him.

'I don't think I'll argue the point with you, Miss Lyne,' said Major Poole, rising.

'Nor I,' said little Willie Rook, rising.

'Nor I,' said the Reverend Mr Jerningham, rising.

'Nor I,' said young Butterworth, rising.

'I should say,' Major Poole went on, 'that we're going to have some rain. Wouldn't you, Jerningham?'

'Yes,' said the parson. 'To-night, I fancy.'

They left the lounge together, followed closely by Messrs Rook and Butterworth. Mrs Jerningham rose and went upstairs.

Arethusa caught the eye of her mother who rose and followed Mrs Jerningham. Arethusa turned to Basil where he sat huddled up in his chair, sucking busily at a cold pipe.

'Well?' she asked defiantly, 'aren't you going to withdraw yourself from the neighbourhood of the pariah, too?'

'No,' he said slowly, 'I'm not, and I want to tell you, Arethusa, that I admire you tremendously for the way you gave it us about poor old George. You're perfectly right. We've been guilty of shocking cruelty to the poor fish, and I'm glad to think that there won't be any more of that rotten work. But I must confess that I'd never hitherto looked upon it in that light. Hitherto, whenever anybody has expressed sympathy for George—as you did, you'll remember, the first night here—I've always made a joke of it, and sworn that George liked nothing better than to be caught. But now—well, I can only tell you that I'm wiser now. I see clearly that we've been no better than, as you say, badger-baiters.' He relit his pipe. 'And,' he concluded steadily, 'I propose to tell those others what I think.'

'Basil!' she cried, finding at last her tongue. 'You're not *serious* about this? You don't *mean* it?'

He looked up at her. He seemed surprised. 'Well, of course I do,' he said. 'Why not?'

'Oh, Basil,' she said, 'I really do now believe you love me.'

'Of course I love you,' he informed her. 'Why not? It's *because* I love you that I can see your point of view in this business.'

'And you're not going to side with the others?'

'When you're in question,' he said simply, 'there are no others. If you'd done in old Wellington or even poisoned the Yeoman, I should still stand by you. If you'd killed George, not out of your beautiful womanly pity, but in sheer lust for his life, I should back you up. Naturally.'

In the face of such perfect loyalty deception was no longer possible to Arethusa.

'But, Basil,' she whispered, 'that's just what I did do.'

'What?' he inquired.

'Why, kill him in sheer lust for his life. When I got him on the bank I instantly forgot everything and whanged him on the head. I was so frightfully excited, Basil. And all that stuff I gave you just now about putting George out of his misery was simply a lot of tosh that I made up in my own defence.'

His face became suddenly illuminated with a great joy,

and he started to his feet. 'The Lord be praised!' he exclaimed. 'I thought you'd begun to be humane.'

He clasped her to his bosom.

'I'll get the car,' he said after a time, 'and we'll take George in to Tavistock to be set up for the hotel. He'll look superb in the lounge.'

'Yes, Basil,' she murmured obediently.

THE LINN OF LOGIE

By PATRICK R. CHALMERS

For PATRICK REGINALD CHALMERS, see p. 81. 'The Linn of Logie' is from chapter XIII of *Where the Spring Salmon Run* (1931) and is here given by permission of the author.

THERE was once a young man in a shooting-lodge among the misty red hills and it was Lammas time. And the rain roared and hammered on roof and windows and, on such a day as yon, you would not be driving a grouse were it ever so. And the young man could not play at bridge for he had not the bridge faculty. But neither had he a fishing-rod, for he had come to shoot grouse and not to catch burn trouts. So he stood in the window and listened to the singing of the showers. And he went to the hall door and opened it, and the West Wind, sweet with the rain and the smell of the pinewoods, went by with a shout and bade him follow it. It was then that his host told that, if a body walked two miles over the hill, that he would come to the Logie Water wherein were trout for the catching. The rod to take them on was still the difficulty. But a rod was borrowed from the bothy. It was a little old two-piece trout-rod and it was lashed with binding and bound about with twine. But it was light and whippy and the handicraft of a great maker of old, and Peter Stuart had had it 'in a present' from 'her leddyship' at Druim this long time ago.

But the young man was not concerned for the genesis of the rod so long as he might get a loan of it. And to this he was kindly welcome. There was a sufficiency of line on the reel too. And, as it passed the not too drastic testing of a line, all was well. Peter had some bait-hooks and a yard or two of gut. The procuring of a 'pucklie' worms, in wet moss and a mustard-tin, would not hinder long. And so the guest was provided for. And presently he swung a game-bag upon his back, for creel there was none, and, syne, he was for away. But not before he had remembered that, in the cap to match with his Lovat mixture of yesterday's wearing, there were a two or three trout-flies. So it was that cap that he would put on. And before he did so he asked about the Logie Water, for he knew it not.

The Logie was, it appeared, a wee stony water on most days and the trout that lived in it were wee trout. About six to the pound? They would be just about that, said the angler's host. But they were plump and golden little trout and dusted on with crimson spots, and sometimes, maybe, there was a half-pounder to be had. The Logie ran into the Waupie of course. And the Waupie was a salmon river? Why, yes, the Waupie was a salmon river, but no salmon were ever in the Logie because they could not get up the Linn of Logie. And a very good reason too, thought the angler as he crossed the hill. And the West Wind was blowing steady and the rain was going out on it. But the hills were full of the roar of waters where the burns ran foaming full. And the mist rose out of the glens and the corries and shifted, like grey smoke, and through it the hills, what a man might see of them, were very dark and blue. And when the angler got to the Logie Water he thought that it was a real bonny little river.

Like all the hill waters the Logie rose like a rocket. But she cleared soon and then she ran in good and swirling ply for a whole fishing day before she fell in and went trickling among the humpbacked stones that huddled in the course of her like a herd of sheep that lie in a park. But there were none of these river-sheep to show to-day. A sleek back here and a sleek back there perhaps, a swirl, a curl, a brown eddy to mark, you'd say, a likely cast, a likely resting place for a running fish. That is, did salmon run the Logie. But no salmon ever ran the Logie because none, as we know, may mount the Linn of Logie. Which was a sad pity, said the angler, for it is a pretty little river, this Logie, and if he, the angler, were Lord Pittenweem, his host's landlord, he'd have the Linn, and the rocks that made it roar, dynamited out of that and a passage made for my lord the salmon.

'This is no *worm* water, anyhow,' thought the fisherman. And he sat down and considered the flies that he wore in his bonnet. There, tied on gut, were a male March brown, a red palmer, two teals-and-red, and a couple more that he could put no name to. 'They'll serve,' said he, 'and if I fish them single they'll see me through the day.'

So our angler took the worms out of the mustard-tin and howked a hole and buried them, moss and all; for he was a young man solicitous of all living things. He mounted the March brown, the March brown that kills well everywhere and, in spite of its specialist title, all the year round.

As he makes his first cast, a slant of sun kisses the water simultaneously with his March brown, and an ouzel speeds upstream and under the angler's very line. The angler notes the pucker where the March brown alights on the Logie Water, and almost before that miniature ring has disappeared there is a flash of gold at the fly. The angler twitches the rod-top, but the trout has missed the March brown. To the repeated cast the fingerling responds with a dash and, hooking himself, tears, for all that he weighs scarce the poor quarter of a pound, a goodly yard of line off a stiffish reel. He is beached (for the angler has never a net) where the Logie, fringed with a lace of foam, sweeps round a tiny curve of sand and small gravel.

The report on the trouts of the Logie has been a true report. This is a remarkable pretty trout, fat and well-liking, high in the shoulder, deep in the golden flank and dotted upon, as it was said that he would be, in crimson dots. So, with a quick tap on his head, the *coup de grâce* that every takeable trout should get ere he be basketed, the game-bag receives him to lie upon two handfuls of hill grass and heather. He is not long alone there for, to the next cast, there is a glancing rise and a trout that might be the twin of the first is making 'her leddyship's' little rod bend and curtsey as he leaps and leaps again. A game and a gallant little fighter he is, but in a minute or so he also is drawn up on to the little circle of sand and his troubles, if ever he had any until now, are over.

The sun is hot by this time and the wet heather is steaming in the kindliness of light and day. The angler can hear the pop of guns somewhere over the march. The tenant of Waupie Lodge has evidently gone to the hill for an after-luncheon hour or two. But our friend is very well content to be where he is. The little Logie trout are worth a lot of grouse and, moreover, none so little as all that are some of them. For on the edge of a smooth *break*, a streaming swirl that marks the sunken boulder, Troll-tossed a million years ago from a mountain top to lie for all time in Logie as the shelter of great trout, the March brown is taken with a devil of a tug. And almost before the angler can raise the point of 'her Leddyship,' for, as such, he has come to know lovingly the little engine at his command, a great trout, every ounce of three-quarters of a pound, fat as butter, golden as guineas, leaps with a shattering leap and, falling with a splash, has gone and the March brown with him.

Well now, that 's a pity and all, but there are over two dozen trout in the game-bag and an uncommon pretty creel they are and uncommon well, no doubt, they will taste, split and fried and eaten with cold fresh butter and a sprig of parsley. And talking of eating it is now three-thirty and the angler has not yet eaten the egg sandwiches that Maggie came running after him with as he went out. He will eat them now therefore. And that done, shall it be the Palmer as a second horse, or one of the anonymous insects—or a teal-and-red ?

A teal-and-red it is, and now the angler will catch another five trouts to make the three dozen and then be facing the lodge-ward two miles up along the march burn, over the rigging, down hill again, and so home. This pool is a real picture of a pool and it is a thousand sorrows that salmon cannot loup the Linn of Logie, for, if they could, you'd say, in this water, that it is here you'd get into a fish. The river shoots and tumbles in peacock tails of amber, over an upheaval of granite it goes, with a flounce of foam, and so, into a deep, fast, porter-coloured pool—a pool that thins out on to a wide shallow of gravel that, in turn, contracts into the rough-and-tumble neck of another important-looking piece of water.

Very quickly the angler catches a further three of the game little trout to whom he has grown accustomed. And the teal-and-red now explores the glassy honey-coloured glide, the fan of clearing river, at the tail of the pool. Then, under dark water, and it all happens in a second of time, there is a welt of sudden silver that shoots athwart just where the teal-and-red—ah, no salmon can loup—but 'her Leddyship's' slight nose is pulled, for all that, most savagely a-down and the line goes off the stiff reel with a shriek.

Twenty yards out and the hooked fish, finding the shallow, throws himself sideways out of the water, clean and beautiful and swift, the salmon who has louped the Linn—the sea-silver salmon who has established a precedent! And back he comes into the dark water with a dash that takes him upstream, up till almost he'd leave the pool at the top of it. Indeed, for a moment he hangs in the very tumult of the entry, then as the angler comes opposite to him, he goes down, down under the boughs of the birks on the far bank and the line buzzing like bees.

Splash, he is on the shallow once more. He jolts and he lunges, and then 'her Leddyship' is pulled almost straight as the rough water at the neck of the next pool takes charge of the fish. Headlong down he goes and headlong the angler follows after him—fifty dividing yards after him, fifty of the sixty yards of line that the reel runs to. The next pool is a bonny pool too—bonny from an artistic point of view anyhow—but rock-staked and swirling, a bad place to beat a fish in. And beaten he must be, for at the tail of this pool boils the Linn itself and plunges over and down in spouts and water-falls. However, there is seventy yards of water to go or ever the fish may make the fall, and half-way thereto is a bit of shelving gravel and backwater which the angler notes well. The fish, six pounds is he, eight perhaps, has had a rattling and if he can be brought to the gravel the rod shall do yet. And so 'her Leddyship' bends and condescends with all her slim might.

And gradually the fish comes to her, heavily now and sometimes with the wedge of his steel-grey tail cutting the surface. The angler holds him as tightly as he dares, gives him such of the butt as he presumes. And the gods are on his side, for, rolling this way and that way, the fish comes to hand. And the angler, with a last guiding pressure, lays him, head and shoulders, on the beach, and dropping 'her Leddyship,' he tails the only salmon that ever louped Logie's Linn.

JACK MULLANY'S FISH STORY

ANONYMOUS

This story appears anonymously in *Irish Pleasantry and Fun* (1892), an anthology of Irish stories published by Messrs M. H. Gill & Son, Dublin.

'YOU see, sir,' said Jack Mullany, 'there's an ould reprobate be the name of Paddy Foley, who rints the grate salmon-ware o' Lismore from the Duke Be the same token, they say that same ware was built by Finn MacCool for the ould monks that Saint Mochuda had there, an', faith, sir, I believe it, for never a one else but giants an' heroes could do sich a work. Well, that's neither here nor there now. Finn an' his heroes, an' Saint Mochuda an' his monks are gone; an' more's the pity, for it's little o' their sort is in Ireland now; but the ware is there yet, an' before ould Paddy lased it the salmon wor so plinty that you could buy 'em for a pinny a pound, when the new fish kem up fresh from the say wid their sides as bright as a shillin', an' the cruds between every flake of the pink cuts as fat as butter. But whin thim steamboats wor invinted, an' ould Foley got a hould o' the ware, the skamin' ould rogue, what does he do, but sinds the fish off to thim English cormorants that before that ate all our fat pigs, an' cows, an' sheep. You see, sir, before the steamboats wor to the fore the English couldn't get the fish fresh from here, an' so the people ate thim themselves. Well, ould Paddy built an ice-house, an' packed the salmon in it, an' sint them off in horseloads every week to Waterford to go be steam to Liverpool, an' thin the ould rogue, not contint with what he caught in the ware an' his nets from Lismore to Blanahowrie, begridges poor fellows like me to get a bit at all, even as much as an ould spint collough [1]; an' so he sets a gang of fellows to mind the rivers all round about, an', bad cess [2] to 'em, many a long day meself, and Pat Donohue, and Pierry Mullowney gave in Waterford Jail through their manes. Though, to give the divil his due, the jailer was never very hard on meself, an' whin I'd be sintinced to a month, or maybe two, at hard labour, ould Triphook 'id keep me the whole time windin' quills for the wavers that wor at work in the jail. But no thanks to Foley or his water-bums for that, you know, nor to ould "Nosey" either, that sintinced me.

'Well, of all the watchmin that ould Foley had on this river or the Finisk, Jack Daly was the wan that annoyed us most. He was here an' there an' everywhere, stuck one time under the eye o' that limekiln yander, watching Poul-na-roothee, where the fish wor fond o' stayin', for they ginirally used to make their scours at the tail o' the hole; another time the spyin' thief would be all day stretched on his belly between two furze bushes, an' whin we'd be afther waitin' for hours an' tryin' every hedge an' ditch within a field o' the glin till we wor sure all was right before we vintured to tie on the gaffs an' dash out up to our middle in the cowld freezin' water, we'd no sooner have the fish on the bank than up the rascal would pop, like a hare from her sate, and cry out, "Well done, me boys, ye'll pay for this work next binch day." I ralely believe some o' the boys were often timpted to drownd him, the spyin' sleveen.[3]

'But sharp as he was, we matched him at last, and this is how we managed it:

'Wan fine frosty mornin', whin the water was as clear as crystal, there wor six as fine salmon as ever you'd wish to set eyes upon in a hole just under that turn o' the cliff below. Some o' the boys wor up bright an' early, takin' a walk be the river for the good o' their health, moryah [4];

[1] very small fish. [2] luck. [3] schemer.
[4] as it were—in the slang sense, I don't think.

but before you could have light to see a white horse in the wather, me bould Jack Daly was standin' sintry on the bank o' the millstream, right above where the salmon wor. We seen him there, an' sint Silve Donohue, Pat's young brother, to see what he was watchin'. Silve soon came back wid the white of his eyes out, as he towld us about the six whoppers he saw in the hole. We felt our teeth watherin' at the story. If we had only tin minutes to ourselves at that hole we could pin every fish ov 'em. We lay down in the grove opposite the spot, where Jack couldn't see us, an' determined to stay there till he wint to breakfast, but deuce a foot he stirred till ould Kate, his mother, kem to call him about tin o'clock. Be that time two of our gang, John Donohue an' meself, had gone round be the bridge, an' hid ourselves in a hedge that ran down to the edge o' the cliff, over Jack's head, an' soon afther we wor joined by young Silve—a regular limb, if ever there was wan.

'To make a long story short, afther a good deal o' coaxin', ould Kate Daly persuaded Jack to go home to the praties [1] while they wor hot, an' she'd stay an' watch the salmon herself, till he kem back, an' as she knew every wan of us, an' had a tongue whose ayquil for bargin' you never heard, we might as well have Jack there as her, if we couldn't get rid ov her, an' that's what we wor detarmined to do, be hook or be crook.

'So, no sooner did Jack go off to his breakfast, than Kate plants herself down on her grug,[2] an' pulls out her stockin' an' begins to knit, keepin' a sharp eye on the salmon all the time. In the manetime John Donohue had packed off Silve up street for a box o' snuff, an' you may be sure the shaver [3] let no grass grow undher his heels on the way. He was soon back, an' thin John sallies round the corner to where Kate was, wid his——

'"Good-mornin', Kate; arrah,[4] what in the world are you doin' here at this time o' day?"

[1] potatoes. [2] haunches. [3] youngster. [4] now.

'"Wisha,[1] thin, John, a vicko,[2] I'm watchin' thim salmon there, while poor Jack was runnin' home to his breakfast, an' I may as well cut me stick out o' the house for iver an' a day, av anything happened to 'em before he comes back, for he says he 's afeerd to trust me, an' he swore like a trooper that he'd be the death o' me av wan ov 'em was missin'. I'm sure I couldn't stop 'em av they took it into their heads to run away out o' that."

'"True for you, Kate, an' 'tis little the vagabones would think of clearin' off under your nose: an' talkin' o' noses puts me in mind o' the snuff." So wid that me lad pulls out the box, an' afther takin' a pinch himself, he asks Kate to take another.

'"Wisha, yes, an' glad to get it, a vicko, for I hadn't a pinch since I got wan from ould Nell Magrath this mornin', as I was gettin' the milk for our breakfast. *Suid or awr slaintha or pinch sniesheen*," [3] sez the poor woman, dippin' in her finger an' thumb for a rousin' pinch, when, jist as she was risin' it to her nose, the young divil Silve slinges [4] up barefooted behind his brother, an' blows the whole contints o' the box into her eyes, mouth, nose, and all.

'The screech the ould woman gev was the signal for the whole ov us, an' while a cat would be lickin' her paw, we had the whole six salmon nabbed, an' in five minutes afther they wor safe undher a pile o' whate in the mill below—for Tom Burke, the miller, was wan of the party.

'Ould Kate's yellin' an' screechin' brought half Barrack-street down through the fields to where she was. You'd think they'd break their necks runnin', for they thought some man was drowned or murdhered; but there was no wan but the ould lady sittin' down, afeered to stir for fear o' fallin' into the river, an' not able to see a stim before her. 'Twasn't long 'till Jack kem runnin' out o' breath; an' the vagabone, thinkin' more o' the salmon

[1] indeed.
[2] my boy.
[3] Here 's to our health in a pinch of snuff.
[4] slinks.

thin he did of his ould mother, didn't stop to ask what ailed her, till he looked into the hole, an' saw some blood on the strand, an' the salmon all gone, an' then he got a'most crazy, an' runnin' up to Kate, he yells out:

'"You ould squallin' hag, where's the salmon gone?"

'"Wisha, may the dickins roast you an' your salmon, an' the curse o' Crummell attind Paddy Foley every day he sees a pavin' stone; sure, 'twas the misfortinit day I ever kem next or near 'em. Oh! me eyes, me eyes!"

'An' so they kep' at it, hammer an' tongs, like two Clonmel gingerbread women, for nearly an hour; an' before half the time was past, the crowd found out how the thing happened; an' tho' some of 'em pretinded to condole wid ould Kate, the never a single sowl of 'em but wor a'most choked with the laughin', an' nayther Jack or his mother ever heard the last of it while they lived.

'The story spread all over the country, an' ould Foley, when he kem to hear it, laughed as loud as any wan at it, for the ould rascal was fond of a joke as well as a decent man like yerself; an', bedad, sir, wan would think you took a pinch o' snuff yerself, now, for the tears are runnin' down yer nose, an' 'tisn't wid cryin' aither. You may be sure 'twas the last time ould Kate volunteered to mount guard for her hopeful vagabone of a son.

'But didn't we come the gamogue [1] on the pair of 'em, sir?'

'Well, Jack, ye got at the blind side of poor Kate, at all events; but what became of Jack after, or did he ever pay you off for the trick?'

'Faith, sir, he hadn't a chance; for ould Paddy gave him the sack, sayin' whin ould women wor sent to do his business, no wonder things went to blazes; an' sure that was true; but Jack couldn't make an honest livin', or do a decent day's work, an' so he turned process-server soon afther.'

[1] trick.

THE ANGLER'S COMPLAINT

By THOMAS TOD STODDART

For THOMAS TOD STODDART, see p. 63. 'The Angler's Complaint' is from Stoddart's *Songs and Poems* (1839).

THEY'VE steekit [1] the waters agen us, Jock,
They've steekit the burnies an' a';
We hae na a chiel to befrien' us, Jock,
Our laird's aye makin' the law.

We'll get neither yallow nor grey-fin, Jock,
Nor bull-heid [2] nor sawmon ava;
The laird he's aye at the savin', Jock,
An' hauds to us weel wi' his law.

Yer flees ye may set them a-bleezin', Jock,
Our wands they may gang to the wa';
It's neither in rhyme nor in reason, Jock,
To coort a kick-up wi' the law.

That ilka intent should miscarry, Jock,
I dinna wunner ava;
Our laird he's kin to the Shirra,[3] Jock,
And sib [4] wi' the loons o' the law.

But faith! ye'll agree it's a hardship, Jock,
To gie up our richts to the craw;
The neist [5] time we meet wi' his lairdship, Jock,
We promise him licks for his law.

[1] closed. [2] bull-trout. [3] sheriff. [4] hand in glove. [5] next.

An' e'en when the mirk is a-nearin', Jock,
  Wi' pock-nets and drag-nets an' a',
We'll gie his bit ponds sic a clearin', Jock,
  Our laird he'll look twice to the law.

We'll no spare a ged[1] or a gudgeon, Jock,
  We'll no spare a fin or a jaw;
Lord pity the crazy curmudgeon, Jock!
  He'll sune tak his leave o' the law!

[1] pike.

THE CORPORAL

By LORD LYTTON

For LORD LYTTON, see p. 66. 'The Corporal' is from Book I, chapter IX, of *Eugene Aram* (1832).

WALTER arrived at the banks of the little brooklet, and was awakened from his reverie by the sound of his own name. He started, and saw the old corporal seated on the stump of a tree, and busily employed in fixing to his line the mimic likeness of what anglers, and, for aught we know, the rest of the world, call the 'violet-fly.'

'Ha! master—at my day's work, you see; fit for nothing else now. When a musket's half worn out, schoolboys buy it—pop it at sparrows. I be like the musket! but never mind—I have not seen the world for nothing. We get reconciled to all things: that's my way—augh! Now, sir, you shall watch me catch the finest trout you have seen this summer: know where he lies—under the bush yonder. Whi-sh! sir, whi-sh!'

The corporal now gave his warrior soul up to the due guidance of the violet-fly: now he whipped it lightly on the wave; now he slid it coquettishly along the surface: now it floated, like an unconscious beauty, carelessly with the tide; and now, like an artful prude, it affected to loiter by the way, or to steal into designing obscurity under the shade of some overhanging bank. But none of these manœuvres captivated the wary old trout, on whose acquisition the corporal had set his heart; and, what was especially provoking, the angler could see distinctly the dark outline of the intended victim as it lay at the bottom—like some well-regulated bachelor, who eyes from afar the charms he has discreetly resolved to neglect.

The corporal waited till he could no longer blind himself to the displeasing fact that the violet-fly was wholly inefficacious; he then drew up his line, and replaced the contemned beauty of the violet-fly with the novel attractions of the yellow-dun.

'Now, sir,' whispered he, lifting up his finger, and nodding sagaciously to Walter. Softly dropped the yellow-dun on the water, and swiftly did it glide before the gaze of the latent trout: and now the trout seemed aroused from his apathy; behold, he moved forward, balancing himself upon his fins: now he slowly ascended towards the surface: you might see all the speckles of his coat—the corporal's heart stood still—he is now at a convenient distance from the yellow-dun; lo, he surveys it steadfastly; he ponders, he see-saws himself to and fro. The yellow-dun sails away in affected indifference; that indifference whets the appetite of the hesitating gazer; he darts forward; he is opposite the yellow-dun—he pushes his nose against it with an eager rudeness—he—no, he does *not* bite, he recoils, he gazes again with surprise and suspicion on the little charmer; he fades back slowly into the deeper water, and then, suddenly turning his tail towards the disappointed bait, he makes off as fast as he can—yonder—yonder, and disappears! No, that's he leaping yonder from the wave: Jupiter! what a noble fellow! What leaps he at?—A real fly! 'Damn his eyes!' growled the corporal.

'You might have caught him with a minnow,' said Walter, speaking for the first time.

'Minnow!' repeated the corporal, gruffly; 'ask your honour's pardon. Minnow!—I have fished with the yellow-dun these twenty years, and never knew it fail before. Minnow!—baugh! But ask pardon; your honour is very welcome to fish with a minnow if you please it.'

'Thank-you, Bunting. And pray what sport have you had to-day?'

'Oh—good, good,' quoth the corporal, snatching up his

basket and closing the cover, lest the young squire should pry into it. No man is more tenacious of his secrets than your true angler. 'Sent the best home two hours ago; one weighed three pounds on the faith of a man; indeed, I'm satisfied now; time to give up': and the corporal began to disjoint his rod.

'Ah, sir!' said he, with a half sigh, 'a pretty river this, don't mean to say it is not; but the river Lea for my money. You know the Lea?—not a morning's walk from Lunnon. Mary Gibson, my first sweetheart, lived by the bridge—caught such a trout there by the by!—had beautiful eyes—black, round as a cherry—five feet eight without shoes—might have listed in the forty-second.'

'Who, Bunting!' said Walter, smiling; 'the lady or the trout?'

A FATAL SUCCESS

By HENRY VAN DYKE

HENRY VAN DYKE (1852-1933), American clergyman, professor of English literature, diplomat, and miscellaneous author, was a skilful angler and became one of the best known of American writers on angling through his *Little Rivers* (1895), *Fisherman's Luck* (1899), from which 'A Fatal Success' is taken, by permission of Messrs Charles Scribner's Sons, and *Days Off* (1907), which has two angling stories.

'*What surprises me in her behaviour*,' *said he*, '*is its thoroughness. Woman seldom does things by halves, but often by doubles*.'— SOLOMON SINGLEWITZ, *The Life of Adam*.

BEEKMAN DE PEYSTER was probably the most passionate and triumphant fisherman in the Petrine Club. He angled with the same dash and confidence that he threw into his operations in the stock-market. He was sure to be the first man to get his flies on the water at the opening of the season. And when we came together for our fall meeting, to compare notes of our wanderings on various streams and make up the fish-stories for the year, Beekman was almost always 'high hook.' We expected, as a matter of course, to hear that he had taken the most and the largest fish.

It was so with everything that he undertook. He was a masterful man. If there was an unusually large trout in a river, Beekman knew about it before anyone else, and got there first and came home with the fish. It did not make him unduly proud, because there was nothing uncommon about it. It was his habit to succeed, and all the rest of us were hardened to it.

When he married Cornelia Cochrane, we were consoled for our partial loss by the apparent fitness and brilliancy of the match. If Beekman was a masterful man, Cornelia was certainly what you might call a mistressful woman. She had been the head of her house since she was eighteen years old. She carried her good looks like the family plate; and when she came into the breakfast-room and said good morning, it was with an air as if she presented every one with a check for a thousand dollars. Her tastes were accepted as judgments, and her preferences had the force of laws. Wherever she wanted to go in the summer-time, there the finger of household destiny pointed. At Newport, at Bar Harbour, at Lenox, at Southampton, she made a record. When she was joined in holy wedlock to Beekman De Peyster, her father and mother heaved a sigh of satisfaction, and settled down for a quiet vacation in Cherry Valley.

It was in the second summer after the wedding that Beekman admitted to a few of his ancient Petrine cronies, in moments of confidence (unjustifiable, but natural), that his wife had one fault.

'It is not exactly a fault,' he said, 'not a positive fault, you know. It is just a kind of a defect, due to her education, of course. In everything else she's magnificent. But she doesn't care for fishing. She says it's stupid—can't see why anyone should like the woods—calls camping out the lunatic's diversion. It's rather awkward for a man with my habits to have his wife take such a view. But it can be changed by training. I intend to educate her and convert her. I shall make an angler of her yet.'

And so he did.

The new education was begun in the Adirondacks, and the first lesson was given at Paul Smith's. It was a complete failure.

Beekman persuaded her to come out with him for a day on Meacham River, and promised to convince her of the charm of angling. She wore a new gown, fawn-colour and violet, with a picture-hat, very taking. But the Meacham River trout was shy that day; not even

Beekman could induce him to rise to the fly. What the trout lacked in confidence the mosquitoes more than made up. Mrs De Peyster came home much sunburned, and expressed a highly unfavourable opinion of fishing as an amusement and of Meacham River as a resort.

'The nice people don't come to the Adirondacks to fish,' said she; 'they come to talk about the fishing twenty years ago. Besides, what do you want to catch that trout for? If you do, the other men will say you bought it, and the hotel will have to put in a new one for the rest of the season.'

The following year Beekman tried Moosehead Lake. Here he found an atmosphere more favourable to his plan of education. There were a good many people who really fished, and short expeditions in the woods were quite fashionable. Cornelia had a camping-costume of the most approved style made by Dewlap on Fifth Avenue—pearl-grey with linings of rose silk—and consented to go with her husband on a trip up Moose River. They pitched their tent the first evening at the mouth of Misery Stream, and a storm came on. The rain sifted through the canvas in a fine spray, and Mrs De Peyster sat up all night in a waterproof cloak, holding an umbrella. The next day they were back at the hotel in time for lunch.

'It was horrid,' she told her most intimate friend, 'perfectly horrid. The idea of sleeping in a shower-bath, and eating your breakfast from a tin plate, just for sake of catching a few silly fish! Why not send your guides out to get them for you?'

But, in spite of this profession of obstinate heresy, Beekman observed with secret joy that there were signs, before the end of the season, that Cornelia was drifting a little, a very little but still perceptibly, in the direction of a change of heart. She began to take an interest, as the big trout came along in September, in the reports of the catches made by the different anglers. She would saunter out with the other people to the corner of the porch to see the fish weighed and spread out on the grass. Several times she went with Beekman in the canoe to Hardscrabble Point, and showed distinct evidences of pleasure when he caught large trout. The last day of the season, when he returned from a successful expedition to Roach River and Lily Bay, she inquired with some particularity about the results of his sport; and in the evening, as the company sat before the great open fire in the hall of the hotel, she was heard to use this information with considerable skill in putting down Mrs Minot Peabody of Boston, who was recounting the details of her husband's catch at Spence Pond. Cornelia was not a person to be contented with the back seat, even in fish-stories.

When Beekman observed these indications he was much encouraged, and resolved to push his educational experiment briskly forward to his customary goal of success.

'Some things can be done, as well as others,' he said in his masterful way, as three of us were walking home together after the autumnal dinner of the Petrine Club, which he always attended as a graduate member. 'A real fisherman never gives up. I told you I'd make an angler out of my wife; and so I will. It has been rather difficult. She is "dour" in rising. But she's beginning to take notice of the fly now. Give me another season, and I'll have her landed.'

Good old Beekman! Little did he think—— But I must not interrupt the story with moral reflections.

The preparations that he made for his final effort at conversion were thorough and prudent. He had a private interview with Dewlap in regard to the construction of a practical fishing-costume for a lady, which resulted in something more reasonable and workmanlike than had ever been turned out by that famous artist. He ordered from Hook & Catchett a lady's angling-outfit of the most enticing description—a split-bamboo rod, light as a girl's wish, and strong as a matron's will; an oxidised silver reel, with a monogram on one side, and a sapphire set in the handle for good luck; a book of flies, of all sizes and colours, with the correct names inscribed in gilt letters on each page. He surrounded his favourite sport with an aureole of elegance and beauty. And then he took Cornelia in September to the Upper Dam at Rangeley.

She went reluctant. She arrived disgusted. She stayed incredulous. She returned—— Wait a bit, and you shall hear how she returned.

The Upper Dam at Rangeley is the place, of all others in the world, where the lunacy of angling may be seen in its incurable stage. There is a cosy little inn, called a camp, at the foot of a big lake. In front of the inn is a huge dam of grey stone, over which the river plunges into a great oval pool, where the trout assemble in the early fall to perpetuate their race. From the tenth of September to the thirtieth, there is not an hour of the day or night when there are no boats floating on that pool, and no anglers trailing the fly across its waters. Before the late fishermen are ready to come in at midnight, the early fishermen may be seen creeping down to the shore with lanterns in order to begin before cock-crow. The number of fish taken is not large—perhaps five or six for the whole company on an average day—but the size is sometimes enormous—nothing under three pounds is counted—and they pervade thought and conversation at the Upper Dam to the exclusion of every other subject. There is no driving, no dancing, no golf, no tennis. There is nothing to do but fish or die.

At first, Cornelia thought she would choose the latter alternative. But a remark of that skilful and morose old angler, McTurk, which she overheard on the verandah after supper, changed her mind.

'Women have no sporting instinct,' said he. 'They only fish because they see men doing it. They are imitative animals.'

That same night she told Beekman, in the subdued tone which the architectural construction of the house imposes upon all confidential communications in the bedrooms, but with resolution in every accent, that she proposed to go fishing with him on the morrow.

'But not on that pool, right in front of the house, you understand. There must be some other place, out on the lake, where we can fish for three or four days, until I get the trick of this wobbly rod. Then I'll show that old bear, McTurk, what kind of an animal woman is.'

Beekman was simply delighted. Five days of diligent practice at the mouth of Mill Brook brought his pupil to the point where he pronounced her safe.

'Of course,' he said patronisingly, 'you haven't learned all about it yet. That will take years. But you can get your fly out thirty feet, and you can keep the tip of your rod up. If you do that, the trout will hook himself, in rapid water, eight times out of ten. For playing him, if you follow my directions, you'll be all right. We will try the pool to-night, and hope for a medium-sized fish.'

Cornelia said nothing, but smiled and nodded. She had her own thoughts.

At about nine o'clock Saturday night, they anchored their boat on the edge of the shoal where the big eddy swings around, put out the lantern and began to fish. Beekman sat in the bow of the boat, with his rod over the left side; Cornelia in the stern, with her rod over the right side. The night was cloudy and very black. Each of them had put on the largest possible fly, one a 'Bee-Pond' and the other a 'Dragon'; but even these were invisible. They measured out the right length of line, and let the flies drift back until they hung over the shoal, in the curly water where the two currents meet.

There were three other boats to the left of them. McTurk was their only neighbour in the darkness on the right. Once they heard him swearing softly to himself, and knew that he had hooked and lost a fish.

Away down at the tail of the pool, dimly visible through the gloom, the furtive fisherman, Parsons, had anchored his boat. No noise ever came from that craft. If he wished to change his position, he did not pull up the anchor and let it down again with a bump. He simply lengthened or shortened his anchor rope. There was no click of the reel when he played a fish. He drew in and paid out the line through the rings by hand, without a sound. What he thought when a fish got away, no one knew, for he never said it. He concealed his angling as if it had been a conspiracy. Twice that night they heard a faint splash in the water near his boat, and twice they saw him put his arm over the side in the darkness and bring it back again very quietly.

'That's the second fish for Parsons,' whispered Beekman, 'what a secretive old Fortunatus he is! He knows more about fishing than any man on the pool, and talks less.'

Cornelia did not answer. Her thoughts were all on the tip of her own rod. About eleven o'clock a fine, drizzling rain set in. The fishing was very slack. All the other boats gave it up in despair, but Cornelia said she wanted to stay out a little longer; they might as well finish up the week.

At precisely fifty minutes past eleven, Beekman reeled up his line, and remarked with firmness that the holy Sabbath day was almost at hand and they ought to go in.

'Not till I've landed this trout,' said Cornelia.

'What? A trout! Have you got one?'

'Certainly; I've had him on for at least fifteen minutes. I'm playing him Mr Parsons's way. You might as well light the lantern and get the net ready; he's coming in towards the boat now.'

Beekman broke three matches before he made the lantern burn; and when he held it up over the gunwale, there was the trout sure enough, gleaming ghostly pale in the dark water, close to the boat, and quite tired out. He slipped the net over the fish and drew it in—a monster.

'I'll carry that trout, if you please,' said Cornelia, as they stepped out of the boat; and she walked into the camp, on the last stroke of midnight, with the fish in her hand, and quietly asked for the steelyard.

Eight pounds and fourteen ounces—that was the weight. Everybody was amazed. It was the 'best fish' of the year. Cornelia showed no sign of exultation, until just as John was carrying the trout to the ice-house. Then she flashed out:

'Quite a fair imitation, Mr McTurk—isn't it?'

Now McTurk's best record for the last fifteen years was seven pounds and twelve ounces.

So far as McTurk is concerned, this is the end of the story. But not for the De Peysters. I wish it were. Beekman went to sleep that night with a contented spirit. He felt that his experiment in education had been a success. He had made his wife an angler.

He had indeed, and to an extent which he little suspected. That Upper Dam trout was to her like the first taste of blood to the tiger. It seemed to change, at once, not so much her character as the direction of her vital energy. She yielded to the lunacy of angling, not by slow degrees (as first a transient delusion, then a fixed idea, then a chronic infirmity, finally a mild insanity), but by a sudden plunge into the most violent mania. So far from being ready to die at Upper Dam, her desire now was to live there—and to live solely for the sake of fishing—as long as the season was open.

There were two hundred and forty hours left to midnight on the thirtieth of September. At least two hundred of these she spent on the pool; and when Beekman was too exhausted to manage the boat and the net and the lantern for her, she engaged a trustworthy guide to take Beekman's place while he slept. At the end of the last day her score was twenty-three, with an average of five pounds and a quarter. His score was nine, with an average of four pounds. He had succeeded far beyond his wildest hopes.

The next year his success became even more astonishing. They went to the Titan Club in Canada. The ugliest and most inaccessible sheet of water in that territory is Lake Pharaoh. But it is famous for the extraordinary fishing at a certain spot near the outlet, where there is just room enough for one canoe. They camped on Lake Pharaoh for six weeks, by Mrs De Peyster's command; and her canoe was always the first to reach the fishing-ground in the morning, and the last to leave it in the evening.

Some one asked him, when he returned to the city, whether he had good luck.

'Quite fair,' he tossed off in a careless way; 'we took over three hundred pounds.'

'To your own rod?' asked the inquirer, in admiration.

'No-o-o,' said Beekman, 'there were two of us.'

There were two of them, also, the following year, when they joined the Natasheebo Salmon Club and fished that celebrated river in Labrador. The custom of drawing lots every night for the water that each member was to angle over the next day, seemed to be especially designed to fit the situation. Mrs De Peyster could fish her own pool and her husband's too. The result of that year's fishing was something phenomenal. She had a score that made a paragraph in the newspapers and called out editorial comment. One editor was so inadequate to the situation as to entitle the article in which he described her triumph 'The Equivalence of Woman.' It was well-meant, but she was not at all pleased with it.

She was now not merely an angler, but a 'record' angler of the most virulent type. Wherever they went, she wanted, and she got, the pick of the water. She seemed to be equally at home on all kinds of streams, large and small. She would pursue the little mountain-brook trout in the early spring, and the Labrador salmon in July, and the huge speckled trout of the northern lakes in September, with the same avidity and resolution. All that she cared for was to get the best and the most of the fishing at each place where she angled. This she always did.

And Beekman—well, for him there were no more long separations from the partner of his life while he went off to fish some favourite stream. There were no more home-comings after a good day's sport to find her clad in cool and dainty raiment on the verandah, ready to welcome him with friendly badinage. There was not even any casting of the fly around Hardscrabble Point while she sat in the canoe reading a novel, looking up with mild and pleasant interest when he caught a larger fish than usual, as an older and wiser person looks at a child playing some innocent game. Those days of a divided interest between man and wife were gone. She was now fully converted, and more. Beekman and Cornelia were one; and she was the one.

The last time I saw the De Peysters he was following her along the Beaverkill, carrying a landing-net and a basket, but no rod. She paused for a moment to exchange greetings, and then strode on down the stream. He lingered for a few minutes longer to light a pipe.

'Well, old man,' I said, 'you certainly have succeeded in making an angler of Mrs De Peyster.'

'Yes, indeed,' he answered—'haven't I?' Then he continued, after a few thoughtful puffs of smoke, 'Do you know, I'm not quite so sure as I used to be that fishing is the best of all sports. I sometimes think of giving it up and going in for croquet.'

THE FROG AND THE TWO FISH

From the PANCHATANTRA

This story from the Panchatantra is in the rendering given in chapter I of Anaryan's (i.e. F. F. Arbuthnot's) *Early Ideas: A Group of Hindoo Stories* (1881).

In a certain reservoir were two fishes, one named Satabuddhi, or the hundred-witted, the other Sahasrabuddhi or the thousand-witted. They had a friend, a frog, named Ekabuddhi or the single-wit, with whom they were in the habit of meeting and conversing at the edge of the water. When the usual party assembled, they saw several fishermen approach with their nets, and heard them say to one another, 'This pool is full of fish, the water is but shallow; we will come to-morrow morning and drag it.' They then went away. When they had departed, the frog said to his friends, 'What is to be done, had we not better make our escape?', at which the thousand-witted laughed and said, 'Never fear, they have only talked of coming. Yet if they should come I will be answerable for your safety as well as my own. I shall be a match for them, as I know all the courses of the water.' The hundred-witted one said, 'My friend here is very right; wherever there is a way for the breeze, for water or its tenants, or for the rays of the sun, the intellect of a sagacious person will penetrate. By following his counsel your life would be in no peril, even had you approached the abodes of the manes. Stay where you are, even I will undertake your safety.' The frog said, 'I have perhaps but limited talent, a mere singleness of sense, but that tells me to flee, and therefore whilst I can I shall withdraw with my mate to another piece of water.' The frog left the pool that night. In the morning the fishermen arrived, and the lake was so beset with nets that all the fish, turtles, crabs, and other tenants of the water, were made prisoners, and amongst them Satabuddhi and Sahasrabuddhi, in spite of their boasted cunning, were caught and killed. The frog saw the fishermen on their return, and recognising Satabuddhi on the head of one man, and Sahasrabuddhi dragged along with cords by another, he pointed them out to his mate, saying, 'See where Satabuddhi or the hundred-witted one is carried on the head, and there also is Sahasrabuddhi or the thousand-witted one, whilst I, who am Ekabuddhi or the single-wit, still can gambol in the crystal stream.'

OF A KEEPER

By WILLIAM CAINE

For William Caine, see p. 251. 'Of a Keeper' is from 'Of Two Keepers' in *An Angler at Large* (1911) and is here given by permission of Messrs Kegan Paul, Trench, Trubner, & Co.

This adventure befell me because one night a kindly-disposed man offered me a day on some priceless water which he had in Hampshire. I was going to Scotland or Manchester or one of those places where there are no chalk streams almost immediately, but I could just sandwich in my day if I took it on the morrow. Therefore I hardly went to bed at all, and at the hour when I was in the habit of recomposing myself to the slumber from which a persistent yet dispirited housemaid had waked me, I got out of the down train into God's second county.

The wind blew soft from the south-west, and the sky looked as if the sun were scotched for the day. I told myself that I should certainly catch a great many trout, and I almost believed it. I swore that an angler's is the only incomparable life, and as I took the high road through the valley I kicked up the dust in clouds for sheer high spirits. This was to be a day of days. And so I came to the cottage of William Pound.

I was naturally anxious to reach the water at the earliest possible moment, but courtesy required me to report myself to William, and nature demanded a breakfast at the Inn. Afterwards I desired to go away by myself and fish. But when I had found William, and had satisfied him of my right to take the lives of his employer's trout (if I could), and had mentioned that I would go and get some food, and that I supposed I should see him later on—which means, in plain English, that I would be happy to compensate him for the loss of my society during the day by a suitable gift at the end of it—when, I say, I had done all this, and made as if to leave him, he asserted that there was no use in fishing before ten-thirty, and invited me to visit his crops of vegetables. Now I had deprived myself so far of a hot breakfast and of several hours' sleep in order to gain the riverside by nine-thirty, and I had no wish to contemplate William's orderly rows of beetroots, lettuces, and cabbages, or even potatoes. My soul was attuned to less earthly things. I felt, however, that a refusal must be churlish, and I consented. Here I made a vital mistake, for from that moment William had me at his mercy.

It was nearly half-past nine, when, having brought his last cauliflower to my notice, William gave me permission to seek my breakfast. He would call for me at the Inn at ten. This was the moment for speaking up. I should have said: 'William, do not call for me at ten; do not follow me to the river. I shall do capitally alone. Do not put yourself out on my account. Stay here, William, and cultivate your garden.' But I had not the courage to say this. It were easier to decline an invitation to Windsor. There is no doubt that he felt that in accompanying me he would be doing me not so much a service as an honour, and to hint that I would rather be without him was beyond me. 'But he will quickly tire,' I reflected, 'of seeing me blundering about and putting down rising fish. He will stay an hour at the most. I shall soon be alone.' And I agreed to wait for him at the Inn till ten. As I ate my eggs and toast I indulged in the hope that after all William might find wire-worms among his carnations, and as I put up my rod and greased my line in the porch, that hope grew stronger with each minute which brought the hand of the clock nearer to the hour, for still no glimpse of William was visible upon the road. At ten precisely he was with me, nor did he forget ponderously to draw out his watch by way of emphasising his punctuality.

We were presently beside a small backwater. 'Here,' said William, 'we can begin to fish. This rod,' he continued (taking it from my hand), 'is no good. I have one up at my cottage which is worth ten of he.' So saying, he selected a fly from his cap, tied it on, and oiled it—all with great deliberation. 'You won't find it easy under this tree, sir,' he remarked, as he got out line. 'There be a whopper lays under that elder. Shall I try for 'un?' It was at this point that I ought to have said: 'No, William; I will.' But he did not wait for my answer, and I could not snatch the rod out of his very hands. He rose the fish and appeared well satisfied. 'Told 'ee so, sir,' he said. 'Now do 'ee cast in among they flags.' I was glad enough to recover the rod, and fished for some minutes without success. 'My, what a whop!' said William, though I could see for myself that the fly had not touched the water very lightly. Presently he said: 'We'd best get down to the bottom of thick meadow. Main stream be easier for 'ee.' Down there we found some fly, and a rising trout, over which I made a number of infamous casts, to the accompaniment of William's 'Too fur to the right. Not up to 'un. 'Ee won't find 'un there, sir. My, what a whop!' and other encouragements. Finally, 'Let me have a whack,' said he, and in sheer curiosity to see if he could cheat the wind and the drag and the trout all together, I gave place to him. Neither the wind nor the drag seemed to present any difficulties to William, though the trout would not come up, and for twenty minutes I was witness of an exhibition of skill which I gladly confess was of the finest quality. What he would have done with the rod up at the cottage I do not know, but with mine he did about fifty things which I shall never learn to do if I fish till I am a hundred—which is William's age.

The sight of a rise in a very attractive spot gave me

courage to ask for a turn, and so I got a nice fish. 'Now,' said I, in a foolish burst of generosity, 'you must get one.' Nothing rose for the next two hundred yards, but William fished the water carefully up to a bridge on which I sat smoking and marvelling at his dexterity. It was midday, and the fly was fairly off the water when he left me to go and get a bit of dinner. He promised to be back in an hour. Had I possessed a spark of courage, I should have told him plainly not to come back. I should have reminded him that I had come all the way from London to fish, and not to sit about and watch him doing it. But my chance of taking a firm stand had gone by, and I could only swear to make the most of my lonely hour. Of it three-quarters passed without incident, and then I got to work on a fair fish that rose irregularly, at what I do not know. I put, perhaps, five flies over him, and was just tying on an alder when I observed the massive figure of William moving remorselessly towards me across the water-meadows. In three minutes he was angling for that trout. Now I had found it and fished for it, and by all the rules of the game it was mine to catch or put down. But I was too cowed to protest. I am not man enough for Williams and people like him. William tried fly after fly, fishing with such delicacy and precision that I almost forgave him. At last he tied on what he called a drake's hare's ear. I did not know the fly, but it looked a likely one, and I up and asserted myself, clutched the rod which he had laid very incautiously on the grass, and at the second throw had the exquisite pleasure of landing the fish before William's eyes.

I was now at peace with all the world, and yielded up the rod without a murmur. At four o'clock William had landed two fish and risen three others, and was engaged at an angle of the stream up to his knees in water (where I could not follow him) over three good trout which he said he could see. Every now and then he would answer me when I spoke, and sometimes when I coughed he would tell me how he was getting on. But most of the time he was quite unconscious of my presence on the bank, and I am sure that he was very happy. I was wet and cold and hungry by this time, and I left him (he hardly turned his head) and went away to the Inn for tea. On my return he was still at the same place. The food must have given me heart, for I found myself able to claim the rod, and in a very short time William had discovered a trout and I had caught it. The custom was now thoroughly established, that after I had grassed a fish William was to have the rod, and I followed him up the stream till six-thirty when he took me to a stretch of water which we had not yet visited. Here there was no fly, so from that time I had the rod to myself until it was too dark for me to see, when William resumed it, and finished the day with an exhibition of long casting under the far bank, in the course of which the spear of the butt fell into the long grass and was lost to me for ever.

SPLENDIDE MENDAX

By 'CHRISTOPHER NORTH'

For 'CHRISTOPHER NORTH', see p. 91. 'Splendide Mendax' is from the *Noctes Ambrosianæ* for June 1830.

Shepherd. Tell me, Mr North, what for ye didna come out to Innerleithen and fish for the silver medal o' the St Ronan's Border Club? I'm thinkin' ye was feared.

North. I have won so many medals, James, that my ambition *αἰεί ἀριστεύειν* [1] is dead—and, besides, I could not think of beating the Major.

Shepherd. You beat the Major! You micht at baggy-mennons,[2] but he could gie ye a stane-wecht either at trouts or fish. He's just a warld's wunner wi' the sweevil, a warlock wi' the worm, and wi' the flee a feenisher. It's a pure pleesur to see him playin' a pounder wi' a single hair. After the first twa-three rushes are ower, he seems to wile them wi' a charm awa' into the side, ontil the gerss or the grevvel, whare they lie in the sunshine as if they were asleep, His tackle, for bricht airless days, is o' gossamere; and at a wee distance aff, you think he's fishin' without ony line ava, till whirr gangs the pirn, and up springs the sea trout, silver-bricht, twa yards out o' the water, by a delicate jerk o' the wrist, hyeucked inextricably by the tongue clean ower the barb o' the Kirby-bend. Midge-flees!

North. I know the Major is a master in the art, James; but I will back the Professor [3] against him for a rump-and-dozen.[4]

Shepherd. You would just then, sir, lose your rump.

[1] always to be best.
[2] minnows.
[3] *i.e.* Professor Wilson, North himself.
[4] rump of beef and a dozen of claret.

The Professor can fish nae better nor yoursell. You would make a pretty pair in a punt at the perches; but as for the Tweed, at trouts or sawmon, I'll back wee Jamie again' ye baith, gin ye'll only let me fish for him the bushy pools.

North. In me the passion of the sport is dead—or say rather dull; yet have I gentle enjoyment still in the 'Angler's silent Trade.' But heavens! my dear James! how in youth—and prime of manhood too—I used to gallop to the glens, like a deer, over a hundred heathery hills, to devour the dark-rolling river, or the blue breezy loch! How leaped my heart to hear the thunder of the nearing waterfall! and lo! yonder flows, at last, the long dim shallow rippling hazel-banked line of music among the broomy braes, all astir with back-fins over its surface; and now, that the feed is on, teeming with swift-shooting, bright-bounding, and silver-shining scaly life, most beauteous to behold, at every soft alighting of the deceptive lure, captivating and irresistible even among a shower of natural leaf-born flies aswarm in the air from the mountain-woods!

Shepherd. Aye, sir, in your younger days you maun hae been a verra deevil. What creelfu's you maun hae killed!

North. A hundred and thirty in one day in Loch Awe, James, as I hope to be saved—not one of them under——

Shepherd. A dizzen pun'—and twa-thirds o' them aboon't. Athegither a ton. If you are gaun to use the lang bow, sir, pu' the string to your lug, never fear the yew crackin', and send the grey-guse-feathered arrow first wi' a lang whiz, and then wi' a short thud, right intill the bull's ee, at ten score, to the astonishment o' the ghost o' Robin Hood, Little John, Adam Bell, Clym o' the Clough, and William o' Cloudeslee.

North. My poor dear old friend McNeil of Hayfield—God rest his soul—it is in heaven—at ninety as lifeful as a boy at nineteen—held up his hands in wonder as under a shady tree I laid the hundred and thirty yellow Shiners on the bank at his feet. Major Mackay,

'A lambkin in peace, and a lion in war,'

acknowledged me as a formidable rival now in angling as in leaping of yore. Auchlian, God bless him, the warm-hearted and the hospitable—long may he live and be happy, among the loving and beloved—from that day began to respect the Lowlanders. And poor Stevenson, mild and brave—a captain in the navy, James—now no more—with his own hands wreathed round my forehead a diadem of heather-bells, and called me King of the Anglers.

Shepherd. Poo! That was nae day's fishin' ava, man, in comparison to ane o' mine on St Mary's Loch. To say naething about the countless sma' anes, twa hunder about half a pun', ae hunder about a haill pun', fifty about twa pun', five-and-twenty about fowre pun', and the lave rinnin' frae half a stane up to a stane and a half, except about half a dizzen, aboon a' wecht, that put Geordie Gudefallow and Huntly Gordon to their mettle to carry them pechin' [1] to Mount Benger on a haun-barrow.

North. Well done, Ulysses.

Shepherd. Anither day, in the Megget, I caucht a cartfu'. As it gaed doon the road, the kintra-folk thocht it was a cartfu' o' herrins—for they were a' preceesely o' ae size to an unce—and though we left twa dizzen at this house—and four dizzen at that house—and a gross at Henderland—on coontin' them at hame in the kitchen, Leezy made them out forty dizzen, and Girzzy forty-twa, aught; sae a dispute haen arisen, and o' coorse a bet, we took the census ower again, and may these be the last words I sall ever speak, gin they didna turn out to be Fourty-Five!

North. The heaviest fish I ever killed was in the river

[1] panting.

Awe—ninety pound neat. I hooked him on a Saturday afternoon—and had small hopes of killing him—as I never break the Sabbath. But I am convinced that, within the hour, he came to know that he was in the hands of Christopher North—and his courage died. I gave him the butt so cruelly, that in two hours he began to wallop; and at the end of three he lay dead at my feet, just as

'The star of Jove, so beautiful and large,'

tipped the crest of Cruachan.

Shepherd. Hoo lang?

North. So beautifully proportioned, that, like that of St Peter's or St Paul's, you did not feel his mighty magnitude till after long contemplation. Then, you indeed knew that he was a sublime fish, and could not choose but smile at the idea of any other salmon.

Tickler. Mr De Quincey, now that these two old fools have got upon angling——

Shepherd. Twa auld fules! You great, starin', Saracen-headed Langshanks! If it werena for bringin' Mr North intill trouble by haen a dead man fund within his premises, deil tak me gin I wudna fractur' your skull wi' ane o' the cut-crystals!

OLD FAITHFUL

By JOHN TAINTOR FOOTE

JOHN TAINTOR FOOTE (born 1881), American story writer and dramatist, noteworthy for his dog, horse-racing, and fishing stories. The now well-known *A Wedding Gift*, from which 'Old Faithful' is taken by permission of the author and of the D. Appleton-Century Company, appeared in 1924 and was followed by a series of other sparkling fishing stories: *Fatal Gesture* (1933), *Change of Idols* (1935), *Daughter of Delilah* (1936), *Broadway Angler* (1937).

'AND you never heard of Old Faithful?' George asked suddenly. 'Evidently not, from what you said a while ago. Well, a lot of people have, believe me. Men have gone to the Cuddiwink district just to see him. As I've already told you, he lay beside a ledge in the pool below Horseshoe Falls. Almost nothing else in the pool. He kept it cleaned out. Worst sort of cannibal, of course—all big trout are. That was the trouble—he wanted something that would stick to his ribs. No flies for him. Did his feeding at night.

'You could see him dimly if you crawled out on a rock that jutted above the pool and looked over. He lay in about ten feet of water, right by his ledge. If he saw you, he'd back under the ledge, slowly, like a submarine going into dock. Think of the biggest thing you've ever seen, and that's the way Old Faithful looked, just lying there as still as the ledge. He never seemed to move anything, not even his gills. When he backed in out of sight he seemed to be drawn under the ledge by some invisible force.

'Ridgway—R. Campbell Ridgway—you may have read his stuff, Brethren of the Wild, that sort of thing—claimed to have seen him move. He told me about it one night. He said he was lying with just his eyes over the edge of the rock, watching the trout. Said he'd been there an hour, when down over the falls came a young red squirrel. It had fallen in above and been carried over. The squirrel was half drowned, but struck out feebly for shore. Well, so Ridgway said—Old Faithful came up and took Mister Squirrel into camp. No hurry; just came drifting up, sort of inhaled the squirrel and sank down to the ledge again. Never made a ripple, Ridgway said; just business.

'I'm telling you all this because it's necessary that you get an idea of that trout in your mind. You'll see why in a minute. No one ever had hold of him. But it was customary, if you fished the Cuddiwink, to make a few casts over him before you left the stream. Not that you ever expected him to rise. It was just a sort of gesture. Everybody did it.

'Knowing that Isabelle had never seen trout taken before, I made a day of it—naturally. The trail to camp leaves the stream just at the falls. It was pretty late when we got to it. Isabelle had her arms full of—heaven knows what—flowers and grass and ferns and fir branches and coloured leaves. She'd lugged the stuff for hours. I remember once that day I was fighting a fourteen-inch fish in swift water and she came to the bank and wanted me to look at a ripe blackberry—I think it was—she'd found. How does that strike you? And listen! I said, "It's a beauty, darling." That's what I said—or something like that. . . . Here, don't you pay that check! Bring it here, waiter!'

'Go on, George!' I said. 'We haven't time to argue about the check. You'd come to the trail for camp at the falls.'

'I told Isabelle to wait at the trail for a few minutes, while I went below the falls and did the customary thing for the edification of Old Faithful. I only intended to make three or four casts with the Number Twelve Fly and the hair-fine leader I had on, but in getting down to the pool I hooked the fly in a bush. In trying to loosen it, I stumbled over something and fell. I snapped the leader like a thread, and since I had to put on another, I tied on a fairly heavy one as a matter of form.

'I had reached for my box for a regulation fly of some sort when I remembered a fool thing that Billy Roach had given me up on the Beaverkill the season before. It was fully two inches long ; I forget what he called it. He said you fished it dry for bass or large trout. He said you worked the tip of your rod and made it wiggle like a dying minnow. I didn't want the contraption, but he'd borrowed some fly oil from me and insisted on my taking it. I'd stuck it in the breast pocket of my fishing-jacket and forgotten it until then.

'Well, I felt in the pocket and there it was. I tied it on and went down to the pool. Now let me show you the exact situation.' George seized a fork. 'This is the pool.' The fork traced an oblong figure on the table-cloth. 'Here is Old Faithful's ledge.' The fork deeply marked this impressive spot. 'Here are the falls, with white water running to here. You can only wade to this point here, and then you have an abrupt six-foot depth. "But you can put a fly from here to here with a long line," you say. No, you can't. You've forgotten to allow for your back cast. Notice this bend here? That tells the story. You're not more than twenty feet from a lot of birch and what not, when you can no longer wade. "Well then, it's impossible to put a decent fly on the water above the sunken ledge," you say. It looks like it, but this is how it's done: right here is a narrow point running to here, where it dwindles off to a single flat rock. If you work out on the point you can jump across to this rock—situated right here—and there you are, with about a thirty-foot cast to the sunken ledge. Deep water all around you, of course, and the rock is slippery;

but—there you are. Now notice this small cove, right here. The water from the falls rushes past it in a froth, but in the cove it forms a deep eddy, with the current moving round and round, like this.' George made a slow circular motion with the fork. 'You know what I mean?'

I nodded.

'I got out on the point and jumped to the rock; got myself balanced, worked out the right amount of line and cast the dingaree Bill had forced on me, just above the sunken ledge. I didn't take the water lightly and I cast again, but I couldn't put it down decently. It would just flop in—too much weight and too many feathers. I suppose I cast it a dozen times, trying to make it settle like a fly. I wasn't thinking of trout—there would be nothing in there except Old Faithful—I was just monkeying with this doodle-bug thing, now that I had it on.

'I gave up at last and let it lie out where I had cast it. I was standing there looking at the falls roaring down, not thinking about anything in particular, when I remembered Isabelle, waiting up on the trail. I raised my rod preparatory to reeling in and the what-you-may-call-'im made a kind of a dive and wiggle out there on the surface. I reached for my reel handle. Then I realised that the thingamajig wasn't on the water. I didn't see it disappear, exactly; I was just looking at it, and then it wasn't there. "That's funny," I thought, and struck instinctively. Well, I was fast—so it seemed—and no snags in there. I gave it the butt three or four times, but the rod only bowed and nothing budged. I tried to figure it out. I thought perhaps a water-logged timber had come diving over the falls and upended right there. Then I noticed the rod take more of a bend and the line began to move through the water. It moved out slowly, very slowly, into the middle of the pool. It was exactly as though I was hooked onto a freight train just getting under way.

'I knew what I had hold of then, and yet I didn't

believe it. I couldn't believe it. I kept thinking it was a dream, I remember. Of course, he could have gone away with everything I had any minute if he'd wanted to, but he didn't. He just kept moving slowly, round and round the pool. I gave him what pressure the tackle would stand, but he never noticed a little thing like that; just kept moving around the pool for hours, it seemed to me. I'd forgotten Isabelle; I admit that. I'd forgotten everything on earth. There didn't seem to be anything else on earth, as a matter of fact, except the falls and the pool and Old Faithful and me. At last Isabelle showed up on the bank above me, still lugging her ferns and what not. She called down to me above the noise of the falls. She asked me how long I expected her to wait alone in the woods, with night coming on.

'I hadn't had the faintest idea how I was going to try to land the fish until then. The water was boiling past the rock I was standing on, and I couldn't jump back to the point without giving him slack and perhaps falling in. I began to look around and figure. Isabelle said, "What on earth are you doing?" I took off my landing-net and tossed it to the bank. I yelled, "Drop that junk quick and pick up that net!" She said, "What for, George?" I said, "Do as I tell you and don't ask questions!" She laid down what she had and picked up the net and I told her to go to the cove and stand ready.

'She said, "Ready for what?" I said, "You'll see what presently. Just stand there." I'll admit I wasn't talking quietly. There was the noise of the falls to begin with, and—well, naturally I wasn't.

'I went to work on the fish again. I began to educate him to lead. I thought if I could lead him into the cove he would swing right past Isabelle and she could net him. It was slow work—a three-ounce rod—imagine! Isabelle called, "Do you know what time it is?" I told her to keep still and stand where she was. She didn't say anything more after that.

'At last the fish began to come. He wasn't tired—he'd never done any fighting, as a matter of fact—but he'd take a suggestion as to where to go from the rod. I kept swinging him nearer and nearer the cove each time he came around. When I saw he was about ready to come, I yelled to Isabelle. I said, "I'm going to bring him right past you, close to the top. All you have to do is to net him."

'When the fish came round again, I steered him into the cove. Just as he was swinging past Isabelle the stuff she'd been lugging began to roll down the bank. She dropped the landing-net on top of the fish and made a dive for those leaves and grasses and things. Fortunately the net handle lodged against the bank, and after she'd put her stuff in a nice safe place she came back and picked up the net again. I never uttered a syllable. I deserve no credit for that. The trout had made a surge and shot out into the pool, and I was too busy just then to give her any idea of what I thought.

'I had a harder job getting him to swing in again. He was a little leery of the cove, but at last he came. I steered him toward Isabelle and lifted him all I dared. He came up nicely, clear to the top. I yelled, "Here he comes! For God's sake, don't miss him!" I put everything on the tackle it would stand and managed to check the fish for an instant right in front of Isabelle.

'And this is what she did: it doesn't seem credible—it doesn't seem humanly possible; but it's a fact that you'll have to take my word for. She lifted the landing-net above her head with both hands and brought it down on top of the fish with all her might! . . . . . . "I didn't miss him, George," I heard Isabelle say.'

BY OTTER'S STREAM

By GILBERT FRANKAU

GILBERT FRANKAU (born 1884), English novelist. The first of the novels, *One of Us* (1912), was in verse. 'By Otter's Stream' is from Canto XVII of this and is here given by permission of the author.

IT is the instant of the evening rise.
  The sun-rim slips behind the corn-clad hill;
Adown the vale a homing heron flies;
  Delicious breezes crinkle mead and rill.
Now from his sedgy lairs, wherein he lies
  Daylong content to flap the scarlet gill,
The Monarch of the Pool swims sauntering out,
Sovereign-contemptuous of the lesser trout.

Monarch, heed well the greenheart's fatal flicker!
  Let eyes be keen to know the man-made dun
That falls so softly where the real flies bicker
  Below the arching bridge of Otterton!
Else shall the cruel creel of Hardy's wicker
  Enfold your corpse before the set of sun;
Else shall the nether water's overlord
Feel the constraining yoke of Rowland Ward.

In the marsh-pasture of the Devon kine—
  So milking-proud that none dare doom them veal—
Low-crouched, Jack spies the tell-tale bubbles shine.
  The rod-point sways; metallic, clicks the reel;
Hums through its rings the deftly lengthened line;
  Far-flung and true, outcurves the feathered steel.
Now—if there's power in hackle, cord or oil—
Mark, and be swift to strike the speckled spoil!

Barely a foot above that greedy throat!
  Another second, and those jaws shall shut!
Watch where the trailing feathers cock and float,
  Watch for the shimmer of the straightened gut!—
A swirl! a leap! a flash of silver coat!
  The greenheart quivers to its agate butt . . .
Struck, and well struck! The barbed death has him fast:
Let but the playing justify the cast.

Taut line until your top-joint nearly smashes,
  There's danger where the waterweeds grow rank!—
Slack him!—but 'ware another of those brashes!—
  Look out! he'll slip you if he gains the bank—
Reel him again—quick!—almost spent he splashes—
  Give him the butt, man!—roll him on his flank—
And ere those Titan struggles start afresh,
Pluck from your belt, and ply, the landing-mesh!

Zest of all zests—no Muse can give to me,
  Whose casts are far from Angler Izaak's rite,
Who may not know that tingling ecstasy
  When the three-pounder, fished-for night by night,
Shall never wrench another Wickham free.
  Proudly Jack stands, still flushing from the fight . . .
And lo! adown the marge of Otter's stream,
Appears the goddess of his journey's dream.

Swiftly she moves; behind her sweeping skirt,
  The kingcups bow: beneath her ample straw,
With loosened curls audacious zephyrs flirt.
  She seems a Dryad of the inner shaw;
Save that arch mouth, disparted, overpert,
  Belies the chill of Artemisian law;
Save that the smiles in azure orbs bewray
The artless damsel of a later day.

Hard at her heels, majestic, deep of jowl,
  Ambles forlorn the melancholy Dane,
Whom hawkers hate and tramps that nightly prowl.
  From Axwell Kennels by the northern main,
Where the cropped Porthos throats a prizeless growl,
  His line is traced through Redgrave's noblest strain.
Though softer limbs may hold romance in fee,
The hound's display the nobler pedigree.

The vole plops bedwards, and the pigeons coo;
  The rushes murmur and the ripples eddy.
Where one head bent before, are bending two,
  Above those great gills stiffening already.
Eyes that admire, meet other eyes that woo;
  Hands that would touch, meet other hands unsteady;
Lips that speak only of a captured fish,
Would fain give utterance to a fonder wish.

The sun is down. The river smoothes to glass.
  Into the leafy woodlands, dark and cool,
Where hart's-tongue fern and foxglove fleck the grass—
  Lover and lass and Monarch of the Pool,
And silver-brindled guardian—they pass.
  Dear Alice, thou who lov'dst him yet at school,
Will thy touch still the passions that destroy?
KEE-OW, the prescient peacocks cry, KEE-OY.

THE KING-FISH

By THOMAS HUGHES

For THOMAS HUGHES, see p. 167. 'The King-fish' is from volume III, chapter III, of *Tom Brown at Oxford* (3 vols 1861).

TOM was out soon after sunrise the next morning. He never wanted to be called when there was a trout-stream within reach; and his fishing instinct told him that, in these sultry dog-days, there would be little chance of sport when the sun was well up. So he let himself gently out of the hall door—paused a moment on the steps to fill his chest with the fresh morning air, as he glanced at the weathercock over the stables—and then set to work to put his tackle together on the lawn, humming a tune to himself as he selected an insinuating red hackle and alder fly from his well-worn book, and tied them on to his cast. Then he slung his creel over his shoulder, picked up his rod, and started for the water.

As he passed the gates of the stable-yard, the keeper came out—a sturdy bullet-headed fellow, in a velveteen coat, and cord breeches and gaiters—and touched his hat. Tom returned the salute, and wished him good morning.

'Mornin', sir; you be about early.'

'Yes; I reckon it's the best time for sport at the end of June.'

''Tis so, sir. Shall I fetch a net and come along?'

'No, thank you, I'll manage the ladle myself. But which do you call the best water?'

'They be both middling good. There ain't much odds atwixt 'em. But I sees most fish movin' o' mornins in the deep water down below.'

'I don't know; the night was too hot,' said Tom, who had examined the water the day before, and made up his mind where he was going. 'I'm for deep water on cold days; I shall begin with the stickles up above. There's a good head of water on, I suppose?'

'Plenty down this last week, sir.'

'Come along, then; we'll walk together, if you're going that way.' So Tom stepped off, brushing through the steaming long grass, gemmed with wild flowers, followed by the keeper; and, as the grasshoppers bounded chirruping out of his way, and the insect life hummed and murmured, and the lark rose and sang above his head, he felt happier than he had done for many a long month. So his heart opened towards his companion, who kept a little behind him.

'What size do you take 'em out, keeper?'

'Anything over nine inches, sir. But there's a smartish few fish of three pounds, for them as can catch 'em.'

'Well, that's good; but they ain't easy caught, eh?'

'I don't rightly know, sir; but there's gents comes as stands close by the water, and flogs downstream with the sun in their backs, and uses all manner o' vlies, wi' long names; and then thay gwoes away, and says, 'tain't no use flying here, 'cos there's so much cadis bait and that like.'

'Ah, very likely,' said Tom, with a chuckle.

'The chaps as catches the big fishes, sir,' went on the keeper, getting confidential, 'is thay cussed night-line poachers. There's one o' they as has come here this last spring-tide—the artfullest chap as ever I come across, and down to every move on the board. He don't use no shove nets nor such-like tackle, not he; I s'pose he don't call that sport. Besides, I got master to stake the whole water, and set old knives and razors about in the holes, so that don't answer; and this joker all'us goes alone—which, in course, he couldn't do with nets. Now, I knows within five or six yards where that chap sets his lines, and I finds 'em, now and again, set the artfullest you ever see. But 'twould take a man's life to look arter him, and I knows he gets maybe a dozen big fish a week, do all as I knows.'

'How is it you can't catch him, keeper?' said Tom, much amused.

'Why, you see, sir, he don't come at any hours. Drat un!' said the keeper, getting hot; 'blessed if I don't think he sometimes comes down among the haymakers and folk at noon, and up lines and off, while thay chaps does nothing but snigger at un—all I knows is, as I've watched till midnight, and then on again at dawn for'n, and no good come on it but once.'

'How was that?'

'Well, one mornin', sir, about last Lady-day, I comes quite quiet upstream about dawn. When I gets to Farmer Giles's piece (that little rough bit, sir, as you sees t'other side the stream, two fields from our outside bounds), I sees un a stooping down and hauling in's line. "Now's your time, Billy," says I, and up the hedge I cuts, hotfoot, to get betwixt he and our bounds. Wether he seen me or not, I can't mind; leastways, when I up's head t'other side the hedge, vorrights where I seen him last, there was he a-trotting upstream quite cool, a-pocketing a two-pounder. Then he seen me, and away we goes side by side for the bounds—he this side the hedge and I t'other; he takin' the fences like our old greyhound-bitch, Clara. We takes the last fence on to that fuzzy field as you sees there, sir (parson's glebe, and out of our liberty), neck and neck, and I turns short to the left, 'cos there warn't no fence now betwixt he and I. Well, I thought he'd a dodged on about the fuz. Not he; he slouches his hat over's eyes, and stands quite cool by fust fuz bush—I minded then as we was out o' our beat. Hows'-ever, my blood was up; so I at's him then and there, no words lost, and fetches a crack at's head wi' my stick. He fends wi' his'n; and then, as I rushes in to collar'n, dash'd if 'e didn't meet I full, and catch I by the thigh and collar and send I slap over's head into a fuz bush. Then he chuckles fit to bust hisself, and cuts his stick, while I creeps out full o' prickles, and wi' my breeches tore shameful. Dang un!' cried the keeper, while Tom roared, 'he's a lissum wosbird, that I 'ool say, but I'll be up sides wi' he next time I sees un. Whorson fool as I was, not to stop and look at un and speak to un! Then I should ha' know'd un again; and now he med be our parish clerk for all as I knows.'

'And you've never met him since?'

'Never sot eye on un, sir, arly or late—wishes I had.'

'Well, keeper, here's half a crown to go towards mending the hole in your breeches, and better luck at the return match. I shall begin fishing here.'

'Thank'ee, sir. You keep your cast pretty nigh that there off bank, and you med have a rare good un ther'. I seen a fish suck there just now as warn't spawned this year, nor last nether.'

And away went the communicative keeper.

'Stanch fellow, the keeper,' said Tom to himself as he reeled out yard after yard of his tapered line, and with a gentle sweep dropped his collar of flies lightly on the water, each cast covering another five feet of the dimpling surface. 'Good fellow, the keeper—don't mind telling a story against himself—can stand being laughed at—more than his master can. Ah, there's the fish he saw sucking, I'll be bound. Now, you beauties, over his nose, and fall light—don't disgrace your bringing up!' and away went the flies quivering through the air and lighting close to the opposite bank, under a bunch of rushes. A slight round eddy followed below the rushes, as the cast came gently back across the current.

'Ah, you see them, do you, old boy?' thought Tom. 'Say your prayers, then, and get shrived!' and away went the flies again, this time a little below. No movement. The third throw, a great lunge and splash, and the next moment the lithe rod bent double, and the gut collar spun along, cutting through the water like mad. Up goes the great fish twice into the air, Tom giving him the point; then upstream again, Tom giving him the butt, and beginning to reel up gently. Down goes the great fish into the swaying weeds, working with his tail like a twelve-horse screw. 'If I can only get my nose to ground,' thinks he. So thinks Tom, and trusts to his tackle, keeping a steady strain on trouty, and creeping gently downstream. 'No go,' says the fish, as he feels his nose steadily hauled round, and turns with a swirl downstream. Away goes Tom, reeling in, and away goes the fish in hopes of a slack—away, for twenty or thirty yards—the fish coming to the top lazily, now and again, and holding on to get his second wind. Now a cart track crossed the stream, no weeds, and shallow water at the side. 'Here we must have it out,' thinks Tom, and turns fish's nose upstream again. The big fish gets sulky, twice drifts towards the shallow, and twice plunges away at the sight of his enemy into the deep water. The third time he comes swaying in, his yellow side gleaming and his mouth open; and, the next moment, Tom scoops him out on to the grass, with a 'whoop' that might have been heard at the house. 'Two-pounder, if he's an ounce,' says Tom, as he gives him the *coup de grâce,* and lays him out lovingly on the fresh green sward.

Tom had splendid sport that summer morning. As the great sun rose higher, the light morning breeze, which had curled the water, died away; the light mist drew up into light cloud, and the light cloud vanished, into cloudland, for anything I know; and still the fish rose, strange to say, though Tom felt it was an affair of minutes, and acted accordingly. At eight o'clock he was about a quarter of a mile from the house, at a point in the stream of rare charms both for the angler and the lover of gentle river beauty. The main stream was crossed by a lock, formed of a solid brick bridge with no parapets, under which the water rushed through four small arches, each of which could be closed in an instant by letting down a heavy wooden lock gate, fitted in grooves on the upper side of the bridge. Such locks are frequent in the west-country streams—even at long distances from mills and millers, for whose behoof they were made in old days, that the supply of water to the mill might be easily regulated. All pious anglers should bless the memories of the old builders of them, for they are the very paradises of the great trout who frequent the old brickwork and timber foundations. The water in its rush through the arches had of course worked for itself a deep hole, and then, some twenty yards below, spread itself out in wanton joyous ripples and eddies over a broad surface some fifty yards across, and dashed away towards a little island some two hundred yards below, or rolled itself slowly back towards the bridge again, up the backwater by the side of the bank, as if longing for another merry rush through one of those narrow arches. The island below was crowned with splendid alders, willows forty feet high, which wept into the water, and two or three poplars; a rich mile of water meadow, with an occasional willow or alder, lay gleaming beyond; and the view was bounded by a glorious wood, which crowned the gentle slope, at the foot of which the river ran. Another considerable body of water, which had been carried off above from the main stream to flush the water meadows, rejoined its parent at this point; it came slowly down a broad artificial ditch running parallel with the main stream; and the narrow strip of land which divided the two streams ended abruptly just below the lock, forming a splendid point for bather or angler. Tom had fixed on this pool as his *bonne bouche*, as a child keeps its plums till the last, and stole over the bridge, stooping low to gain the point above indicated. Having gained it, he glanced round to be aware of the dwarf ash-trees and willows which were scattered along the strip and might catch heedless collars and spoil sport, when, lying lazily almost on the surface where the backwater met the stream from the meadows, he beheld the great-grandfather of all trout—a fellow two feet long and a foot in girth at the shoulders, just moving fin enough to keep him from turning over on to his back. He threw himself flat on the ground and crept away to the other side of the strip; the king-fish had not seen him; and the next moment Tom saw him suck in a bee, laden with his morning's load of honey, who touched the water unwarily close to his nose. With a trembling hand, Tom took off his tail fly, and, on his knees, substituted a governor; then, shortening his line after wetting his mimic bee in the pool behind him, tossed it gently into the monster's very jaws. For a moment the fish seemed scared, but, the next, conscious in his strength, lifted his nose slowly to the surface and sucked in the bait.

Tom struck gently, and then sprang to his feet. But the Heavens had other work for the king-fish, who dived swiftly under the bank; a slight jar followed, and Tom's rod was straight over his head, the line and scarce a yard of his trusty gut collar dangling about his face. He seized this remnant with horror and unsatisfied longing, and examined it with care. Could he have overlooked any fraying which the gut might have got in the morning's work? No; he had gone over every inch of it not five minutes before, as he neared the pool. Besides, it was cut clean through, not a trace of bruise or fray about it. How could it have happened? He went to the spot and looked into the water; it was slightly discoloured, and he could not see the bottom. He threw his fishing coat off, rolled up the sleeve of his flannel shirt, and, lying on his side, felt about the bank and tried to reach the bottom, but couldn't. So, hearing the half-hour bell ring, he deferred further inquiry and stripped in silent disgust for a plunge in the pool. Three times he hurled himself into the delicious rush of the cold chalk stream, with that utter abandon in which man, whose bones are brittle, can only indulge when there are six or seven feet of water between him and mother earth; and, letting the stream bear him away at its own sweet will to the shallows below, struck up again through the rush and the roar to his plunging place. Then, slowly and luxuriously dressing, he lit his short pipe—companion of meditation—and began to ruminate on the escape of the king-fish. What could have cut his collar? The more he thought the less he could make it out. When suddenly he was aware of the keeper on his way back to the house for orders and breakfast.

'What sport, sir?'

'Pretty fair,' said Tom, carelessly, lugging five plump speckled fellows, weighing some seven and a half pounds, out of his creel, and laying them out for the keeper's inspection.

'Well, they be in prime order, sir, surely,' says the keeper, handling them; 'they allus gets mortal thick across the shoulders while the May-fly be on. Lose any, sir?'

'I put in some little ones up above, and lost one screamer just up the back ditch there. He must have been a four-pounder, and went off, and be hanged to him, with two yards of my collar, and a couple of first-rate flies. How on earth he got off I can't tell!' and he went on to unfold the particulars of the short struggle.

The keeper could hardly keep down a grin. 'Ah, sir,' said he, 'I thinks I knows what spwiled your sport. You owes it all to that chap as I was a-telling you of, or my name's not Willum Goddard'; and then, fishing the lock-pole with a hook at the end of it out of the rushes, he began groping under the bank, and presently hauled up a sort of infernal machine, consisting of a heavy lump of wood, a yard or so long, in which were carefully inserted the blades of four or five old knives and razors, while a crop of rusty jagged nails filled up the spare space.

Tom looked at it in wonder. 'What devil's work have you got hold of there?' he said at last.

'Bless you, sir,' said the keeper, ''tis only our shove-net traps as I wur a-telling you of. I keeps hard upon a dozen on 'em, and shifts 'em about in the likeliest holes; and I takes care to let the men as is about the water meadows see me a-sharpening on 'em up a bit, wi' a file, now and again. And, since master gev me orders to put 'em in, I don't think they tries that game on not once a month.'

'Well, but where do you and your master expect to go to if you set such things as those about?' said Tom, looking serious. 'Why, you'll be cutting some fellow's hand or foot half off one of these days. Suppose I'd waded up the bank to see what had become of my cast?'

'Lor', sir, I never thought o' that,' said the keeper, looking sheepish, and lifting the back of his short hat off his head to make room for a scratch; 'but,' added he, turning the subject, 'if you wants to keep thay artful wosbirds off the water you must frighten 'em wi' summat out o' the way. Drattle 'em, I knows they puts me to my wits' end; but you'd never 'a' had five such fish as them before breakfast, sir, if we didn't stake the waters.'

CLEOPATRA AND ANTONY

By PLUTARCH

PLUTARCH (*c.* A.D. 46-120) in his life of Antony in the *Parallel Lives* tells what must be one of the best of angling stories, as well as one of the oldest. It is here given in Sir Thomas North's translation (1579). Shakespeare, after Plutarch, touches also on the theme in Act II, scene V, of his *Antony and Cleopatra.*

ON a time Antonius went to angle for fish, and when he could take none, he was as angrie as could be, bicause Cleopatra stoode by. Wherefore he secretly commaunded the fisher men, that when he cast in his line, they should straight dive under the water, and put a fishe on his hooke which they had taken before: and so snatched up his angling rodde, and brought up fish twise or thrise. Cleopatra found it straight, yet she seemed not to see it, but wondred at his excellent fishing: but when she was alone by her selfe among her owne people, she told them howe it was, and bad them the next morning to be on the water to see the fishing. A number of people came to the haven, and got into the fisher boates to see this fishing. Antonius then threw in his line and Cleopatra straight commaunded one of her men to dive under water before Antonius' men, and to put some old salte fish upon his baite, like unto those that are brought out of the contrie of Pont. When he had hong the fish on his hooke, Antonius thinking he had taken a fishe in deede, snatched up his line presently. Then they all fell a laughing. Cleopatra laughing also, said unto him: Leave us (my Lord) Ægyptians (which dwell in the contrie of Pharus and Canobus) your angling rodde: this is not thy profession: thou must hunt after conquering of realmes and contries.

POACHER JOCK

By NORMAN MACLEOD

NORMAN MACLEOD (1812-1872), one of the greatest of Scottish divines, was distinguished also as a writer, and 'Poacher Jock' is from chapter VII of *The Starling* (1867), one of his stories.

'WHAT luck, Johnnie?' asked Hugh, the keeper, as his son entered with his fishing-basket over his shoulder.

'Middling only,' replied John, 'the water was raither low, and the tak' wasna guid. There were plenty o' rises, but they were unco shy. But I hae gotten, for a' that, a wheen [1] for breakfast'; and he unslung his basket and poured out from it a number of fine trout.

Jock's attention was now excited. Here was evidence of an art which he flattered himself he understood and could speak about.

'Pretty fair,' was his remark, as he rose and examined them; 'whaur got ye them?'

'In the Blackcraig water,' the boy replied.

'Let me luik at yer flee, laddie?' asked Jock. The boy produced it. 'Broon heckle—bad!—ye should hae tried a teal's feather on a day like this.'

Johnnie looked with respect at the stranger.

'Are *ye* a fisher?' he asked.

'I hae tried my han',' said Jock. And so the conversation began, until soon the two were seated together at the window. Then followed such a talk on the mysteries of the craft as none but students of the angle could understand—the arrangement and effect of various 'dressings' of wings, bodies, heckles, etc., being discussed with intense interest, until all felt they had in Jock a master.

[1] few.

'Ye seem to understan' the business weel,' remarked Hugh.

'I wad need,' replied Jock. 'When a man's life, no to speak o' his pleasure, depen's on 't, he needs to fish wi' a watchfu' e'e and canny han'. But at a' times, toom [1] or fu', it's a great diverteesement!'

Both Johnnie and his father cordially assented to the truth of the sentiment.

'Eh, man! what a conceit it is whan ye reach a fine run on a warm spring mornin', the wuds [2] hotchin' [3] wi' birds, an' dauds [4] o' licht noos and thans glintin' on the water; an' the water itsel' in trim order, a wee doon, after a nicht's spate, and wi' a drap o' porter in't, an' rowin' [5] and bubblin' ower the big stanes, curlin' into the linn and oot o't; and you up tae the henches in a dark neuk whaur the fish canna see ye; an' than to get a lang cast in the breeze that soughs in the bushes, an' see yer flee licht in the verra place ye want, quiet as a midge lichts on yer nose, or a bumbee on a flower o' clover, an'——'

Johnnie was bursting with almost as much excitement as Jock, but did not interrupt him except with a laugh expressive of his delight.

'An' then,' continued Jock, 'whan a muckle chiel o' a salmon, wi'oot time to consider whether yer flee is for his wame [6] or only for his mouth—whether it's made by natur' or by Jock Hall—plays flap! and by mistak' gangs to digest what he has gotten for his breakfast, but canna swallow the line alang wi' his mornin' meal till he taks some exercise!—an' than to see the line ticht, and the rod bendin' like a heuk, and tae fin' something gaun frae the fish up the line and rod till it reaches yer verra heart that thumps *pit pat* at yer throat, in spite o' you; until the bonnie cratur', after rinnin' up and doon like mad, skulkin' beside a stane to cure his teethache, and

[1] empty. [2] woods. [3] alive with.
[4] great patches. [5] rolling. [6] stomach.

trying every dodge, at last gies in, comes to yer han' beat in fair play, and lies on the shore sayin' "Wae's me" wi' his tail an' makin' his will wi' his gills and mouth time aboot!—eh, man! it's splendid!' Jock wearied himself with the description.

'Whaur hae ye fished?' asked Hugh, after a pause in which he had evidently enjoyed Jock's description.

'In the wast water and east water; in the big linn and wee linn, in the Loch o' the Whinns, in the Red Burn, an' in——'

'I dinna ken thae waters at a',' remarked the keeper, interrupting him, 'nor ever heard o' them!'

'Maybe no,' said Jock with a laugh, 'for they're in the back o' the beyonts, and that's a place few folk hae seen, I do assure you—ha! ha! ha!' Jock had, in fact, fished the best streams watched by the keepers throughout the whole district.

Johnnie was delighted with this new acquaintance, and looked up to him with the greatest reverence.

'What kin' o' flee do ye fish wi'?' he asked. 'Hae ye ony aboot ye enoo [1]?'

'I hae a few,' said Jock, as he unbuttoned his waistcoat, displaying a tattered shirt within. Then diving into some hidden recess near his heart, he drew forth a large old pocket-book and placed it on the table. He opened it with caution and circumspection, and spread out before the delighted Johnnie and his no less interested father, entwined circles of gut, with flies innumerable. 'That's the ane,' Jock would say, holding up a small, black, hairy thing, 'I killed ten dizzen wi'—thumpers tae, three pun's some o' them—afore twa o'clock. Eh, man, he's a murderin' chiel this!' exhibiting another. 'But it was this ither ane,' holding up one larger and more gaudy, 'that nicked four salmon in three hours to their great surprise! And thae flees,' taking up other favourites, 'wi' the muirfowl wing and black body, are guid killers; but isna this

[1] just now.

a cracker wi' the wee touch o' silver? It killt mair salmon —whaur, ye needna speir—than I could carry hame on a heather wuddie[1]! But,' he added after a pause, 'I maun, as yer frien', warn ye that it's no the flee, nor the water nor the rod, the win', nor the licht, can do the job wi'oot the watchfu' e'e and steady han'! I think I could maist catch fish in a boyne[2] o' water if there were ony tae catch!'

[1] rope. [2] tub.

CHAFER'S PATTERN

By FRANCIS FRANCIS

For Francis Francis, see p. 29. 'Chafer's Pattern' is from 'A Week on the Brattle' in *Hot Pot* (1880).

'Chap here last week, name of Chafer; out-and-out good fisherman,' said Charley in course of conversation at Mrs Wadlow's angling inn, 'but so jealous that he hates to see any fellow anywhere on the water. Catches baskets and baskets of good fish, even in quite still quiet places, you know, where I never could raise one.'

'What fly did he use?'

'Ah, that's the point! Nobody knew.'

'But wouldn't he tell you?'

'Not he. If you asked him, he'd say, with a sort of confiding smile, a smile that was childlike and bland, "Oh! a little dun, you know—a little dun," as if there weren't forty little duns; and I knew he was lying too, ever so far, because I was once reclining on the bank, closer than he thought, on the other side, when he passed, and I saw his fly fall on the quiet water, and it was a jolly big one—I could see that much.'

'But couldn't you ever get a sight of his book?'

'Not likely. He took it to bed with him, and never parted with it on any pretence. He's worse than Jock Grant of Kennaweell, who said to me once, "A loe ma brither verra, verra dearly; oh, verra dearly, inteet; but'd no trust him wi' ma flee buik on any pratance, d' ye ken."'

'What an infernal skunk! That's a sort of man I would have no hesitation in lifting up the hatches on, and sending any amount of weed down on him, on the first day of the Mayfly. Well?'

'Wait a bit. I had him at last.'

'No! How did you sarcumvent that weasel?'

'Well, I'll tell you. Just below Pwnwddel Wood at the end, under a bush, there's a nice, smart little run close under the bank. It's a rare place for good fish, but you never hardly see them rise, because there's an eddy there that sucks your line, as well as most flies, and such light matters, under water. There's always a rattling trout or two there, and it is a very favourite cast of Chafer's. I was peeping in there over the bank one day, when I saw a big root under the bank, and an idea struck me I thought might be worth trying. I went and got a nice little blackthorn bush, got a bit of bell-wire, and fastened it to the stump of the bush, then made it fast to the old root, sinking the bush about two inches under water. The next morning I went down the same side again, got up into the wood about fifty yards or so from the river, where I could sight the proceedings without being seen, and waited. I had been there about half an hour, when I saw Chafer coming down the opposite bank, and I chuckled as he stopped overright my trap. Swish, swoop! The fly went across, just above the eddy; the line tightened. Chafer thought he had a fish, and struck merrily, and then I saw his rod bend. "You're in it this time, old chap!" said I; and so he was, sure enough. "What the—etc., etc., etc.—is this?" growled old Chafer; "never knew anything settle there before. Some beastly bramble hung up, I expect; but it will come presently"; and he tried a steady strain. But blackthorn and bell-wire were too much for gut and horsehair, and, after trying all he knew (as it was too deep to wade), he had at last to conclude for a break, which he effected, losing half his casting-line. "Humph!" he grunted, as he stumped off; "come home up that bank to-night, and get that fly back; never do to leave it there." "Will you, my angel?" says I, as soon as he was out of sight; "not if this child knows it." I went to the place, took off my coat, fisted the bush, undid the wire, and there on the topmost branch of all was the coveted fly. This I featly removed, chucked the bush away, carefully destroyed all trace of my intervention, and walked quietly home with my prize—and there it is.

'It was a big sandy-red hackle, with a lemon-yellow silk body. I have seen this fly on several rivers, and, though it is used of double or treble the size of the ordinary flies, somehow this fly kills most of the big fish, and that even in bright weather and stillish water at times, though best for afternoons and evenings. What the trout take it for I can't conceive.

'Chafer came home that evening profoundly disturbed. He was awfully sulky and puzzled, but never opened on his loss, for fear someone should go a-hunting for the fly. Ha, ha! he little knew that it was snug in my pocket. I always have a small stock of feathers and silk, in cases of emergency, and the next day I had the best bag I ever had; and ha! ha! I beat Chafer. Mrs Wadlow told me, with a chuckle, that Chafer saw my dish in the cellar, and glowered like thunder at it; and whether or no he thought that I had had any hand in the fly job I don't know, but the next day he went home quite suddenly, and I sent at once to you. Here you are, and to-morrow we'll try Chafer's pattern.'

ISAAC ON A CHALK STREAM

By WILLIAM CAINE

For WILLIAM CAINE, see p. 251. 'Isaac on a Chalk Stream' is from 'Of Purfling Again, with a Colloquy' in *An Angler at Large* (1911) and is here given by permission of Messrs Kegan Paul, Trench, Trubner, & Co.

(Piscator; Venator; Raptor, a pot-hunter; Corydon)

Piscator. Well met, my loving scholar. You have prevented me, I see.

Venator. Ay, marry, good master. I have awaited your coming this hour. Shall we be walking towards the river?

Piscator. Nay, sir, you have been betimes indeed. But there is no cause to be so brisk. Trust me, on such a dull day we shall find no fly on the water thus early. And it is my purpose to drink my morning's draught in this same good ale-house where you have so patiently expected me. Hostess, a cup of your best drink. Another. Come, I will try a third.

Venator. But, sir, were it not better to be by the waterside? There is no chance of a fish here.

Piscator. As much, my honest scholar, as beside the very stream. The fly will not show before seven minutes after eleven of the clock, at soonest. Hostess, a draught of ale.

Venator. Good master, you do amaze me. How know you this so surely?

Piscator. Let me tell you, sir, that your fly is a creature very obedient to the action of the elements. On a grey morning, such as we have to-day, he lacketh the genial warmth of the sun to bring him forth. But forth he must come, will he, nill he, and that he will do this morning at seven after eleven. Nor will he fail us. Come, will you drink a civil glass with me?

Venator. Most gladly, sir; but I had rather be a-fishing. See, the sun is shining now.

Piscator. Fear not, worthy scholar; the fly will appear neither sooner nor later than I say.

Venator. I pray you, master, tell me how you have got this prodigious knowledge?

Piscator. Marry, sir, by learning. But I confess that no direction can be given to make weatherwise a man of dull capacity. Your good health, my impatient scholar.

Venator. But, sir, may we not take some trouts, though there be no fly?

Piscator. Scholar, you are young to the angle, and so you stand excused. This is the talk of your pot-hunting fishers who do not scruple to throw an alder to a trout that is breakfasting on green drakes. Let me tell you, scholar, that no honest angler will wet a line until the fly be up. Hostess, a pot of ale.

Venator. Good master, I crave your pardon. Shall we not be going?

Piscator. Why, my honest scholar, I think we shall, for it is now eleven of the clock, and it is no more than seven minutes' walk to Willows Bridge, where I do purpose to begin.

. . . . . .

Venator. Sir, there is a gentleman on the bridge.

Piscator. An angler, by his rod; and, by his reaching the river at this hour, one who hath skill in the craft. Good-day, sir.

Raptor. Good-morrow, sir. What sport?

Piscator. Why, sir, none.

Raptor. None, sir? You have been fishing to ill purpose then.

Piscator. Nay, sir, I have been fishing to no ill purpose, for I have not been fishing at all.

Raptor. Then, sir, you have my sympathy, for a merrier hour's work I have never known. I have taken the number limit, three brace of as fine trouts as ever were seen. There is eighteen pounds weight here, in my fish-bag.

Venator. This is some pot-hunting fisherman, I fear.

Piscator. Why, sir, you have indeed been fortunate. But I am told that a silver doctor, run through these Clere hatch-holes——

Raptor. A murrain o' your silver doctors, sir! It was a dark olive quill.

Piscator. Indeed, sir?

Raptor. Ay, marry! The rise of a lifetime, sir. The fly came on at nine of the clock, but there hath been none for this half-hour, and so I am for home with my three brace.

Piscator. To sell them at the fishmonger's, sir?

Raptor. Good-day, sir.

Venator. Alas, I fear we have lost some noble sport.

Piscator. I fear that this good gentleman is a liar. Did you mark, scholar, how he made no offer to show us this great catch of trouts?

Venator. True, good master. Then we are to doubt his story?

Piscator. Most shrewdly.

Venator. I see no fly, and it is eight minutes past the hour.

Piscator. Nay, my most particular scholar, would you hold me to a minute? No man may be so nice as to the moment of its coming. We shall see it in good time, never fear. Hand me your rod; a pretty tool indeed, but ill-balanced and something too limber for our manner of fishing. See, this is mine; stiff, springy, and lovable. I use no other. With this rod, no matter how bloweth the wind, I will lay my fly on a sixpence at twenty-five yards in the first throw. It is to yours, scholar, as the day is to the night.

Venator. Indeed, master, I have so little of the art that I can find no difference between them. The tackle-maker hath served me ill, for he sold me this same rod as a perfect copy of your own.

Piscator. These tackle-makers are for the most part arrant knaves. But, scholar, I see that you have already tied on your fly; and a detached badger—a most unworthy contrivance. Trust me, this is not what honest fishermen are used to do.

Venator. Nay, master, never scold me; I did but wish to be ready.

Piscator. Trust me, you do but waste your time; for while it hath been computed that there are no less than seven thousand six hundred and forty-three different sorts of fly tied by these same scoundrelly tackle-merchants, there can be but one or two natural kinds of insects on the river's surface. Thus, scholar, it is in the neighbourhood of four thousand to one that when the fly comes (and it is a plaguy long time a-coming) you must take off this lure and put up another.

Venator. Well, sir, I have a goodly store. See how many sorts are in this pretty box of mine, each in its separate compartment. Is there not a brave show here?

Piscator. A brave show, I warrant you. Oh, my poor scholar! How many hath the villain sold you? One, two—twelve! Trust me, scholar, no honest fisherman needs more than three.

Venator. Then have I been tricked most vilely. Tell me, sir, what are these three patterns of which you speak?

Piscator. The olive quill, light and dark, and the Piscator's Fancy, so called because your unworthy master devised it. See, it is a little similar to the Wickham, but with this essential difference: the silk is turned around the hook to the right instead of to the left. With these three flies I will catch trouts at any time, I'll hold you two to one, nor will I ask for any other pattern.

Venator. See, master, there is a great trout.

Piscator. Where? Where?

Venator. There, good master—a most lovely fish.

Piscator. Scholar, you must get you sharper eyes. Do you not see it is a bit of weed?

Venator. But look, dear master. There—it riseth.

Piscator. Lend me your rod. I have no fly tied on.

Venator. Nay, master, you know that I have a detached badger. Would you use such a lure?

Piscator. Why, scholar, it will prove merry sport to take him so. Come, your rod; I warrant you I will fit you with a trout for supper. Note, scholar, how I shall lay my fly three inches above his nose. A plague take the wind!

Venator. Methought five yards too much on this side.

Piscator. Nay, this was but a trial cast. So, I have got his length. There—that was another trial. No man may fish in such a gale with such a rod.

Venator. Good master, do you take your own, and while you tie on a fly let me angle for this trout.

Piscator. Prithee, fair scholar, cut me off this willow branch that I may regain my hook. Come, we must try other measures with this gentleman. My Fancy shall go forth in quest of him. Scholar, I must again crave your aid; it is somewhere in the small of my jacket.

Venator. Now, sir, you are fancy free. I pray you, let me have my rod.

Piscator. These olives will not tempt him. He is a dainty fellow. See with what scorn he regardeth the pink Wickham; and the ginger quill fareth no better than the sherry spinner, nor the Welshman's button, neither. We must e'en put up a red caterpillar. No? Then an orange tag.

Venator. Now, sir, I have given you all my patterns.

Piscator. The fiend run away with this fish! Have you any salmon flies about you?

Venator. Nay, sweet master.

Piscator. Then do you essay to catch him. Is a foe worthy of your steel.

Venator. Thank you, sir. I will try this same detached badger once again. See, master, I have him.

Piscator. Well done, scholar. Keep up your point or all is lost. Reel in your line, scholar—give him line. Oh me! These weeds must be your undoing, I fear. Bravely, scholar, bravely! Give him line—reel in—he is a prodigious stout fish. Shall I take the rod?

Venator. No.

Piscator. Well, you have bungled through, scholar, and now he is your own. Well done, sir! A pound if he is an ounce, and were a good fish an he were in season; but I do find him something lean and lousy and unwholesome. Shall we not throw him in again and let him grow till he is more worthy of your anger?

Venator. Nay, sir, my scales make two pounds and one quarter, and I do think him to be a vastly fine trout. There—he is dead.

Piscator. See, sir, there is some fly coming down, as I said it would.

Venator. Then, master, we may look for more sport, I trust, for I do protest that I am quite in love with this fishing. My dear master, what are you doing?

Piscator. Marry, scholar, I am catching one of these same flies, for let me tell you that unless your lure is to the shadow of a shade the same as the fly that these trouts are taking, you shall labour to more purpose in yonder three-acre pasture.

Venator. Well, good master, I will e'en try my detached badger over yonder trout that I see busy by the willow.

Piscator. You will not take him. Here cometh a fly, close in, if I can but reach him. Zounds! I am in to the waist.

Venator. Give me your hand, dear master. Nay, sir, you are woefully stuck.

Piscator. . . .

Venator. Here is help. Good fellow, lend me your aid.

Corydon. Marnin', gentlemen both. Lar, naow, if it bean't Measter Piscator. Zure as my name be Corydon, 'tis. Swimmin', be 'ee, zur? Cayn't catch these-air trouts thataway, zur. Haw! Haw!

Piscator. . . .

Venator. Nay, good master, this honest man meaneth well by us. Prithee, brave Corydon.

Corydon. Naow, zur—one, two, three—and up comes the——

Piscator. Donkey!

Corydon. If you please, zur.

Piscator. I am soundly drenched. Corydon, are you not keeper here, and is not that your cottage?

Corydon. Ay, zur.

Piscator. Then, friend, you shall fit me with a dry pair of breeches. Scholar, I will presently return.

Venator. And while you are gone, I will match my poor skill against yonder lusty fish.

Piscator. Nay, scholar, he is too far for you, trust me. Leave him, and on my return I shall show you a pretty piece of angling. Make your way below bridge where I do see some tidy trouts busy, who are more within your capacity. Come, good Corydon.

. . . . . .

Venator. Nay, I will angle for these sprats no longer; there is no hooking them. I will e'en go try for the big fellow, for I do believe that I can reach him. Ay, he is still at work. Marry, by his rise he is a trout indeed. So, another cast and I cover him.

Piscator. Why, most naughty scholar, do I find you so heedless of my counsels?

Venator. My loving master, are you back already?

Piscator. Ay, our worthy keeper, Corydon, hath furnished me out with these coarse, rough small-clothes. I would they fitted me less straitly, but beggars may not be choosers, eh, honest Corydon?

Corydon. Why, zur, there wasn' no more'n they two pay-er fer 'ee to chuse amongst; but 'ee did zurely chuse the best.

Piscator. There is a penny for you.

Corydon. Thank 'ee, zur.

Piscator. Spend it wisely; let us not find you bemused with liquor this evening, when we come to leave the water. And now we do not need an attendant, so go your ways, for I mean to catch yonder trout for this gentleman's supper. Come, scholar, give place, and you shall soon see him at closer quarters.

Venator. Dear master, I have but this moment got his length.

Piscator. Nay, sir, you cannot take him; you have not the skill to throw so far; you will surely crack off your fly. Catch me one of these trouts below the bridge, them that I told you of.

Venator. Oh, sir, they are little things.

Corydon. They be daace, zur.

Piscator. Go your ways, Corydon; I tell you that they are trouts. Well, scholar, perhaps you will be better employed watching me. Why, it is a long cast, beshrew me! How now? My fly is gone! Mark this, scholar, and learn how the best may be caught napping. The gut hath been overlong drying and hath broken. Now, I am ready again. There—I think that was pretty well.

Venator. Your fly is in the tree, sir.

Piscator. Ah, scholar, this time your eyes have not deceived you; it is as you say. Oh me! I am most evilly hung up. Now, while I am mending the damage, let me tell you, sir, that when I shall hook yonder fish I must manage him yarely. Do you see these beds of green weeds? He will surely run for them, and once among them, he is lost to us, but you shall see how I shall master him.

Venator. That was a fine cast, sir. Oh, he hath taken it.

Piscator. Ay, hath he, and he is mine own.

Venator. Have a care, sir; he is for the weeds.

Piscator. . . .

Venator. Oh, sir, what is to be done now?

Piscator. Marry, a strong fish; no man alive could have held him; but I have not done with him, scholar. Mark now, how I shall play him with the hand. See, a gentle pull and draw; a steady sawing motion of the arm, and——

Corydon. Haw! Haw!

Piscator. Corydon, we do not desire your company. Come, scholar, let us be going, for there is a notable pool beyond this meadow where I have seen as many as twenty valiant trouts feeding at a time. And when we are come to this pool we will sit beneath one of those tall elms and rest from our toil awhile. For let me tell you that the sun is now so hot and high that it is odds against our seeing anything to repay our casting. But there we will take our dinner pleasantly, feasting blamelessly among the buttercups like these same silly kine; and I will give you yet more directions, for I would fain make you an artist.

Venator. Well, sir, I will confess that a sandwich will not come amiss.

Piscator. Nay, scholar, an your stomach be for sandwiches I must pity you; for let me tell you, sir, that I do abhor your sandwiches. A greasy, soft, and flimsy food, more fitted for the tea-table of a gentlewoman than for the dinner of an honest angler. It is ever my way to carry with me in my fish-bag a cold pullet's leg and a lettuce, a piece of good, dry wheaten bread, and such fruit as is in season. Ah hah! sir, I see your mouth begin to water. What say you to the providence of an old angler? Come, scholar, here is our tree, and now let us fall to.

Venator. Oh, master, what is the matter?

Piscator. That feather-brained wench hath forgotten to furnish me with my dinner. A murrain——

Venator. Nay, my loving master, will you not share mine? A sandwich——

Piscator. Oh, my dear scholar, shall I not be robbing you? Thank you, sir, I will try another. I protest that these sandwiches are vastly well; though this one hath more gristle in it that I could wish. Nay, sir, but one more and I am filled. No more, I thank you.

Venator. Why, sir, I shall not eat it; would you see it wasted?

Piscator. Nay, that were a sin, and I would rather have it on my stomach than on my conscience.

Venator. You are merry, sir.

Piscator. That is a gallant hunch of cake.

Venator. Will you try it, sir?

Piscator. Very gladly, scholar. What goodly plums are here! Oh me! your cake hath stones in it, sir. Whither now, good scholar?

Venator. A fish rose, sir.

Piscator. Can you point him out?

Venator. Nay, sir, I have my eye upon the very spot in the middle of the pool, but I should be hard put to it to show it to you. Why, I have him at the first attempt.

Piscator. I will put the net under him for you, for let me tell you, scholar, that this feat is no easy one, and not to be essayed by an unskilful hand. For if in landing of a fish the net do but touch the line, he shall break all. Bring him nearer to this tussock—so——

Venator. Alas, master, he is gone.

Piscator. Scholar, you will do better yet, but I must tell you that you managed clumsily. Why did you suffer the line to touch the net?

Venator. Dear master, it seemed to me——

Piscator. No matter, sir. You will do better, trust me. I have in you a towardly scholar, but no one may learn this art in a morning's fishing. I protest that the day is over sultry; I will sit awhile beneath this fine tree and read old Epictetus in the shade. Angle, if you will; but, trust me, you may not look for sport before evening.

. . . . . .

Venator. Up, dear master, the trouts are rising madly.

Piscator. My shaving-water, Thomas.

Venator. Nay, sweet master, awake. It is six of the clock, and there is great sport toward.

Piscator. As I live, I do believe that I have nodded. Ay, scholar, the trouts are rising gallantly. Let me tell you that this is the evening rise, called amongst us old anglers Tom Fool's Light, because it would seem that the veriest bungler must enjoy sport when the fish are so ready to feed. But you must know, sir, that this name is ill-chosen. For all their boldness it taketh a master hand to deceive them at this time.

Venator. Yet have I landed a leash in this very pool.

Piscator. Then I will go higher yet, and try conclusions with them in the next meadow.

. . . . . .

Venator. Well, master, the sun hath set upon a fair day and a happy one for me. I have taken another brace since we parted company. How hath fortune smiled upon you, good master, beside this tumbling bay?

Piscator. Why, sir, sourly, for I have wasted all this fine rise fishing for one trout, which, when I had caught him, proved too small for keeping. So I gave him his liberty.

Venator. Why, sir, what fly is this? Here is a woundily big hook, and here is a brave show of silver tinsel and peacock herl.

Piscator. It is a sedge-fly that came by accident among my tackle.

Venator. Here comes friend Corydon, the keeper, to lead you to your dry clothes.

Piscator. Prithee, sweet scholar, not a word about the sedge-fly. Our day is ended, and I am glad to see that you have profited so well by my instruction.

Venator. And by your example, fair master.

ANGLERS' WIVES

By C. R. GREEN

This story is from *Chambers's Journal* for December 1929.

LITTLE Mrs Trimble stood on the top step of the Flyfishers' Hotel and watched her husband moving off towards the river. He was festooned with accessories of the chase—fishing-bag, mackintosh, and collapsible landing-net—and shod with mighty brogues. He looked back once, and the trout-rod that he was carrying waggled blithely. Little Mrs Trimble, after waving a small handkerchief vigorously in reply, remained on tiptoe in her eagerness to keep him in view till the last possible moment. He swung through the ornamental gateway at the bottom of the drive, crossed the white road beyond, and was lost to sight, all but the tip of his rod, behind the hedge. He had not looked round again. Mrs Trimble strained her eyes until he had quite disappeared, and then turned to enter the hotel. Her smile had flickered out, and she looked a little woebegone. Inside the porch she even sniffed, in a tentative way, and applied the handkerchief to the corner of one eye.

Out of the dining-room and along the hall came Mrs Benson, the only other woman staying in the hotel, with her horn-rimmed spectacles in one hand and the *Daily Mirror* in the other. The call of the river had been answered by Mr Benson half an hour before; his wife had remained in possession of their table to absorb an unhurried third cup of coffee and the news. The procedure was invariable. Mrs Trimble had remarked it every morning since her arrival, five days ago.

Mrs Benson's glance, as she neared Mrs Trimble, was

kind and shrewd. She was large, middle-aged, and placid, with the demeanour of a perfect housewife. Until to-day she and Mrs Trimble had exchanged no more than a conventional word or two. But she had heard the faint sniff and seen the handkerchief, and she plunged.

'Is anything the matter?' asked Mrs Benson.

Mrs Trimble shook her head, and replied 'Nothing, thanks.' And then, unluckily, she sniffed again.

'You must let me help you if I can,' said Mrs Benson persuasively. 'I'm sometimes rather good at helping people. And I can see there is something.'

Mrs Trimble steadied herself with a long breath. 'There's nothing at all,' she insisted. 'Only——'

She stopped and turned to go. But by this time Mrs Benson had laid a hand on her arm, and was steering her into the tiny drawing-room of the hotel. A maid who was dusting furniture slipped out, leaving them alone. Mrs Benson led her companion to a settee facing the empty fireplace. 'Now, dear,' she said, 'tell me.' And little Mrs Trimble began to cry into her handkerchief.

'I know I oughtn't to tell you,' said Mrs Trimble in a small voice, 'but I daren't say anything to P-Percy, and I can't keep it to myself any longer. Oh, how I *hate* fishing!'

Mrs Benson nodded intelligently. 'This is your honeymoon, isn't it?'

Mrs Trimble, sobbing gently, nodded also.

'You poor child,' said Mrs Benson. 'I'm an angler's wife myself, and I think I understand. But I should have thought that you would both have wanted a different honeymoon from this.'

'It was partly my fault,' Mrs Trimble answered mournfully. 'I knew how tremendously keen he was on fishing, and I knew it would probably be his last chance this summer. So I encouraged him to bring me here. But I never expected it would be as bad as this.'

'Couldn't you go down to the river with him?' suggested Mrs Benson.

'He doesn't want me there—I can see that. I did go with him, the first morning. He took no notice of me whatever for most of the time, except to tell me I was frightening the fish when I came anywhere near him. If I spoke, he usually didn't answer. And when anything went wrong, he used such horrible words that I couldn't bear to hear him. So I came back.'

Mrs Benson nodded again. 'He belongs to the same school of fishermen as my husband,' she observed: 'the articulate school.'

'Another time,' pursued Mrs Trimble, 'we arranged to meet on the bank at one o'clock and have lunch together. I took some sandwiches with me, as Percy does every day. When I reached the place I couldn't see him anywhere. I found him half a mile off. He was up to his knees in the water, gulping his sandwiches and fishing at the same time. He'd been afraid he would miss the rise—whatever that is—if he came away, he said.'

'I can't tell you how sorry I am, dear,' said Mrs Benson. 'Of course *I'm* used to it. We were married a good many years ago, and Mr Benson has always been like that.'

'How long does it take to get used to it?' inquired Mrs Trimble, not at all hopefully.

'I suppose it depends on oneself. Some women never do. They're like poor Mrs Wilkinson, whom we used to meet with her husband in Devonshire. John does hardly anything but fish the whole year round, you know. We move about from one hotel to another, and run across the same people year after year.'

'What happened to Mrs Wilkinson?'

'I was going to tell you. After a few years of this she took up fishing herself. It wasn't that she was particularly interested, but she decided that anything would be an improvement on mooning about hotels by herself for the rest of her life.'

'I'm sure it would,' Mrs Trimble said with feeling.

'She persuaded her husband to teach her. She was an intelligent woman, and she became so clever at it that she once brought back three trout on a day when neither her husband nor the other men in the hotel could catch one. It was more than her husband could stand. She was explaining how she had nearly landed another when he struck her. They never forgave each other, and it came to a separation in the end.'

Mrs Trimble shivered. 'I wish you hadn't told me.' She brooded for a space, and then went on: 'I shouldn't feel it quite so much if I could get Percy to myself in the evenings. He's promised to take me for a walk after dinner to-night; it will be the first time. He usually sneaks off to the smoke-room, and stays there talking with the other men—about fishing, I suppose—till bed-time.'

'They all do,' Mrs Benson agreed. 'Personally, I prefer John to talk over his exploits with them, rather than with me.'

There slipped from her a sigh, and instantly Mrs Trimble was remorseful. 'I'm behaving very selfishly,' she exclaimed. 'Here I am howling over my own troubles, when yours must be every bit as hard to bear.'

Mrs Benson pulled herself up sharply. 'My dear,' she replied, 'don't bother your head about *me*. As a fisherman's helpmeet I'm a very old hand by this time, I assure you. Between ourselves'—she lowered her voice mysteriously—'I even extract a certain amount of entertainment from it.'

'Entertainment?'

'Amusement,' asseverated Mrs Benson. 'Fun. Though I never owned up to it to a living soul until this minute.' Her hands were demurely folded in her lap as she made this surprising statement. 'Now I've said so much I'll go further. I can trust you, can't I? I get very nearly as much enjoyment out of John's fishing as he does himself, and occasionally a good deal more.'

'But how on earth——' began the bewildered Mrs Trimble.

'Give me a minute to fetch my work,' Mrs Benson interrupted, 'and then we can talk comfortably.' A little later she was back beside Mrs Trimble on the settee, armed with silks and knitting-needles and an embryo scarf. 'I know it's old-fashioned of me, but I never could sit with my hands idle,' she apologised, with a matronly smile. 'And now I'm going to tell you secrets.'

The needles began to click. 'I suppose no normal woman can understand why men fish at all,' said Mrs Benson. 'It looks a slow and messy occupation at the best. At its worst—well, every day has been fine since you arrived, and you haven't yet seen your husband after a really unpleasant day on the river, soaked to the skin, half-frozen, and resembling a drowned rat generally. The only thing that can interrupt my husband's fishing is a raging flood; and when that happens he spends most of the day watching the river, to see whether it's rising or falling. You must have noticed already how a fisherman will go miles out of his way at any time to look at water, and how he stands and gazes solemnly at it, even if it's only a duck-puddle in a farm-yard. I grew so tired of it, years ago, that I vowed I'd never go for a country walk with Mr Benson again.

'But whatever the explanation, men who fish evidently do see something very fascinating in the sport. I've known my husband go out every day for a fortnight without catching anything bigger than a sardine the whole time, and grumble because we couldn't stay longer. It wasn't much fun for me, and I couldn't see what satisfaction there was in it for him. I told him so once or twice, in fact. After the way he answered me I didn't pursue the subject. (One of the things you'll learn, my dear, is not to expect an angler to see reason; and another is to spare him embarrassing questions. Above all, never say "Any luck?" when your husband comes in at the end of the day. Wait till he volunteers the information, or doesn't.) But I began to wonder if there was *anything* that could effectually discourage a fisherman—to the point, I mean, at which he would see for himself the futility of the whole silly business. It was mainly just curiosity, I think, that made me ask myself that question. I admit that I was interested in the answer for my own sake. But there was something else besides: this modern spirit of inquiry that one hears about must have seized on me, I suppose. I thought it over carefully. There didn't seem to be many ways in which fishing could be more unpleasant than it looked already, but I decided to explore them.

'My first experiment I remember very clearly. It was one August, at a little inn on the Ribble. John was there for the sea-trout fishing, and I was there because I'd married John a few years earlier; and as the river was so low and clear that fishing in daylight was a waste of time, he was spending most of the day in bed and not going near the water till it was quite dark. I rose early one morning, while John was asleep after his night's outing, and went downstairs with my scissors before anyone else was about. John uses one of those collapsible nets like your husband's; when it isn't actually in use the net part hangs down the handle in a bunch. It had occurred to me that he wouldn't be at all likely to discover a hole in his net before the moment came for using it, and then it would be dark. I snipped a fair-sized slit across the meshes.

'He returned from his next expedition at about three in the morning. I confess I was curious to know what had happened; but I hadn't reckoned on his keeping me awake for an hour and a half while he recounted his remarkable experience. He was hardly inside the bedroom door before he greeted me with what I can only describe as a whispered shout.

'"Jane! Jane! Wake up, Jane, and listen!"

'"What is it, dear?" I said, not so sleepily as I sounded.

'"The most extraordinary thing! Are you listening? I'd been fishing for a couple of hours or so without a rise, when"—and he launched into a minute account of the affair. It appeared that he had hooked a powerful fish, and after tiring it out hauled the creature near enough to put the net under it. And then, he said, for some unaccountable reason the fish slipped through the net, the line got into a terrible mess in the dark, and it was quite forty minutes before he managed to drag the fish up the bank, with the net and the line and the sea-trout in one huge tangle. It weighed very nearly four pounds, and he was positively delirious at his victory over such tremendous obstacles. I heard every detail of the story at least six times before he went to sleep. Of course, he wasn't quite so pleased when he examined his net more carefully next day and saw that the hole hadn't come in it by accident. He offended a lot of people in the hotel by inquiring if they knew anything about it, but he didn't ask me.

'It wasn't a very promising start, as you'll agree, my dear. But I kept on. The most vulnerable part of an angler's equipment, I found, is his waders. A stout bodkin will make quite a serviceable puncture in them. You wouldn't notice it unless you made a particular search, but it's sufficient to cause an uncomfortable leak. Like every other fisherman, Mr Benson occasionally wades in too deep and the water enters the tops of his wading-stockings, and so in a sense he's accustomed to wet feet. But somehow it seems to irritate a man quite unreasonably to feel his waders letting in water when he doesn't expect it; and then there is the nuisance of patching them with the tyre-repairing outfit out of the car before he can wear them again. I don't attempt it too often, you know. I fall back on the bodkin just now and then, when I haven't thought of anything more interesting lately.

'I take an interest also in his casts. You're new to the subject, dear, and I mustn't expect you to know the meaning of these technical terms. Casts are the thin transparent stuff that fishermen fasten on the end of their line, and the fly is tied to the end of that. They're made of gut, which comes out of silkworms—or is it cats? Once, before starting off on a long fishing trip to the west of Scotland, John bought a lot of casts—five or six dozen—which turned out to be rotten. He said so, anyway. Every night when he came back to the hotel he cursed them afresh, and said he'd lost I don't know how many trout again that day because the gut had snapped at the crucial instant. In the end he wired to a shop in Edinburgh for some more, and threw the old lot away. When his back was turned I rescued them. I still have a few left, tucked away at the bottom of my work-basket. They look exactly like the ones he always buys, and when he puts a new cast into the soap-dish in the bedroom to soak (which is another habit of fishermen you'll make acquaintance with) I watch for a chance to abstract it and put one of the old ones I've been treasuring in its place. Gut always goes weaker with age, so Mr Benson's fishing-books tell me, and if these were bad to begin with they should be a good deal worse after the years I've had them.

'All these are little things that can be done anywhere. There are others that suggest themselves in particular places. I always try to look at any new stretch of river we visit with an open mind. I remember that on the Scottish trip I've mentioned, I used to give a village boy twopence every morning to bathe in my husband's favourite pool, at about the time he was due to reach it at his regular rate of progress upstream. The boy always ran away when he saw John approaching, and John would abuse him unmercifully; but by that time all the trout, of course, were miles away. And that reminds me of Charlie and Miss Winstanley.

'It was in this very hotel that it happened. Miss Winstanley came in the middle of our annual three weeks' visit, six or seven years ago. She was an artist. There was nothing specially interesting about her outwardly, poor old thing, but she was the most persevering artist—in spite of a good many set-backs in a longish career—that I ever came across. For the first day or two she wandered about making little pencil sketches of anything that caught her fancy, but she confided to me, one evening, that as soon as she had found the right subject she intended to start upon a landscape in oils, with the idea of sending it to the Royal Academy. It had been the dream of her life to be hung at the Academy, and she believed she would find her inspiration here, among the hills of Derbyshire.

'I asked her if she hadn't seen anything suitable along the river.

'"I've seen three or four delightful bits that I should love to paint," she answered; "but the road runs so close beside the river that I should be pestered to death by all the motor-cars and char-à-bancs and the crowds of picnickers that seem to swarm there every day."

'"Have you tried the Hall grounds?" I asked.

'"I thought they were private."

'You know, I expect, that the Hall and its grounds really belong to the proprietor of this hotel, and the men who come here fish regularly up the river inside the grounds. When I told her this, she said she would explore the place next day.

'It was while I was lying awake that night that the possibilities of the situation first struck me. This brings me to Charlie. I don't suppose you'll have heard of Charlie, but in those days I heard a great deal about him from Mr Benson and his brother anglers. Charlie was a trout, and he picked up a comfortable living a few yards below the Roman bridge in the Hall grounds. He was famous as the biggest fish known to anyone in these parts, and they had all been after him for years. My husband must have spent hundreds of hours, I should think, standing below the spot where Charlie usually lay with his head upstream, and flinging every known pattern of artificial fly over him. But that trout was as cunning as a monkey. This year John was making a supreme effort. He'd brought with him from town some Mayflies of a patent kind that were highly spoken of, and it was generally agreed that if Charlie couldn't be taken in the Mayfly season he was not to be caught at all.

'The evening before Miss Winstanley arrived at the hotel, John had returned from the Hall grounds making ecstatic noises because Charlie had risen at one of the new Mayflies. It was true he'd risen "short," as they say; but to find him paying any attention whatever to an imitation insect—the real ones he swallowed by the gross—had moved John to the depths of his being. "I've a feeling that I shall get him this year," he said to me impressively that night. I thought it not at all impossible, for John is a really clever fisherman—which is the first kind word you've heard from me about him, I fancy.

'Well, some time during the small hours I determined to take a stroll with Miss Winstanley through the Hall grounds, if she had no objection, and point out to her that bit of river just below the Roman bridge. I felt sure it would appeal to her, and I knew of a flat patch of turf, between a buttress of the bridge and the water's edge, which had always seemed to me the perfect place from which to appreciate its full beauty.

'So I suggested, after breakfast, that if she didn't mind my company I should be glad to show her the pleasantest way down to the river, round the back of the Hall. She seemed grateful; and we first came in sight of the river at the bridge. The view from that grassy corner delighted her, and it really made a delicious picture that morning, with the water bubbling white over the gravel on the far side and flowing clear and strong in the middle, and the sunshine caught in the overhanging trees.

'"It's gorgeous," she murmured. "I shall bring my easel here and start on my picture directly after lunch."

'Apparently John didn't encounter her that afternoon; I think he had wasted the best hours of the morning over Charlie and given him up in disgust for the rest of the day. When he arrived next morning, Miss Winstanley was in possession. Her easel was planted on the extreme edge of the bank, and directly in the line of vision of Charlie if he had stayed to watch her, though I don't suppose for a moment that he had. John simply said "Good morning," climbed out of the water, and started to fish again above the bridge. He was not quite so affable when he returned in the late afternoon and found her still at work. He inquired whether she was likely to be there very long; and when she informed him that in all probability, being a careful worker, she would be at the same spot all day and every day for some weeks to come, he made a rather disagreeable exhibition of himself. But Miss Winstanley was firm. She felt, no doubt, that here was her chance to paint the picture of her career, and she didn't mean to be side-tracked by a mere fisherman. She didn't admire fishermen anyway—I'd gathered that from our first conversation, and she said as much to John now. In her opinion they were the embodiment of cruelty, she told him, and she looked forward to the day when all blood-sports, including fishing, would be put down by law. In the meantime she proposed to go on with her painting without consulting him.

'The following morning John was there first, having given orders overnight for an early breakfast. But Miss Winstanley had this advantage, that whereas she could have gone on with her picture even with John fishing under her nose, *he* would have been simply wasting his time. John continued to rise early—I was thankful he didn't insist on my doing so too—and to spend all the time he could over Charlie until Miss Winstanley appeared on the bank with her paraphernalia and sent them both packing for the day. But Charlie apparently preferred to wait till a little later in the morning for his breakfast, and my husband had no better luck when he tried in the evenings after dinner.

'However, John won, if winning is the right word in all the circumstances. Sunday came round, and Miss Winstanley was old-fashioned enough to treat it as a *dies non*. She left the painting on its easel in one of the garages, where it always spent the night, and attended morning service in the village. John, who didn't share her Sabbatarian scruples, took out his rod as usual after breakfast. I hadn't expected him back till evening. But he returned at one o'clock, with the excuse that the sandwiches the hotel staff had given him were uneatable, and then disappeared until he judged the rest of us had gone in to lunch.

'You've seen how at the end of the day every fisherman here lays out his catch upon a plate, and leaves it on the table in the hall for the rest of the company to admire. Miss Winstanley came in late that Sunday morning. She was hurrying to the dining-room when she saw on the hall table an unusually large fish, which was Charlie. My husband has a quite unnecessary habit of washing his trophies under the tap in the yard, or in any other convenient place, so that they'll be looking their best when he lays them out for inspection. But on this occasion the wash-and-brush-up had been omitted, and Charlie had a good deal of mud and wet grass attached to him. The reason why I mention it is that he was reposing on Miss Winstanley's oil-painting.

'Neither I nor anyone else except my husband had the slightest inkling of all this. John, as he explained to me later, had intended to surprise and humble us all by contriving that Charlie should burst on our vision as we left the dining-room. He had dished him up on Miss Winstanley's picture as an afterthought, and as a graceful intimation to the artist that a good man was not to be kept down. The first news we received of her discovery was a shriek that easily penetrated to the dining-room. It was followed by Miss Winstanley in person. In four strides she was at our table, waving Charlie by the tail; and with the one word "Cut-throat!"—I never quite understood why—she smacked John's face with him. Then she collapsed in hysterics.

'After that there was a lot of unpleasantness, to which the proprietor of the hotel contributed, and John didn't come well out of it. We left the place the same afternoon, in fact, in disgrace, and this is our first return visit. *I* should have been content to remain an absentee for the rest of my life; but my husband was never the man to let pride stand between him and a stretch of really good water like this, and when he heard lately that the hotel had changed hands it was all he'd been waiting for. Whether Miss Winstanley managed to clean her picture and finish it, and whether it was ever hung at the Academy, I never heard. I hope it was, poor dear.'

Mrs Trimble had heard the tale of duplicities thus far without interrupting. But it was evident that it had shocked her, and her manner was politely hostile when she spoke.

'I see, of course, that it's very clever of you,' said Mrs Trimble. 'But *why*? None of these—complications seems to have damped your husband's ardour in the slightest. Then what *good* is all this?'

Mrs Benson lowered her knitting and looked thoughtfully at a stuffed heron which was meditating on a bracket in the corner. 'I'm trying to remember,' she said at length, 'exactly when it was that the same point first occurred to me. For quite a long time before that, I think, I'd really given up hoping for any practical results, but without being conscious of it. And then it suddenly became quite clear to me. I saw that the rivers would all run dry before John of his own free will stopped fishing.'

'And still you kept on?'

'It's rather difficult to explain. At the very moment when I realised this, I discovered also that, however John felt about it, *I* was enjoying myself immensely. And so, as you say, I kept on. I hope you won't think me very wicked, dear. But I do so look forward to these little breaks in the monotony; and after all, you know, they keep me out of mischief. I believe in the old saying—"Satan finds some mischief still for idle hands to do"—and I always like to be occupied with something. And really I believe you'd forgive me if you saw how funny my husband can be sometimes. One of these days, when he's overhauling his waders for the hole my bodkin has made in them, you must come with me and study his expression. It's for all the world like a peevish monkey looking for fleas.'

'I know I oughtn't to preach,' said Mrs Trimble slowly, 'but I can't help feeling that it's rather dreadful. He is your husband, isn't he? I shouldn't——' She rose abruptly from her seat beside Mrs Benson, who had begun to look a little miserable, and stared out of the window. 'You can trust me not to say anything,' she added, after a pause.

'Thank you, dear,' Mrs Benson murmured, and there was again a silence.

It was broken presently by Mrs Trimble. 'Here's Mr Benson coming up the drive,' she observed. 'Can anything be the matter?'

Mrs Benson joined her at the window. 'I'm sure I don't know; unless it's his line.'

'His line?'

'Something might have gone wrong with it, perhaps.'

Mrs Trimble spun round. 'What have you done this time?' she demanded.

'John was exceedingly naughty last night,' said Mrs

Benson virtuously. 'I caught him washing his fish in the wash-hand basin in our bedroom.'

'And what has happened to his line?'

'You know how badly lighted the hall is at nights.' The tone was that of one accused unjustly. 'I *had* to strike a light on my way to bed, for fear of bumping into the rod-rack. I simply held the match against John's line, the part of it that was on the reel, as I was passing. Now I expect he's broken it.'

Mrs Trimble said no more, but almost shuddered.

Mrs Benson, on the contrary, seemed to have regained her cheerfulness. 'I must meet him at the door and ask if anything's the matter,' she said, and left the room.

From her post at the window Mrs Trimble heard only the beginnings of the duologue. Mingled with the words of wifely solicitude that reached her, however, she heard enough to prove that Mrs Benson had made no empty claim in numbering her husband with the articulate school of fishermen. Feeling that she would be safer out of earshot lest worse should follow, Mrs Trimble slipped quietly off to her room, nor did she reappear till summoned by the gong to lunch.

It was early evening. The long July day promised yet an hour or two of tempered light, but in this tranquil half-hour before dinner the wind had died away, and the shadows were slowly broadening as the sun dipped nearer to the top of Pincushion Hill. Tired anglers trudged up to the hotel at intervals, and with a nod to Mrs Trimble, who occupied a deck-chair under the smoke-room window, went heavily on to shed their gear round the corner. Mrs Trimble's finger was between the pages of a book, but her eyes were turned to the gateway at the far end of the drive. Her air of quiet anticipation contrasted shiningly with the unhappiness which Mrs Benson had discerned in her that morning.

Mrs Benson came out of the hotel and joined her.

During the afternoon she had been in to Ashbourne in the car with Mr Benson, for the purpose of buying a new line, she explained. Mrs Trimble answered absently. Thereafter Mrs Benson sat and sewed beside her, and they said little.

At last the dun-coloured figure for which Mrs Trimble had been watching was espied. It came slowly up the trying slope.

'Here he is,' said Mrs Trimble gladly, and started down the drive to meet him.

'Hullo, old thing,' said the fisherman. 'How goes it?'

'Had a good day, dear?'

'Not too bad—a brace and a half.'

'*How* many?'

'Well, if you prefer it, three. The best was almost a pound.'

'That's splendid,' said Mrs Trimble. They were walking up the drive together now.

There was a pause before Mr Trimble spoke again. 'I say, Molly,'—the tone was elaborately casual—'would you mind very much if I went down to the river again after dinner for an hour?'

'I thought we were to have a little walk together,' Mrs Trimble faltered.

'I was looking forward to it tremendously. But I spotted an enormous fish this afternoon, under the alder at the tail of the Colonel's Pool, and I fancy I might do something with him later on. I hate to disappoint you . . . but do you think we could postpone the walk till to-morrow?'

'Of course, if you'd rather.' She said it bravely, but with a glint of the eye that would have been new to her husband had he noted it. But his mind was otherwise occupied, for he was already beginning to tell her of the trout he had pricked and lost that day in the deep stretch beyond the second meadow.

Mrs Benson was still sewing under the smoke-room

window. As they came level with her Mrs Trimble halted.

'Just a minute, Percy dear,' she said.—'Mrs Benson, I wonder if you'd mind lending me your big bodkin?'

'I have it with me,' said Mrs Benson. 'There. Don't hurry about returning it.'

'It's sweet of you,' said Mrs Trimble.—'Go on with your story, darling.'

BLACK DOG

By HENRY WILLIAMSON

HENRY WILLIAMSON (born 1897), English author, best known perhaps for his animal sagas—*The Old Stag* (1926), *Tarka the Otter* (1927), *Salar the Salmon* (1935). 'Black Dog' is from chapter XIII of the last-named and is here given by permission of the author and of Messrs Faber & Faber.

SALAR slept. The water lightened with sunrise. He lay in shadow. His eyes were fixed, passively susceptible to all movement. The sun rose up. Leaves and stalks of loose weed and water-moss passing were seen but unnoticed by the automatic stimulus of each eye's retina. The eyes worked together with the unconscious brain, while the nerves, centres of direct feeling, rested themselves. One eye noticed a trout hovering in the water above, but Salar did not see it.

The sun rose higher, and shone down on the river, and slowly the shadow of the ledge shrank into its base. Light revealed Salar, a grey-green uncertain dimness behind a small pale spot appearing and disappearing regularly.

Down there Salar's right eye was filled with the sun's blazing fog. His left eye saw the wall of rock and the water above. The trout right forward of him swam up, inspected that which had attracted it, and swam down again; but Salar's eye perceived no movement. The shadow of the trout in movement did not fall on the salmon's right eye.

A few moments later there was a slight splash left forward of Salar. Something swung over, casting the thinnest shadow; but it was seen by the eye, which awakened the conscious brain. Salar was immediately alert.

The thing vanished. A few moments later, it appeared nearer to him.

With his left eye Salar watched the thing moving overhead. It swam in small jerks, across the current and just under the surface, opening and shutting, gleaming, glinting, something trying to get away. Salar, curious and alert, watched it until it was disappearing, and then he swam up and around to take it ahead of its arc of movement. The surface water, however, was flowing faster than the river at mid-stream, and he misjudged the opening of his mouth, and the thing, which recalled sea feeding, escaped.

On the bank upriver fifteen yards away a fisherman with fourteen-foot split-cane rod said to himself, excitedly, 'Rising short'; and pulling loops of line between reel and lowest ring of rod, he took a small pair of scissors from a pocket and snipped off the thing which had attracted Salar.

No wonder Salar had felt curious about it, for human thought had ranged the entire world to imagine that lure. It was called a fly: but no fly like it ever swam in air or flew through water. Its tag, which had glinted, was of silver from Nevada and silk of a moth from Formosa; its tail, from the feather of an Indian crow; its butt, black herl of African ostrich; its body, yellow floss-silk veiled with orange breast-feathers of the South American toucan, and black Macclesfield silk ribbed with silver tinsel. This fly was given the additional attraction of wings for water-flight, made of strips of feathers from many birds: turkey from Canada, peahen and peacock from Japan, swan from Ireland, bustard from Arabia, golden-pheasant from China, teal and wild duck and mallard from the Hebrides. Its throat was made of the feather of an English speckled hen, its side of Bengal jungle-cock's neck feathers, its cheeks came from a French kingfisher, its horns from the tail of an Amazonian macaw. Wax, varnish, and enamel secured the 'marriage' of the feathers. It was one of hundreds of charms, or materialised riverside incantations, made by men to persuade sleepy or depressed salmon to rise and take. Invented after a bout of seasickness by a Celt as he sailed the German Ocean between England and Norway, for nearly a hundred years this fly had borne his name, Jock Scott.

While the fisherman was tying a smaller pattern of the same fly to the end of the gut cast, dark stained by nitrate of silver against under-water glint, Salar rose to mid-water and hovered there. Behind him lay the trout, which, scared by the sudden flash of the big fish turning, had dropped back a yard. So Salar had hovered three years before in his native river, when, as parr spotted like a trout, and later as silvery smolt descending to the sea, he had fed eagerly on nymphs of the olive dun and other ephemeridæ coming down with the current.

He opened his mouth and sucked in a nymph as it was swimming to the surface. The fisherman saw a swirl on the water, and threw his fly, with swish of double-handed rod, above and to the right of the swirl. Then, lowering the rod point until it was almost parallel to the water, he let the current take the fly slowly across the stream, lifting the rod tip and lowering it slightly and regularly to make the fly appear to be swimming.

Salar saw the fly and slowly swam up to look at it. He saw it clear in the bright water and sank away again, uninterested in the lifelessness of its bright colours. Again it reappeared, well within his skylight window. He ignored it, and it moved out of sight. Then it fell directly over him, jigging about in the water, and with it a dark thin thing which he regarded cautiously. This was the gut cast. Once more it passed over, and then again, but he saw only the dark thinness moving there. It was harmless. He ignored it. Two other salmon below Salar, one in a cleft of rock and the other beside a sodden oak log wedged under the bank, also saw the too-bright thing, and found no vital interest in it.

The fisherman pulled in the line through the rod-rings. It was of plaited silk, tapered and enamelled for ease of casting. The line fell over his boot. Standing still, he cut off the fly, and began a search for another in a metal box, wherein scores of mixed feathers were ranged on rows of metal clasps. First he moved one with his forefinger, then another, staring at this one and frowning at that one, recalling in its connection past occasions of comparative temperatures of air and river, of heights and clearness of water, of sun and shade, while the angler's familiar feeling, of obscurity mingled with hope and frustration, came over him. While from the air he tried to conjure certainty for a choice of fly, Salar, who had taken several nymphs of the olive dun during the time the angler had been cogitating, leapt and fell back with a splash that made the old fellow take a small Black Doctor and tie the gut to the loop of the steel hook with a single Cairnton-jam knot.

Salar saw this lure and fixed one eye on it as it approached and then ignored it, a thing without life. As it was being withdrawn from the water a smolt which had seen it only then leapt open-mouthed at a sudden glint and fell back, having missed it.

Many times a similar sort of thing moved over Salar, who no longer heeded their passing. He enjoyed crushing the tiny nymphs on his tongue, and tasting their flavour. Salar was not feeding, he was not hungry; but he was enjoying remembrance of his river-life with awareness of an unknown great excitement before him. He was living by the spirit of running water. Indeed Salar's life was now the river: as he explored it higher, so would he discover his life.

On the bank the fisherman sat down and perplexedly re-examined his rows and rows of flies. He had tried all recommended for the water, and several others as well; and after one short rise, no fish had come to the fly. Mar Lodge and Silver Grey, Dunkeld and Black

Fairy, Beauly Snow Fly, Fiery Brown, Silver Wilkinson, Thunder and Lightning, Butcher, Green Highlander, Blue Charm, Candlestick Maker, Bumbee, Little Inky Boy, all were no good. Then in one corner of the case he saw an old fly of which most of the mixed plumage was gone: a Black Dog which had belonged to his grandfather. Grubs of moths had fretted away hackle, wing, and topping. It was thin and bedraggled. Feeling that it did not matter much what fly was used, he sharpened the point with a slip of stone, tied it on, and carelessly flipped it into the water. He was no longer fishing; he was no longer intent, he was about to go home; the cast did not fall straight, but crooked; the line also was crooked. Without splash the fly moved down a little less fast than the current, coming thus into Salar's skylight. It was like the nymphs he had been taking, only larger; and with a leisurely sweep he rose and turned across the current, and took it, holding it between tongue and vomer as he went down to his lie again, where he would crush and taste it. The sudden resistance of the line to his movement caused the point of the hook to prick the corner of his mouth. He shook his head to rid himself of it, and this action drove the point into the gristle, as far as the barb.

A moment later, the fisherman, feeling a weight on the line, lifted the rod-point, and tightened the line, and had hardly thought to himself, *salmon*, when the blue-grey tail of a fish broke half out of water and its descending weight bended the rod.

Salar knew of neither fisherman nor rod nor line. He swam down to the ledge of rock and tried to rub the painful thing in the corner of his mouth against it. But his head was pulled away from the rock. He saw the line, and was fearful of it. He bored down to his lodge at the base of the rock, to get away from the line, while the small brown trout swam behind his tail, curious to know what was happening.

Salar could not reach his lodge. He shook his head violently, and, failing to get free, turned downstream and swam away strongly, pursued by the line and a curious buzzing vibration just outside his jaw.

Below the pool the shallow water jabbled before surging in broken white crests over a succession of rocky ledges. Salar had gone about sixty yards from his lodge, swimming hard against the backward pull of line, when the pull slackened, and he turned head to current, and lay close to a stone, to hide from his enemy.

When the salmon had almost reached the jabble, the fisherman, fearing it would break away in the rough water, had started to run down the bank, pulling line from the reel as he did so. By thus releasing direct pull on the fish, he had turned it. Then, by letting the current drag line in a loop below it, he made Salar believe that the enemy was behind him. Feeling the small pull of the line from behind, Salar swam up into deeper water, to get away from it. The fisherman was now behind the salmon, in a position to make it tire itself by swimming upstream against the current.

Salar, returning to his lodge, saw it occupied by another fish, which his rush, and the humming line cutting the water, had disturbed from the lie by the sodden log. This was Gralaks the grilse. Again Salar tried to rub the thing against the rock, again the pull, sideways and upwards, was too strong for him. He swam downwards, but could make no progress towards the rock. This terrified him and he turned upwards and swam with all his strength, to shake it from his mouth. He leapt clear of the water and fell back on his side, still shaking his head.

On the top of the leap the fisherman had lowered his rod, lest the fly be torn away as the salmon struck the water.

Unable to get free by leaping, Salar sank down again and settled himself to swim away from the enemy. Drawing the line after him, and beset again by the buzzing vibration, he travelled a hundred yards to the throat of the pool, where water quickened over gravel. He lay in the riffle spreading away from a large stone, making himself heavy, his swim-bladder shrunken, trying to press himself into the gravel which was his first hiding-place in life. The backward pull on his head nearly lifted him into the fast water, but he held himself down, for nearly five minutes, until his body ached and he weakened and he found himself being taken down sideways by the force of shallow water. He recalled the sunken tree and it became a refuge, and he swam down fast, and the pull ceased with the buzz against his jaw. Feeling relief, he swam less fast over his lodge, from which Gralaks sped away, alarmed by the line following Salar.

But before he could reach the tree the weight was pulling him back, and he turned and bored down to bottom, scattering a drove of little grey shadows which were startled trout. Again the pull was too much for him, and he felt the ache of his body spreading back to his tail. He tried to turn on his side to rub the corner of his mouth on something lying on the bed of the pool—an old cartwheel—again and again, but he could not reach it.

A jackdaw flying silent over the river, paper in beak for nest-lining, saw the dull yellow flashes and flew faster in alarm of them and the man with the long curving danger.

Fatigued and aching, Salar turned downstream once more, to swim away with the river, to escape the enemy which seemed so much bigger because he could not close his mouth. As he grew heavier, slower, uncertain, he desired above all to be in the deeps of the sea, to lie on ribbed sand and rest and rest and rest. He came to rough water, and let it take him down, too tired to swim. He bumped into a rock, and was carried by the current around it, on his side, while the gut cast, tautened by the dragging weight, twanged and jerked his head upstream, and he breathed again, gulping water quickly and irregularly. Still the pull was trying to take him forward, so with a renewal by fear he turned and re-entered fast water and went down and down, until he was in another deep pool at a bend of the river. Here he remembered a hole under the roots of a tree, and tried to hide there, but had not strength enough to reach the refuge of darkness.

Again he felt release, and swam forward slowly, seeking the deepest part of the pool, to lie on the bottom with his mouth open. Then he was on his side, dazed and weary, and the broken-quicksilvery surface of the pool was becoming whiter. He tried to swim away, but the water was too thick-heavy; and after a dozen sinuations it became solid. His head was out of water. A shock passed through him as he tried to breathe. He lay there, held by line taut over fisherman's shoulder. He felt himself being drawn along just under the surface, and only then did he see his enemy—flattened, tremulant-spreading image of the fisherman. A new power of fear broke in the darkness of his lost self. When it saw the tailer coming down to it, the surface of the water was lashed by the desperately scattered self. The weight of the body falling over backwards struck the taut line; the tail-fin was split. The gut broke just above the hook, where it had been frayed on the rock. Salar saw himself sinking down into the pool, and he lay there, scattered about himself and unable to move away, his tail curved round a stone, feeling only a distorted head joined to the immovable river-bed.

MASTER AND MAN

By SIR HENRY NEWBOLT

SIR HENRY JOHN NEWBOLT (1862-1938), in the collected edition of his verse, *Poems: New and Old* (1919), gives one angling piece. It is here reproduced by permission of the author's son and of Messrs John Murray.

Do ye ken hoo to fush for the salmon?
  If ye'll listen I'll tell ye,
Dinna trust to the books and their gammon,
  They're but trying to sell ye.
Leave professors to read their ain cackle
  And fush their ain style;
Come awa', sir, we'll oot wi' oor tackle
  And be busy the while.

'Tis a wee bit ower bright, ye were thinkin'?
  Aw, ye'll no be the loser;
'Tis better ten baskin' and blinkin'
  Than ane that's a cruiser.
If ye're bent, as I tak it, on slatter,
  Ye should pray for the droot,
For the salmon's her ain when there's watter,
  But she's oors when it's oot.

Ye may just put your flee-book behind ye,
  Ane hook wull be plenty;
If they'll no come for this, my man, mind ye,
  They'll no come for twenty.
Ay, a rod; but the shorter the stranger
  And the nearer to strike;
For myself I prefare it nae langer
  Than a yard or the like.

Noo, ye'll stand awa' back while I'm creepin'
  Wi' my snoot i' the gowans;
There's a bonny twalve-poonder a-sleepin'
  I' the shade o' yon rowans.
Man, man! I was fearin' I'd stirred her,
  But I've got her the noo!
Hoot! fushin's as easy as murrder
  When ye ken what to do.

Na, na, sir, I doot na ye're willin'
  But I canna permit ye;
For I'm thinkin' that yon kind o' killin'
  Wad hardly befit ye.
And some work is deefficult hushin',
  There'd be havers and chaff:
'Twull be best, sir, for you to be fushin'
  And me wi' the gaff.

PETE AND THE BIG TROUT

By HENRY WARD BEECHER

HENRY WARD BEECHER (1813-87), famous American preacher. His published work includes one novel, *Norwood, or Village Life in New England* (3 vols 1867), and from volume I, chapter XII, of this 'Pete and the Big Trout' is taken.

PETE ain't growed away from natur' so far but what he knows what's goin' on in beast and bird. There ain't his equal at fishin' in these parts. The fish just cum, I do believe, and ask him to catch 'em.

He don't take on airs about it neither. He ain't stingy. He'd just as soon take you to the best brooks and the best places as not. But then that's nothin'. Very like you can't catch a fish. The trout knows who's after 'em. They want Pete to catch 'em, not Tom, Dick, and Harry.

You mind that time he caught that trout out of Hulcomb's mill-pond, don't you?—No? Well, it had been known that there was an awful big fellow living in there. And I know a hundred folks had tried for him. Gentlemen had come up from New Haven, and from Bridgeport, and from down to New York, a-fishin', and ever so many of 'em had wound up with tryin' their luck for that big trout, and they had all sorts of riggin'. One he tried flies, and another worms; sometimes they took the mornin', and sometimes the evenin'. They knew the hole where he lay. He's been seen breaking the water for one thing and another, but allus when nobody was fishin'. He was a curious trout. I believe he knew Sunday just as well as Deacon Marble did. At any rate the deacon thought the trout meant to aggravate him. The deacon, you know, is a little waggish. He often tells about that trout. Sez he: 'One Sunday morning, just as I got along by the willows, I heard an awful splash, and not ten feet from shore I saw the trout, as long as my arm, just curving over like a bow, and going down with something for breakfast. "Gracious!" says I, and I almost jumped out of the waggon. But my wife Polly, says she: "What on airth are you thinkin' of, Deacon? It's Sabbath-day, and you're goin' to meetin'! It's a pretty business for a deacon!" That sort of talk cooled me off. But I do say, that for about a minute I wished I wasn't a deacon. But 'twouldn't made any difference, for I came down next day to mill on purpose, and I came down once or twice more, and nothin' was to be seen, tho' I tried him with the most temptin' things. Wall, next Sunday I came along agin', and to save my life I couldn't keep off worldly and wandering thoughts. I tried to be sayin' my Catechism. But I couldn't keep my eyes off the pond as we came up to the willows. I'd got along in the Catechism as smooth as the road, to the Fourth Commandment, and was sayin' it out loud for Polly, and jist as I was sayin': "What is required in the Fourth Commandment?" I heard a splash, and there was the trout, and afore I could think, I said: "Gracious, Polly; I must have that trout." She almost riz right up: "I knew you wan't sayin' your Catechism hearty. Is this the way you answer the question about keepin' the Lord's day? I'm ashamed, Deacon Marble," says she. "You'd better change your road, and go to meetin' on the road over the hill. If I was a deacon, I wouldn't let a fish's tail whisk the whole Catechism out of my head";—and I had to go to meetin' on the hill road all the rest of the summer.'

Wall, Pete he worked down to the mill for a week or two—that's as long as he stays anywhere, except at Dr Wentworth's, and he lets him come and go about as he pleases. And so, one day, says he: 'I'm goin' to catch that big trout.' So, after the sun was gone down, and just as the moon riz and lighted up the tops of the bushes, but didn't touch the water—Pete, he took a little mouse he'd caught, and hooked his hook through his skin, on the back, so that it didn't hurt him or hinder his being lively, and he threw him in about as far as a mouse could have jumped from the branches that hung over. Of course, the mouse he put out lively to swim for his life. Quick as a flash of lightnin', the water opened with a rush, and the mouse went under; but he came up again, and the trout with him, and he weighed between three and four pound.

TURNING THE TABLES

By T. C. HALIBURTON

For THOMAS CHANDLER HALIBURTON, see p. 71. 'Turning the Tables' is from *Traits of American Humour* (1852) and there has the title 'A Shark Story.'

'WELL, gentlemen, I'll go ahead, if you say so. Here's the story. It is true, upon my honour, from beginning to end—every word of it. I once crossed over to Faulkner's island to fish for *tautaugs*, as the north-side people call black fish, on the reefs hard by, in the Long Island Sound. Tim Titus (who died of the dropsy down at Shinnecock point, last spring) lived there then. Tim was a right good fellow, only he drank rather too much.

'It was during the latter part of July; the sharks and the dog-fish had just begun to spoil sport. When Tim told me about the sharks, I resolved to go prepared to entertain these aquatic savages with all becoming attention and regard, if there should chance to be any interloping about our fishing-ground. So we rigged out a set of extra large hooks, and shipped some rope-yarn and steel chain, an axe, a couple of clubs, and an old harpoon, in addition to our ordinary equipments, and off we started. We threw out our anchor at half ebb-tide, and took some thumping large fish; two of them weighed thirteen pounds—so you may judge. The reef where we lay was about half a mile from the island, and, perhaps, a mile from the Connecticut shore. We floated there, very quietly, throwing out and hauling in, until the breaking of my line, with a sudden and severe jerk, informed me that the sea attorneys were in waiting downstairs; and we accordingly prepared to give them a retainer. A salt pork cloak upon one of our magnum hooks forthwith engaged one of the gentlemen in our service. We got him alongside, and by dint of piercing, and thrusting, and banging, we accomplished a most exciting and merry murder. We had business enough of the kind to keep us employed until near low water. By this time the sharks had all cleared out, and the black fish were biting again; the rock began to make its appearance above the water, and in a little while its hard bald head was entirely dry. Tim now proposed to set me out upon the rock, while he rowed ashore to get the jug, which, strange to say, we had left at the house. I assented to this proposition; first, because I began to feel the effects of the sun upon my tongue, and needed something to take, by the way of medicine; and secondly, because the rock was a favourite spot for rod and reel, and famous for luck: so I took my traps, and a box of bait, and jumped upon my new station. Tim made for the island.

'Not many men would willingly have been left upon a little barren reef that was covered by every flow of the tide, in the midst of a waste of waters, at such a distance from the shore, even with an assurance from a companion more to be depended upon than mine, that he would return immediately and take him off. But somehow or other, the excitement of the sport was so high, and the romance of the situation was so delightful, that I thought of nothing else but the prospect of my fun, and the contemplation of the novelty and beauty of the scene. It was a mild, pleasant afternoon, in harvest time. The sky was clear and pure. The deep blue sound, heaving all around me, was studded with craft of all descriptions and dimensions, from the dipping sail-boat to the rolling merchantman, sinking and rising like sea-birds sporting with their white wings in the surge. The grain and grass on the neighbouring farms were gold and green, and gracefully they bent obeisance to a gently breathing south-wester. Farther off, the high upland,

and the distant coast, gave a dim relief to the prominent features of the landscape, and seemed the rich but dusky frame of a brilliant fairy picture. Then, how still it was! Not a sound could be heard, except the occasional rustling of my own motion, and the water beating against the sides, or gurgling in the fissures of the rock, or except now and then the cry of a solitary saucy gull, who would come out of his way in the firmament, to see what I was doing without a boat, all alone, in the middle of the sound; and who would hover, and cry, and chatter, and make two or three circling swoops and dashes at me, and then, after having satisfied his curiosity, glide away in search of some other food to scream at.

'I soon became half indolent, and quite indifferent about fishing; so I stretched myself out at full length upon the rock and gave myself up to the luxury of looking and thinking. The divine exercise soon put me fast asleep. I dreamed away a couple of hours, and longer might have dreamed, but for a tired fish-hawk who chose to make my head his resting-place, and who waked and started me to my feet.

'"Where is Tim Titus?" I muttered to myself, as I strained my eyes over the now darkened water. But none was near me to answer that interesting question, and nothing was to be seen of either Tim or his boat. "He should have been here long ere this," thought I, "and he promised faithfully not to stay long—could he have forgotten? or has he paid too much devotion to the jug?"

'I began to feel uneasy, for the tide was rising fast, and soon would cover the top of the rock, and high water-mark was at least a foot above my head. I buttoned up my coat, for either the coming coolness of the evening, or else my growing apprehensions, had set me trembling and chattering most painfully. I braced my nerves, and set my teeth, and tried to hum "Begone, dull care," keeping time with my fists upon my thighs. But what music! what melancholy merriment! I started and shuddered at the doleful sound of my own voice. I am not naturally a coward; but I should like to know the man who would not, in such a situation, be alarmed. It is a cruel death to die to be merely drowned, and to go through the ordinary commonplaces of suffocation; but to see your death gradually rising to your eyes, to feel the water rising, inch by inch, upon your shivering sides, and to anticipate the certainly coming, choking struggle for your last breath, when, with the gurgling sound of an overflowing brook taking a new direction, the cold brine pours into mouth, ears, and nostrils, usurping the seat and avenues of health and life, and, with gradual flow, stifling—smothering—suffocating! It were better to die a thousand common deaths.

'This is one of the instances in which, it must be admitted, salt water is not a pleasant subject of contemplation. However, the rock was not yet covered, and hope, blessed hope, stuck faithfully by me. To beguile, if possible, the weary time, I put on a bait, and threw out for fish. I was sooner successful than I could have wished to be, for hardly had my line struck the water, before the hook was swallowed, and my rod was bent with the dead hard pull of a twelve-foot shark. I let him run about fifty yards, and then reeled up. He appeared not at all alarmed, and I could scarcely feel him bear upon my fine hair line. He followed the pull gently and unresisting, came up to the rock, laid his nose upon its side, and looked up into my face, not as if utterly unconcerned, but with a sort of quizzical impudence, as though he perfectly understood the precarious nature of my situation. The conduct of my captive renewed and increased my alarm. And well it might; for the tide was now running over a corner of the rock behind me, and a small stream rushed through a cleft, or fissure, by my side, and formed a puddle at my very feet. I broke my hook out of the monster's mouth, and leaned upon my rod for support.

'"Where is Tim Titus?" I cried aloud. "Curse on the drunken vagabond! Will he never come?"

'My ejaculations did no good. No Timothy appeared. It became evident that I must prepare for drowning, or for action. The reef was completely covered, and the water was above the soles of my feet. I was not much of a swimmer, and as to ever reaching the island, I could not even hope for that. However, there was no alternative, and I tried to encourage myself, by reflecting that necessity was the mother of invention, and that desperation will sometimes ensure success. Besides, too, I considered and took comfort from the thought that I could wait for Tim, so long as I had a foothold, and then commit myself to the uncertain strength of my arms and legs for salvation. So I turned my bait-box upside down, and mounting upon that, endeavoured to comfort my spirits, and to be courageous, but submissive to my fate. I thought of death, and what it might bring with it, and I tried to repent of the multiplied iniquities of my almost wasted life; but I found that that was no place for a sinner to settle his accounts. Wretched soul, pray I could not.

'The water had not got above my ankles, when, to my inexpressible joy, I saw a sloop bending down towards me, with the evident intention of picking me up. No man can imagine what were the sensations of gratitude which filled my bosom at that moment.

'When she got within a hundred yards of the reef, I sung out to the man at the helm to luff up, and lie by, and lower the boat; but to my amazement, I could get no reply, nor notice of my request. I entreated them, for the love of heaven, to take me off; and I promised I know not what rewards, that were entirely beyond my power of bestowal. But the brutal wretch of a captain, muttering something to the effect of "that he hadn't time to stop," and giving me the kind and sensible advice to pull off my coat and swim ashore, put the helm hard down, and away bore the sloop on the other tack.

'"Heartless villain!" I shrieked out, in the torture of my disappointment; "may God reward your inhumanity."

'The crew answered my prayer with a coarse, loud laugh; and the cook asked me through a speaking-trumpet if I was not afraid of catching cold.—The black rascal!

'It now was time to strip; for my knees felt the cool tide, and the wind dying away, left a heavy swell, that swayed and shook the box upon which I was mounted, so that I had occasionally to stoop, and paddle with my hands against the water in order to preserve my perpendicular. The setting sun sent his almost horizontal streams of fire across the dark waters, making them gloomy and terrific, by the contrast of his amber and purple glories.

'Something glided by me in the water, and then made a sudden halt. I looked upon the black mass, and, as my eye ran along its dark outline, I saw, with horror, that it was a shark; the identical monster out of whose mouth I had just broken my hook. He was fishing now for me, and was evidently only waiting for the tide to rise high enough above the rock, to glut at once his hunger and revenge. As the water continued to mount above my knees, he seemed to grow more hungry and familiar. At last, he made a desperate dash, and approaching within an inch of my legs, turned upon his back, and opened his huge jaws for an attack. With desperate strength, I thrust the end of my rod violently at his mouth; and the brass head, ringing against his teeth, threw him back into the deep current, and I lost sight of him entirely. This, however, was but a momentary repulse; for in the next minute he was close behind my back, and pulling at the skirts of my fustian coat, which hung dipping into the water. I leaned forward hastily, and endeavoured to extricate myself from the dangerous grasp; but the monster's teeth were too firmly set, and his immense strength nearly drew me over. So, down flew my rod, and off went my jacket, devoted peace-offerings to my voracious visitor.

'In an instant the waves all round me were lashed into froth and foam. No sooner was my poor old sporting friend drawn under the surface, than it was fought for by at least a dozen enormous combatants! The battle raged upon every side. High black fins rushed now here, now there, and long, strong tails scattered sleet and froth, and the brine was thrown up in jets, and eddied and curled, and fell, and swelled, like a whirlpool in Hell-gate.

'Of no long duration, however, was this fishy tourney. It seemed soon to be discovered that the prize contended for contained nothing edible but cheese and crackers, and no flesh; and as its mutilated fragments rose to the surface, the waves subsided into their former smooth condition. Not till then did I experience the real terrors of my situation. As I looked around me to see what had become of the robbers, I counted one, two, three, yes, up to twelve, successively, of the largest sharks I ever saw, floating in a circle around me, like divergent rays, all mathematically equidistant from the rock, and from each other; each perfectly motionless, and with his gloating, fiery eye, fixed full and fierce upon me. Basilisks and rattlesnakes! how the fire of their steady eyes entered into my heart! I was the centre of a circle, whose radii were sharks! I was the unsprung, or rather *unchewed* game, at which a pack of hunting sea-dogs were making a dead point!

'There was one old fellow, that kept within the circumference of the circle. He seemed to be a sort of captain, or leader of the band; or, rather, he acted as the coroner for the other twelve of the inquisition, that were summoned to sit on, and eat up my body. He glided around and about, and every now and then would stop, and touch his nose against some one of his comrades, and seem to consult, or to give instructions as to the time and mode of operation. Occasionally, he would skull himself up towards me, and examine the condition of my flesh, and then again glide back, and rejoin the troupe, and flap his tail, and have another confabulation. The old rascal had, no doubt, been out into the highways and byways, and collected this company of his friends and kin-fish, and invited them to supper.

'I must confess, that horribly as I felt, I could not help but think of a tea-party of demure old maids, sitting in a solemn circle, with their skinny hands in their laps, licking their expectant lips, while their hostess bustles about in the important functions of her preparations. With what an eye have I seen such appurtenances of humanity survey the location and adjustment of some special condiment, which is about to be submitted to criticism and consumption.

'My sensations began to be now most exquisite indeed; but I will not attempt to describe them. I was neither hot nor cold, frightened nor composed; but I had a combination of all kinds of feelings and emotions. The present, past, future, heaven, earth, my father and mother, a little girl I knew once, and the sharks, were all confusedly mixed up together, and swelled my crazy brain almost to bursting. I cried, and laughed, and spouted, and screamed for Tim Titus.

'In a fit of most wise madness I opened my broad-bladed fishing-knife, and waved it around my head with an air of defiance. As the tide continued to rise, my extravagance of madness mounted. At one time I became persuaded that my tide-waiters were reasonable beings, who might be talked into mercy and humanity, if a body could only hit upon the right text. So I bowed, and gesticulated, and threw out my hands, and talked to them, as friends and brothers, members of my family, cousins, uncles, aunts, people waiting to have their bills paid; I scolded them as my servants; I abused them as duns; I implored them as jurymen sitting on the question of my life; I congratulated and flattered them as my comrades upon some glorious enterprise; I sung and ranted to them, now as an actor in a play-house, and now as an elder at a camp-meeting; in one moment, roaring,

'"On this cold flinty rock I will lay down my head,"—

and in the next, giving out to my attentive hearers for singing, a hymn of Dr Watts's so admirably appropriate to the occasion:

'"On slippery rocks I see them stand,
While fiery billows roll below."

'What said I, what did I not say! Prose and poetry, Scripture and drama, romance and ratiocination—out it came. "Quamdiu, Catalina, nostra patientia abutere?" —I sung out to the old captain, to begin with: "My brave associates, partners of my toil,"—so ran the strain. "On which side soever I turn my eyes,"—"Gentlemen of the jury,"—"I come not here to steal away your hearts,"—"You are not wood, you are not stones, but"— "Hah!"—"Begin, ye tormentors, your tortures are vain," —"Good friends, sweet friends, let me not stir you up to any sudden flood,"—"The angry flood that lashed her groaning sides,"—"Ladies and gentlemen,"—"My very noble and approved good masters,"—"Avaunt! and quit my sight; let the earth hide ye,"—"Lie lightly on his head, O earth!"—"O, heaven and earth, that it should come to this!"—"The torrent roared, and we did buffet it with lusty sinews, stemming it aside and oaring it with hearts of controversy,"—"Give me some drink, Titinius," —"Drink, boys, drink, and drown dull sorrow,"—"For liquor it doth roll such comfort to the soul,"—"Romans, countrymen and lovers, hear me for my cause, and be silent that you may hear,"—"Fellow-citizens, assembled as we are upon this interesting occasion, impressed with the truth and beauty,"—"Isle of beauty, fare thee well,"

—"The quality of mercy is not strained,"—"Magna veritas et prevalebit,"—"Truth is potent, and"—"Most potent, grave, and reverend seigniors":

> '"Oh, now you weep; and I perceive you feel
> The dint of pity: these are gracious drops.
> Kind souls, what, weep you when you but behold
> Our Cæsar's vesture wounded?"—

Ha! ha! ha!—and I broke out in a fit of most horrible laughter, as I thought of the mince-meat particles of my lacerated jacket.

'In the meantime, the water had got well up towards my shoulders, and while I was shaking, and vibrating upon my uncertain foothold, I felt the cold nose of the captain of the band snubbing against my side. Desperately, and without a definite object, I struck my knife at one of his eyes, and, by some singular fortune, cut it out clean from the socket. The shark darted back, and halted. In an instant hope and reason came to my relief; and it occurred to me, that if I could only blind the monster, I might yet escape. Accordingly, I stood ready for the next attack. The loss of an eye did not seem to affect him much, for after shaking his head once or twice, he came up to me again, and when he was about half an inch off, turned upon his back. This was the critical moment. With a most unaccountable presence of mind, I laid hold of his nose with my left hand, and with my right scooped out his remaining organ of vision. He opened his big mouth, and champed his long teeth at me, in despair. But it was all over with him. I raised my right foot and gave him a hard shove, and he glided off into deep water, and went to the bottom.

'Well, gentlemen, I suppose you'd think it a hard story, but it's none the less a fact, that I served every remaining one of those nineteen sharks in the same fashion. They all came up to me, one by one, regularly and in order, and I scooped their eyes out, and gave them a shove, and they went off into deep water, just like so many lambs. By the time I had scooped out and blinded a couple of dozen of them, they began to seem so scarce that I thought I would swim for the island, and fight the rest for fun, on the way; but just then, Tim Titus hove in sight, and it had got to be almost dark, and I concluded to get aboard and rest myself.'

THE FOOLISH FISHERMAN

From *THE ARABIAN NIGHTS*

This story from *The Arabian Nights* is from volume IX of Sir Richard F. Burton's edition (16 vols 1885-8).

A FISHERMAN went forth to a river for fishing therein as was his wont; and when he came thither and walked upon the bridge, he saw a great fish and said in himself, ''Twill not serve me to abide here, but I will follow yonder fish whitherso it goeth, till I catch it, for it will relieve me from fishing for days and days.' So he did off his clothes and plunged into the river after the fish. The current bore him along till he overtook it and laid hold of it, when he turned and found himself far from the bank. But albeit he saw what the stream had done with him, he would not loose the fish and return, but ventured life and gripping it fast with both hands, let his body float with the flow, which carried him on till it cast him into a whirlpool none might enter and come out therefrom. With this he fell to crying out and saying, 'Save a drowning man!' And there came to him folk of the keepers of the river and said to him, 'What ailed thee to cast thyself into this great peril?' Quoth he, 'It was I myself who forsook the plain way wherein was salvation and gave myself over to concupiscence and perdition.' Quoth they, 'O fellow, why didst thou leave the way of safety and cast thyself into this destruction, knowing from of old that none may enter herein and be saved? What hindered thee from throwing away what was in thy hand and saving thyself? So hadst thou escaped with thy life and not fallen into this perdition, whence there is no deliverance; and now not one of us can rescue thee from this thy ruin.' Accordingly the man cut off all his hopes of life and lost that which was in his hand and for which his flesh had prompted him to venture himself, and died a miserable death.

FISH AND A 'FISH'

By WILLIAM SCROPE

For WILLIAM SCROPE, see p. 136. 'Fish and a "Fish"' is from chapter IV of *Days and Nights of Salmon Fishing in the Tweed* (1843).

I WENT forth, after my arrival at Selkirk town, at the hour of prime. I asked no questions, for I cannot endure to hear beforehand what sort of sport I am likely to have. Sober truth is sometimes exceedingly distressing, and brings one's mind to a lull; it puts an end to the sublimity of extravagant speculation, which I hold to be the chief duty of a sportsman. So, as I said, I asked no questions; but I saw the river Ettrick before me taking her free course beneath the misty hills, and, brushing away the dewdrops with my steps, I rushed impatiently through the broom and gorse with torn hose and smarting legs, till I arrived at the margin of that wild river, where the birch hung its ringlets over the waters.

Out came my trusty rod from a case of 'filthy dowlass.' Top varnished it was, and the work of the famous Higginbotham: not he the hero of an hundred engines, who was afeard of nothing, and whose 'fireman's soul was all on fire' [1]; but Higginbotham of the Strand, who was such an artist in the rod line as never appeared before, or has ever been seen since. 'He never joyed since the price of hiccory wood rose,' and was soon after gathered to the tomb of his fathers. I look upon him, and old Kirby the quondam maker of hooks, to be two

[1] Correctly Higginbottom, fireman hero in a 'Tale of Drury Lane,' Horace Smith's parody of Sir Walter Scott in the *Rejected Addresses* (1812).

of the greatest men the world ever saw; not even excepting Eustace Ude,[1] or Michael Angelo Buonarroti.

But to business. The rod was hastily put together; a beautiful new azure line passed through the rings; a casting line, made like the waist of Prior's Emma, appended, with two trout flies attached to it of the manufacture even of me, Harry Otter. An eager throw to begin with: round came the flies intact. Three, four, five, six throws—a dozen: no better result. The fish were stern and contemptuous. At length some favourable change took place in the clouds, or atmosphere, and I caught sundry small trout; and finally, in the cheek of a boiler, I fairly hauled out a two-pounder. A jewel of a fish he was—quite a treasure all over. After I had performed the satisfactory office of bagging him, I came to a part of the river which, being contracted, rushed forward in a heap, rolling with great impetuosity. Here, after a little flogging, I hooked a lusty fellow, strong as an elephant, and swift as a thunderbolt. How I was agitated say ye who best can tell, ye fellow tyros! Every moment did I expect my trout tackle, for such it was, to part company. At length, after various runs of dubious result, the caitiff began to yield; and at the expiration of about half an hour, I wooed him to the shore. What a sight then struck my optics! A fair five-pounder at the least; not fisherman's weight, mark me, but such as would pass muster with the most conscientious lord mayor of London during the high price of bread. Long did I gaze on him, not without self-applause. All too large he was for my basket; I therefore laid the darling at full length on the ground, under a birch tree, and covered over the precious deposit with some wet bracken, that it might not suffer from the sunbeam.

I had not long completed this immortal achievement ere I saw a native approaching, armed with a prodigious

[1] Louis Eustache Ude, a famous late 18th and early 19th century French-English cook.

fishing-rod of simple construction, guiltless of colour or varnish. He had a belt round his waist, to which was fastened a large wooden reel or pirn, and the line passed from it through the rings of his rod: a sort of Wat Tinlinn he was to look at. The whole affair seemed so primitive—there was such an absolute indigence of ornament, and poverty of conception, that I felt somewhat fastidious about it. I could not, however, let a brother of the craft pass unnoticed, albeit somewhat rude in his attire; so, 'What sport,' said I, 'my good friend?'

'I canna say that I hae had muckle deversion; for she is quite fallen in, and there wull be no good fishing till there comes a spate.'

Now, after this remark, I waxed more proud of my success; but I did not come down upon him at once with it, but said somewhat slyly, and with mock modesty—

'Then you think there is not much chance for any one, and least of all for a stranger like myself?'

'I dinna think the like o' ye can do muckle; though I will no say but ye may light on a wee bit troot, or may be on a happening fish. That's a bonny little wand you've got; and she shimmers so with varnish, that I'm thinking that when she is in the eye o' the sun the fish will come aneath her, as they do to the blaze in the water.'

Sandy was evidently lampooning my Higginbotham. I therefore replied that she certainly had more shining qualities than were often met with on the northern side of the Tweed. At this personality, my pleasant friend took out a large mull from his pocket, and, applying a copious quantity of its contents to his nose, very politely responded—

'Ye needna fash[1] yoursel to observe aboot the like o' her; she is no worth this pinch o' snuff.'

He then very courteously handed his mull to me.

'Well,' said I, still modestly, 'she will do well enough for a bungler like me.' I was trolling for a compliment.

[1] trouble.

'Ay, that will she,' said he.

Though a little mortified, I was not sorry to get him to this point; for I knew I could overwhelm him with facts, and the more diffidently I conducted myself the more complete would be my triumph. So laying down my pet rod on the channel, I very deliberately took out my two-pounder, as a feeler. He looked particularly well; for I had tied up his mouth, that he might keep his shape, and moistened him, as I before said, with soaked fern to preserve his colour. I fear I looked a little elate on the occasion; assuredly I felt so.

'There's a fine fish now—a perfect beauty!'

'Hoot-toot! that's no fish ava.'

'No fish, man! What the deuce is it, then? Is it a rabbit, or a wild duck, or a water-rat?'

'Ye are joost gin daft. Do ye no ken a troot when ye see it?'

I could make nothing of this answer, for I thought that a trout was a fish; but it seems I was mistaken. However, I saw the envy of the man; so I determined to inflict him with a settler at once. For this purpose I inveigled him to where my five-pounder was deposited; then kneeling down, and proudly removing the bracken I had placed over him, there lay the monster most manifest, extended in all his glory. The light—the eye of the landscape—before whose brilliant sides Runjeet Singh's diamond, called 'the mountain of light,' would sink into the deep obscure; dazzled with the magnificent sight, I chuckled in the plenitude of victory. This was unbecoming in me, I own, for I should have borne my faculties meekly; but I was young and sanguine; so (*horresco referens*) I gave a smart turn of my body, and, placing an arm akimbo, said, in an exulting tone, and with a scrutinising look, 'There, what do you think of that?' I did not see the astonishment in Sawny's face that I had anticipated, neither did he seem to regard me with the least degree of veneration; but, giving my pet a shove with his nasty iron-shod shoes, he simply said:

'Hoot! that's a wee bit gilse.'

This was laconic. I could hold no longer, for I hate a detractor; so I roundly told him that I did not think he had ever caught so large a fish in all his life.

'Did you, now?—own.'

'I suppose I have.'

'Suppose! But don't you know?'

'I suppose I have.'

'Speak decidedly, yes or no. That is no answer.'

'Well, then, I suppose I have.'

And this was the sum total of what I could extract from this *nil admirari* fellow.

A third person now joined us, whom I afterwards discovered to be the renter of that part of the river. He had a rod and tackle of the selfsame fashion with the apathetic man. He touched his bonnet to me; and if he did not eye me with approval, at least he did not look envious or sarcastic.

'Well, Sandy,' said he to his piscatorial friend, my new acquaintance, 'what luck the morn?'

'I canna speecify that I hae had muckle; for they hae bin at the sheep-washing up bye, and she is foul, ye ken. But I hae ta'en twa saumon—ane wi' Nancy, and the ither wi' a Toppy—baith in Faldon-side Burn fut.'[1]

And twisting round a coarse linen bag which was slung at his back, and which I had supposed to contain some common lumber, he drew forth by the tail a never-ending monster of a salmon, dazzling and lusty to the view; and then a second, fit consort to the first. Could you believe it? One proved to be fifteen pounds, and the other twelve! At the sudden appearance of these whales I was shivered to atoms: dumbfoundered I was, like the Laird of Cockpen when Mrs Jean refused the honour of his hand. I felt as small as Flimnap the treasurer in the presence of Gulliver. Little did I say; but that little, I hope, was becoming a youth in my situation.

[1] foot.

PARADISE BUMBLE

By EDEN PHILLPOTTS

EDEN PHILLPOTTS (born 1862), English novelist, short-story writer, dramatist, and poet. 'Paradise Bumble' is from chapter XI of *Folly and Fresh Air* (1891), a novel of a fishing holiday in Devonshire, and is here given by permission of Messrs Hurst & Blackett Ltd. 'Brake Fern Weir,' in *Down Dartmoor Way* (1896), has a river-poaching background, and in *Three Birds With One Stone* (1903), a short story, there are good descriptions of fishing and of fishing scenery.

THE Doctor started along the river's bank, and I followed mechanically. Presently we found a little, round-shouldered, dwarfish fellow with a long beard. He was fishing, and singing to himself stray snatches of old country melodies.

'Will you show my brother some of those wonderful home-made flies of yours,' said the Doctor.

'Awnly tu pleased, I assure 'e,' answered the little man, and, putting down his rod, he got from some obscure pocket a strange book made of old newspaper. This contained trout-flies which the Doctor's quaint friend had himself manufactured. He proved a complete authority on local sport, abounded with odd rustic sayings, and showed keen pleasure at exhibiting the clever work of his hands to us. My brother had given him a fly or two as patterns, and in return received some infallible specimens, manufactured from live models which the little man had himself caught on the water. They had also exchanged lunches, which accounted for the singular meal I found my brother engaged upon. It was cheese, not soap, as I at first feared, which the Doctor had been eating.

'Water-rats' fur be very gude fashioned stuff for fly-bodies. Then you gets feathers from the farm-yards, and makes any shade to the wings and such as you've a mind,' explained the artist. 'Now that theer's a proper tied fly, though I sez it—a proper tied fly, so true to the livin' hinsec as may be. It's my partickler, that is.'

The little gentleman's 'partickler' was a rather loud fly with a bit of peacock's feather in it, and I mentally determined to try my prentice hand in secret at fashioning just such another, and so astonishing the Doctor and perhaps getting admiration from him. I made mental notes of the thing, and recollected that there were peacocks' feathers in vases in our sitting-room. As to water-rats' fur, it seemed a pity to kill a whole rat just for the small part of it I should require. No, I rather thought I saw a simple way out of that difficulty. Our new friend said he would be down again in the dusk of evening to try for a peel; so we arranged to meet him about seven o'clock, and also try for a peel. With three goodish fishermen all trying together for a peel, the numerical strength of that fish in this stream should be reduced. And possibly the fly I am going to make will take some peel's fancy, and so reward my labours. It would be a good and pleasant circumstance to catch a peel on a fly you yourself have tied.

The first thing I had to do was to get my brother out of the way. This I managed rather cleverly after returning for a cup of tea. I said:

'Would it not be as well to find out at the station about trains to Maryford?'

He fell into the trap immediately, and marched off to worry the people at the railway, thus leaving me free to my task. I began by choosing a big, naked hook from my collection. Of these I had several, with a view to using a worm some day for the trout, if there chanced to be a flood; for a friend had told me that it was a fine thing to fish for trout with a worm in a flood. The hook ready, I cut a piece off one of the landlady's peacocks' feathers, and started. Then it became necessary to procure fur, and the cat being available, this difficulty was surmounted exactly as I had foreseen. The cat entered the window just about the time I wanted him, had a dish of milk, and cleaned his claws on the leg of the table. Then he sat down and gazed at me without winking, as cats will gaze at a man when they are trying to get at his real private opinion of them.

It was just the sort of animal for a fly-maker, being much variegated in colour, with brown patches and white. I took my fishing scissors and chipped off a lock or two from the cat, and it purred and fussed about, of course not realising what I was doing. Then, as ill-luck would have it, our landlady came in to clear away the tea-things. I admit it looked strange and undesirable at first sight, to see a grown man sitting on the floor cutting tufts off a cat; but there was no occasion for such a volcanic outburst as I now suffered from Mrs Vallack. Had I been brutally vivisecting the cat, she could not have showed greater severity. I tried to pass it off with a jest, but she was too vexed to appreciate the fun of the situation. She said I couldn't keep my hands off a single thing in the house. She implied that I was making her life a burden to her. She finally picked up the astounded cat by his neck and bounced out of the room. I own I was annoyed with the woman. I had intended to tell her all about the peacock's feather, and even buy it outright if there was any unpleasantness. But now I determined to say nothing, nor should I offer any apology for my conduct to the cat. 'Hang it all, I'm down here for pleasure,' I said to myself; and then went on making the fly.

The insect began to grow under my hands. It had rather a tropical look, I fancied; one would have naturally expected to see such an affair buzzing about in the neighbourhood of the equator, but it appeared out of place at home. It might, I thought, after further struggles with it, be now easily mistaken for a caterpillar with wings. This was not true to nature, and the trout would know it. Cat's fur is very difficult to work with. I needed a further supply, but dared not ask for the cat. One thing I knew—there was no other local cat that matched ours. Then I added a trifle more feather, and the fly began to grow lifelike, with a fantastic, unearthly animation all its own. I felt as Frankenstein perhaps felt; I half expected to see the thing rise up and hum round the room and bang against the window. A wasp noticed it, and fell off the table in her hurry to get away. Now this I regarded as a perfect test. I had evidently imitated a real insect so exactly that other flies feared it and hastened to escape from it.

I put the finished creation on the mantelpiece as the Doctor returned. Presently his eye fell upon it, and he said:

'Good Lord! What's that beast?'

Then he picked up a book and crept forward with a view of smashing it. My triumph was complete; my work had deceived man!

'Stay your hand!' I cried, and picked it up and showed it to him. 'Alone I did it,' I declared, with quiet pride.

'You made this?' he asked, examining it.

'Every atom of it,' I told him.

'Why?' he said.

This is another of his idiotic questions. I cooled down in a moment.

'Why are artificial flies made?' I inquired.

'But you don't mean to assert you are going to fish with this?' he murmured, looking first at me and then at my handiwork.

'I certainly am,' I replied calmly.

He thought about the matter for some time before speaking again. Then he said: 'What d' you call it?'

I pretended not to hear him, and, seeing he had me in difficulties, he repeated the question.

'As to naming it,' I answered at length, 'I have not yet thought of that. It will probably become a classic fly, without which no fisherman's outfit would be considered complete. I shall very likely call it the "Paradise Bumble."'

He reflected again with his hand held up to the side of his head. After a pause, he observed:

'It might pass on a Christmas-tree, but as to supposing any ordinary fish would look at it—well!'

'I'm not going to try for an ordinary fish,' I said. 'When you see a ten-pound peel gasping on the bank you'll understand.'

Then I left the house, and took out the fly to pit it against anything that swam. Yet, curiously enough, why I shall never know, the thing was not a success at all. One trout saw it, and I think fainted, for it sank like a stone. Then the local angler came along and examined it and looked at me, and I felt that the look meant I had forfeited his respect.

'My stars!' he said, 'wonnerful fly, sure'nough—a reg'lar pantomime of a fly, sir.'

Then we fished about for peel in such places as he considered might harbour them. He told many remarkable stories on peel-catching, more, I suspect, to keep our spirits up than because the stories in themselves possessed any truth or value. It appears hard in discoursing of great adventures to help adding a little colour sometimes. I have denied myself so far, and kept well within the bounds of human experience and common-sense, but the struggle is perpetual. I find it necessary to watch my pen narrowly, and even occasionally to make it run out that which it has written down. This attempt to circumvent peel, for instance, might easily be managed so as to read very differently. Had I caused the Doctor to catch a peel, or our companion to kill a big one, or even myself to secure a couple of small fish, you would have been quite disposed to believe it. But no, I take my stand on bald veracity; and, as the first angler that ever did such a thing, may reasonably hope that some day a statue shall be raised depicting me in the aforesaid position. We did not catch a peel or anything at all. The little man failed to understand it; he affected to be grievously disappointed and surprised; but I don't fancy he felt very deeply about it in his heart, and he was delighted when we said we were going to stop fishing, and invited him in to supper.

CRUEL DIVERSION

By GEORGE BORROW

GEORGE HENRY BORROW (1803-1881), passionate lover of nature's scene, tells of his fishing in chapter XV of *Lavengro* (1851), comparing the sport unfavourably with shooting, and then goes on to relate the incident given below. Earlier, in chapter VI, he has told memorably, though not at the moment as an angler, of his first view of the Tweed at its mouth.

AT some distance from the city, behind a range of hilly ground which rises towards the south-west, is a small river, the waters of which, after many meanderings, eventually enter the principal river of the district, and assist to swell the tide which it rolls down to the ocean. It is a sweet rivulet, and pleasant it is to trace its course from its spring-head, high up in the remote regions of Eastern Anglia, till it arrives in the valley behind yon rising ground; and pleasant is that valley, truly a goodly spot, but most lovely where yonder bridge crosses the little stream. Beneath its arch the waters rush garrulously into a blue pool, and are there stilled for a time, for the pool is deep, and they appear to have sunk to sleep. Farther on, however, you hear their voice again, where they ripple gaily over yon gravelly shallow. On the left, the hill slopes gently down to the margin of the stream. On the right is a green level, a smiling meadow, grass of the richest decks the side of the slope; mighty trees also adorn it, giant elms, the nearest of which, when the sun is nigh its meridian, fling a broad shadow upon the face of the pool; through yon vista you catch a glimpse of the ancient brick of an old English hall. It has a stately look, that old building, indistinctly seen, as it is, among those umbrageous trees; you might almost suppose it an earl's home; and such it was, or rather upon its site stood an earl's home, in days of old.

I was in the habit of spending many an hour on the banks of that rivulet with my rod in my hand, and, when tired with angling, would stretch myself on the grass, and gaze upon the waters as they glided past, and not unfrequently, divesting myself of my dress, I would plunge into the deep pool which I have already mentioned, for I had long since learned to swim. And it came to pass, that on one hot summer's day, after bathing in the pool, I passed along the meadow till I came to a shallow part, and, wading over to the opposite side, I adjusted my dress, and commenced fishing in another pool, beside which was a small clump of hazels.

And there I sat upon the bank at the bottom of the hill which slopes down from 'the Earl's home'; my float was on the waters, and my back was towards the old hall. I drew up many fish, small and great, which I took from off the hook mechanically, and flung upon the bank, for I was almost unconscious of what I was about, for my mind was not with my fish. I was thinking of my earlier years—of the Scottish crags and the heaths of Ireland—and sometimes my mind would dwell on my studies—on the sonorous stanzas of Dante, rising and falling like the waves of the sea—or would strive to remember a couplet or two of poor Monsieur Boileau.

'Canst thou answer to thy conscience for pulling all those fish out of the water, and leaving them to gasp in the sun?' said a voice, clear and sonorous as a bell.

I started, and looked round. Close behind me stood the tall figure of a man, dressed in raiment of quaint and singular fashion, but of goodly materials. He was in the prime and vigour of manhood; his features handsome and noble, but full of calmness and benevolence; at least I thought so, though they were somewhat shaded by a hat of finest beaver, with broad drooping eaves.

'Surely that is a very cruel diversion in which thou indulgest, my young friend?' he continued.

'I am sorry for it, if it be, sir,' said I, rising; 'but I do not think it cruel to fish.'

'What are thy reasons for not thinking so?'

'Fishing is mentioned frequently in Scripture. Simon Peter was a fisherman.'

'True; and Andrew and his brother. But thou forgettest: they did not follow fishing as a diversion, as I fear thou doest.—Thou readest the Scriptures?'

'Sometimes.'

'Sometimes?—not daily?—that is to be regretted. What profession dost thou make?—I mean to what religious denomination dost thou belong, my young friend?'

'Church.'

'It is a very good profession—there is much of Scripture contained in its liturgy. Dost thou read aught beside the Scriptures?'

'Sometimes.'

'What dost thou read besides?'

'Greek, and Dante.'

'Indeed; then thou hast the advantage over myself; I can only read the former. Well, I am rejoiced to find that thou hast other pursuits beside thy cruel fishing. Farewell!'

And the man of peace departed, and left me on the bank of the stream. Whether from the effect of his words, or from want of inclination to the sport, I know not, but from that day I became less and less a practitioner of that 'cruel fishing.' I rarely flung line and angle into the water, but I not unfrequently wandered by the banks of the pleasant rivulet.

THE LAKE OF THE RED TROUT

By H. A. MANHOOD

HAROLD ALFRED MANHOOD (born 1904), English short-story writer. 'The Lake of the Red Trout,' here given by permission of the author and of Messrs Jonathan Cape Ltd, is from *Crack of Whips* (1934), which has other fishing stories; and there are also fishing stories in the author's *Nightseed* (1928), *Apples by Night* (1932), *Sunday Bugles* (1939).

THE two of us, fisherman and novice, came upon the mountain lake quite unexpectedly in the evening of a long, dusty, sun-blurred day, and the discovery was as refreshing as ice in the mouth. Trout were everywhere rising with the quiet ripple of earnest feeders, the successive targets having the likeness of eyes widening in merry, welcoming surprise. This was the wine of the mountains for which we searched, we assured each other, as we gazed from a pike-head ledge: a lake of decided character, wonderfully cupped in curiously knotted stone, and sternly different from the greenpan lowland waters in which we had fished for twenty days past.

Since dayspring we had travelled roads without regard for their surfaces or thought for the car, viewing many lakes with critical eyes, questioning warmly interested cottagers (who, at first, misled by our odd clothes and black-sheeted burden of collapsible boat and camping gear, invariably mistook us for journeymen undertakers or outriders of a circus) on the subject of fish and weather, and pondering secretly at times on the wisdom of travelling without maps; fortifying ourselves with promises of a rich discovery, recalling old thrills, old camps found without compass, Rich only hoping always with the strange, illogical faith of the true fisherman, who, as it is said, sees fish in every soup-plate, and hatches flies in his armpits when nature fails in her covenants. We crossed sunken bogs veined and fretted like old leaves, where turf had been cut since the Saints were young, and virgin bogs with remote cuttings glowing like the marks of branding irons, all brightly fleeced with cotton-grass upon which melancholy asses browsed as if in the hope of renewing their grey and matted hairs. We searched for the arms of signposts which had fallen from their sockets, but only undecipherable snail-shine marked the bleached wood. Villages blinked awake as we passed, pigs turning in their sleep and fowls skipping from comfortable dust-pits in the road with hysterical comment. Heads peered from doorways like flowers drawn in the wind, bright wondering eyes following us in our course. The civic guard would pause in the nursing of his infant son to regard us good-humouredly, prepared to advise us minutely, no whit dismayed or affronted when we passed with no more than a choking gift of dust. Sometimes a dog raced with us, and Rich would talk encouragingly, holding the car at level speed. A worthy runner was rewarded with a ship's biscuit and a poor one with a hoot of derision which must have penetrated deeply, if drooping, woebegone head and tail and shambling gait fairly indicated the way of the spirit.

Eight o'clock found us some forty miles west of Cork on a well-graded but peculiarly stony road rising towards a great half-moon range of mountains. A stream ran beside the valley road—a pleasant stream with dark trouty pools and hissing falls. Ruminating on the brink, we imagined a mountain-shadowed lake, a fine oval mirror linked to this handsome splinter necklace. The vision became an enticing fact after conversation with a toothless, barefooted old dame, who carried a splendid crown of butter on a bit of slate. Approaching nimbly down the road, avoiding flints by enviable instinct, she stood and laughed at the metal rabbit on the radiator cap, and then came and peered shyly round at us, feet deftly shuffling a space clear of larger piercing stones. Was a lake connected with the stream, we asked, and she answered with her eyes on the tobacco with which Rich was filling his pipe—

'Surely! Surely! As grand a lake as the Holy One ever made is away up there in the lap of the mountains. 'Tis called Nam-brach-derg, it is, and 'twill be glad to see ye, for 'tis lonely it must be with only Moriarty and his woman living on the verge and them a little mad with the bleakness of it all.'

And were there fish in the lake?

The old woman smiled and nodded wisely: 'Surely! Surely! for didn't Nam-brach-derg mean the Lake of the Red Trout, and isn't it a pity ye have no Irish to be understanding the country properly. But there, 'tis past understanding entirely we are, and the Irish a dying fire at the back of the world.' She sighed and scratched one foot with the other, eyeing us shrewdly, smiling delightedly when Rich offered his pouch. Adroitly balancing the butter slate in the crook of her arm, she pressed tobacco into her cheek and returned the pouch with a merry wink, blessing us in well-sounding Irish as we climbed into the car. Turning back for a last sight of her we saw her standing with her red skirt folded over the butter to shield it from our dust. She had not yet begun to chew the tobacco, but was saving it for her solitude as a child might save a rare sweet. 'So long!' we called, and she nodded, and, without lowering her eyes, scooped a finger-tuft of butter to her mouth to improve the tobacco. We wished that we had asked her name. 'A fine old Friday Soul,' commented Rich, and so she became for us the Friday Soul, always to be remembered for her mixing of butter and tobacco.

Very soon the road parted with the stream. Hedges dropped away, and only occasional wind-twisted thorns and knuckles of gorse appeared above the cliff edge on our left. We passed a derelict cottage of fire-blackened stone, empty save for a truculent yellow-eyed ram, and a shabby pair of crows nested in the crumbling lichen-patched chimney. Mountain sheep stared down at us from the higher slopes, pausing momentarily in their chewing, the lambs simulating an elderly indifference until an unexpected bumping or slide of locked wheels broke their nerve and sent them panicking in all directions. Already we had climbed two miles. The road could be seen ahead, a dark bristle-edged line swinging in a wide upward curve against the olive-green and rock-littered mountains. Four miles at least to go before we should reach the only basin which seemed at all likely to contain a lake, and from which the stream appeared to drain. The road in its surface and bends reminded us of a river-bed. We recalled the Gap of Dunloe and a particular coast road in Donegal, and endeavoured to make merry over present difficulties. Sometimes a spray of stones would rattle over the edge as we rounded elephant rocks and leaning bastions, and unexpected echoes would rise like brisk laughter at our expense. With a show of carelessness we tried to distinguish a back axle note above the bumpings of the springs, but so many were the squeaks and grunts that accuracy in diagnosis was impossible. 'If she goes, she goes,' declared Rich with philosophic emphasis, adding happily, 'Anyway, the lake can hardly be overfished, even by birds.'

A cold upsweeping wind brought the smell of burning turf to our nostrils, and we saw, far down the valley, a black and smoking strip of bogland. 'It was probably burning long before the Friday Soul was born. . . .' The thought occupied us for many minutes and, slowly, the genius of the mountains entered into us, and we were cool and content where we had been fevered and out of humour. A well-rounded green-tinged mass of cloud vanished behind a serrated ridge like a bunch of grapes into a hungry mouth, and it seemed an appropriate nourishment, an explanation of the grape-bloom that was now upon every crag and slope. A distant water-splash sparkled as might wine leaking to waste. Two bell-wethers wrangled together in the valley, making merry jangling music suggestive of convivial occasions. The frenzied boiling of the radiator, and the snatch and lunge of the car over outcropping rocks, seemed but matter for amusement in such a perfect cradle of poetry.

The road ended suddenly, unexpectedly. Driving through tunnelled rocks, we emerged into a quarry-like arena from which sheep-paths only meandered onwards. The place was like the inside of a shell, and as sound is prisoned in a shell, so were our thoughts prisoned. Where was the lake? Evidently we should have to climb. We had cherished hopes of driving to the brink and pitching camp between car and lake. So often had we done this that it had become a habit of mind to anticipate absolute convenience. Still, wasn't this the Lake of the Red Trout, something different and new in our experience? Its inaccessibility was part of its charm. So we argued as we stood there, cut off from the wind, and solemnly regarded by five elderly sheep, who stood like a suspicious reception committee close-grouped upon the path which appeared most likely to lead to heart's desire. Only at the last moment of approach did they turn tail, and we laughed at their undignified flight and were at once silent again, for violent echoes filled the craggy shell, the sounds damping us by their piercing strangeness. Thoughtfully we climbed out of the basin into the wind again, stepping among tufted heath and cotton-grass, casting about for a direction. A magnificent perpendicular cliff-face towered ahead, silvered here and there with slow-sliding water that was like a queer breaking sweat. But the dividing slope that prevented a glimpse of its heels was vividly green, water-nourished, as we discovered after a tentative move. Time, however, was fast making its round. We were anxious for a sight of the promised water, and camp must soon be fixed. There seemed no way round the treacherous green, so we stepped squarely forward, water bubbling high, the whole slope quaking as we floundered on, loud sucking noises sounding long after we had passed. An anxious minute and we were safely across, hurrying over heath and great humped rocks that were like peering heads, to a lichened rampart which barred us from clear vision. Jostling each other in our eagerness, we craned forward, and were together awed and comforted. Stretching downwards under our eyes was a great broken slope, toothed with white-bleached tree-stumps and limestone quoins, and gloomy with burnt heather, among which scorched-looking sheep browsed with fatalistic determination. At the foot of the slope was the lake, large and splendid and ringed by breaking trout, walled by the earlier seen cliff which descended straightly into the water the oval length of the lake, dropping in magnificent crags and overlips down to meet the heather slopes on either side. It was as if the seat of a massive straight-backed throne had been made to hold water. A sinister place, Rich thought, in the present light, only redeemed by the breaking trout. We could hear the wind against the cliff, a low defeated sound in the stillness. The rock-face was deep-seamed and creviced, as if anciently scribbled over by a master-graver, splashed with white in curious manner as if someone of lighter soul—perhaps old Moriarty, of whom the Friday Soul had told us—had sought to efface some part of the runic warning. Now a mass of cloud settled upon the cliff-top, and it was as if a great fist were scratching the ragged pate in perplexity at our coming. Distant at the end of the lake, Moriarty's cottage lay like an old lobster-pot, and near it was a boat, a fish to bait the same pot, the Novice thought, then started, for Rich had seen the boat, and was wondering aloud whether we might borrow it. 'Better than the collapsible,' he mused. A wild sad cry, perfectly expressing the dour spirit of the place, surprised us both, echoing as a stone echoes in its bouncing down a well, and we saw a buzzard soar out from the cliff, circling and hovering by a miracle of physical understanding of wind and air, swerving inwards again to its white-splashed roost while echoes of its cry still were flung the length of the dreaming lake.

Sighing a little at the dying light, Rich turned away. 'Time enough for a cast or so before dark,' he said, and lurched and splashed his way hurriedly back to the car.

'But what of the camp?' Practical and with a care for comfort, the Novice followed.

'Pitch it where you like.'

'And supper?'

'Biscuits and chocolate will do if you can't manage to trim a fire.'

'Imbecile!' retorted the Novice lovingly.

Very well we understand each other, the one in his simplicity valuing a good fish well caught far above food and comfort; and the other, being but a novice and with a truly English need of snugness, finding utter pleasure in the tight line only when assured that house and belly are in happy order. Quickly but with care, Rich unstraps rods and reaches for the tackle-bags. He will not stop for waders, and hurries off with a length of gut soaking in his mouth and his hands occupied with the screwing of landing-net into handle and the fitting of rod joints together.

'Good luck!' calls the Novice as he begins his search for kindling and level tent square, and Rich mumbles a characteristic reply, 'There's no such thing as luck in good fishing—but I know what you mean.'

Within half an hour the camp was fixed for the night, the tent secure against unlikely yet possible wind and rain, sleeping-bags disposed, water brought from a rock trickle fifty yards away, fire burning well, coffee simmering; and a rabbit, killed that morning by a wheel of the car, frying in the pan in butter which we had helped to churn. Enamel plates are propped to heat, food-box spread as table; jam, biscuits, chocolate, and apples piled close to hand, and all is ready. But the Novice hesitates to whistle. He climbs and peers down at the lake, beautiful in the last reflected light, steel-blue and shining in its lapping as if dusted with powdered gems; sees Rich casting from a spoon-point with unfailing artistry. The trout have ceased to rise, but he is reaching for them in their water pockets. Five more minutes and the lake will be dimmed. At the extreme end of the lake, where Moriarty's cottage seems to cower under its ledge, a figure watches; Moriarty himself, it must be, come like a spider to the edge of his web, waiting and watching without movement. Is he resentful of our intrusion? We should have approached him before fishing, but time was so short. The morning would do as well. After explanation and apology he might, as Rich hoped, offer his boat with true Irish generosity. 'Sure and ye must take she whenever's the fancy's upon ye. 'Tis sorry I am she's untidy a bit, but there, bless ye, I had no feeling at all ye were coming. *Next* year now and I'll have her grand for ye, ladylike enough to mix with the best from Athlone.' So another had promised us and so might Moriarty. Strange and chilling to the soul it must be to live always in the shadow of such a masterful cliff. The Novice sedulously nurses his feeling for comfort, and loudly whistles for the return of the enthusiast, the sound seeming to race round and round that enormous stone cup and curl itself snakily, restrainingly, about the arm of Rich; for he pauses, then waves emphatically and winds in his line, trudging upwards with thoughtful air.

The Novice waits by the camp fire, toasting a fragment of cheese. He hears Rich cross the quaggy slope, breathing hard, then pause to stamp moisture from his shoes before marching to the fire. 'Smells good!' he declares, and sits to unlace his shoes, pull off soaked stockings, and wriggle his feet perilously close to the glowing turf.

'What luck?' The Novice empties fat from the pan

with sympathetic gesture. Already he has seen the empty net and translated the absent-minded expression upon the face of Rich.

'Just one bite.' Transferring a leg of rabbit from one hand to the other, Rich reaches into a pocket and tosses a miserable, muddy-coloured, four-inch trout across. 'And I nearly broke the net in landing him! Happened to slip on some hair weed. Plenty of fish rising, but 'twas a kind of bat and ball they played with my flies. Can't understand it at all.'

'Perhaps the clouds were the wrong shape for good fishing, or maybe the wind was in the wrong key. Did you try the May-bee?' Gently the Novice quizzes and offers excuse, having long ago realised the necessity of excuse to the unlucky fisherman.

But Rich is in no mood for banter. 'Not a bit funny!' He flings a bone from sight and rakes an ember to fire his pipe, gazing reflectively. 'It was queer down there by the water; like trying to fish inside a glass bowl, yourself inside and the fish beyond the glass. I could hear the flies scraping across the water. Trout came and whacked them with their tails, breaking wild, as they say, but not so much wildly as with intelligent sarcasm, it seemed to me. It was just as if someone had told them that those flies weren't good to eat. Fine trout, most of them, well over half a pound. But still, there it is. To-morrow we'll borrow that boat down the lake and spend all we know, and if we haven't enough trout for a reunion supper by night, well, I'll take to prawning!'

The Novice nods over the coffee-pot. Slowly the fire crumbled, surrounding rocks glowing like the great red cheeks of approving giants. Night is fast soaking down upon us. Far down the valley a light swings in erratic dance for several minutes; then blinks out as the cottager, satisfied that cows and fowls are secure, re-enters his dwelling. Now a cold wind drives like a tide across the mountains, filling every niche, whipping sparks from our fire, and shaking heath and gorse until the air is loud with a creaking and sighing as of flailing broken wings.

Rich taps the dottle from his pipe, and carefully damps the fire, hanging shoes and stockings where the wind will dry them. 'To bed, my son.'

Five minutes later we are comfortably relaxed. The wind bumps against the tent, but we are not disturbed. Rich sighs and turns a little. 'We'll try Eagan's May-flies to-morrow.' The Novice drowsily imagines a great Mayfly swooping like a gull and lifting trout to our ready net. 'Sure, and can't we fly them like kites?' But only a derisive grunt answers him, and presently we sleep.

We awoke late the following morning for all our firm resolves. A great wedge of sunlight seemed to be forcing the tent in two. We rolled over and eyed each other, guessing at the hour, full of amiable blame. Scattering his clothes in a movement, Rich found his watch. 'Half-past nine, mother o' mine!' Hastily he wriggled from the sleeping-bag, snatched a towel, and scrambled out of the tent. But, instead of prancing to the water dip across the way, he stood and stared, hand pausing in its scratching. 'Hello!' A slow voice answered him, 'Good morning t'ye,' and Rich recovered from his astonishment sufficiently to cap the greeting. Intensely curious, the Novice rolled forward, peering between the legs of Rich, seeing no one at first, then meeting the gaze of a ragged old man squatting upon an upturned bucket against the car, his great hands stroking the fishing-rods loosely tied upon the running-board. He was a quaint old fellow, with a white bristling growth of beard upon his brown starved-looking face. Pale blue eyes gazed from sunken sockets, fierce curling lashes looking like old thorns above deep pools. His sharp nose seemed to sail over the broken waves of his lips. His hat appeared to be the top half of the sleeve of a frieze jacket, roughly folded and stitched. A thick, black, woollen scarf was round his neck, although the day was already hot enough to suggest sunspots. Great vari-coloured patches covered his jacket and trousers, like crusts of lichen, while his boots were astonishingly like little barrels.

At sight of the Novice he nodded extravagantly. 'I thought there were two of ye,' he said slowly, and grinned amiably. Producing a stumpy pipe, so burnt that it looked like a cinder raked from the fire, he began filling it with a mixture of tobacco and dust and wool emptied from a pocket. Hastily, perhaps remembering occasions when he himself had been forced to smoke a similar mixture, Rich rummaged for his pouch, forcing it upon the old man. 'Help yourself.'

'Me?' The old fellow scratched his nose in a startled way, examined the tobacco closely, and accepted a meagre pinch. 'I'll try it,' he said, as if uncertain whether it would suit his palate. He stared up. 'I'm Moriarty. I live down there. I saw ye last night.'

'Ah, yes, we were coming to see you.'

'About the fishing? Ye've heard maybe of the monster that is below, and would be catching him and earning fame the world over? Well, maybe ye will, and 'tis Moriarty himself will be helping ye, for 'tis a curse and a terror this beast is. Down below the cliff he lies in a sort of castle under water. 'Twas my sonny did see him first twelve years agone, and 'twas so frightened he was, and him no more than a child, that he fell and was drowned. That's why we must be catching the beast, d' ye understand me? Ye've strong tackle?'

'The strongest there is.' Rich went and sat beside the old man. 'Tell me more. What kind of a fish would it be, this monster? And have none fished for it before?'

'God only knows what kind it is, but for sure 'tis of a kind and size ye've never heard of before. One of the priests from the village did fish for him once, but he sickened and died within a week, and I'm thinking 'twas the fish that blackened his soul with its spite and wished him dead. 'Tis big as a curragh he is, this fish, if fish ye can call him, and him all scarred as if he'd been stabbed and stoned and his teeth all broken with the age of him. Terrible teeth they are still. Often I find great trout floating down there, and 'tis bitten in two they are, clean as ye'd slice a stick, and 'tis that is the old devil's idea of fun, to be murdering them gaily.'

'Is it a pike?'

'Nay, 'tis a greater than a pike, but there, 'tis yourselves shall see, and that soon, God willing. Will ye try for him?' The old man eyed us anxiously in turn.

'That we will,' Rich reassured him quickly, 'and be glad of the opportunity. We shall be needing a boat, though.'

''Tis mine ye shall have and myself to be showing ye the place.' The old man flapped his long arms in his excitement. 'Quick now! 'Tis a great day this will be and the end of that great murdering devil if only your gear is strong enough to be holding him. Give me something to be carrying now, and I'll away down below and fix the boat. . . .'

'Little enough to be carrying, and that we can manage.'

'But he's a hell of a great beast.'

'The bigger the better. We like them that way, and will come prepared.' Rich's confidence had a calming effect. Moriarty banged his pipe upon a stone with splintering force as if killing a fish, and shambled away, shouting directions.

We watched him go. Rich, still holding the towel in one hand, careless of flies on his naked body, began raking over the contents of a tackle-bag. 'Where did we put the Circus Spoon?'

The Circus Spoon was an enormous spinner bought years before after reading a volume of Irish fishing stories. Never yet used, it nevertheless figures in several excellent tales which Rich tells, preferably by night, when none can see our shudders of amusement. Now it seems that the moment of the Circus Spoon has come. The Novice ponders and names its whereabouts.

'An odd yarn. What did you make of it?'

'It sounds rather like a pike. Logically it can't be anything else. Theoretically pike exterminate trout in a lake, but they've been known to be neighbours before. Whatever it is we'll try for it and pick up some trout by the way.'

'Good. It would be great to be hooked into something quite outside the range of *The Fishing Gazette*—a giant pike or some other entirely outlandish fish. Just think. . . .'

'I'm thinking.'

Rich and the Novice imagine great scenes, the one superintending the transport and stuffing of the monster, and the other writing a precise account of the capture with full details of the difficulty in weighing it accurately; how a small boy was seized with convulsions at sight of the fish; of strange things found in its belly. In later years fishermen would visit the lake, row reverently over the spot where it was hooked, recount the long struggle towards the shore, how the gunwale was splintered by a blow of the great tail, of the blood that streamed from its eyes when it was finally killed with hatchet blows. . . .

The Novice stared bemusedly as Rich spoke. 'What about breakfast?'

Ah, yes, breakfast! It was soon over, that particular breakfast. Unwashed crocks were piled together, and the tent secured against the beasts of the mountain. Stout sea rods were tied with dainty split canes and greenhearts for the passage to the lake. The largest of the three gaffs was filed to a needle-point. The Circus Spoon lay with a nine-inch tope reel among wire traces and lesser spoons. Materials for lunch were tossed together. A last survey and we were ready, hardly conscious that we had neither shaved nor combed our hair nor cleaned our teeth.

The morning was altogether too perfect from a fisherman's point of view. The light was too strong, shadows too crisp. We could only hope that a little night-gloom remained on the lake. Occasional clouds raced before a strong west wind like scattered hounds upon a scent. A heat shimmer was in the valley and rocks were scorching to the touch. Sheep grazed with dreamy persistence. A hot scent of gorse and heather came in quick breaths. The descent to the lake was quickly made. Together we trotted and stumbled precariously among great bleached stumps and rocks, holding the rods high above our heads for safety, Rich humming softly to himself in happy preoccupation. The lake was magnificent in the full light of morning, the wind breaking it into a silvery fleece. The buzzard was waiting high on its pitch, a lonely barb against the blue of the sky. Distant mountains were beautifully furred, and it was as if leopards basked in the stillness of pure physical delight. Now the shadow of a cloud strode across the cliff-face like a moth across a wall and was gone. Bright threads of water that trickled over high crags were like silver-haired wens on a great brooding face. At one point a stream sprayed outwards in a fine plumy fan which seemed to consume itself.

Now a boat was crossing the length of the lake, impelled, it seemed, by bright tumbling blades, Moriarty bending heroically over the oars. We waited upon the stony shore for him, Rich busy with casts and lines, assembling rods and discussing the merits of flies in loving phrases. As the boat came nearer we could hear the thrust of water, the squeaking of ungreased thole-pins and the wheezy breath of Moriarty himself, all strangely loud and clear in the stillness. At twenty yards he hailed us excitedly, breaking his stroke to peer round and point at a spot directly under the opposite cliff. 'That's where he is!' his shout bumping and echoing explosively.

'The echo might explain why the trout are so shy. They hear too much.' Rich spun the Circus Spoon on its swivel and pulled with all his strength. 'If we do hook Old Mystery he'll have to dance to our tune.'

The boat grounded, Moriarty splashing ashore through two feet of water as if the water were but an illusion. 'Are ye ready?' He seemed younger as he peered closely at Rich as he tied a cast. 'Begob, and that's a gentleman's knot.' Sighting the Circus Spoon he pounced upon it, stroking it and trying the hooks in his horny thumb. 'And is this for *him*? 'Tis the best ye have? Well, we'll be trying it, but, mind ye, 'tis a terrible brute he is, and him with the drowning of my sonny on his soul, and no pity at all inside him.'

Splashing again to the boat, he dragged it ashore, climbed inside, and began bailing out gallons of water with an old saucepan. ''Tis a bit wet she is what with the sun beating on her, and she not tasting water since Holy Thursday; but ye'll not be minding that, for won't our minds be on the catching of that great devil and not on the dampness of feet? If ye can but make him splash, then 'tis meself will be finishing him!' Proudly he unwound an old sack, revealing a rusted flintlock gun to our astonished gaze. 'One fair shot at him and he'll be finished entirely!'

'And ourselves, too,' Rich murmured, and we resolved privately that never should that gun be fired while we were near. Fishing had ceased to be the quiet meditative pastime that the Novice had once imagined it to be. Doubt had entered his cautious soul. Ever since the day we had ferried a drunken squireen, together with his bicycle and a frantic pig, across Corrib on a day of squalls, and been upset on the way, he had pondered a disclaimer of the common belief. But now was no time for studied inquiry. All was ready, we were assured, and Rich stepped forward with extreme care into the stern, methodically damping the flintlock with a handful of water while Moriarty peered at a weakness in the keel. Next, Moriarty himself scrambled aboard, muddling the oars and calling instructions which the Novice, in his own interest, could only ignore. A heave, and an anxious moment balanced upon the bow, and the boat was afloat and the Novice inboard. Two eggs were in the bows together with a litter of old canvas and straw. Search failed to reveal the hen, and the Novice settled down to watch the straining back of Moriarty, wondering whether he should offer to take an oar, but dismissing the thought after a glance at the patched and splintered pair in use. Already, on that trip, he had broken two perfectly sound oars, as they said, and the breaking of another would weigh too heavily upon an unreliable conscience.

We crossed the lake at a fair pace, Rich casting in the hope of a trout, somewhat to Moriarty's amusement. 'Why don't ye be trying a worm or a mite of bacon instead of they bits o' feather?' His astonishment was complete when Rich brought to net a nice twelve-ouncer. 'Sure and it's just luck! I'm only hoping we'll have the same with him we're after.'

Rich smiled his own sure smile, and, before we had reached the head of the lake, had hooked and missed a second trout, smaller than the first, but sizable, whereat Moriarty scrubbed his nose on his sleeve. 'Just luck,' he reiterated; 'ye might just as well try and catch 'em with a needle and cotton. Sport? Why yes, I suppose 'tis sport, but 'tis like buying time to waste and an empty belly for your trouble!'

Still his respect for Rich had increased, and he now did exactly as he was directed, not quite willingly, for he still had the idea of sport in mind, and thought perhaps that Old Mystery had interested us less than our plans for the capture of him. Rich questioned him again as to the whereabouts of the monster; but Moriarty was compass-sure, and we moved slowly within a dozen yards of the rock-face under the cliff, Rich trolling the Circus Spoon and the Novice casting where he would, Moriarty rowing in a kind of breathless daze, listening, his eyes on the gun beside him. Evidently he was thinking of the moment when he would snatch up the gun and empty it into the head of Old Mystery. The Novice pricked a trout, and muttered in his annoyance, the cliff snatching his words away, rolling them into a deep grumble, which blent ominously with the heavy fall of water-drops from jutting lips.

The great wall, split and knotted like old oak, was cold and grey and forbidding for all the warmth of sunlight upon it. It seemed apart from the daylight, a bulk out of time, a great face which had outstared all humanity with hardly a change of expression, unaware of sunlight, undisturbed even by the regularity of daylight. Daylight could hardly impress a bulk that could remember the original night in which the world was sunk like a grape-seed in wine . . . the wine of a God's idea. Deep lay the water at its feet, flood-lines marked evenly upon it. Dark glimmered the stone, then vanished. In his reverie the Novice missed a second fish, and Rich chid him gently. 'Better take a button-hook to them. Remember we came for fish and not great thoughts on the nature of things.'

Moriarty judges that we are passing over the deeps private to Old Mystery. ''Tis down there he lies in a sort of castle. On a clear day ye can see him from the top, big as a curragh and ugly as the devil himself when God denied him. 'Twas so my sonny saw him, and 'twas frightened he was and down he fell. The water split his face and blinded him, and he was drowned with his soul all broken, and all the time that big bastard was down there laughing away at the trick. Have I ever seen him on the surface? Ay, surely! Times there are when the trout fly like splinters, and ye'll see the water heave and break and a tail go splash so's ye'd think the world had cracked like a ball of glass! And bubbles go floating along the edge, bubbles big as eggs, and ye'll maybe see black bits of oak and ugly weeds that he've loosened in his wandering.' The thole-pins squeaked as with suppressed excitement. 'That brass of yours must be moving over him now. Take care!'

But nothing happened. We rowed beyond the stronghold, and the tension relaxed. Rich sighed and felt for his pipe. The Novice cast again with jaunty air, and was astonished when a trout snatched the dropper—so astonished that he struck as if mastering a wild pony, and the fly was left in the mouth of the fish.

'Bad! bad!' came a murmur from Rich, who would make of the Novice an artist like himself, and then he hummed violently, for the match had scorched his fingers, and the Novice was saved further censure.

By now it is time to turn. We judge the lake to be rather more than half a mile from end to end. Again we will tempt Old Mystery with the Circus Spoon. Rich reels in, examines spoon and trace with scientific intentness, and declares himself ready. After prolonged discussion the Novice takes the oars, Moriarty busying himself with the bailing-tin and hammering fast odd nails which have crept from their holes like dark maggots under the strain of rowing. The Circus Spoon vanished astern, and we imagine it spinning seductively. Easily the Novice rows, damping the thole-pins to quiet their plaint, pleased with the smooth progress of the boat and the vigorous chuckle of water; it is as if we are weaving a stout cloth. High above the buzzard watches, perhaps with amusement in its amber-ringed eyes. Without doubt it sees the drowned rabbit floating on our left, but will not relax dignity to pounce while we are close. The Novice imagines the fall of the rabbit from the cliff. Perhaps it had screamed, and then the scream was lost in the wind-whistle of its fall. So must the son of Moriarty have screamed and fallen. Fortunately Moriarty has not seen the rabbit, and is not again reminded of the tragedy. Wasn't it odd that Old Mystery hadn't gulped the rabbit? The Novice watches the trailing line, how it quivers and tears the bubbling water; watches the quiet muscular hands of Rich, waiting like recumbent wrestlers for the moment when they may spend their strength. Moriarty has finished his labours with the bailing-can, and is staring overside as if hopeful for a glimpse of the giant. His lips move in constant talk as he examines his thoughts. Now he looks up at the cliff, clearly remembering the flesh that had fallen so cruelly. He spits into the water, peering closely. '’Tis level with that Jesus-crust he lies,' he fumed, and bent past all comfort, his reflection streaming in the water, an appropriate figure-head. By Jesus-crust he meant a reddish-purple cruciform marking upon the cliff, an ironstone eruption which certainly resembled blood-encrusted flesh. An apt name, but then such thoughts were the certain harvest of those who lived in loneliness. . . .

The Novice became alert. Rich had felt unusual movement on the line, and was sitting tensed, waiting, prepared to strike and play the monster. Glowing ash fell from his pipe on to his hand, but he did not move to brush it away. Any moment. . . . All waited. The spinner would be about level with the Jesus-crust. Had Old Mystery mouthed it experimentally? Maybe now he was moving round it in curiosity, wondering at the impudence of this shining fish-shape which drove so steadily through his domain. Moriarty thought he saw something breaking astern and stamped in his excitement, and that stamping was our undoing. A rotten strake was splintered and water fountained into the boat. Moriarty stared stupidly; Rich nodded as if he had expected as much; and the Novice, after one surprised moment, dropped the oars and stuffed the jersey upon which he had been sitting into the splintered hole.

'Better pull inshore.' Rich gave his attention to the line again, but we were now well past the lie of the giant, and there was little hope of a strike. Moriarty was on his knees, holding the jersey into the hole, grumbling in his disappointment.

'But there, 'tis a little job, and ye can be resting while I'm patching her and then we'll after him again.'

He looked up for our approval, and Rich comforted him. 'To be sure that's what we'll do. We'll hook him yet, and no bother at all.'

The boat scraped on stones, and Moriarty hopped into the shallows, impatiently hauling the boat high, scarcely waiting for us to climb ashore with all our gear before straining to cock the boat. A concerted movement, and the *Diresome*, as we had already named her, was overturned, and we saw how little had divided us from the depths. The entire hull was patched and cross-patched, both with wood and metal, until hardly a square foot of the original timber was to be seen.

'A good boat,' said Rich with gentle irony.

But Moriarty was busy tugging splinters loose, and could only mumble offhandedly, ''E yes, a good boat. 'Twas built by himself, my father that was, but 't 'as been badly used by the weather. Rain driving on it in winter and the sun tearing at it in summer. 'Tis terrible the way weather does destroy a boat.'

It was in our minds to speak of the uses of boat-houses, but we held our peace, remembering poverty and the way it can cramp a mind past all reason. Gratefully we settled among heather to enjoy food, calling Moriarty to join us. For a moment he paid no heed, and then came slowly to see what we had to offer. Trout in vinegar interested him not at all, but baked beans brought an enthusiastic grunt. Slowly he spelt out the label on the tin, begging the tin for use as a patch on the *Diresome*. Tomatoes he had never before seen, and he refused them after long study and questioning on their qualities. Cheese brought a smile, and he remembered cheese that his mother had made from the milk of goats. 'Fine cheese that ye'd never be thinking could be stirred from the crud of a goat. . . .' He accepted ship's biscuits, and thought he would eat them for supper pulped in milk. ''Tis the teeth of me, ye understand. They don't grow good in these parts under the mountains, the good God He knows why.' Our butter angered and amused him. 'For hadn't it been whipped from sour cream by some bitch of a Mary too lazy to be making the scald from day to day. . . .' Chocolate delighted him, and he folded the tablet carefully in paper and tucked it into a difficult pocket, ambling ten yards away to eat in comparative privacy.

When, later, Rich tossed an apple and begged a question, he shuffled himself nearer on his backside, face wrinkling, tongue licking the corners of his mouth in search of fragments, hands stroking the apple.

'Have I lived here always? Surely! And my father, too, and the father of him, with no difference in the house except a crust of thatch when the old wears thin. And f'why not, for isn't it a grand place to be living, all peace ye might say, but for that bloody great murdering monster in the lake. A bit cold in the winter, maybe, but what's the harm when the turf is burning well and there's bacon in the chimney and flour in the tub? Sometimes, when the wind runs wild, rocks do bounce down from above, but 'tis what we do expect and no harm at all to us who've nothing to lose. Do I labour? For the foreigners in the valley d'ye mean? Surely not, and f'why should I when there's me own property to be tending and saving from ruin and the thieves who would be skinning the very stones of your hearth if ye did but give 'em the ghost of a chance! My woman, she do work a bit, and likes to think she'm propping the house; but there, she's a Philbin, and the Philbins are all cock-heavy and good for nothing but talk.' He sighed and scratched his nose and stared uneasily across the lake, eyes chancing upon the boat, purpose returning. 'Damn we all for wasting time and she waiting to be patched, and that devil waiting and grinning till the lake do boil. D'ye see?'

He pointed with sudden excitement and we stared across the lake, expecting revelation. But it was no more than a gust of wind agitating the waters. We said as much, and he turned fiercely. 'Fools! If ye'd seen what I've seen. . . . But there, how can ye be knowing the size and temper of him? Once he came and snatched at my oar, smashing it like you'd break a twig. Another time he whipped water with his tail until it touched a cloud, and the cloud broke and we were damned near drowned with the power of water that fell. That's the spite and temper of him. But I'll not talk. I'll pray that he grabs that brass of yours and then ye'll see.'

He stared down at the apple in his hands and bit at it suddenly, fishily, in illustration; then scrambled to his feet and bolted away down the shore, presently reaching the cottage, careering in and out of it like a wasp in an old apple, gathering tools for the repair of the *Diresome*. After a long time he came slowly back along the shore, stopping once to shake his fist at, perhaps, a cormorant on the lake, stepping on, singing huskily, bringing with him on a half plate 'a toothful of good butter to be tasting,' together with many useless tools for our inspection. The butter eaten and justly praised and the tools examined, he crossed to the boat and ceremoniously began the repair, hammering out the tin which had contained the beans, and pegging it awkwardly into place over a wad of canvas. The bulging tin, shining in the sunlight, suggested that the *Diresome* had been badly stung. And then Moriarty tenderly painted the patch with tar, lingering over it, finding other places in need of attention, bending low over them, peering shortsightedly, sweating and muttering to himself.

We tired of watching him, and, rolling our jackets for pillows, fell comfortably asleep, sinking in the honey-scented warmth, the Novice dreaming of a gigantic Moby pursued by a gawky Ahab Moriarty. A dramatic and fitting culmination was prevented by an impatient shout from Moriarty.

'All ready, if you please!'

We stretched and yawned, and became alive again to opportunity. We had wasted time enough. The afternoon was almost gone, and we were no nearer the capture, no nearer to fame. The Novice, yet remembering his dream, visualised a magnificent fish plunging and fighting; himself waiting with the useless gaff, waiting through the hours while Rich played him to a finish, Rich who was never so sure of hand and mind as when occupied with a good fish. It would be the triumph of his life, and the Novice, too, would be able to say, 'I was there. . . .' We should need the camera. 'Come on, my lad!' Bundling our gear together we made for the boat, Moriarty beckoning us tetchily forward. By some untold feat of strength he had managed to refloat the *Diresome*, and was paddling and stamping in the shallows.

'He's on the move, I'm thinking,' he called excitedly. 'Did ye hear the black bishop scream just now? They hate each other, I'm telling ye.'

The black bishop was his name for the buzzard. It was possible that the bird could see movement in deep water. Rich settled again in the stern, Moriarty took the oars, and the Novice pushed off. Rich ordered a wide circuit, and Moriarty pulled jerkily, strenuously, straining boat and oars at every stroke.

'Easy! easy!' called Rich, 'else you'll spoil our chances.'

With sober face Moriarty accepted reproof, slowing to an easy trolling speed, straightening the boat for the row down under the cliff.

'Let down the brass,' he begged Rich. 'He roves like a priest when the fancy's on him, and there's no knowing where ye'll touch him.'

In his own time Rich paid out the line. The Circus Spoon vanished. The Novice, with apparent unconcern, assembled a fly rod and made tentative casts, keeping well down in the boat to avoid warning shadows. An eighteen-ounce fish hooked itself when he turned to look at Rich's hands, and he played it in ungentlemanly fashion, dragging it aboard without waiting for the net, the whole performance earning sharp comment from Moriarty.

'Why the hell can't ye keep quiet instead of jigging about like a frog after flies?'

The Novice apologised, winking at Rich; but Rich's whole attention was on the Circus Spoon. He could not be bothered with trifles. Now we were level with the Jesus-crust. Moriarty peered continually overside, lips twisting in the intensity of feeling. Once he broke his stroke to reassure himself that the flintlock was to hand. The Circus Spoon must be flashing deep down. But then, if Old Mystery was as big as Moriarty implied, he would scarcely see such a lure. Big and very old, he was probably half blind as well. Did fish become blind with age? Certainly we had caught some elderly specimens whose eyes were queerly coloured and malformed. An interesting point, but . . .

'My God!' Rich struck hard, and his winch screamed. 'Check the boat!'

Moriarty, at the first alarm, had dropped the oars, and was fumbling with the gun. With a warning, 'Drop that damned thing!' the Novice butted him from his seat and got the oars into reverse action. The boat was checked, but not before much line had run out. Moriarty raised himself on his knees, questioning:

'Have ye got him?'

'Got something,' replied Rich shortly, winding slowly. He frowned. 'Not a move. Must be a rock.'

'That's him! That's him! Cunning he is, big and cunning, remember that!' Moriarty dribbled in his excitement and caught his breath painfully.

Rich worked quietly, winding in, never slackening the line for an instant. He was obviously puzzled. His fingers read the vibrations of the line. 'Queer,' he said. Bracing himself, he heaved suddenly, the reel braked against mishap. We saw the rod bend and the line slide slowly to the right. 'He moved then all right! His head seemed to swing, and then he rolled like a pig. The line is quivering . . . you can almost feel something thinking down there. Damned queer! Either he's a monster or it's a turtle we've hooked. . . .'

''Tis him! 'Tis him! Drag at him! Make him jump!' Moriarty could not endure calm supposition. He swung from side to side, nursing the flintlock. 'Pull, man, pull, for the love of Mary! Remember, remember . . .!' He could not control himself. 'Damn ye!' Dropping the gun, he made a grab at the rod, half snatching it from the unprepared hands of Rich. The boat rocked. Rich swore and tried to force Moriarty back without breaking the strain. 'Hold the damned fool!' he called, but the Novice could do little. Added weight and motion in the stern would simply cause the *Diresome* to roll over. Moriarty struggled frantically for possession of the rod. A decisive blow sent him sprawling into the bottom of the boat, Rich after him, for he still held the rod. The winch rasped and the line ran suddenly slack. The Novice fell upon Moriarty, and Rich regained the rod. Breathing hard, he wound in, but all strain was gone from the line. Water dropped steadily from the reel. A sudden flicking through the rings and the end of the line came in sight, the Spoon gone, wrenched from the trace in inexplicable manner, a topmost happy-chance triangle of hooks only remaining. Rich sat loosely, staring at Moriarty.

'Gone?' whispered Moriarty.

Rich nodded, not trusting himself to speak. Sighing deeply, he felt for his pipe, filling and lighting it with care.

None cared to break the silence. Moriarty sat in the bilge and pulled threads from his jacket. The Novice found a scrap of biscuit in his pocket and chewed hungrily, pondering darkly, all his fine hopes gone. The boat drifted towards the cliff. A vicious gust of wind swept across the lake, and we heard it hiss and whistle like evil laughter against the wall. A cormorant rose from the lake, and the echoing clap of its wings was like mocking applause. We watched it drive steadily from sight, and with it went our last hopes. Now we were in deep cold shadow. Looking up, the cliff seemed to sway over us. The Novice shivered.

'Where to?'

Rich shrugged, puffing steadily at his pipe. Moriarty raised himself to his seat, crestfallen and ashamed. Spitting upon his hands, he thumped the thole-pins tight and balanced the oars, working them slowly, turning the boat towards his cottage. 'Maybe ye'd like some drink, a sip of black·cream?' He could do no more to compensate us for his folly. We could not hurt him with a refusal. Steadily now he pulled. He looked like one who had been terribly scorched, and yet was without wound or scars. Presently Rich smiled at him. 'Come, man, cheer up! No bones broken and no great loss.'

But Moriarty was sick with disappointment and could only mutter disjointed threats involving dynamite and quicklime. We neared the shore and the ramshackle cottage, and we saw it to be a miserable place indeed, sunk in loneliness. The thatch was rotten, and had been patched with sail-cloth. Mud had been daubed upon the unmortared walls in ineffective attempt to keep out the wind and the rain. The two windows were no larger than biscuit tins, and were grey with the grime of years. Fowls strutted in and out of the dark interior. An untidy pile of turf was by the door, the crumbs trodden everywhere. In the doorway a figure waited, unseen as yet by Moriarty. The boat grounded in a rough quay-way, and we stepped ashore, followed by Moriarty. He waved us towards the cottage, then stopped short with an expression of shame and fear as he saw the woman standing there. Thin and sour-faced she was; toothless, judging by her sunken mouth. Her thin hair straggled untidily, and her boots were laced with twine. A hard worker, but one without grace of body or mind. Rich greeted her with his unfailing courtesy, and she nodded curtly.

'We have been trying for the big fellow under the cliff.'

''Tis great fools ye must be entirely, then, for there's naught there but an old log. *He* told ye 'twas a fish, I suppose, and ye not knowing that 'tis mad he's been since the drowning of our Michael. Always simple and then mad, so that they shut him away for a year and gave me peace of him. But they wouldn't keep him, and now he spends his days like an addled child, not thinking of the hours I must slave to be filling his belly. . . .'

'I am sorry.'

'No blame to ye at all!' The woman turned away, picked up a dinted bucket, and went off to milk a sulky cow standing in a threadbare acre beyond the cottage. We looked for Moriarty, but he had hidden himself, and we were glad, for we felt that we had added to his madness by our belief. We called our thanks, but heard no answer. Leaving silver on the window ledge, we hurried away, the woman watching us with her bleak unfriendly eyes. We still felt that she was watching even when we had broken camp and were ready to start. Short had been our talk.

''Tis a great pity to be leaving such trout to play with themselves, but the place is unhappy and not kind to us at all. Foolish to stay. . . .' Thus Rich.

'Agreed. And no regrets?'

Not at once did Rich reply. We got under way, and presently, when we were once more in the valley and the lake miles behind, the Novice repeated his question, disturbed by a curious glint in Rich's eyes.

'Regrets?' Rich smiled in a melancholy way. 'Only one.' He hesitated, then felt for a long time in a pocket, producing at last a strange thing, a fish-scale big as a halfpenny and tough as horn. 'I found that caught on the triangle,' he said sorrowfully, and began softly to sing a song that was like a keen, saying never another word to the Novice for all the understanding that was between them.

THE HINMOST CAST

By NORMAN HALKETT

NORMAN HALKETT (born 1910), Scottish banker. 'The Hinmost Cast' here appears for the first time.

WHEN cauldrife [1] age, wi' canny tread,
The human frame o' strength has bled,
When creaking joint and thowless [2] limb
Our hardy pleasures fain wad dim,
How fondly turns the heart forlorn,
What anxious hopes are daily born,
To do again the things we did,
And dwell anew the scenes amid,
Where in our youth each pool was fraught
Wi' marvels mony, wonders wrought.

This truth befell an aged man,
Wha wi' a laddie's saughy wan',[3]
That instrument o' daughty deed,
At Brokentrodder first drew bluid,
A salmon, great as Jonah's whale,
That wi' the years sae raxt [4] its tail,
Till noo, beyond the 'lotted span,
Nae man could mind whar it began;
But sure the mem'ry o' that fish
Gave birth tae Sandy's dying wish.
He girnt [5] and pined and hankert sair
In Brokentrodder's rocky lair
Tae throw that canny, cautious cast
Wad catch a fish, his very last,
Syne happy, wi' his cup sae fill,
He'd sit him doon and wait God's will.

[1] chilly. [2] pithless. [3] willow rod. [4] stretched. [5] whined.

Wi' Wullie Rough he priggit sair
Tae tak him owre the hills aince mair,
Tae steer him throwe the foggy moss
And help him a' the bogs across,
For these were days wi' nae bus route,
The journey maun be made on foot,
Oot owre the Clashmach's frosty pow [1]
By droving road noo kent tae fyow;
And Wullie, dootfu' o' the plan,
At lang length took the job in han',
Gave sweir [2] consent and set the date
When Sandy's fish wad ken its fate.

The ancient noo for days was thrang [3]
Wi' preparations great and lang,
And like a bairnie fu' o'ts toy,
Each item but increased his joy,
As deep within the roomy creel
He packed the muckle salmon reel,
Hooks and sweevels, flees and casts,
Lines and sinkers, fusky flasks,
And a' that's kent as our regalia
He stappit [4] 'mang the para'nalia,
Syne lest a wee thing'd been forgot,
He'd till't [5] again, teem oot [6] the lot,
And search it a' till doubly sure
He hadna miss't ae single lure.
Oh, wae's me, wives o' fishermen,
What trying moments ye maun ken,
What cankert,[7] fashious [8] reprimands,
And urgent, ill-advised demands
Are cast upon your eident [9] care,
Whatever's tint,[10] the brunt ye bear.
And Sandy's wifie, true tae cast,
Was tychaavin' [11] hard wi' fingers fast,

[1] head. [2] reluctant. [3] busy. [4] stuffed. [5] at it. [6] empty out. [7] cross. [8] peevish. [9] diligent. [10] lost. [11] struggling.

For kennin' fine this Day o' Days,
This hinmost cast 'mang Cabrach braes,
Wad see her guidman's fishin' dune,
She pleitered [1] lang wi' bowl and spune
Tae mak' a piece wad shame a poet
Tae sing the very fineness o't—
A Yirdie Tam [2] o' guid oatmeal,
Brochan [3] bree'd o' cheese's heel,
Bere-meal bannocks, traikle spread,
Trig wee scones o' floormeal made,
And tho' her siller ne'er was plenty,
She bakit galshochs [4] sweet and dainty,
Weel flavourt a' wi' kindly graces,
It surely was the Prince o' Pieces.

Upon the scene has dawned the morn,
And furth upon the breerin' [5] corn
The fishers press wi' anxious haste
Tae pierce the Clashmach's mornin' mist;
And up the hill's historic flanks
Gaed Sandy's ancient withert shanks,
As fleet's a roe, nor cried a stop,
His very feet were winged wi' hope.
Syne forrit owre the lanely moors,
Wi' hags and bogs tae try his poo'ers,
(And Wullie, canny, settin' snares,
That fore the nicht wad fill wi' hares),
They passed alang the Gromack's broo
Till Cabrach glens appeared in view,
A twa-three miles and there below
Shone Brokentrodder's broken flow.
Puir Sandy gazed wi' glist'nin' e'e,
The place he'd hardly hoped tae see,
Except frae oot some Heavenly clood
Wi' angels ruggin' at his shrood,

[1] worked messily. [2] dumpling. [3] gruel. [4] titbits. [5] sprouting.

Lay sparklin' there in wild caprice,
And a' his soul was filled wi' peace.

The curlew piped, the grouse-cock crew,
The tychoochit [1] near and nearer flew,
As forth upon the mornin' air
Cam clear a note, a wordless prayer;
The soople sough o' Sandy's wan'
Was cravin' help o' god and man,
As ilka searchin', sweepin' swish,
Grew louder in its whine for fish,
And e'en the ancient, raspin' reel
Wi' ratchet tongue made shrill appeal.
But na! the mornin's silv'ry gleam
Had turned a dour and sulky stream,
And tho' his castin' ne'er devaalled [2]
Nae salmon broke the foamy fauld;
The mavie fusslin' [3] on the brae
Frae sympathy had calmed her lay,
The mawkin [4] keeked wi' bated breath,
The wastlin wind died on the heath,
Throwe a' the lift a stillness brewed,
The hills like silent mourners stood,
A' Nature waited, sad, constrained,
The answer Sandy's gods wad send.

When grim misfortune sair besets
And battle-tides are thrang wi' threats—
That hour when men o' little faith
Maun surely dee an early death,
That hour when tae the mortal frail
The power o' prayer seems fairy tale,
That hour when man forsakes his gods
And vanquished, sinks beneath the odds,
That very hour tae man was given
To prove the michty power o' Heaven;

[1] lapwing. [2] ceased. [3] whistling. [4] mountain hare.

And Sandy's faith, noo limp wi' dool,[1]
Hung weeping owre the sulky pool,
His cherished gods bereft o' power
In this his needfu' gloaming hour.
His palsied muscles shook wi' strain,
His glist'nin' e'e was glazed wi' pain,
When tug! the weary, warpit wan'
A wild and sprightly dance began;
Its saughy sinews shook and shivered,
Its straining timbers bent and quivered,
And sweet in tune the trusty reel
Rang forth its loudest, fiercest peal,
The mavie burst afresh in sang,
The mawkin frae its hunkers [2] sprang,
And high abune the changeling lair
Leapt forth a shape, an answered prayer—
A salmon cleft the trembling air.

But mortal path is fraught wi' snares,
The humble man the better fares:
Achievement brews a heidy potion,
Humility's a cooling lotion,
Man's ever prone tae exultation,
Nor fills his cup wi' moderation:
And Sandy, hoppin' daft wi' glee,
Had drunk owre deep achievement's bree.
He heedless leapt frae rock tae rock,
Whene'er the fish the surface broke,
Till, prood's a peacock, puffed wi' pride,
He stumbled in his cocky stride,
And forrit in a sprawlin' heap
Gaed heelster-gowdie [3] in the deep.

As Wullie hastened tae the scene,
The eldritch [4] yells tore oot abune,

[1] sorrow. [2] haunches. [3] head over heels. [4] frightful.

For Bedlam babel, Huntly Square
At brak o' market, a' was there,
And quickly loupin' owre the rocks
He saw a beard and snaw white locks
Afloat upon the foamy flow,
While striving limbs focht hard below,
And fast within his droonin' han'
The ancient clutched the wavin' wan'.
The salmon reart and loupt and splasht,
While Sandy roart and skriegh [1] and thrasht.
Young Wullie, soople, stoot, and strang,
His prowess on the waters flang,
Cut deep across wi' powerfu' stroke,
Fast grabbed his man and gained a rock,
A moment hung for space tae breathe,
Syne forrit tae the shore he dreeve,[2]
Drappt his burden safe on lan',
Seized the ancient's trusty wan',
Reeled the slack and brocht t' bay
That wilfu' salmon's wayward play;
Some twists and turns, some desp'rate tries,
And gleaming on the strand he lies,
His measured length, four feet o' grun',
A salmon weel owre twenty pun'.

And noo my tale is nearly dune,
For hoo can I describe the scene,
Whar on the bank auld Sandy lies,
A mortal humble, sad, and wise.
Frae ilka cloot the water seeps,
His every vestment trimmed wi' dreeps.
Wi' ebbing floods he nearly chowked,[3]
As loud he paiched [4] and sair he cowked,[5]
The water forth in spouts he blew,
The spray frae oot his nostrils flew,

[1] screamed. [2] drove. [3] choked. [4] panted. [5] vomited.

And doon his dreepin', dragglt beard
The wee cascades their course careered:
And Wullie, feart he'd tak a dwaam,[1]
Poured doon his throat an unco dram:
Syne wi' a michty, raxin' hoast [2]
The ancient fand the speech he'd lost,
Quo he, when's tongue had won release,
'Lor' michty, Wull, *I've wet my piece!*'

[1] faint. [2] racking cough.

INDEX